PRAEDAMUS

LET US PREY

. . . To Rob; Plunder

Selling Heaven

**Overcoming Tribalism
(Narcissism)**

*Connecting the dots between class, gender,
religion and racism*

*Taking ignorance, outdated superstition and
mythology, disguised as faith, out of theology*

Spears Publishing LLC
New Orleans, Louisiana

Copyright © 2015, 2017, 2019, 2021
New Orleans, Louisiana
All rights reserved
Printed and Bound in the United States of America

Published by:
Spears Publishing
New Orleans, Louisiana
Donspears1@yahoo.com   www.donspearstheauthor.com

Consulting by:
Professional Publishing House
1425 W. Manchester Ave. Ste B
Los Angeles, California 90047
323-750-3592
Email: professionalpublishinghouse@yahoo.com
www.Professionalpublishinghouse.com

First printing January 2015
Second printing April 2017
Third printing (Revised) January 2019
Fourth printing (Revised) March 2021

978-0-69234921-2
1098765

Illustrations: William Jamison, Afromation Art, New York, NY
                Gail Pomes, Franklinton, LA

Technical Assistance: Diana D. Spears, New Orleans, LA
Theresa Wellman, Perfect Papers, New Orleans, LA

Interior Design:Jessica Tilles of TWA Solutions.com

Research: Dr. Luther G. Williams, Ph.D., New Orleans, LA
Fortunata Jefferson, New Orleans, LA
Dr. Rosie Milligan, Professional Business, Consultants, Los Angeles, CA

Cover design:Don Spears, New Orleans, LA
Cherrae Stuart, New Orleans, LA

This book is the product of a broad variety of resources and investigation over a period of nine years following Hurricane Katrina. I take this opportunity to apologize in advance for any sources I have overlooked or failed to acknowledge.

All rights reserved. No part of this publication may be reproduced, stored in a retrieval system, or transmitted in any form or by any means—electronic, mechanical, photocopy, recording, or any other—except for brief quotations and in printed reviews, without the prior permission of the publisher.

This book is dedicated to my wife Diana D. Spears, my parents Julius and Ruth Spears, my son Patrick Shannon Spears, my siblings Julius and Juanita Spears, and to everyone else who has helped me discover and live a meaningful, purpose driven life.

Other books by Don Spears

In Search of Goodpussy
Playing for Keeps

TABLE OF CONTENTS

Preface 1
Chapter 1: Jesus in Black and White..19
Chapter 2 Paul The Image Maker, Shaman, Disciples..................40
Chapter 3: The Herod Clan...55
Chapter 4: Fighting Nuns and Sweetheart Deals...........................67
Chapter 5: Scandals & Constantine's Consolidation.....................79
Chapter 6: Reasons for Christianity's Survival 94
Chapter 7: Who was the Real Jesus? 106
Chapter 8: Mary Magdalene 118
Chapter 9: Jesus' Divinity or Not...131
Chapter 10: Did Moses Borrow from Ancient Wisdom?.............141
Chapter 11: Church Politicking 157
Chapter 12: Magic..182
Chapter 13: Leaning, Leaning...188
Chapter 14: The Role of the Benjamins..199
Chapter 15: Past and Present Examples of Lynchings 207
Chapter 16: Will the Real Jesus Please Stand Up 236
Chapter 17: Abraham's Story 246
Chapter 18: Some "Not So Simple" Questions 251
Chapter 19: The Bible, Adam & Eve..261
Chapter 20: Times Have Changed 281
Chapter 21: Church—Big Business 302
Chapter 22: Blind Obedience, A Slave to Religion 332
Chapter 23: American Negrophobia 345
Chapter 24: Homosexuality in History 356
Chapter 25: Brainwashed 369
Chapter 26: What the Good Book Really Says.............................376
Chapter 27: Willie Lynch and Plato 393
Food for Thought 413
Bibliography/Recommended Readings 424
Index...431

LET US PREY

The Bible has always proven to be an excellent management tool in the arts of miseducation and suppression. It has been especially effective in the domination, subordination, and oppression of black people, brown people, gays and women as a marginalized societal subculture. And while the Bible has been the source of immeasurable inspiration and achievement, it has fueled endless and unspeakable pain, suffering, and hatred, all in the name of "God"—deeds sanctified by the three words:

"Let us pray!"

One constant in a belligerent world history is two thousand years of Christianity, and for a troubled American history five hundred years of Christianity.
– Don Spears

And call no man your father on earth, for you Have one Father, who is in heaven.
–Jesus - Matthew 23:9

Religion is the opiate of the people.
– Karl Marx

If you want to hide something from a black person put it in a book.
– Unknown

Life is not kind, or easy, or your friend, but merely the act of living, the opposite of death, and nothing more.
– Don Spears

Intelligence is no match for stupidity.
– Unknown

The only thing necessary for the triumph of evil is for good men to do nothing.
– Edmund Burke

Opinions are like assholes; everybody has one.
– Unknown

I think, therefore I am.
– René Descartes

The most segregated hour of Christian America is 11:00 o'clock on Sunday morning.
- Dr. Martin Luther King, Jr.

Life is not always a straight line or a smooth road.
- Unknown

I was sent only to the lost sheep of the house of Israel.
- Jesus – Matthew 15:24

Every damn fool thing you do in this life you pay for.
-Edith Piaf

Lighthouses are more important than churches.
-Benjamin Franklin

Can a man stand in a bucket and lift himself up by the handle?
-Winston Churchill

No lie can live forever.
-Dr. Martin Luther King, Jr.

Racism in America is little more than classism and old fashioned tribalism, descent claimed from four common ancestors. God, Jesus, Adam and Eve.
-Don Spears

Life is a bitch and then you die
-Unknown

PREFACE

As a Hurricane Katrina survivor from New Orleans, it goes without saying that I have experienced at least one horrific event during my lifetime. Another, however, was Hurricane Betsy in 1965. I, and others like myself, bore witness to nature's fury and to the devastating effect of unimaginable tragedy. Friends and family members missing; homes, cars, clothes, pictures—all lost. Neighbors and your neighborhood gone, the corner grocery store, and even the old lady who lived across the street for as long as you can remember—vanished. Almost everything about your life that was comfortable and familiar to you was destroyed or changed in an instant. And since Katrina, others in this country have suffered as well. Victimized by tornadoes in Tuscaloosa, Alabama, or the horrific flooding in Joplin, Missouri and Colorado, or wildfires in California. It is crystal clear that life is indeed unpredictable. Tragedies in other countries are common, but catastrophes of such magnitude rarely touch American soil. How do we continue? And what do we do when we know that the cavalry will not be coming?

For two years after Hurricane Katrina, my new wife and I lived in Birmingham, Alabama. She went back to school to become an accountant, living in a house we rented, while I drove 350 miles, four-and-one-half hours twice a week, back to New Orleans from Monday through Friday to renovate a building we own. The people of Birmingham were most accommodating, and I thank them profoundly.

In New Orleans I lived in one of the infamous FEMA trailers, sleeping with my loaded .38 under my pillow. Driving through Mississippi on weekends I saw thousands of new white trailers, seemingly for miles, deserted, unusable, parked on hilltops and rotting like surrealistic headstones in some giant cemetery because of the dangerously high levels of formaldehyde in them that made people sick. New trailers the American people had already paid for.

With the exception of downtown and a few other areas, New Orleans was pitch-black at night and eerily dangerous. In addition to strangers who had infiltrated the city (many of them criminals), there were also snakes, packs of wild dogs, nutrias, hundreds of thousands of rats and other animals that had come here to live. The only comforting signs of relief were the police, state troopers, and the National Guard carrying loaded M-16s, patrolling the city in gun-mounted Hummers to prevent looting, vandalism, and any other illicit activity. For all practical purposes, New Orleans had of necessity become an occupied city.

House-high piles of debris lay everywhere, with bloated dead animals on the streets, and occasionally dead people being found in empty houses by first responders and sometimes construction workers. One of the worse things was the putrid, vomit-like smell of rotting flesh saturating the air, and stale, slimy, muddy, bacteria-filled oily water.

Thankfully, most people have no idea what it's like being forced to leave home, without any real warning, with whatever you can carry, almost overnight. And not really knowing where you're going, what you'll find when you get there, if you'll ever be going back home, or if there will even be a home to get back to. The only money you have is the cash in your pockets or credit cards because your own bank has no branches where you go. You have to buy food and gas. You've got to stop and sleep somewhere. Traffic is bumper-to-bumper, creeping along inch by inch for 100 miles. Every rest stop and every gas station overflow with people and sell out of everything, including gas. Nothing is the same or ever will be again, and almost everything happening to you is beyond your control. You're powerless among a sea of others who are also powerless.

A black child, raised in the Deep South in the '50s and '60s, I witnessed racism's atrocities firsthand, sitting behind the "colored" sign on public transportation, going to the "colored" side window for bread, and walking in civil rights marches on hot summer days, harassed by seething mob-like hecklers. Even white preachers supported segregation.

In September of 1965, just as I was set to begin my first semester of college at Dillard University, Hurricane Betsy struck the Gulf Coast decimating New Orleans. Flooding claimed many lives then as well, especially in the Ninth Ward where black residents reported hearing levees being blown up so that uptown New Orleans—where white people lived and where most businesses were could be spared. Men like Samuel Dupre, a bricklayer who would become my future father-in-law, and his brother-in-law Luther Williams, a school teacher, were the real heroes. Everybody had a boat, and they used them to rescue people who were desperate and stranded. In 1965 there was no FEMA, no Morial Convention Center, and no Mercedes Benz Superdome. Hundreds died, drowned in attics by water that rose above rooftops when Betsy, a category 4 storm, slammed into New Orleans at 110 miles per hour. Betsy was the first hurricane to cause more than $1 billion in damages.

What most people do not realize, however, is that there had been another horrific disaster in 1927 when the Mississippi River broke its levees. It was called "The Great Mississippi River Flood of 1927." Many people died, and that was the first time the levees were blown up to save New Orleans.

On that occasion the neighboring town of Chalmette flooded too, just as it did during Hurricane Katrina. Businessmen and politicians from New Orleans promised the people there that after the emergency was over they would be compensated, but of course that never happened. Like residents of the lower Ninth Ward, they were screwed.

Forty years later the Vietnam War was tearing our country apart, with anger, hostility, violence, and still more marches protesting the war. Many of my high school classmates were drafted and killed. Only a year earlier they were in the school yard with me laughing and shooting hoops. Almost daily their pictures would appear in the obituary section of our local newspaper, *The Times-Picayune*. I got a 4-F classification from my draft board because I was attending college and married, with a wife and child. That was how I missed the Vietnam War and the horrors of being a long way from home in the hot, steamy jungles of Southeast Asia.

The Civil Rights Movement, which started as a demonstration against a segregated bus line in Montgomery, Alabama in the mid-1950s was successful. By the '60s, integration had become the "unofficial" law of the land. The Jim Crow system of racial separation and discrimination against blacks I grew up under, based on religion and white supremacy, had been in effect since shortly after the Civil War. Wherever black people went we were reminded of white supremacy and black subordination. I remember my grandfather (my mother's father), a self-employed businessman in New Orleans, and my grandmother (my father's mother), who lived on a farm in Clinton, Louisiana, always addressing any white man or any white woman as "mister" or "miss", and never looking at them directly. Other Colored people even called white children as young as four years old mister or miss. When I became old enough to understand segregation and what was going on, the racism and white lawlessness they had witnessed, and their sacrifices to give us a better life, I loved and respected my humble elders even more. *Ironically, most of the people exercising racial abuses called themselves Christians.*

In the early 70s I became a school teacher, and as such, I was proudly held up in my community, especially my church, as a credit to my race. The leading sisters in the congregation and my father's relatives (female educators), were instrumental in directing my life. As a small boy I was always drawing something, especially cars, so they were the ones who encouraged me to go to college and to pursue a career as an artist. With the early seventies, however, also came my first divorce, jolting me into a dark reality I had never known before. Something new had come along and life in America would never be the same again. It was called a "quickie divorce," and you could have one, uncontested, in six months. That was my first experience with real solitude and the emptiness of being alone. Luckily, I was still teaching and I had my family, so however difficult, I survived. Family really had meaning back then. We were devoted. And family wasn't just another word or an empty expression.

By 1981 I was married again, to my best friend of seven years, an almost white, green-eyed Louisiana Creole beauty, which was a real prize in the color conscious '70s and '80s, but that marriage was short-lived too, not even seeing a one-year anniversary.

Another "quickie divorce."

My papers were in the mail. And just as the Civil Rights Movement was changing America, so was something else, the "Women's Liberation Movement." Many so-called educated or progressive black women were only too eager to jump on board "to discover themselves," no matter what or whom they were leaving behind. It was a white women's liberation movement (modeled after the black civil rights movement), because surely black women in this country did not need to be liberated from emasculated, powerless black men.

At any rate, divorce number two was even more earth-shattering than the first one. This time I had gotten married when I was older and more mature, or so I thought (thirty-three), and nobody could have told me that it wasn't going to last. Silly, silly, poor naïve little me. I had lived a sheltered, protected life and here I was divorced for the second time, still too young to really know anything about the real world. It was also more difficult this time since I had given up my "good teaching job" because of my ambitions. I wanted to write and to make movies, which at that time was considered an impossible dream for almost anybody. There were few known black writers except for people like James Baldwin and Iceberg Slim, or black moviemakers like Gordon Parks and Melvin Van Peebles...In my mind, as an original thinker and a trained artist, *WHY NOT ME TOO?* I became an associate in a small advertising agency while managing a popular nightclub after dark. Whenever there was a spare moment I was reading, researching and writing. Because of unforeseen circumstances, both the ad agency and the nightclub failed at about the same time. Literally, overnight I was unemployed.

Severely depressed for over a year, cut off from the outside world by self-imposed isolation and barely eating, my wonderful life had fallen apart for the second time. Before that things were fantastic, and I had often remarked that every day was Christmas. Life was indeed wonderful. At 23 years old I was already driving my first Corvette and owned a beautiful home, living the American Dream. Forty years ago having a car like that was even more of a fleeting fantasy than it is today. But there I was, in a bottomless pit by myself, with no visible way out. I was jobless in the 1980s when the Republicans had taken over and America's economy was in the toilet again. My wife was gone, my life was seemingly over, and everybody else I knew was still going on with theirs.

The other scary thing was that none of my friends had the slightest clue as to how to help me. What could they say? "Oh, you'll be ok," or "Just hang in there, it'll be all right." Well, they couldn't do that either, because times were relatively innocent and divorce was still an uncommon phenomenon, especially for sheltered young people like me. But before long almost everybody would be getting one. A divorce.

Divorce. The word itself seems innocent enough, but it's much more than that. Divorce is no simple thing. It changes your life forever. Divorce becomes your life at that time. You lose friends. You lose confidence, and you may even lose financial security and stability. A divorce is also psychological, emotional, and perhaps even spiritual. Divorce—don't get one unless it's absolutely unavoidable. Today it's a 50-billion-dollar industry, run by crooked lawyers and judges, and half of all marriages in the United States end in divorce. You can't win. My own parents, no matter how disappointed and disillusioned they were with each other, were smart enough to realize that. No divorce!

Living under the same roof families stayed together, regardless of how dysfunctional they were, including extended family and friends who were proxy family members. That's what we knew because that's what we saw and what we expected. Marriage was forever. Working together and supporting each other was what had sustained black families in particular, both during and after slavery. And throughout Jim Crow. American apartheid! *Perhaps slavery's horrors created deeper bonds.*

Over time, I followed my grandmother's heart-felt advice. I held my head high and I handled my business. She told me, "You can cry inside, but once you step outside that door it's a different story. Nobody else needs to know how much you're hurting but you." I found out later, the hard way, that they don't care either. My mother told me to just keep putting one foot in front of the other until I got where I was going ... I followed her advice too, picking myself up and moving on. I was a young black man, after suffering the second-biggest setback of my young life, again being comforted and counseled by women. My father did the best he could, but like so many men, even today, he was busy fighting his own battles.

Just as I was fighting mine.

My dad had survived World War II, and even segregation. He had also managed to outlive bouts of malaria, but was never able to watch war movies on our black and white television set. I can still remember some of the dark conversations we had about his military career. Once as a sergeant in the infantry, he was stuck in a foxhole for almost two days, eating cans of beans, sitting on top of one of his men who had died after having half of his face shot off.

As for me, a year after divorce number two I was back on top again. Running another world-class nightclub, hosting celebrities like Stevie Wonder, Eddie Murphy, Mohammad Ali and Oprah Winfrey. Dressed in a tuxedo and driving another Corvette. Once, I actually experienced a genuine James Bond moment. I had left the club at about 4:00 in the morning and decided to drive to Bourbon Street, with the top down, still wearing my tuxedo. The barricades were removed and Bourbon Street was reopened for vehicular traffic. My beautiful orange Corvette and I were the only car in sight, slowly cruising past noisy bars and festive tourists. People whistled and clapped and cheered. They were probably shocked, seeing a handsome young black man in a tuxedo driving a convertible Stingray at 4:00 in the morning, on one of the most famous streets in the world during the late 1980s.

Life was great again ... until one day I started urinating blood. Never one to be a follower, I was terrified about it being the big "C." I was only thirty-five, and the word cancer wasn't generally used back then. X-rays in the emergency room revealed a mass in my kidney, so the doctors kept me at the hospital for more tests, and then surgery. A workaholic, I was even writing in my hospital room, sitting on the side of my bed with an IV in my arm until a nurse came in and said, "Mr. Spears, this is a hospital. You've gotta' stop! You can't do that in here! Put that stuff away."

The nurse also told me I had a visitor, an attractive young woman who had followed her in. Terri gave me a peck on the lips, plopped down in a chair beside my bed, and we talked. She and I had dated a couple of times before, but never anything intimate. Flirtatiously, my sexy visitor went on to tell me she had never made love in a hospital before and wondered what it might be like, which was all I needed to hear. The two of us quietly moved into the small bathroom, IV and all. Unfortunately, we were pressed against the wall and the call button kept going off in the nurses' station.

"Mr. Spears . . . Mr. Spears, are you all right?" I heard the nurse asking from the other side of the bathroom door.

"I'm fine, I'm fine." I answered. When my IV and I arrived at the elevator with my guest, all the nurses were grinning and smiling. They knew that I wasn't in that bathroom alone. (I'm in the bathroom, in the hospital, screwing around, waiting to be operated on. Are men crazy or what?)

The night before surgery there was a big party in my hospital room (did I mention that my brother was the administrator?). My time there was a ball, with hospital staff pampering me and bringing copies of *Penthouse* and *Playboy Magazine*. But a very funny thing happened that night after the party. Will, a gay male nurse's aide came in to shave my groin area, prepping me for surgery the following morning. I wanted to know where my favorite pretty, young nurse Claire was, and he told me that most men didn't like being shaved below the waist by females. He said, "that's why I'm here." Will gave an effeminate smile, tilted his head slightly to the side and placed his hand on my leg. When Claire entered the room I told her I wasn't like most men. I wanted both of them to shave me, one on each side, and we would see who gave me the best shave. Afterward, the three of us laughed about it, then Claire inconspicuously slipped me her phone number. She was about to leave town for two weeks on vacation.

Surgery went well, but I became an old man overnight. The pain was excruciating. I had been slit right down the middle like a pig at a barbecue, from my chest to just past my naval. Moving even a fraction of an inch was agonizingly painful, and for months afterward I believed I would never be able to stand up straight again. Wearing slippers and pajamas, I was walking bent over and taking tiny baby steps like an eighty-year-old man. Luckily, several of my nurses, including Claire, were taking very good care of me at home.

Finally, I went back to teaching for a short while, eventually self-publishing my first book, *In Search of Goodpussy*, explaining important lessons I had at times painfully learned over the years. Surprisingly, it quickly became a national best seller. And from then on, jealous or envious people who were glad to see me doing badly before were standing in line this time to kiss my ass. After all, I was famous. I had become a national and international celebrity, seemingly overnight.

In Search of Goodpussy. That's one helluva' title. Everywhere I went people wanted to know how I came up with such an outrageous idea. I then told them something they already knew. That whether it was a nightclub, a ball game, or a church it was always about sex too. In one way or another everything is about sex. Women deal with other women one way but with men in an entirely different manner, no matter who he is, with the possible exception of gay men who are more like sisters. A black male's identity is almost always tied to his sexual persona.

Men deal with other men differently than they do women. They want to be "macho men" in front of women, and sometimes cocky, irrational super men around other males. As members of the animal kingdom, it's simply human nature.

I was *"The Man"* again. But as they say, all that glitters is not gold. Many hypocritical, self-righteous people, especially some black women, rejected the title of my book as being sexist and obscene without even taking the time to understand what I, as a black man, was trying to tell them about black men and their experiences. Ironically, most of my readers were other black women who did want to know. Perhaps some of those same women who were unwilling to listen (who may have been divorced or were injured products of failed relationships) might have learned a thing or two. One woman, who was obviously not open-minded, said if she could give *In Search of Goodpussy* a zero rating she would.

Traveling almost nonstop for about five years, I slept on airport floors and missed most weekends and holidays at home with my family and friends, at least those who were still around. On two occasions I became temporarily paralyzed on my left side and had to be rushed to hospitals in Chicago and in New Orleans. Once at the Los Angeles Convention Center for a book signing, I was lying on a cot and hearing sirens wailing. The paramedics were actually coming for me. I felt paralyzed again but refused attempts to be transported to an emergency room. It would have been embarrassing, to say the least, especially for *"The Man," "Mr. Goodpussy,"* as I was frequently called. Nobody was rolling me out of anywhere on a stretcher. Period. I guess it's a "man thang."

Three years after Katrina New Orleans was still devastated. Relatively speaking, things hadn't changed very much at all. Half of the city's houses and businesses remained dark and dilapidated. Hundreds of homeless people were living on the streets (the working poor, as well as home owners whose property was destroyed by Katrina), camped across the street from the mayor's office in city hall, sleeping outside in the cold and darkness. Progress was slow. Tens of thousands of residents were displaced and living in other cities, and many across America, facing their own dilemmas, were tired of hearing about New Orleans and its problems.

What we all need to remember, however, is that America is one country and that we must respect and be sympathetic to the needs of all her people, black, white, Hispanic, Native American, Asian, European, African, Middle Easterner or whatever. That's true for rich or poor, gay or straight, Yankee or Southerner, Muslim, Christian, Buddhist, Baha'i, Jew, agnostic, or atheist. "One for all, and all for one." It's a far-fetched and probably impossible goal, but remember, "shit happens" to everybody, eventually. Sooner or later it's your turn. Hopefully, telling you my story will remind you of that.

I call my own style of writing conversational, for modern thinkers, and my purpose for writing this particular book is relatively simple. I'm tired of seeing the world "going to hell in a hand basket," the world in which I have no choice but to live. I'm frustrated at seeing black people either being denigrated, degraded, acting like fools, or living in denial. It seems we're either the lower class glorifying ignorance, the middle class asleep at the wheel, or an upper class failing to accept its blackness "outside" of the white man's world. *No matter who some bourgeois black people think they are, as Malcolm X once said, "to many they're still niggers."* Niggers who definitely don't want to hear anything about Africa or be too black. Their belief that they are accepted and included among the white majority is an unhealthy illusion. It may be the 21st Century, but black people and white people are still living in different worlds.

What about white people and the insulated world they are living in, that gives them a sense of comfort and security? All I can say is, it's only minutes from Manhattan to Harlem. We are all living on the same planet. Quoting Congresswoman Shirley Chisholm, "We came on different ships but we're in the same boat now."

Religion plays an important part in most people's lives, profoundly influencing how we think and what we do, affecting attitudes and decision making on a daily basis. Many of us have absolute and often blind faith in the churches we attend. But is such dedication and unconditional loyalty well-founded, or even smart? *Is it good for people to live their fragile lives based on stories told to them by someone who is not an informed, trusted family member, or a loyal and devoted friend?* Somebody they don't really know at all, giving them instructions from a Bible they've probably never read deeply and analytically, then accepting their interpretation of it. After ten years of research I still have questions.

Speaking of that, just how much do you know about your own church, its religious tradition, its history, and its beliefs? If you are an American, then the answer is probably not very much. Likewise, how much do you know and understand about the Bible? Your Bible. From earliest recorded time to the present, man has routinely been involved in self-aggrandizement. He has stolen, cheated, and killed barbarically all the way back to Adam and Eve in the name of God. And he has used both the pulpit and the Bible as his platform in doing so.

Let Us Prey takes a brief look at organized religion and its attendant, ominous consequences. It is an attempt to help you understand and appreciate how and why your secular world and spiritual world work, or do not work. Life itself is much too short, and time much too precious to keep going around in circles, only to find yourself cheated out of most of both in the end.

But on to a more fundamental question. Why have Christian churches kept their members in the dark for over 2,000 years? And why were the beliefs of others deliberately kept secret? What were some of the things known two millennia ago that have been continuously hidden or destroyed, that we still don't understand or know about even now? Why does the church continue to keep secrets and will that always be the case?

That is exactly the point of *Let Us Prey*. Many of the answers we deserve have been historically obscured. Why weren't early Christians allowed to read other books besides the Bible? And for many years, not even the Bible. What did the church hierarchy actually know that wasn't being shared? And why not? *Let Us Prey* is the very readable story of the story of the greatest story never told.

The subtitle is *Selling Heaven,* and I certainly believe that to be true. Everybody, including priests and preachers, God's bullies, is busy chasing that buck. *SELLING HEAVEN!* (They must have been listening to comedian Mike Epps when he said "Getcha' money man")! Making sure people remain Christians is, after all, how the church pays its bills, *and* the good bishop. Organized religion, like so many other institutions, is also based on an illusion. In my humble opinion, *life itself is an illusion*. One requiring further examination and transparency.

After posing the question to some of my associates, what is the key to life, I received all kinds of answers: hard work, a good education, faith, discipline, love, etc. While I believe those things are important, I am convinced that the real answer is commerce. Whether you're a stock trader on Wall Street, a schoolteacher in Minnesota, a bus driver in Mississippi or a girl dancing in a strip club in New Orleans you need money to live, and you've got to find a way to get it. The same thing is true for religion. It obviously takes commerce too. Money.

Without food and shelter gained through commerce or having something of value, tangible or intangible to sell or barter, you won't survive. Nothing will. That's exactly what this critically important book is about. Survival. Skipping past distortions and illusions, and giving yourself a better chance to weather life's ever-present challenges. Even in the richest country on earth, the United States, we see dissidence and despair more and more every day as AMERICA, THE LAND OF OPPORTUNITY, IS INCREASINGLY BECOMING A TROUBLED LAND OF HOPELESSNESS AND LESS OPPORTUNITY. Is "The American Dream" actually dying?

John Adams, the famous American statesman said, "there was never a democracy that did not commit suicide." Are we still being bamboozled; scammed by lying politicians? Today, 47 million Americans (1 in 7) live in poverty and participate in the SNAP program receiving food stamps, averaging $133.00 a month, or $1.50 a meal. A recent Gallup Poll showed that at some point, 20% of Americans don't have enough money to buy food to eat, and that most of them are children and old people. (16 million kids in American struggle with hunger. Food insecurity). Quoting Ghandi, *"Poverty is the worst form of violence."*

In schools across the United States poor children are having their lunches taken away and thrown into garbage cans in front of them, with their hands stamped when there is not enough money in their accounts to pay for their meals. (Two in five black and Latino students attend segregated schools while whites are primarily in private or charter schools, which comes at a cost to public neighborhood schools.) During a National Prayer Breakfast, President Obama said that "religion strengthens America", but does it? Try telling that to the youngsters whose stomachs were left empty when their breakfast or lunch was trashed. *At school.* Imagine any child suffering that kind of abuse and public humiliation, not to mention the psychological trauma of never knowing when it might happen again, *in a Christian nation.* At the other end of the spectrum, in 2013 Wall Street paid out 26.7 billion dollars in bonuses and Americans spent 56 billion dollars on their pets, especially dogs.

In addition to having their lunches trashed, in a USA Today article Greg Toppo writes, "Black students face harsher discipline plus lower paid, less qualified teachers. The Education Department says that among high schools serving the highest percentage of African American and Latino students, one in three don't offer a single chemistry course, and one in four don't offer a math course more advanced than Algebra I.

Black students are suspended and expelled at a rate more than three times as high as white students (16% vs. 5%). Even in public preschools, black pupils represent only 18% of the student population, but account for 48% of those receiving more than one suspension. *More racism against children, in a so-called Christian county.* From the youngest to the oldest Americans are in pain, and angry.

A recent Yale University study has found that implicit bias (unconscious racial profiling and prejudice) begins in preschool. Many suspensions are in fact based on adult decisions and preconceived stereotypical notions (precipitated by the teacher's own fears and experiences), especially in the case of black boys. Even in preschool there is often little empathy shown for black males who are routinely viewed as older and less innocent (tougher) and black girls who are perceived as being less ladylike (harder). Involuntarily activated, teachers aren't aware that they unfairly and automatically treat certain children differently and are racists. Implicit bias may actually follow some children from the classroom, to the courtroom, to the unemployment line primed by stereotypical concepts like violence, weapons, and poverty.

Racially and ethnically minorities are disproportionately kicked out of school for the same behavior that white children are not. Something as simple as not wearing the right socks can make a black child or a Latino child lose precious hours in class.

Pedro Noguera, a New York University sociologist and others talk about the "school to prison pipeline." Left on their own [after being thrown out of school for simple infractions], kids get arrested, convicted of a crime, and end up incarcerated. That also means that they are probably unemployable and will never live the American dream.

Retirees who will be living a lot longer will be a lot poorer. Fifty-seven percent have less than $25,000 saved, and at least 28 percent don't ever see retirement on the horizon. A new survey has also shown that four out of five Americans have been close to poverty at some point in their lives, primarily because of globalization, the widening gap between the rich and the poor, and the loss of good-paying manufacturing jobs. *As evidenced by today's homelessness and the "hunger crisis", capitalism in America is obviously no longer working. The stock market may be soaring for the top 15%, but poor people in what is called "the richest country on earth", are starving and sleeping under bridges.*

There are 7 billion people on this planet and you're only one of them. By 2026 there will be 8 billion, and 9 billion by 2050. Because of pandemics and advances in technology, millions of jobs will be stripped away and they're not coming back. Computers and robots are predicted to take 50% of all jobs at some point. (Ninety-one million Americans, 37%, are not working and aren't even looking.) One half of college students are moving back home after graduation while 15% remain unemployed. In some suburban neighborhoods there are more pets than children. Energy consumption is fast eroding our supply of fossil fuels, and as they say, "God ain't making land anymore," or water either, which is increasingly in short supply as well. It was Steve Jobs, the deceased genius at Apple who famously said "real artists ship." Sure, it's a pretty painting, but you need to be able and willing to sell it. Certainly, lots of things are more important than money, but all of them cost money.

Today, 46 million Americans, or one in five, consider themselves religiously unaffiliated but spiritual. Sixty two percent believe Christianity is a myth. They question how what they are seeing and being told is even vaguely Christ-like, if there really is such a thing. Ten percent of Protestants, 21 percent of Roman Catholics and 52 percent of Jews do not believe in God. Now most people even go to church less than once a month. According to another Pew Research Study, 77 percent of people surveyed say *religion is losing its influence.* And one-third of those under age thirty say they are not religious. They condemn the church's hypocrisy in not practicing what it preaches, especially when it comes to pursuing money and power, and its lack of empathy and compassion for the poor. They take particular exception to the Bible's account of the virgin birth, and believe that you can do good without God. Most people don't think they need either preachers or priests to tell them how to be good, or for that matter, what "good" even is. In fact, by observing some religious leaders, it's easy to see that they don't appear to know the difference between "right and wrong" themselves.

Interpretations and beliefs we have about God and the Bible came to us from imperialistic, misogynistic, xenophobic, tribal white European males giving us their version of the truth. Racism in our society is passed down through Christianity. <u>American Christianity created American racism, giving white people authority.</u> That's why so many of us remain slaves to Euro-American images, traditions and white iconography today. How do we change that long-held scenario, so everyone finally benefits instead of the usual select few? Just as the influence of white, European male dominance is eroding and in decline, so are their religious institutions and doctrines. And why is it that America has to reshape other nations in its own white English speaking Christian image, purposely eliminating indigenous languages? How can we ever separate fact from implicitly biased fiction?

Many Generation X'ers grew up either not going to church at all, or not going regularly. The fact of the matter is that for quite a few men and women today, even the concept of a physical church is outdated. Being spiritual rather than religious, people can access their higher being in a nice park on a beautiful sunshiny day, alone or with friends, or even in a cluttered, messed up garage at home. Witnessing injustice and suffering as they have, or as someone they know has, people are neither looking for the right church nor the right preacher or priest. Many doubt that such a person exists at all. Today more and more individuals are simply seeking truth and a better life. And because they can take care of it themselves, today's church is indeed in trouble. There was even an apology line (Dial Atone), where you could use your cell phone to call in your own little confession if you felt the need, without a priest. (Talk about convenience!) Because of science and technology people know more, are no longer living in fear, and no longer need God's protection from the great unknown. For many religion is also too boring and old-fashioned, especially when it denies provable science and intelligence by saying things like the earth is only 7,000 years old.

We know that's simply not true. The bones of a two year old Neanderthal child who lived during the Middle Palaeolithic era (200,000 to 40,000 years ago) were recently discovered in Syria. Modern humans lived there 100,000 years ago, developing a primitive language. Between 10,000 BC and 3,000 BC, because of bronze and copper tools, agricultural communities and cattle breeding developed in preference to hunting, during the late Neolithic and Bronze Ages. Domesticating animals meant settling down and staying put (establishing towns and cities), with children guaranteeing a labor force. Staying put meant defending families, animals and crops that had to be stored; combining resources and developing culture, laws, religion and political systems.

Next came trade in cities like Hamoukar 8,000 years ago, religion and writing. Syria had a cuneiform alphabet as far back as the 14th Century BC, 1,400 years before Jesus was born. Roughly around the time Moses led the Israelites out of Egypt. An 11,000 year old red, black and white Neolithic wall painting, believed the world's oldest, was found near the city of Aleppo. For conservative Christians I have but one question. If the world is only 7,000 years old as they claim, how can an 11,000 year old painting exist; or all the other artifacts and discoveries we know about? And dinosaurs, like the 77 million year old bones found in Argentina. Aborigines were in Australia 50,000 years ago.

The Bible tells us that God created Adam and Eve; where did transgender individuals come from? Who created the people who were here two million years ago, and what about Lucy, the fossil of a prehistoric woman who lived three and one half million years ago?

Surely, today everybody knows about cavemen. But what about you? For example, did you know that Kennewick Man lived here in America nine thousand years ago? That's right, right here in the good ole' U.S.A., around Kennewick, Washington. Seven thousand years before Jesus was born.

The Holy Bible mentions primitive animals like the Leviathan in the Book of Job, a sea monster that sneezes lightening, spits sparks and fire, and has smoke coming out of its nose. The Bible talks about an ancient monster; not ancient man. The likely reason is that the writers didn't know about prehistoric man, and because prehistoric man wasn't an Israelite. Jews considered people before Adam and Eve inferior, morally unclean savages, beasts without souls. Animals! *Only Jews were people. God's people!*

Another factor is that authority these days is no longer vertical. You know, the pope, the cardinals, the bishops and archbishops, and so forth, who told us what their truth was. Authority today is horizontal. *People are in charge of their own lives and making their own decisions.* They feel that they no longer need either permission or approval from somebody else to do something . . . or not do it. Christianity is no longer a factor in their lives, and today fewer Americans, especially young people, think of themselves as Christians or about going to heaven.

Exactly where do you fit in, and are you being affected positively or negatively by your own religious beliefs? Instead of giving your hard earned cash to the church, couldn't you more wisely be investing in yourself? Investing in your family. Investing in your own future and your own dreams. In America, we love to live now, but it's time to seriously reconsider how we live, who we're living for, and finally whether our actions are ultimately improving our lives or not?

Mrs. Royal, my ninety-year-old neighbor, who was always in great shape for her age often quipped, "if I had known I was going to live this long, I would have taken better care of myself." Isn't it time you started taking better care of yourself too, while you still can? *This isn't play-life, it's real life, and it's already later than you think.*

CHAPTER 1

Jesus in Black and White

⇌

Disclaimer—It is not my intention to harm anyone or to destroy their faith, but rather to bring understanding, common sense and accountability where I can. Before proceeding I need to establish at least one logical, reasonable frame of reference. According to the Bible, after Cain murdered Abel he ran off to the Land of Nod, *East of Eden*, and got married. If only four people existed up to that time (Adam, Eve, Cain and Abel), where did Cain's wife come from? *Cain's wife was a foreigner, not descended from Adam and Eve. A stranger.* The first family of Genesis were not the only people living on earth. Their world was small, a tiny community. Perhaps they didn't know about other people and their cultures, or they simply didn't care. Just as ancient Africans wouldn't have known or cared about polar ice caps and Eskimos, and Eskimos wouldn't have known or cared about camels or the Sahara Desert. There's no mystery. Life on earth didn't just start with two people named Adam and Eve in a pretty garden populating the entire planet, an idea based on primitive legends. The Bible's Old Testament's God created the first white man on earth.

Early on, after Abel has been murdered, there's a contradiction in Genesis 4:14. Fearful that he may die too, Cain tells the Lord "I shall be a fugitive and wanderer on the earth, and anyone who meets me may kill me." Then the Lord put a mark on him, like a king's seal or a passport, so that wouldn't happen. So who wouldn't kill him, if there were no other people? Who lived in Enoch, the city Cain built, *East of Eden*?

After Abel was killed Adam and Eve had Seth, plus a bunch of other sons and daughters. According to Josephus, the ancient Jewish historian, they gave birth to 33 sons and 23 daughters. Brothers and sisters who were free to marry each other until the time of Moses when it became a sin to intermarry. So, another explanation for who Cain married is that he either married one of his sisters, Awan, or one of his nieces.

According to German philosopher Friedrich Nietzsche, 1844–1900, *"In heaven, all the interesting people are missing."* I have also heard it said that "you can learn more from sinners than you can from saints." It is therefore my sincere hope that after reading *Let Us Prey*, you will be prompted to ask difficult questions, and inspired to learn to think for yourself if you don't already do so. *To become one of the interesting people.* And thinking for yourself is exactly what's necessary if your desire is to discover what is truly best for you. To become a Free Thinker, an Independent Thinker. As so eloquently stated by the English philosopher Bertrand Russell, "no man's authority can establish truth by decree; that we should submit to truth; that truth is above human authority." (*Just saying something is the truth doesn't actually make it true.*) Or, as stated so succinctly in God's Holy Bible, "trust no man!"

I'll begin by asking three basic questions. First, is today's church helping or crippling its members? Second, given the state of today's families and black families in particular (divorce, skyrocketing male and female homosexuality, single mothers raising children alone, under education, incarceration and gross unemployment, especially among black males), is the church a benefit, a liability, or even relevant in the twenty-first century? And third, certainly the church has been a deterrent for some who might have pursued a life of crime or some other destructive behavior. But what about others who might have made greater personal gains or contributed more to society had they not been stifled by religion, having become apathetic, passive, and indifferent instead of being aggressive, responsible, and proactive in making decisions about their own lives and the lives of those dear to them?

When dealing with issues of race, gender, class, politics and religion, I fully realize that there is no one single question or one single answer that will fully address such intensely powerful and deeply interrelated personal and social problems, but hopefully some light will be cast.

In addition to greed and corruption witnessed by today's churchgoers, there is yet another lingering question for many, including myself. A matter of identity. Preachers preach and teach that the words found in the Bible came directly from God and Jesus, but how can anyone be so certain about something said over 2,000 years ago? Black and white preachers can't even find common ground on what Jesus actually looked like, or when his real birth date was. Nobody knows because no detailed records were kept of when some poor baby was born during Herod's reign. Jesus' birthday was certainly not December 25th of the year A. D. 1 when we celebrate it, due to a monk's miscalculation (perhaps on purpose to fulfill Jewish prophecy, and probably around 4 BC). In the year 349, December 25th became the date Pope Julius I decided would be the official celebration, coinciding with the ancient birth of the sun, Mithra, the Persian sun god's birthday, the birthday of the Roman god known as the "Unconquered Sun", revered by Emperor Constantine, and the winter solstice, when the sun is reborn each year, so existing celebration days wouldn't be disrupted or get mixed up. *December 25th was simply convenient for everybody!*

In *Jesus of Nazareth: The Infancy Narratives*, Pope Benedict XVI admits that Jesus' birthday was not December 25th, the date the Catholic Church lied about for 2,000 years. Like Mark and John, the Pope said there were no donkeys, oxen, singing angels or wise men present.

As the Bible story goes, Joseph, a much-older man than teenaged Mary, was even going to call the wedding off when she told him she was pregnant. Joseph was humiliated because everybody in town would know that Mary was already expecting. Did he believe her? And who was the father? Poor Joseph was feeling both disappointment and anger. We learn that an angel came to him in a dream explaining what was going on. In his supernatural dream the angel told him to name the child Jesus, meaning "the Lord saves," according to Jewish prophecy. Can you imagine that? JOSEPH WAS ONLY DREAMING ABOUT THE ANGEL. HE WAS SLEEPING. KNOCKED OUT! He would later dream that an angel told him to run and hide with his family, then have yet another dream where the angel warned him not to go back to Nazareth, a sleepy backwood boonie in the middle of nowhere where troublemakers lived. (Joseph dreamed a lot!) What was he doing before falling asleep and starting to dream (seeing and hearing things), that an angel was standing in front of him? Was the angel real or only a part of his dream? *In the Bible Joseph never speaks one word.* What he was doing before nodding off just might be significant, like Moses, and Abraham-the father of all Jews, who'll be discussed later. *In ancient times, mythical experiences often involved trances, visions, and a loss of reality.*

An angel (messenger), Gabriel, stopped by to see Mary telling her the same thing. But as young as she was, Mary could already see where this was going and wanted no parts of any "baby mama drama" in her life. *"No daddy, no baby. No way!"* Then Gabriel, who must have been one helluva salesman, told her to name the child Jesus, and that he would be called "Emmanuel, God with us," and "holy, the Son of God." In the original Hebrew, the word *elohim* meant "mighty ones," or "gods," plural, not one "God". Genesis 1:26 "Let us make man in our image". The *elohim* were the ones who told about Jesus. Gabriel, after doing some really heavy selling, finally convinced her, and Joseph and Mary (a very young girl) got married. (A much-older man marrying a tender young teenager is definitely a no-brainer, even today.) Joseph was dreaming but Gabriel, who had lots of angelic things to do, was kind enough and thoughtful enough to drop in for a visit with Mary to talk about her baby. Such a nice angel. At first she didn't tell her parents about Gabriel. *(Or maybe thirteen-year-old Mary was dreaming too.)* Think about how young and immature any thirteen-year-old is, riding 100 miles on a donkey to have a baby with a ninety year old husband chosen by her parents.

The following is taken from *Who's Who In The Bible* published by Reader's Digest in 1994 and addresses Mary's childhood.

> According to the second-century Protoevangelium of James, Mary was miraculously born to a rich man named Joachim and his barren wife, Anne—a story obviously

based on the Old Testament account of Samuel's birth to Hannah. From the age of six months, the child was kept pure in a "sanctuary in her bedchamber," cared for by "the undefiled daughters of the Hebrews." At three, Mary was taken to live in the temple at Jerusalem, there to be fed by "the hand of an angel." *As she approached puberty, when she would be forced to leave the sacred precincts, Mary was given over to the care of the aged widower, Joseph.*

Unlike the canonical Gospels of Matthew and Luke, the Protoevangelium makes Mary rather than Jesus the central character of its narrative. It is she who is the long anticipated child, her childhood that reflects Old Testament tales, she who is raised to serve the Lord, her name that is to be remembered by future generations. [Chose by God, Mary was more important than Jesus, and stories about the great mother, the miraculous child, and the wondrous resurrection have been around forever.]

Mary's mother, Anne, was barren when an angel came along and told her she would have a child, and both Anne and her husband Joachim, who was wealthy, are saints now. *(Jesus' grandfather was an ancient millionaire, and many of his other relatives were wealthy.)* So, was Mary also conceived by Immaculate Conception? *Mary, who was pure and free from sin, conceived Jesus who was pure and free from sin.* Denying Jesus' virgin birth denied his deity. Early gospel writers, Jewish fanatics, were not interested in Mary, nor the facts. If the account in the Protoevangelium is true, she lived a sheltered life and would have believed almost anything, especially coming from people she trusted, who were keeping her pure. Anne promised Mary to God, turning her bedroom into a shrine until she was three years old, before sending her to the Temple of God. Needless to say, *"Mary was green as grass!"*

Engaged at thirteen, customarily for an entire year without sex, Mary probably gave birth to Jesus when she was fourteen years old. A child by our standards. Today, Joseph would have been arrested as a pedophile, with uncomplimentary pictures floated around the neighborhood, and labeled a sex offender and a sexual predator for the rest of his life. *Jesus' daddy.* For the ancients, however, it seemed obvious that if Mary was old enough to menstruate and to produce offspring, she logically was old enough to marry. It was only natural, but as usual egotistical men had to invent rules and laws that superseded even nature. (In today's world, you're supposed to be of legal age before having sex. Nature, fortunately or unfortunately, takes a backseat.)

In their infinite wisdom, about 200 years ago men started making laws that overruled even biology and Mother Nature. In the old days, an older man and a younger woman were considered a good match because of the older man's ability to provide for the young lady, including protecting her.

In the "Song of Solomon," King Solomon, a much-older man who is already married to several women, falls in love with "the Shulamite maiden," a very young teenager. Solomon called her his girl companion, and she was so young that she was still living at home with mama. According to her brothers, *"we have a little sister who hardly has breasts yet,"* while their young sister said that *"my breasts are like towers."* Even though men ordained (and God permitted) this story to go into his Bible, and Solomon was the wisest man on earth, today he would have found himself locked up in the cell next to Joseph, also labeled a pedophile and a sexual predator. But Solomon's problem really was women. In the "Testament of Solomon," he is said to be a sorcerer *(magician)* and master of demons, having been given a powerful ring by the angel Michael. (Invading dreams, visiting pregnant women, passing out magic rings, when did angels have time to sleep? Or maybe just have a few dreams of their own?)

Some speculate that being naïve and only thirteen or fourteen years old, Mary may have easily been taken advantage of, perhaps by some Roman soldier in a shiny uniform that glistened in the sunlight, looking like a "god," or a first-century "rock star" to someone as inexperienced as she was. Being pregnant and unmarried was very serious. *(Joseph could have had Mary stoned to death for fornication and adultery.*) He paid the bride price, $400 to $1,600 today, but Mary was pregnant before the marriage was consummated. Joseph wanted a quick, *quiet* divorce. It was a real "who-done-it".

Joseph doubting Mary's chastity was why he wanted to call the wedding off. Roman soldiers passed on the main road, and Joseph hadn't touched her. While he was building a house in Sepphoris, Mary went to Judea to visit Elizabeth, her cousin, and came back three months later, pregnant. Was she running away, hiding something? She wasn't caught doing anything. Did Mary walk 120 miles by herself? For protection people traveled in large groups. Would Joseph shame her and her family feel betrayed by scandal and gossip? *Had Mary already had sex with Joseph?* In the Protoevangelium of James, when Salome sticks her finger inside Mary to prove that she is indeed a virgin, her hand is consumed by fire. (A lewd pregnancy would have derailed Jewish prophecy.) Another problem was the idea that mortals could be impregnated by gods. And Mary being impregnated by God was undeniably a pagan concept. *Could the story of a virgin birth protect her?*

According to the Hebrew word *almah (Isaiah 7:14)*, the mother of the messiah would simply be "a young woman" or "a young maiden." When translated to Greek, the church's sacred language, the word *parthenos* in Matthew, Mary becomes a virgin. (The correct Hebrew word for virgin is *bethulah*.) Consistent with Jewish prophecy, a virgin birth was foretold by ancient prophets of the Hebrew Scriptures and the early church leader Isaiah, who was mistranslated. In 735 BCE Mary wasn't that virgin. *It was a commonly accepted belief during ancient times that special people had special births, magnificence, and it doesn't get any more special than your moms being a virgin, and God being your pops.*

In The Good News Bible translation, Isaiah 7:14, a child is to be born soon, whose mother is pregnant at that time. (The kid is on his way now, not way off somewhere in the distant future.) "They shall name him Emmanuel," meaning "God with us," 700 years before Jesus was born. At that time the idea of a virgin birth would have been more in keeping with Greek and Roman culture, or paganism, which makes such a prediction better understood. Greco-Roman birth stories led to Jesus' virgin birth mythology 50 to 60 years after Christianity thrived. Gospel writers reworked stories fulfilling Old Testament prophecies to legitimize Christianity. The prophecy was stretched to fit Jesus, but not about him.

The Catholic Church maintains that Mary's conception happened without sin in her mother's womb. She was perfect even though Jesus himself wasn't. According to the *Catholic Church's "Assumption of Mary," Mary's body went up to heaven, where she is Queen, without actually dying.* (Really?) The Scriptures, however, do not say Mary was without sin. Romans 3:23 says all have sinned, which I believe includes Mary. But does the Bible say that Mary was "full of grace" (always perfect) or "with grace," the original Greek translation? According to Catholic doctrine, even though something may not be in the Scriptures officially, as long as it's not contradicted by the Scriptures it's acceptable. Here again, I have but one question. What makes Catholics claim they're always right in speaking for God, that they alone are the arbitrators and final answer for what the truth really is? Because of their devout belief in God and Jesus, Catholics are now claiming to be the actual lost sheep of Israel. *Jews?* Most Catholics considered the bread and wine they received during Holy Communion not to be symbolic, but the actual blood and body of Christ. *Do today's Catholics still believe that, that they are drinking real blood and actually eating Jesus' flesh? Real pieces of Jesus' body.* Mithras had communion; bread and wine 4000 years before Jesus.

In Genesis 6:2 and 4, the Bible says that elite angels "the sons of God [benei elohim in Hebrew], saw that the daughters of men were fair, and took wives of all they desired and chose." That "the sons of God lived with the daughters of men, and they bore children of them."

Today, interpreters do say that God's sons and human women had children together. But why is it that only God's sons came to earth and picked out all the prettiest women to "knock up"? How did they get here and why were their own women left behind? Besides that, just who are their offspring, the children of God's sons who hooked up with earth's women? According to the banned Book of Enoch, the sons of God were

200 rebel angels who were hot for earth's sexy women, and after having sex the women became pregnant, producing bloodthirsty giants called Nephlin in Genesis, who stretched to the clouds. Is it possible that Mary became pregnant by one of God's sons, a giant, instead of God himself, since the Bible plainly says God's sons had sex with earth's women? Whoever Mary became pregnant by wasn't human. We don't take Greek mythology seriously, but this sounds a lot like mythology to me. Greek and Roman gods lived on Mt. Olympus, the Christians' God was on Mt. Sinai. *Mythology*. Jesus as God, first written in The New Testament in Greek by Paul, the most important person in Christianity after Jesus.

Two of my favorite references to mythology and history come from the American scholar and mythologist Joseph Campbell, a devotee of Friedrich Nietzsche, Thomas Mann, James Joyce, Sigmund Freud, Carl Jung, and his good friend John Steinbeck. Campbell, a prolific writer said *"Myth is more important and true than history. History is just journalism and you know how reliable that is."* He also said that *"life is like arriving late for a movie, having to figure out what was going on without bothering everybody with a lot of questions, and then being unexpectedly called away before you find out how it ends."*

It's also important to understand that dreams, subconscious brain activity, are a critical part of mythology. Remember Joseph was dreaming, and so were quite a few other main Christian characters. In Hinduism, it is said the god Vishnu even dreamed the world into existence.

With respect to Christian mythology, Mary was the epitome of innocence, *but not God's mother*, until the Catholic Church's Council of Ephesus in 431. In a patrilineal system like Christianity, women were kept in their place and subordinate to men. Mary would never have been characterized as a central figure to be revered or venerated. Even being Jesus' mom was no big deal and didn't mean very much. *Mary may as well have been the donkey she rode into Bethlehem to have Jesus in the first place.* Esteemed positions were reserved for men who were obstinate and unyielding in their grip on power and authority. The patrilineal Bible has never been a fair or equal opportunity account. In a war against women, Mary was short-changed.

Several women do make a grand appearance: Deborah, Esther, Judith, Ruth, and a few more. In Romans 16, Paul talks about Phoebe, a church deacon, and Junia-a Greek speaking Jew who was an apostle before he was. Paul himself had a female disciple whose name was Theckla. Theckla, a rich young virgin, was almost a saint and often compared to Mary. (Paul had Theckla while Jesus had Mary Magdalene). Being unmarried, Theckla was not under the authority of any man, preaching and even baptizing, but of course you won't find that recorded anywhere in your Bible. Unmarried women also owned property.

In Jesus' day nobody paid attention to when somebody was born. It was a miracle if the baby survived at all. During the 1st Century the standard of pre-natal care was abysmal. No sterilization and women often died giving birth. The Bible never says anything about there being three wise men at Jesus' birth, and no camels. Because of the gold, frankincense, and myrrh, we naturally assume there were three. But maybe there were only two, or four, and each of them brought all three gifts. *One, Balthazar, was said to be black, with a beard.* The wise men, magi (magicians), prominent citizens with knowledge of the stars (Zoroastrian astrologers/astronomers-fortunetellers who could predict the future), sent by Herod the Great, the ruler of Galilee and Palestine to find Jesus "the baby king" so he could be killed, were warned by God, *in a dream*, not to tell Herod where the "young child" was. Not infant. THE WISE MEN WERE DREAMING TOO! (God only spoke in dreams and visions). Only Matthew's Gospel mentions wise men and a star. Like Herod the Great, the wise men didn't know who the baby was either. Finely dressed and riding Persian steeds, their huge caravans shocked neighbors, with slaves, soldiers and livestock.

Were the wise men really dreaming, or was dreaming only an excuse to run in the other direction, away from Judea? Remember, they were smart. Visionaries. Maybe they just smelled a rat and realized that Herod, feeling threatened by a real Jewish messiah, was lying all along when he told them that his reason for wanting to find the blessed infant was so he could worship him. Afterall, his family already had a well-deserved reputation as murderous madmen. Remember, Joseph was warned *in a dream* too, that Herod intended to kill his son that night and to take off, but maybe he wasn't dreaming either. Maybe it was just plain, old, good, common sense. (Get out of Dodge before it's too late!)

Only the wise men saw the star. The Star of Bethlehem was an expected astrological configuration, an omen; not just a bright light. Traveling 1000 miles from Persia, *in the East,* Jesus may have been two years old when they arrived, walking and talking. *No babe in the manger.* Alexander the Great's birth in Greece in 356 B.C. was symbolized by a new star. Jesus' model, Augustus, the son of Apollo, followed Alexander in 63 BC. How could a star, a huge planet, stand still over one house or barn casting light for two years? Did the wise men see a star or were they reading the stars for signs, the prophecy? Like Mary, they knew about the messiah's foretold birth in Judea. Is the star another stolen mythological pagan concept? *A fairy tale.*

We can't forget the shepherds Luke wrote about decades later but never saw, and no wise men. They must have been freezing their buns off out there in the field at night, in the middle of December tending their flocks (shivering). Is it possible that the light everybody saw was Jesus himself, the bright morning star? A symbol.

Some scholars even believe that the "Slaughter of Innocents" where Herod the Great ordered all males under two years old murdered, either never happened, or was not nearly as significant. Since there were about one thousand people living in the area, that may have meant that as few as twenty babies were killed. Today what most of us don't realize is that Herod the Great, a corrupt Jewish leader, was ordering the murder of innocent Jewish children, his own people, to keep his job. (Herod was a scumbag who believed Jewish prophecy was a myth and prophets were liars).

There may be evidence that Jesus wasn't born in a manger in a stable as Luke said, but in the lower room of a home, a cave basement, like today's wine cellar, as Matthew said. (I remember a song sung at church "In the Upper Room", but we had no idea that in ancient Palestine *"upper room"* only meant upstairs). Downstairs, fourteen-year-old Mary would have had more privacy during delivery, a very perilous ordeal, and often animals, which were valuable, were kept there. This was true during the harsh winter when Jesus was born. Joseph and Mary were not dirt-poor or they might not have been traveling from Nazareth to Bethlehem, with Mary riding on a donkey instead of walking (transportation). A donkey would also be important when Jesus rides into Jerusalem during Passover before his crucifixion because the donkey was part of uncle Zechariah's prophecy announcing the messiah. The reason they didn't stay at the inn (a cozy bed and breakfast), wasn't because they couldn't afford to, but because Bethlehem was very small and there was no inn there. They probably stayed in the crowded home of one of Joseph's relatives. Surely Mary wasn't being pampered and overprotected so she could be sent off to marry some destitute, old, broken down pauper.

It was cold, 30 degrees at night and raining. The treacherous trip from Nazareth to Bethlehem would have taken several days, seven to ten. Mary was riding on a donkey, about to have a baby, eating bread and drinking water. *Was Mary Jesus' first disciple before becoming his mother?* The thirteenth apostle. Scholars now believe Jesus was conceived in December (Christmas), and born around September, when it was warmer and traveling easier. Besides criminals and thugs lying in wait to rob them, there were snakes, scorpions, lions, bears and wild boars.

Almost all depictions of Jesus' birth show him in the manger, with his parents beside him and animals in the background. But in one painting at an ancient church, the baby Jesus, complete with halo, appears being cradled in his mother's arms on a donkey. His father Joseph is on one side of the donkey, and his big brother James, as a teenager, is on the other side. A fourteenth-century painting in Padua, Italy, called *Flight Into Egypt* shows almost the same thing. Mary is riding on a donkey and holding Jesus in her arms, with a halo encircling his head. But in this painting, both Joseph and James are leading the donkey from the same side. *Most paintings leave James out because God's son having a big brother was incredible and probably a bit too much to swallow.*

In a Greek monastery deep in the Judean desert, there is a portrait of a young Jesus being carried on Joseph's shoulder. This time Mary is riding on a donkey behind them, with big brother James walking behind Mary. All four have golden halos encircling their heads. There were thousands of similar paintings, most of which were intentionally destroyed. *In order to make Christianity work, the church had to rewrite Jesus' life, beginning with his family and where he was born.*

According to Dr. Bart D. Ehrman, professor of religious studies at the University of North Carolina, and author of *Did Jesus Exist? Forged,* and *Jesus, Interrupted,* as the legend goes,

> Joseph himself observed time stand still at the moment when Jesus came into the world: he sees birds stopped in midair, a group of men eating with hands frozen halfway to their mouths; a shepherd striking his sheep with his arm posed but unmoving.

and

> Joseph has gone off to fetch a midwife to assist Mary in her labor, but when they arrive, it is too late: the cave (not a stable) is filled with a blinding light, the child has already appeared, and in fact he walks (within an hour of his birth!) over to his mother and takes her breast.

This was Joseph's account of how Jesus was born. *Mary had gone into labor halfway to Bethlehem when he went off to find a mid-wife. (Not in Bethlehem, but on her way to Bethlehem.)* Some scholars however, do not believe Jesus was born in or near Bethlehem at all, but in Nazareth. The story of Jesus being born in Bethlehem was contrived to reinforce Jewish prophecy, as foretold by ancient sages (wise men) and the prophet Micah. It was Micah who said the messiah would be born in Bethlehem. Still, others believe that it was a different Bethlehem, one closer to Nazareth, only four miles away. *But to fulfill the messianic prophecy, Jesus had to be born in the other Bethlehem, the one near Jerusalem.* (Any witnesses who might testify to the contrary were either missing or dead already, and any written accounts of Jesus' life didn't begin until twenty-five to thirty-five years after his crucifixion.)

There are those who believe that Mary herself was responsible for the myth of Jesus being born in Bethlehem, to fulfill ancient predictions. That Mary wasn't some naïve child who had been used. There was a cover up! Mary was headstrong and engineered everything, along with Elizabeth and others, like Simeon, a pious elder. They manipulated facts to make them fit circumstances (pregnancy), and Isaiah's prophecy. Mary made Joseph, her much older honey-do, go to Bethlehem so Jesus would be born there and recognized as the messiah (King Jesus). *No Bethlehem, no David. No David, no Jesus the messiah.* Two great Hebrew heroes.

Only Matthew and Luke discuss Jesus' birth, but there are inconsistencies. In the Gospel of Luke, Joseph lives in Nazareth but goes to Bethlehem because of a Roman census requirement, so Jesus is born in Bethlehem. In Matthew's Gospel Joseph lives in Bethlehem, the city of David, his ancestor, where Jesus is born, then moves to Nazareth after Herod dies. And what was the reason for Joseph being in Bethlehem: a census or taxes? *The patriarchal stories are not historically accurate.*

There was another problem for Jews according to Jewish prophecy. The messiah was to be descended from David on his father's side, and if Mary was a virgin Jesus had no daddy, at least not one related to David. *God was his father so there was absolutely no way Jesus was descended from David. Joseph was Jesus' legal father, not his biological father!* JESUS HAD NO HUMAN FATHER!

For Jews Jesus being God's son was as unthinkable as Mary, a virgin, having a baby for God was. Some even argued that if Jesus actually had a human father it might have been easier for him to be accepted as their messiah. While Mark's and John's Gospels omit discussion of Jesus' birth altogether, Mark wasn't interested in who Jesus' father was either, possibly because of his perceived illegitimacy, nor Jesus' resurrection. *(No miracles.)* Jesus just shows up to be baptized, a fully grown man.

In Matthew's Gospel Mary was a virgin because of an incorrect interpretation of Isaiah's prophesy. Luke said God himself impregnated her. *When?* In Luke, Gabriel visited Mary. In Matthew an unknown angel visited Joseph. Luke 2:19-20 says Mary never told anybody about God's baby. Is that why early Christian writers knew nothing about Jesus' miraculous birth? There was also the Christian doctrine that Jesus existed as a divine being before he was born. *Before Jesus became Jesus he was already God.* After Jesus was born, God was only being himself in two places, at the same time. He chose the Jews because they were a pure race, making a special promise to them alone. *Is God a bigot?*

What about Joseph's family, his brother Clopas, his sister-in-law Mary, their children, parents and grandparents? The wedding celebration in Cana where Jesus turned water into wine (only in John's Gospel), after three days of partying was a family affair. Maybe not Joseph's family, but he had a family somewhere, as did Mary. They just didn't make it into the gospels recognized under Constantine's reign, like so many other things that have been conveniently left out. *Every family has a few secrets and skeletons in a closet somewhere, but what didn't they want us to know about Jesus' family and their skeletons?* There were people running around town who knew some of those secrets and where the bodies were buried. In the *Acts of Thomas* Jesus has a twin brother.

Nobody even knows Joseph's last name. In Luke 3:23 his father is Heli, but Matthew 1:16 says Jacob was his father, thereby tracing his family linage back to King David. Paul wrote so much about Jesus, but why didn't he ever talk about Joseph? Joseph wasn't at the wedding. He wasn't around during Jesus' ministry and he wasn't at his crucifixion . . . Why? Mark, the oldest or earliest gospel skips right past Joseph, just like Paul does.

A genealogy of the family would have told who Joseph and Mary were, and given glimpses of the rest of the family and what they were doing at that time. That would have meant a lot of questions from everybody. But more problematic, a genealogy would have told that Mary and Joseph, Middle Eastern Jews, looked like Middle Eastern Jews and not Caucasians. They were probably short and dark complexioned, with dark hair and eyes, until European artists finished with them. Both Joseph and Mary were descendants of Judah, the darkest tribe.

St. Jerome (Eusebius Sophronius Hieronymus), another early church leader, born in 347 AD, went so far as to say that Jesus' brothers and sisters weren't brothers and sisters, but close relatives. St. Jerome said Joseph was a widower whose wife Salome died, and that Joseph and Mary were betrothed but not married. Jesus' brothers and sisters are Joseph's and Salome's children. In the Protoevangelism of James, Joseph is an old man chosen by lot, God flipping a coin, to watch over the Virgin. Joseph is too old for sex. One account says he was 90 when Mary was only 12. Jesus' virgin birth supported claims of his exceptionalism as the messiah. Again, a genealogy might have shown that Jesus was not white but a person of color. Yet another reason why the Romans, who were colonizing the Middle East and North Africa might have hated him. A dark-skinned Jew!

Again, one other critical piece of the puzzle is whether Mary and Joseph had more children. As Perpetual Virginity, a Catholic doctrine during the sixteenth century, the accepted belief became that not only was Mary a virgin when Jesus was conceived, Mary did not have sex at any time, not even with Joseph. Not one time. Never! *Mary was "semper virgo," a virgin all her life.* There was no way she could have had any other children. Matthew's Gospel talks about sex after Jesus' birth. Such beliefs, along with God's son having brothers and sisters, and sons of God coming down from heaven would have been confusing to anybody.

Anne and Joachim, Mary's mother and father, couldn't have children, then an angel told Joachim that Mary was on the way. Emerentia, Mary's grandmother and Jesus' great-grandmother was a virgin who lived near the Carmelite monks until the monks had a vision of the Savior of the World being a descendant of hers. Emerentia, a pious woman who had no interest in sex, had to marry seven times before Joachim, who was also pious came along, and then they became the proud parents of Anne and her sister Esmeria, Mary's aunt. Emerentia's first six husbands were naturally interested in sex, and it is said that all six of them died unexpectedly, probably by poisoning.

According to Rose Eveleth, a writer for Smart News, marital sex during ancient times was not for pleasure, and people who were married had to abstain from having sex sometimes to avoid becoming lustful and sinful. Even kids who were born because their married parents were *"knockin' boots"* at the wrong time were problematic. If the Church's calendar said the parents should not have been having sex because of the wife's reproductive cycle; the children were considered bastards. *(Damn!)* Sex was neither a right nor a gift from God; only to be exercised in procreation. *(No sex for pleasure, ever.)*

No fondling! No lewd kissing! No oral sex! No strange positions! And only once! Fornicating with an effeminate male, another man, or an animal meant fasting for 10 years, or death. (Early believers were definitely repressed and frustrated, having had more than a few sexual issues.) And of course the rules were made-up by men.

As you quickly begin to see, there are just so many holes, unanswered questions and complicated circumstances that are beyond imagination. The only thing we can be reasonably sure of is the fact that Jesus did indeed exist, and that he was an orthodox Jew, an Essene, a property-sharing monastic brotherhood who believed in piety and celibacy, and that the body was immoral and sordid. The Essenes, who thought the end of the world was near, freaked the Romans out. They didn't believe in living by either Jewish or Roman rule and moved to the wilderness where they would be left alone, anxiously awaiting the cleansing of the Temple in Jerusalem and the reform of its leadership. Naturally, the murderous Romans (Italians) obliterated the Essenes.

To be closer to God, it's possible that Jesus' early life was spent in the wilderness where John the Baptist was, wearing torn camel hair rags, half-starved and living on locusts and wild honey with other Essenes, people laughing at them. For some, Jesus was a rabbi or teacher. For others, a sage, *magician*, faith healer, a prophet, an ancient philosopher, and even an exorcist. Joseph, Jesus' father, was possibly a stone mason (tekton in

Greek, an artisan who works with his hands), or even a laborer instead of a carpenter, because stone was abundant and widely used in building primitive houses, while wood was scarce. Nobody really knows anything else either (like the story of the wise men), because none of us were there. And as they so aptly say in court, "it's all hearsay," from a long, long, very long time ago. Absolute hearsay, because people didn't start writing down what Jesus said until the middle of the first century.

Do you have any idea what the world must have been like for most people 2,000 years ago, without reading and writing? Only stories and word of mouth with no record or proof of anything, and no way of permanently retaining and sharing information. Everything in Jesus' world that was known was learned through stories. Much like a rumor being spread day after day and year after year, Jesus' story changed and he became divine. (Incidentally, Egyptian priests had already been writing for 2,000 years.) How much could any one person, especially uneducated possibly understand? How could any new ideas be exchanged with someone far away, and how much could the average person know? The answer is not very much, and the church in particular wanted to keep it that way. (Any dissent or deviation from orthodoxy was taboo.) Most people were ignorant and uninformed about their world. How could anyone know what Jesus thought or said?

Among the Jews there were Sadducees and Pharisees who didn't get along at all. Sadducees, the empowered elite, much like Republicans today, were the wealthy high priests (descendants of Moses), people with money who cared little about the masses. Today's upper class. The Sadducees also maintained good relations with the people they had to answer to, the Romans, who ruled them and kept them in power. Pharisees were like today's middle-class scholars and rabbis: devout, open to new ideas, politically involved, and focused on education and responsibility. Their lives were comfortable. *Like today, during Jesus' time they were dealing with rifts too, among the upper class, the middle class, and the powerless lower class who were being exploited.*

Jesus and his followers were impoverished Jews, like today's working poor who are living on minimum wages. And much like today's poor, lower class, people were seeking justice and a better life. They hated both the Romans and their own leaders who were selling them out. Jesus and Christianity were the answer. They trusted his message that "God will provide." That and Christianity's promise of "the kingdom of heaven where their suffering would end," and common people would be equal to wealthy powerful people were the solutions they were desperate for. Jesus and his followers believed that once the evil forces controlling the world were defeated by God all suffering would be over, at least in human consciousness. They could live with dignity again.

The world at that time was brutal, ignorant, and filled with hatred. The fishermen who followed Jesus suffered a hard life. Through taxes Roman conquerors were taking land and everything else of value, and using the money to build temples to their gods. The gap between rich and poor was even worse than it is today. The Romans rigidly enforced export taxes, import taxes, land taxes, fishing taxes, and even a head tax. This, while embittered Jews felt that taxes were legitimate only for God, paid at the Temple in Jerusalem. People were beaten and their money and food seized when they had nothing else the Romans wanted. Jews were controlled with an iron fist, and any resistance meant certain death. Disease, famine, and drought ran rampant, with most children dying by the time they were five years old, and most adults by thirty. A charismatic young preacher, Jesus gave people hope that someday they would be liberated from the Romans and their arduous rule. Attention to everyday needs and the idea of life after death were driving forces behind the people's affection for Jesus and his new movement's popularity. His alone was the one belief that could both help you and save you from eternal damnation.

The Jewish Temple in Jerusalem was always at the center of Jewish life, both socially and politically because God lived there. Gnostics and John the Baptist believed God was everywhere, and preached that there was no need to go to town or to the Temple once a year to worship and for ritual cleansing, and no need for priests, a threat to the status quo that infuriated the jealous holy men who were being sustained by believers offerings. According to Jewish law, one day in the week was for rest and for studying the Torah, read in the Hebrew synagogue. Not having to make the dangerous pilgrimage to the Temple was one of the main reasons why Christianity survived. Imagine not having to take a long, costly trip or buy sacrificial animals, and how much easier that made it for John the Baptist, Jesus, and his disciples to gain converts and become leaders compared to the old, expensive, inconvenient ways.

People were happy that Jesus was confronting the high-handed, moneygrubbing priests and defying Herod Antipas' extravagance. Thousands believed God really would deliver them. Naturally, the holy men hated all the attention Jesus was getting as a healer and a miracle worker, but a battle with him was the very last thing they wanted. The Romans and the Jewish leadership, their go-betweens, demanded quiet obedience. They had to shut Jesus up in a hurry.

Some were so angry that they didn't want to go to the Temple anymore. Because they were collaborating with the Romans, the priests had money and were "living the good life". Holding power, they enjoyed a monopoly while poor people were becoming an irrelevant nuisance. Needless to say Jesus and his disciples were not impressed. Their reaction was quite the opposite, that being rich and living the way the priests did was a disgrace. Poor Jews were well aware that they meant nothing to the elitist holy men, and they were fed up with being misused.

Religious leaders often confronted Jesus. Miracles and talk about freedom really got people excited, especially since it was coming from somebody who was one of them. For the holy men and the Romans there was an easy solution. Anybody defying them and any challenge to their authority was blasphemous and punishable by a horrible death. Jesus was ready to send them packin' and they knew it. *He was the one who had to go.*

JESUS, THE HEALER AND MIRACLE WORKER, REALLY WAS THE WORLD'S FIRST SUPERSTAR! Like paganism, healing and miracles were still a big deal. But while John the Baptist stayed close to the water so he could make a quick getaway if he had to, four miles and he was home free, out of Herod Antipas' jurisdiction (planning ahead),

Jesus, on the other hand, sometimes went to town looking for trouble (knowing he would find it, or it would find him). Confrontation was in his DNA (but not from Joseph), and by saying he was the son of God, if he said it, Jesus was challenging the implicit authority of the emperor and absolute power of the state. The emperor was already a god, but Christians were refusing to bow down to him and claiming a God of their own. Their Kingdom of God was diametrically opposed to the emperor's Kingdom of Rome. *The exact opposite.*

CHAPTER 2

Paul the Image Maker, Shamans, Disciples

―⇒―

I believe there are a number of reasons why Christianity has survived and thrived all these years. For one thing JESUS CHRIST ISN'T ONLY SEEN AS AN UNMISTAKABLE NAME, BUT A "BRAND" AS WELL. JESUS BECAME HIS OWN PRODUCT, WHICH UNINTENTIONALLY BECAME THE WORLD'S FIRST EXAMPLE OF MARKETING GENIUS (LIKE FORD, COKE, MICHAEL JACKSON, OR ELVIS), MAKING JESUS A HOUSEHOLD NAME AND ONE OF THE MOST IMPORTANT MEN WHO EVER LIVED. In advertising and marketing there is something called an *imprint*, which means that after hearing something at least five times you automatically remember it. And after hearing about Jesus over and over again, etched into your brain, you didn't need money to learn more about Christianity or to sign up. Membership was cheap, FREE, in the only religion that focused on how much "GOD LOVES YOU!" (Not selfish, egotistical gods fighting among themselves, but one God who was on your side.) Love is that magic word in Christianity that separates it from other religions. *The good news!*

It's fascinating with everything written or said about Jesus, he never wrote anything himself. IN THIRTY THREE YEARS JESUS NEVER WROTE A SINGLE WORD. Did Jesus, a carpenter's son (only in Matthew's Gospel), from an insignificant little village ever learn to read and write? *No Gospel of Jesus was ever recorded by Jesus or by anybody else.* John 7:15 says Jesus never studied. What did it mean if Jesus, who was said to be the son of God was illiterate? SUPPOSE JESUS COULDN'T READ OR WRITE. Learning to do so was difficult and very expensive. Some argue that while being taught Hebrew and Jewish law, Jesus learned to read and write at his little synagogue. Most young men worked with their fathers learning a trade. (For Jesus, a carpenter, mason or a general contractor.) Everybody contributed to the family. Contrary to what many people think, Paul was not one of the twelve original disciples or an apostle of Jesus, nor James, Jesus' brother. The only original apostles Paul knew were Peter and Barnabas. Mark knew Peter, Luke, and Barnabas, his own cousin. Mark was like a son to Peter. Some apostles never met. Years later actual gospel writers, professional scribes, didn't know each other. After Jesus' death, James saw Paul as a false teacher perverting Jesus' message. Matthew was a corrupt tax collector, and Luke was a physician. Who else among Jesus' followers could read and write? What if a Gospel of Jesus existed, but it too was destroyed or never revealed?

In biblical patriarchy, only men are inspired by God, even though Jesus' message of love and compassion was more attractive to women than men, just as it is in today's churches. During the first century, once they were inside the synagogue, the women had to sit in a different section with their backs to the men. A rabbi wasn't allowed to talk to a woman in public, not even his wife. Because women didn't write, leaving records of their influence and accomplishments, whatever accounts there are came from men. Women were written out of history. They were the ones, like nurses and nuns, who took care of those who were sick and dying, often risking their lives.

The words *Christianity* and *Jesus*, inextricably tied to the man known almost universally as the son of God, have been used billions, if not trillions of times over the last 2,000 years. They were also specific to Jesus of Nazareth, instead of the real reference to the anointed one, who may or may not have been Joseph and Mary's son, the man we acknowledge today as the messiah. (The real messiah could have been someone else or even a different Jesus.)

I also believe there was a plan. Jesus was in the right place at the right time, or so it seems. The members of his clan were probably savvy individuals who were determined to rescue Judaism and save their faith as Paul implied, "by any means necessary!" *Was Jesus the self-sacrificing martyr we believe him to be, or was his persona actually created by Paul, perhaps the world's first image maker?* The message for believers was simple. Jesus would save them. But was the whole story of Jesus Christ only a myth and a product of Paul's very vivid imagination? *Did Paul actually invent Jesus?* It was Paul, who knew about Osiris, the Egyptian god of death and the afterlife, who wrote about the crucifixion and miraculous resurrection in the New Testament. (Was Paul, Christianity's CEO and creator only looking for his big payday?) More people knew who Paul was and about his preaching than Jesus. It was Paul who said, "*In the next life salvation was for anybody.*" (Paul's letters were twitter for the 1st Century).

Paul, however, wasn't just another Jew or another ruling class Pharisee. As Saul, a young man, he was a radical, militant Shammaite Pharisee who didn't believe in compromise or concessions regarding pagans, and no submission to Gentiles. Hillel Pharisees, on the other hand, were not so strict. The revolutionary Shammaites sole master was God himself, and they believed that only students who were worthy should study the Torah, while Hillels believed that anyone could be taught. The radical Shammaites were extremist zealots for God, and violence against their enemies, including other Jews they saw as traitors to paganism was the protocol. Everything was to go according to Torah and prophecy. Another group of dangerous fanatics, the infamous Sicarii, the dagger-men, murdered with small daggers hidden under their robes, even slitting the high priest's throat in broad daylight during the feast of Passover. The Sicarii plundered fellow Jews' property, drove their cattle off and burned their houses down, believing that any Jew who cooperated with the Romans was a traitor. For many that was only an excuse. Jews butchering other Jews! *God himself had said that "without the shedding of blood there can be no remission of sins."*

Before switching teams, Paul (Saul), a fanatical Jewish zealot who never met Jesus fiercely guarded the Jewish faith. He gave Jesus' followers hell, having many of them locked up after storming into their houses. Tracking them down like some bounty hunter. Paul was a real Jesus hater. Unlike Jesus and the other Jews, he was also a free Roman citizen with rights. From different worlds, Paul didn't understand their fears, admonishing slaves to obey their masters. Paul (Saul) was a gangster for the high priest, just like a "strong-arm" for the mafia is today. Saul, a thug, was one of the men responsible for Stephen being stoned to death.

Stephen, who helped the poor and gave them food was one of the first seven Christian deacons. A Greek-speaking Jew who converted many Greeks to Christianity. Living in Corinth for three years, Paul spoke fluent Greek. In Corinth he was exposed to Greek philosophy, but more importantly to Apollo-god of healing, and Greek mythology.

One of the things that got Stephen killed was his insistence, like Greek speaking Gnostics and John the Baptist, that God wasn't only in the Temple, and Jesus was standing by the side of God instead of sitting. Jews considered that blasphemy. Stephen said, "yet not in houses made by hands does the Most High dwell." *(God is not in the Temple or in any of man's idols, such as church icons.)* If distortions of God were made up by the church, are a white or black Jesus not also false idols? Is that in itself not blasphemy, another word made up by the Catholic church?

The priestly hierarchy were infuriated by Stephen. He even called them "stiff necked," condemning them for murdering Jesus. This time it was the scribes and elders who went ballistic. They bribed people to lie about Stephen, then a mob of angry Jews dragged him out of town and stoned him to death, making Stephen the first Christian martyr. They had to get rid of him quick too, and Paul approved. Killing somebody who helped poor people and gave them food was still serving God. But what was Paul really up to, preaching that in Christ Jews and Gentiles were the same? *Have lazy, superstitious, unthinking Christians actually been tricked into drinking Paul's spiked Kool-Aid for over 2000 years?*

After recovering from three days of temporary blindness on the dusty road to Damascus where Jesus' voice spoke to him (according to Luke, Paul's teenage gofer, who never met Jesus either), Paul became one of Christianity's top figures, with Jesus and James. In Damascus, Ananias laid hands on Saul, scales fell from his eyes; he could see again. Like John the Baptist, Paul, a strategist, played a crucial role, announcing that Jesus, a descendent of Abraham, fulfilled Jewish prophecy. *Jesus never heard of Paul or Christianity.* The same thing with Luke (like a 1st Century CNN investigative reporter), proclaiming Jesus as God's son. (The bigger the lie the easier to sell.) Luke, a historian, did research, interviewed people and collected evidence. *Hearsay evidence!*

A thinker, turning away from earlier Jewish teachings, Paul's better crafted inspirational theology evolved and included "justification by faith" instead of simply obeying laws, having found failures in the way Judaism was being taught, believed, and practiced. (Like paganism and not keeping the Sabbath, instead honoring Sol Invictus, the Roman sun-god. Even today Christian services are held on Sunday, Sun-Day). Essential was believing in Jesus' death and resurrection. Christianity's cornerstones. Having become an apostle to Gentiles after Jews rejected his teachings, Paul saw a way to alter the status quo. Jews fully believed the end was near and coming at any moment (apocalyptic Judaism, not the end of the world but of biblical Judaism, like the end of Christianity). Through Paul's doctrine of "being in Christ," hope and faith replaced the Jews' "end of the world" doctrine. (Hope vs. the end of the world.) After Paul found salvation in 34 AD he turned away from Judaism, but he never talked about Jesus' miracles, Mary's virginity, Joseph, or Jesus the man. His was the "new knowledge." God in Christ had defeated evil, and Jesus was the true king, proven by his resurrection. *King of the world, Jesus and "The One God" were the same.*

In terms of class status, Jesus, compared to Paul, Paul saw Jesus as just another poor Jew who had never gone anywhere or seen anything. He, on the other hand, was an educated intellectual with insight and vision. The Jews, including Jesus, believed in monotheism, one God, while Paul was both thinking and talking about God when he spoke about Jesus, which was a completely different way of seeing things. But Paul, who was probably a genius, had had an epiphany, discovering another way of knowing God, or at least appearing to know him. Previously, as a Shammaite Pharisee, succeeding by any means necessary meant confrontation and violence, but no longer. All that changed. Gentiles, including persecuted Roman converts, didn't even have to follow Mosaic Law.

Living in Christ meant living a new way, through grace, faith and righteousness instead of rituals, regardless of class, race or gender. Welcoming Gentiles to Christianity who rejected Jewish customs and Rome's state religion, giving them ideas they could accept and understand. *Paul could clearly see that Jesus and his disciples were on to something, fighting corrupt priests and the Romans. Sadly, being uneducated and illiterate, they couldn't really get their act together.* Something had to be done and he was the man to do it, combining Christianity, Judaism and the Roman culture to compete in the widening world and gain followers. *It was Paul who established Christianity as we know it today. Not Jesus.*

"By any means necessary" was the same way leaders of the Orthodox Church did whatever was essential in maintaining their privileged way of life. Like witch doctors and shamans who were given chickens, goats, and other goodies, priests lived relatively well compared to the masses, becoming their own middle class. There was easy money to be made and they knew how to get it. Paul, however, was not a Levite, therefore not of the priestly caste. Was Paul actually looking for money too, or did he really believe what he was preaching? And ironically, of the top three, *Paul, who thought he was doing God's work by having Christians killed, the man who wrote half of the New Testament, thirteen of the twenty-seven books, about twenty years after Jesus had died and a year or two after his own conversion, was eventually beheaded.* Maybe Paul, who knew a good thing when he saw it (rich, corrupt priests), just pushed the envelope a bit too far in designing Christianity. Before converting Paul was fanatical in following Jewish law, but he eventually realized that the bar was set too high, even for him. Doing his best to become a good Jew he grew to hate the hopelessness of Jewish law. There was no way to change things. Nietzsche called Paul "the first Christian, the inventor of Christianess". It was time for a new religion. Paul made up his own.

Paul (Saul) was from Tarsus, one of the largest cities in ancient Syria. And in Syria the worship of the god Ashur was based on monotheism, one god who was all powerful. Did Paul combine Judaism and the Assyrian religion to write the books he wrote in the New Testament to immortalize Jesus and to shape Christianity? Without the apostle Paul, the letters he wrote about Jesus dying for our sins and Christians telling his stories, there is no Christianity. *No Last Supper, no Christianity!*

Like Jesus, Peter was crucified and James, known as Jesus' brother in the books of Galatians and Corinthians, was stoned to death by the Jews, with his brains bashed in in Jerusalem when he was ninety-four. Judas had already hung himself. It was Herod Agrippa, Herod Antipas's brother-in-law who had the apostle James beheaded to keep the Jews happy. The only disciple who didn't die violently was John, even though the Romans tried to boil him to death. "Baptism in blood," dying a martyr, meant going directly to heaven. Being willing to die for the cause meant something, including fighting other Christians who disagreed.

In his book *The Evolution of God*, author Robert Wright says, *"once there was belief in the supernatural, there was a demand for people who claimed to fathom it. In hunter-gatherer society that demand was met by the shaman, meaning one who knows"*. Wright says that "whenever people compete in the realm of explanation, prediction, and intervention, some of them get a reputation for success. Success in explaining 'nature,' and why good and bad things happen, to predict their happening, and if possible to intervene."

"People who appear to demonstrate certain abilities like healing and miracles become leaders in their field." Hence, shamans became the first holy men or spiritual experts. (Today's preachers, bishops, and priests. Shamans became the first political leaders too.)

Robert Wright also notes that "shamans have often been good at converting their powers into material gains" and that "high social status, however intangible, can ultimately bring tangible benefits" (cash). For the shaman, it meant that in addition to goats and chickens, he might also receive blankets, beads, or even an extra wife. (Shamans got gifts, today's preachers and bishops receive love offerings.) And like today's healers and fixers (doctors, lawyers, preachers, and politicians), the more the shaman did to help someone, the greater his compensation. (That is, the more you had to pay.) Depending on how hard he had to work, a few chickens and goats might not be enough. Shamans portrayed gods as "good guys," so the holy men could trick believers into thinking that if they paid them off, the shamans could hook them up by putting in a "good word" with their "main man." (And let's not forget that nobody wanted to cheat or double-cross them either, for fear of having a curse put on them and their family.)

Like today's "holy men," the Shaman business also became a chain or franchise (a monopoly), and often a family business as well (his wife, sons, and nephews). That meant using trickery and deception to keep the loot coming in. Robert Wright observes that some shamans even used ventriloquism to fool people into thinking they were talking to the dead. And watching documentaries, I have seen tricks Eskimo shamans used to deceive tribesmen, stabbing themselves and bleeding severely, with bloody animal bladders secretly hidden under their clothes. Another way to put something over on their neighbors was to trick them into believing the shaman was sucking some object out of a sick person's body, then showing it to all who were present. (Holy men found unholy ways of getting paid thousands of years ago too.)

In the beginning . . . Well, why not? In the beginning Wright says that *"gods arose as illusions, and that the subsequent history of the idea of god is, in some sense, the evolution of an illusion"* and that *"the illusion has gotten less and less illusory."* What was only a vision became accepted as a fact, as reality, something that was true even though it obviously wasn't. *Unlike ourselves, however, one thing primitives didn't believe was that everything their gods did was good, or right, and that they knew everything and could do anything, as most Christians still believe today about their Lord.* (Ancients knew a good lie when they heard one, never expecting the truth.) Even primitives recognized a tale or a myth.

Early on there was animism, the belief that everything had a life and a spirit, whether it was a deer or a rock. Each deer and each rock had its own spirit, which evolved into one god for all deer and one god for all rocks. From that evolved a god of nature for all deer and all rocks, then polytheism—many gods, and ultimately monotheism—only one god. The Old Testament had a vindictive "eye for an eye" God. Today's "one kind merciful God who knows everything and can do anything!"

Again, hunter-gathers didn't worship their gods or think they were perfect. Some of their gods were downright rotten. According to Wright, the god Kmutamtch was always trying to have sex with the wife of his son Aishish, and the god Goana raped his son's wife and ate two brothers-in-law. *Hunter-gatherers basically treated their gods as if they were human, and there was no heaven where good people go or hell where bad people go. Their gods were neither religious nor deserving of praise.*

Jesus and his followers are constantly viewed as uniquely religious icons, when they should perhaps be considered social and political revolutionaries who were not quite so dogmatically religious. Even anarchists or defiant rebels, martyrs and insurrectionists who would die for a cause they believed in, much like those who resist injustice today. Not one of Jesus' early followers was a scholar or a rabbi. They were just plain, ordinary, common folks. But reforming the church, which was out of control was their mission. In the early days, Jesus and his disciples were not saintly, but people who reasoned, debated, disagreed, got pissed off and even argued. Real people, some of the world's first political prisoners, revolutionaries, and freedom fighters, determined not to live as second-class citizens. Especially Simon, a zealot (radical extremist), who hated tax collectors and the Romans who terrorized Jews, controlling their social, political, and economic life. Judas the Galilean and his gang attacked the city of Sepphoris, brazenly seizing Roman weapons and supplies. Jesus' followers rebelled too. Remember, Moses was a rebel. *(Today some scholars believe that even Mary, Jesus' mother, was not wimpish, but a rabble rousing revolutionary like the heroine in Arnold Schwarzenegger's movie "Terminator", who fights to protect her child.)*

In his contemporary best seller *Zealot,* Reza Aslan explains in great detail that many of the early Jews were not the passive sheep many assume them to be, but patriots who fought countless bloody battles against Rome and their own corrupt leaders. Zealots were "warriors of God." Quoting Aslan:

Think of the Temple as a kind of feudal state, employing thousands of priests, singers, porters, servants, and ministers while maintaining vast tracts of fertile land tilled by Temple slaves on behalf of the high priest and for his benefit. Add to this the revenue raked in by the Temple tax and the constant stream of gifts and offerings from visitors and pilgrims—not to mention the huge sums that passed through the hands of the merchants and money changers, of which the Temple takes a cut—and it is easy to see why so many Jews view the entire priestly nobility, and the high priest in particular, as nothing but a band of avaricious "lovers of luxury," quoting Josephus, the non-Christian born after Jesus' execution.

The peasantry were not only obligated to continue paying their taxes and their tithes to the Temple priesthood, they were now forced to pay a heavy tribute to Rome. For farmers, the total could amount to nearly half their annual yield. Those who managed to remain on their wasted fields often had no choice but to borrow heavily from the landed aristocracy, at exorbitant interest rates. [The Temple's money changers were unscrupulous loan sharks.] Never mind that Jewish law forbade the charging of interest on loans. The peasant's land could be confiscated and the peasant kept on the farm as a tenant toiling (debt slave), on behalf of its new owner. [Poor landless farmers made their way to the city of Sapphoris, just as destitute black slaves would move into large cities in America following the Civil War.]

But in Galilee, a handful of displaced farmers and landowners exchanged their plows for swords and began fighting back against those they deemed responsible for their woes. Like Jewish Robin Hoods, they robbed the rich, and on occasion, gave to the poor. They called them *lestai*. Bandits. The bandits claimed to be agents of God's retribution.

They would drown the land in blood. They would smash the heads of the heathens and the gentiles, burn their idols to the ground, slaughter their wives and their children. They would slay the idolaters and bathe their feet in the blood of their enemies, just as the Lord commanded."

"The Twelve", as the apostles were called, were twelve Jewish men who had had enough. They would still struggle and do without beside Jesus for two more years. It was time to kick butt, cast off Roman oppression and form their own nation. Luke 22:36 says, *"The one who has no sword must sell his cloak and buy one."* In Matthew 10:34, Jesus says, *"Think not that I am come to send peace to the earth. I have not come to bring peace, but a sword."* (Living under the Romans was like living under Hitler, when many Jews, feeling betrayed by God lost faith.) They remembered how courageous Jewish rebels like Judas of Gamala were tortured and crucified by the bloodthirsty Romans, then put on public display. Men, women and children were literally being beaten to death.

Even disciples didn't agree on everything. For example, after Jesus died a debate arose among his disciples about whether Gentiles needed to be circumcised to become one of them. Paul's answer was no, while Peter who initially approved, eventually felt that no matter what anybody else said, resurrection was only for Jews. (Peter was an emotional roller coaster, always up and down.) James, Jesus' brother, eventually agreed with Paul in deciding that Gentiles didn't need circumcision. James also said that evil masters would get what they had coming to them in the next life. He was talking *"payback,"* not forgiveness. So, the top three Christians couldn't even agree on how to become one. Besides that, there were no Bibles or gospels to help them figure things out.

Another looming question was did Gentiles have to become Jews first to follow Jesus and to worship a Jewish God? They were not simply abstract philosophical or academic discussions, but hotly debated, emotionally charged issues. Then, as now, some two millennia later, religious convictions were at the very core of many people's daily lives. (There wasn't a whole lot to do back then because leisure time hadn't been invented yet. Race mixing was a crime so they became haters too.)

Speaking of being emotionally charged, let's not forget about Peter, who was so angry that he sliced off the ear of Malchus, servant of Caiaphas, the wealthy Jewish high priest who was a Sadducee, the man who set Jesus up after Judas gave the signal embracing him. (Do you think

they weren't serious, one Jew cutting off another Jew's ear?) It was that serious. After his conversion the Jews wanted to kill Paul too.

Peter used a knife, just as the other disciples, fearing the Romans and the high priest's soldiers carried weapons. The Last Supper, 1st Communion, was held upstairs *at Mary's house*, young Mark's mom, who sold land and gave money to the church. Hearing stories, Mark, Peter's scribe, learned about Jesus from Peter, not his own eyewitness accounts. Leonardo da Vinci's *Last Supper*, painted 1500 years after Jesus was crucified depicted no rebels or weapons. Only Jesus and twelve loving disciples, including Luke and Mark, who were children at that time.

While Judas has been demonized as the apostle who betrayed Jesus for 30 pieces of silver, the accusation doesn't really make any sense because everybody already knew who Jesus was, including the Romans who also knew how to find him. Jesus was already being watched, often moving about undercover similar to the way those who are attempting to avoid detection do today. Afterall, he was advocating a violent overthrow of the Roman government. After conquering Judea and Galilee, the Romans never needed any excuse to massacre Jews or make them slaves, especially instigators. Jesus wanted to destroy the Romans, his mortal enemies (not love them).Not to mention enemies who wanted them dead, and bandits in general. Almost everybody was *strapped* and *packin'* (carrying weapons), even 2000 years ago.

Jewish leaders were terrified by the Romans, fearing that they might be destroyed because of Jesus. Naturally, they argued that it was better for Jesus to die, one man instead of all Jews. Would Jesus continue to endanger their way of life by challenging the Romans? That was anybody's guess, but Jesus was a loose cannon.

Did Judas hang himself out of guilt, for having betrayed Jesus, or simply because he had become severely depressed and suicidal? Was Judas in fact unfairly made a scape-goat? Some have even suggested that Jesus, and Judas who was very smart, actually conspired in Jesus' crucifixion to fulfill prophecy. Judas thought the others were fools.

Peter too was proof that Christians and even disciples weren't timid and always turning the other cheek. *(Jesus wasn't a turn the other cheek kind of guy either.)* They couldn't be, not getting their behinds kicked every other day. Early Christians were definitely not "easy marks." They lived by The Old Testament law "An eye for an eye". Convinced that Jesus was the Jewish messiah, they were determined to see things through, fighting to the end if necessary, "FIGHTING FIRE WITH FIRE, NOT LOVE!" As you might expect, however, Jesus healed Malchus's ear (made it good as new). But Herod later had Malchus assassinated after he found out that he had had his father Antipater poisoned.

In Edom, where the Herod's had come from there was a more advanced society than in Judea, with commerce, agriculture, copper and iron mining, and impressive houses and villages. For much of its history Edomites, descendants of Esau (who was born red), and Judaeans had been fighting each other. Were the first Hebrews and Egyptians actually people of color? Carrying out a genocidal campaign during his reign, David slaughtered 18,000 Edomites. Herod, the new Jewish king, who wasn't a real Jew but a half-Jew, had 2000 bodyguards. Like other Edomites Herod hated the Jews and they hated him. Paul's Christians eventually destroyed them.

CHAPTER 3

The Herod Clan

Greedy Jewish Pharisees accepted Herod the Great's tyrannical rule as a judgment of God, even though he was an Idumean (Edomite) who had only converted to Judaism. This, despite the fact that Herod, fearing a takeover, had Aristobulus, his brother-in-law drowned. Judea was in such anarchy that power-hungry, psychopathic Herod had to escape to Rome, where the Senate declared him client-king (puppet-mayor) of Judea. (In 135 AD Judea was renamed Palestine.)

Returning to Judea, Herod married his second wife, Mariamne, a Hasmonean princess and granddaughter of the high priest. Having been responsible for the murders of 45 members of the Jewish Sanhedrin, taking their property and selling their positions, he had made more than a few enemies. His mother-in-law even tried to talk Cleopatra of Jerusalem, one of his many wives, into helping her "take him out." Herod also killed his father-in-law and several of his other wives.

His brother Pheroas and his sister Salome schemed to make sure they got their piece of the pie before Mariamne's two sons did after Herod had her killed. Jealous and insecure because of the boys' popularity, Herod then had his own sons strangled. On his deathbed, he found out that Antipater, his oldest son, was scheming against him too, to have his own father murdered. When Herod the Great died in 4BC, after ruling Judea for 30 years, the Jews in Galilee, feeling empowered, rebelled against the dictatorial Romans.

Herod the Great was soon replaced by his eighteen year old heir, Archelaus, one of the sons he had with Malthace (a Samarian). But at one point he had changed his will and named his youngest son Antipas to succeed him. On his death-bed however, Herod the Great changed his mind again, appointing Archelaus to the throne. (At that time many thought the old man had been tricked into changing his will, and to avoid any opposition his co-conspirators already had an army in place to support Archelaus).

At first people were happy that Archelaus was their new ruler. He promised to be more conciliatory, but they soon realized Archelaus was just as evil and tyrannical as his father was. Two popular Jewish teachers, Judas and Mathias insisted that the Roman golden eagle Herod had placed at the entrance of the Temple be removed. According to The Ten Commandments they were blasphemous, sinful idols. The teachers and about 40 students were arrested and burned alive.

Jews mourning in the Temple were edged on to retaliate, and when Archelaus sent soldiers and representatives to reason with them the soldiers were stoned to death. The mourners went back to mourning and sacrificing. Archelaus then sent his entire army to the Temple, where they killed about 3000 people, using soldiers on horseback to trample them to death. On that occasion God didn't save the Jews from either the Romans or their own corrupt leaders. After that Archelaus cancelled Passover. (In addition to his cruelty he had also married Glaphyra, his widowed sister-in-law, which was also a sin.)

While Archelaus was in Rome trying to get official confirmation from Caesar Augustus, he realized that Antipas, his brother, because of a second will, still believed that he was Herod's real choice. Many of the Jews however, remained thoroughly disillusioned, wanting none of Herod's relatives running anything. During Archelaus' absence riots broke out in Palestine. Sabinus, the temporary replacement Augustus sent was just as greedy and merciless as Archelaus was. Including robbing the Temple treasury. Sabinas' army was overwhelmed by the Jews, and before order was restored several thousand Roman troops were killed.

But Augustus was shrewd. Because of Archelaus' cruelty and the problems he was creating, especially for the Romans, who hadn't authorized him to take his father's place, there was a real problem. Augustus decided to make Judea a tetrarchy, dividing Herod's empire into three portions, ruled separately by his three sons, with Antipas receiving Galilee and Perea. None of them would become king.

Herod Archelaus' merciless blood thirst was one of the reasons why Joseph and Mary moved from Galilee. They were fierce times, and that was the brutal environment Jesus was growing up in. Governed by ruthless Romans and Jews. (Today, people can't truly imagine how dangerous life was for Jesus, his disciples, and for everybody else.)

Ironically, it was another Archelaus, a Greek philosopher who lived during the 5th Century BCE, possibly a student of Socrates, who claimed that the principal of motion was the separation of hot from cold. That was how he explained the formation of the earth, and the creation of animals and humans. (A theory of evolution before Jesus was born.) The juxtaposition of cold and warm air was to have produced a slimy earth, and while the earth was hardening, the action of heat upon its moisture gave birth to animals, which at first were nourished by mud from which they sprang. (Centuries later the Bible told how Adam and Eve were created from dirt.) In Africa? *Were Adam and Eve black?*

Herod the Great and his entire Herodian dynasty were all rotten SOBs, but that was all right with the Jewish priests as long as they got their share of the wealth. The Romans also needed the Herods and vice versa. As you can see, just about everybody was busy scheming and plotting against everybody else, including Christians and Jews.

Another one of those stubborn Jews was Daniel. A slave in the Old Testament narrative, he refused to honor Babylonian religious traditions, and as a result was thrown in among a bunch of hungry lions. *Repeatedly we see that while Hebrews and Christians were not always the aggressors, they were absolutely not passive or submissive.* They had guts and were resilient, different in many ways from today's spineless flocks who have quietly given in, acquiescing to what some call the Bible's philosophy of subservience and being humble. Believers docilely go about their activities, holding their heads high as peace-loving Christians, totally unaware of the corruption and evil alluded to in the book by which they live and are inspired. They remain ignorant of the fact that by being passive business goes on as usual (monkey business), and that IN THE PAST CHRISTIANS WERE FIGHTERS, NOT PUSHOVERS! It took guts to tell the Romans that their Christian God was better than their pagan gods, and to go to hell! (Today's detached, passive Christians are not behaving as ancient Christians would have expected).

The people responsible for the Bible's existence had power, position, and money. They were not Jesus' buddies. Serving to maintain upper-class advantage by making sure perceptions of Jesus and his followers remained submissive rather than confrontational were characters like Constantine and King James. It was the two of them, an emperor and a king, who helped engineer a dominating brand of Christianity. I can hardly imagine today's political and religious leaders saying, "You don't have to put up with our bullshit anymore." "Stop turning the other cheek!" "Stand up and fight back!"... No, the Bible says just the opposite, and so do church leaders and politicians who tout Christianity. (God is my man and he wants you to be obedient!) There are however, many examples of civil disobedience in the Bible.

Why are pain, sacrifice, and suffering always seen as a sign of faith and humility for women and poor people, but never for the dominant class? Jesus said "the poor will always be with you." But he never said poor people should kiss anybody's butt. What Jesus said and did was just the opposite. So, why is submission encouraged by the church and by political figures instead of resistance and fighting back against exploitation? And why should suffering be considered God's will when being willing to suffer is often tantamount to accepting hopelessness? (The simple answer is that it's a script that makes politicians' and church leaders' lives easier.) All it requires from its peddlers is talk, and they don't have to get their hands dirty or bloody. *Whenever there is a serious problem the only thing preachers and politicians want you to do is pray, sing, and march!* If God actually told Jesus that his suffering would save us, then why are we still suffering 2,000 years later?

There is an ancient tradition of men trying to be more like their gods, but that was then (thousands of years ago), and this is now. And again, when did God himself suffer? Not Jesus, but God. In the ancient world being more like the gods meant having greater power, not being weaker. Hence, imitating and being in touch with Jesus (God), and being more like Jesus, our own personal Savior, should give us power and strength. Not make us weak and impotent.

Understanding that, do yourself a favor and try a little critical thinking for a minute. Ask yourself these questions: "Who wrote the Bible, and why did they write it? Was the goal to tell about Jesus, or was it to create a deliberate, undetected, universal method of domination and control?" And why must the poor always turn the other cheek?

The answer is obvious.

Remember, during Jesus' day life was no bed of roses, filled with lawlessness and violence. Christians had to be tough too, fighting against fellow citizens who were often dangerous, the Romans who were tyrannical, plus their own lying scribes and Pharisees. There is no way to overlook Jesus turning over the money changers' tables in the Temple, whipping money lenders and vendors, and driving out anybody who was buying and selling, one of the ways the orthodox religious system survived. The money changers charged a fee for exchanging Roman currency to Temple shekels, just as there is a fee for converting foreign currency into euros today. (Sacrifices and indulgences were also sold.) During Passover untold numbers of pilgrims visited the city, which meant big bucks for Sadducees running the Temple, collecting tithes and overseeing ritual sacrifices. Like anybody else, Jesus had a serious temper too, when something got under his skin. The money game and the party atmosphere inside the Temple was the last straw. *(Jesus lost it. He went apeshit!)* Challenging what the priests and the Temple represented, Jesus was exposing their corruption.

John 2:15 says *in cleansing the Temple Jesus used a scourge (a whip, or a switch in America), that he made from small twigs to drive the money changers out of the Temple, saying they were turning his Father's house into a den of robbers. (Jesus wasn't foolin' around, scaring the hell out of everybody, and the animals too.)* Remember, in the Old Testament God didn't fool around

either. James and John were so hot-tempered that Jesus nicknamed them "sons of thunder". Even Jesus had attitude. In Matthew 12:48, when told that his mother and brothers were outside waiting to speak to him, Jesus held out his hands toward his disciples saying "Who is my mother and who are my brothers? Here are my mother and my brothers."

What Jesus was saying was all well and good, but as an obedient son why wasn't he at home helping his family, instead of hanging out preaching, and then being impudent and flip about it? Never taking advice of listening to anybody else. *Did Jesus have too much attitude? Dissing his family for not believing in him.* Was Jesus arrogant and even cocky? Others defend Jesus' actions, saying that he was simply a young man who was driven . . . And stressed out.

In addition to turning over the tables in the Temple, Jesus released valuable sacrificial animals: cows, oxen, goats, sheep, and doves the priests were selling to religious pilgrims, animals required for Passover sacrifices at the altars in Herod's Temple. Including the lamb concession owned by the family of Joseph Caiaphas the high priest. The priests sold their ritually-clean animals, sacrificed them, skinned the carcasses, then kept part of the meat to eat later, or sell. The pilgrims were allowed to keep some for celebration meals. (What a scam!) And the animals had to be perfect. If something was wrong with any animal, the pilgrim had to buy another one. Tens of thousands of lambs. *How do you think priests got to be so rich?* The high priest was making a killing. Other than rebels prowling the streets, things generally went well, except for the hideous smell of blood and burned animal flesh during the sacrifice where sins were passed on from humans to animals. *A smell God loved.* The only thing pilgrims got for their hard earned cash was the shaft, with no Vaseline. The money changers paid the priest off too. (Today instead of sacrificial animals, believers are paying for post cards, candles, books, CDs and DVDs.)

In the real world, even our heroes are people with human frailties and limitations. Why wasn't Peter locked up after cutting Malchus up? (Yes, the first pope was a brawler and a slasher.) That's easy. Peter, the first bishop, turned tail and ran, the same way he later abandoned Jesus.

The only problem is that when Peter ran away he left Jesus behind to fend for himself. Even Jesus, not wanting to die and be eaten by ravenous vultures, cried on the cross, like anybody else would have with huge nails being driven into them, and people heckling and cursing them, throwing things and spitting on them, screaming, "If you're the son of God, prove it! Come down!" (Jesus' answer should have been *"just you wait, my old man's got somethin' for your ass!"*)

Caiaphas, the high priest, was being slick and did what real people do, waiting until the Passover was over before snatching Jesus and having him brought to his house because he was afraid the crowd would riot and come after him. *And he was probably right.* That Caiaphas, Jerusalem's most powerful citizen was living large on his ill-gotten gains while everybody else suffered had the Jews really pissed off, including Jesus. These days scholars are aware that the rich high priest was also a descendant of Aaron, Moses' brother, which could have made him one of Jesus' relatives too, through Jacob's son Judah.

Jesus and his disciples disagreed with other Jews, especially Jewish leaders. So, Caiaphas' justification for seeing to it that Jesus would die was predictable—blasphemy, the ultimate crime for which death was the maximum penalty.

While high priests who were Pharisees during Jesus' day recognized the Prophets as being authoritative, Sadducees like Caiaphas, who were in charge didn't. They didn't accept Jesus as the messiah, believe in angels and demons (little devils), or the prophesied bodily resurrection which was to come. *No afterlife!* Jesus' resurrection is the foundation of Christianity. *No resurrection, no Christianity!*

By the time Jesus went before the corrupt Jewish Sanhedrin (court), his fate was already sealed. "Problem solved." Remember, talk about a kingdom of heaven was the complete opposite of views held by Roman leaders, and casting Herod Antipas, Rome's client-king in a bad light, making it appear that he couldn't control the people he was responsible for. Herod owed his position to Rome. Jesus was the fall guy, and Antipas's present to the Romans. Dealing with Jesus and other revolutionaries was the only way he could keep his job, and stay on top.

For Herod Antipas, Herod the Great's other son by Malthace, who like Archelaus was part Jew and part Arab, Jesus and his disciples were dangerous outlaws, subversives, traitors and terrorists who threatened Roman authority, especially for believing that slaves were of equal status to their masters. They were troublemakers who were both a religious and a political threat to someone like him, a scoundrel who was always sucking up to the Romans, even dressing like them, and supporting Greek customs and attitudes. Like his father Herod the Great, and his brother Archelaus, Herod Antipas was a heartless Jewish butcher too. Seeing how slick Antipas was, Jesus himself, who was no fool either, actually called Antipas a fox. Everyday living in fear of him.

Naturally Christians considered their own oppressive domination unjust, especially the murders, rape of their women, and seizing of their land. Peter and his brother Andrew, and James and his brother John were fishermen, which tells you something else about them. They didn't put up with any bull, the same as men who work hard on the water today, and like most fishermen they were prone to exaggeration, like lies about the size of the one that got away. They were real people with explosive tempers. Jews were always great storytellers and known for stretching the truth. (Hollywood in the first century.)

Jesus and his disciples were outraged at the way the Jewish hierarchy were not being true to the tenets of Judaism; erecting pagan status, greed, eating meat that had been dedicated for sacrifice, committing sexual sins with women and various other crimes that were against their beliefs and traditions, *laws Moses made up.* Jewish leaders were ballin' big time out in the open. (Not to mention the craziness you've already read about.) Emperor Herod Antipas divorced his first wife, then married Herodias, his half-brother Herod Philip's wife, which was clearly against Jewish law. Antipas had met her while visiting Phillip and fallen in love. The marriage was incestuous because Herodias was also his niece, and the granddaughter of his father Herod the Great. Because of his open criticism, Herodias, Antipas' new wife, wanted John the Baptist locked up in the Hasmonaean fortress. (John was bad-mouthin' 'em all over the place, and Herodias didn't appreciate it one bit.)

Antipas, getting edgy because of John's fame, refused his wife's request until he saw sixteen year old Salome, Herodias' daughter, dancing at his birthday party. Herod got so hot and bothered *(horny)*, that he promised Salome whatever she wanted. She requested John's head on a platter, which she got, and then gave to her mother Herodias as a gift. John the Baptist's disciples collected his body and then told Jesus, who took a boat and hid out. Jesus and his disciples thought they might be next. (To get a man's head cut off and delivered to you on a platter, that must have been one really nasty, nasty, dance, not to mention the fact that Antipas was plastered.) Remember, Herod the Great, Antipas's father, was the ruthless Jewish SOB who had had his own wife and mother-in-law murdered, plus his two sons. *Jesus and the other Jews were witnessing all this craziness first hand,* being committed by their leaders. *They were out of control.* Meanwhile Antipas was having a few problems of his own. He was freaking out because he kept thinking that Jesus was John the Baptist coming to pay him back for having his head chopped off. He also feared a revolt by John's followers.

In the end, Herod Agrippa I, Herodias's brother, became a king, accused Antipas of treason, and had him kicked out of the kingdom. Herodias, standing by her man, left town with Antipas. Scheming and ruthlessness were a part of everyday life, even in ancient times, and especially among figures in the Bible. And in the Bible, flaws and blemishes in man's true nature are exposed, including Jews, so-called Christians and saints. *(The Bible's own shortcomings are also exposed.)*

Pontius Pilate, the unscrupulous Roman governor hated Jerusalem and only went there when he had to. He was essentially a prefect, from the Latin, meaning "make in front" or "put in charge," representing the Romans who were only occupiers and greatly outnumbered. Known as the hanging judge, he was a cold-blooded disciplinarian who didn't need any problems from his bosses either. Jesus' message that God was the only Emperor and not Tiberius was becoming a real problem. Some thought back then that Pilate even admired Jesus in his own way, and that he might have given him a break if not for pressure from the low-life Jewish priests to get rid of Jesus. He needed their cooperation to keep Emperor Tiberius happy.

Pilate's wife Claudia Procula, who married Pilate because of her own lust for money and power, had had a dream on the morning of Jesus' trial and tried to save him. Matthew 27: 17-26 says that Pontius Pilate asked the Jews who they wanted released, Barabbas, a murderer, or Jesus, and the crowd answered Barabbas. When Pilate asked what should he do with Jesus who called himself the messiah, the unruly mob shouted "Let him be crucified!" To avoid a riot Pilate took some water and washed his hands, saying *"I am innocent of this man's blood, see to it yourselves."* Then the people answered *"His blood be on us and on our children."* Which is why so many hate Jews today. Barabbas was released. Pilate says there are no grounds for killing Jesus, but has him flogged so severely that blood is pouring from his wounds and he can barely stand up. But the Temple priests still want Jesus' life, so he is turned over to be crucified. <u>Dying for Jews who believed in him.</u>

Some felt that Pilate, who had thousands of Jews crucified, was too evil and too bloodthirsty to care about anybody but himself. Others thought that Pilate, a Gentile, had become a believer, which was highly unlikely. Jews, not Romans, sent Jesus to the cross. *Christ killers.*

Did Jesus die to save mankind, or was his death orchestrated to fulfill Jewish prophecy, and ultimately to elevate Christianity? Jews claimed that Jesus' crucifixion proved who he was, king of God's people, and when Pilate had Jesus killed he had the right man. Of course, the real reason Jesus had to be taken out was because he was creating too many headaches for the Romans, as well as the chief Jewish priests and scribes. He was messing up their "good thing", including selling sacrificial animals. So, blasphemy, and being accused of committing crimes against the state (treason), were two of the reasons why Jesus was murdered. Jesus was arrested for sedition and crucified as a revolutionary, a political prisoner, an insurrectionist and a terrorist, not for claiming to be God or the son of God, but King of the Jews. In spite of everything, it was his death that served to solidify and give life to Christianity. Jesus was never thought of as God, or being the son of God while he lived. Not until his crucifixion and resurrection!

The first Jewish Christians, Ebionites (poor Jews who lived in poverty), and Nazarenes who knew Jesus believed James was Jesus' true successor and that Paul was a traitor for mixing with inferior Gentiles. For Ebionites Jesus was just a man, the Jewish messiah sent by the Jewish God to save the Jewish people, fulfilling Jewish Scripture. *Laws meant only for Jews*. He was born the normal way to his biological parents Joseph and Mary with no supernatural powers. Being the son of God or humans being God's children was metaphorical, figurative not factual before Constantine. Because Jesus kept Moses' Laws so well, upon his baptism Ebionites believed he was adopted by God and after his crucifixion raised directly up to heaven. Before that Jesus was 100% human. In Luke 2:49 when Mary and Joseph found Jesus in the synagogue and he asked them didn't they know he was in his father's house or doing his father's business, Luke 2:50 says they didn't understand what he was saying. Why not, if Jesus was indeed God's son?

CHAPTER 4

Fighting Nuns and a Sweetheart Deal

If you've ever seen the film *Romeo and Juliet*, by Franco Zeffirelli, or read Shakespeare's plays, you already understand that people who lived in those days were just as smart and just as unscrupulous as people are today. They were human. And certainly the Catholic Church couldn't be any more religious, but the Catholic Church owns billions of dollars in real estate globally, has its own government, its own prison, its own bank called the "Institute of Religious Works," and even its own Vatican peacekeeping force, or rather four of them, military and police: the Swiss Guard, the Gendarme, the Palatine Guard and the Noble Guard.

In an investigation ordered by the Vatican concerning corruption, cronyism, sexual abuse and financial mismanagement within the Catholic Church, an exiting Pope Benedict said he wasn't sharing the findings with anyone except his successor, the new pope. Was that fair? Was it ethical? Was it even Christ-like, especially since it also concerns information about people's children? Is withholding knowledge of criminal activity not also a crime?

Pope Francis unexpectedly announced that there is corruption inside the Vatican (surprise, surprise), and a gay lobby as well (a clique including gay priests). By the way, there are more gays in the clergy than the general population. To quote "In The Curia," the central Catholic bureaucracy, "there are holy people. But there is also a *stream of corruption*" (Perhaps there's a gay lobby in the Protestant church too).

During his pilgrimage to Rio de Janeiro for World Youth Day, when asked about some gay lobby, the pope joked, "I have yet to find on a Vatican identity card the word gay. If a person is gay and seeks the Lord and has good will, who am I to judge that person? The problem is not the tendency [to homosexuality]; no, we must be brothers. This is the first matter." Francis wants to include gays. (Sign 'em up, quick.)

Pope Francis says that the Catholic Church needs to be reformed. He no longer wants it to be Vatican-centric (centered). The "G8" or "C8"—a group of eight cardinals selected by the pope—will be his advisors. According to Pope Francis, "We need to include those who have been excluded." *(Sign everybody up!)*

The Catholic Church still maintains that homosexuality is "objectively disordered," since the practice is condemned in the Scriptures and cannot lead to having children. Benedict, with his "aristocratic pomposity" did judge, and said just the opposite. That homosexuality is incompatible with the priestly vocation. *Since the pope is never wrong, how can both popes be right when they say just the opposite, at nearly the same time? If popes don't know what they're talking about, who does?*

The problem, however, especially for Catholics who claim higher moral ground, is that it opens up the possibility of *blackmail*. (There's that negative *black* connotation again. You know, a *black* cat, a *black* hole, *black* magic.) According to the Italian newspaper *La Repubblica* and the news magazine *Panorama*, two of Italy's top news sources, in addition to the homosexual subculture at the Vatican, high-ranking gay prelates (cardinals, abbots, archbishops, bishops, etc.) were being blackmailed too. That might mean pressure from insiders on "the down-low" to influence or even betray the pope's ability in decision making.

Incidentally, even now there are nuns who are trying to be more active within the Catholic Church, who are being denigrated and labeled by the priestly hierarchy as subversive, radical feminists, just as some women were during the first century.

If a group of nuns can stand up against the Vatican (men) to do what's best for themselves and for everybody else, shouldn't the rest of us at least exercise the same courage as they? The nuns wear regular street clothes, unlike priests and bishops who seek to intimidate and be set apart by wearing their collars. JUST AS BLACKS GET ACCUSED

OF PLAYING THE "RACE CARD," MANY SO-CALLED HOLY MEN PLAY THE "COLLAR CARD." The nuns work in soup kitchens and homeless shelters, places where high-ranking prelates definitely *ain't* going. PRIESTS ARE "GOD'S BOYS CLUB," his chosen, while nuns obviously aren't. Even when priests retire they get a reasonable pension, but customarily nuns are marginalized.

The Sisters of St. Francis of Philadelphia confronted Goldman Sachs about a pension dispute, and the Daughters of St. Paul in Boston sued the archbishop of Boston, Cardinal Sean P. O'Malley, in a dispute over their settlements. Before 1972, nuns couldn't participate in Social Security and were taken care of by their order, many of them small. The nuns were even referred to as "Boston pension abuse victims." As servants of the church, women were to be seen and not heard. The priests had pensions because they were employed by the diocese. Are nuns the only ones who take a vow of poverty and chastity, and not priests, cardinals, or popes? (In 494, it was Pope Gelasius who decreed that women who had once served as priests could no longer be ordained.) At one time women were actually church leaders, until excluded by men. Jesus himself was a revolutionary who empowered women, treating them as equals.

During the 1990s there were allegations of sexual abuse of nuns by priests, especially in Africa. The priests were allegedly raping nuns because by having sex with virgins, they didn't have to worry about HIV and AIDS. When informed of the allegations, Pope John Paul passively acknowledged the assaults . . . but did nothing. The brides of Christ appeared to be abandoned by their own Catholic Church.

The Vatican doesn't like the fact that the nuns are standing up for the sick and poor, and fighting for the ordination of women, instead of protesting against gay rights and abortion. One of their leaders, Sister Margaret Farley, has even written her own book, *Just Love,* dealing with female masturbation, while Sister Simone Campbell runs Network, a Catholic lobbying social justice group. *Nuns fighting priests for justice. What a novel idea.*

Today, 59 percent of U.S. Catholics believe that women should be ordained. Yet, the Catholic Church continues to condemn other faiths as being unforgiving and nonprogressive toward women, in spite of the fact that there is no theological or spiritual objection to women being ordained. *The priests ain't givin' up nothin'!* All that power, authority, and intimidation belongs to them alone. *The Vatican still teaches that the ordination of women is "a grave sin comparable to child sex abuse."* Nevertheless, sexual molestation of children is forgivable for priests after a little therapy, while nuns continue to be condemned and demonized, simply because they want to become priests too. (But priests can abuse children, while nuns can't even masturbate.)

Unlike the Roman Catholic Church, as it moves into the 21st Century the Church of England has now overturned centuries of tradition by voting to allow women to become bishops. The Most Rev. Justin Welby, Archbishop of Canterbury and the spiritual leader of the Anglican Church, said that the public would find the exclusion of women "almost incomprehensible." Women in the Anglican Church were ordained as priests over 20 years ago. (Is the Catholic Church ever going to wake-up and catch-up?)

In *The Other Catholics* Julie Byrne talks about a new movement of independent Catholics with at least one million members in the United States. They have no formal affiliation with the pope or Rome. Divorced members can take communion, women are ordained, and priest can be married just as gays can. In America there are at least two hundred communities, happy that they can handle their own affairs.

Coincidentally, the Vatican Bank, one of the most secretive in the world, is still in trouble for money laundering. In July 2013, Monsignor Nunzio Scarano, a senior Vatican bank official, along with two other men, was arrested for trying to smuggle 26 million dollars in cash into Italy from Switzerland, using an Italian government plane. *For years the Vatican bank, which reportedly employs 33,400 accountants has been under investigation.* Before Francis became pope, cardinals serving on the Vatican Bank's Board of Supervisors were paid annual bonuses of €25,000 euros, about $34,335.00 US dollars a year. *(Why?)* According to church historian Alistair Sear, "I can't speak about the specific merits of the case (smuggling), but there is no doubt about corruption inside the Holy See. This is not the end of things. It's just the start." Of course there is talk of reforming the bank, with its numerous private accounts, but the Curia doesn't relish the idea of outsiders getting involved in its business.

Even the Pope acknowledged that the Vatican Bank is too capitalistic, money-centric, and has no ethics. Pope Francis said he will close it, fix it, or fix it a little bit more. (But the Bank has some real power brokers behind it, and it's been around a lot longer than he has.)

Obviously, the Catholic Church is political too, and multinational, even if it isn't registered as a corporation. The Catholic Church reportedly has one million employees, with an annual budget of one hundred billion dollars, and assets estimated at seven billion dollars.

What the Vatican really is, however, according to International Law, is extraterritorial, a sovereign territory. THE VATICAN IS A COUNTRY OF ITS OWN WITH ITS OWN LAWS, INHABITED BY ABOUT 800 PEOPLE, AND NO CHILDREN. It is not a part of Rome or Italy. Vatican City is an absolute theocratic monarchy controlled by the pope and the cardinals under the Lateran Treaty of 1929, making it the independent and sovereign Vatican City-State. It's a world on its own. *There is no highly-touted separation of church and state because the church is the state.* Any function of government is guided and dictated by religion, and all state functions are headed by clergy. Thanks to a sweetheart deal cut with the horrific, power-hungry fascist Benito Mussolini, who signed the agreement on behalf of the king of Italy, even the Italian authorities are powerless when it comes to the Vatican and the Catholic Church. The Roman Catholic Church had full autonomy, just as Mussolini's government did. *(That's what I call one helluva' heavenly deal.)*

The Roman Catholic Church conspired with a tyrant and one of the world's worst human rights violators, who believed that everybody should work, but nobody should work against the state. So, the Roman Catholic Church too is totalitarian, globally, also believing that nobody should defy it. WHAT POSSIBLE JUSTIFICATION COULD THE VATICAN, AND MORE PRECISELY THE POPE, HAVE HAD

FOR MAKING A DEAL WITH THE DEVIL? Vatican inhabitants can't be taxed, subpoenaed, or even forced to appear in court by the Italian government. (Now *that's* power. The Vatican is a monarchy where absolute power is absolutely free to corrupt, the same way it is with today's unchecked Protestant church, like the mafia.)

In 2012, Monsignor George Ganswein, one of the pope's personal secretaries, was accused of stealing papers from the pontiff's desk (the Vatileaks scandal). The papers that were leaked contained allegations of corruption, incompetence and nepotism against the Vatican secretary of state, Cardinal Tarcisio Bertone. (No, not corruption at the Vatican too. Impossible?) The pope's butler Paolo Gabriele was arrested (the scapegoat), even though he argued his innocence. After being sentenced to prison, he was pardoned by the pope and guaranteed a job as long as he kept what he knew secret. (Secrets. Secrets. And still more secrets).

Pope John Paul II's secretary Stanislaw Dziwisz has written his own book *"Very Much In God's Hands. Personal Notes 1962-2003"*, against the will of the pope. The pope had ordered his trusted confidant to burn the notes upon his death, so is Dziwisz a hero for wanting the world to know John Paul personally, or a traitor for defying him? At any rate, somebody's going to make a ton of money.

The real problem is politics and conspiracy inside the Vatican, which has been going on since its inception. Pope Benedict, who was already eighty-five years old, decided to step down for health reasons (so he said), which meant a new election, with tailors and shoemakers in Rome being very busy. Benedict, the first pope to resign in nearly six-hundred years, retired to a magnificent Italian villa, Castel Gandolfo, with his own personal staff for a life of prayer, from then on being known as the Pope Emeritus. *Can God's representative just quit, or be fired?*

Other popes who have resigned include Benedict IX, who quit to get married in 1045, even though he went back to being pope when the bride-to-be stood him up. He also had to leave town in a hurry after being accused of adultery and murder. For 22 days, beginning in 1045, after Benedict IX's retreat, Sylvester III served as pope, dying in exile after Benedict managed to have him excommunicated. Clement II was pope from 1046 to 1047, when he died of suspected poisoning. Gregory VI then paid his godchild Benedict IX to be pope, but buying the papacy didn't work for him either, and he was forced to resign a year later. So Benedict IX was the only man who ever lived who was pope twice.

With the exception of John Paul II and Benedict, the last forty-five popes have been Italians. ARE ITALIANS REALLY GOD'S CHOSEN PEOPLE AND NOT THE JEWS? Why doesn't God ever choose women? Maybe that's because not even one woman is a priest, bishop, or cardinal. And the Catholic hierarchy would like to keep it that way. *Imagine God's Boys' Club being infiltrated.*

Although Benedict XVI claimed health concerns to be the reason for his resignation, there has always been talk about sex, money, power, and criminal activity inside the Vatican. Scottish Cardinal Keith O'Brien even resigned amid charges of homosexual activity with male prostitutes, and a homosexual ring of gay priests.

Even gay popes however, are nothing new, like Pope Paul II, Pope Sixtus IV, Pope Leo X, who had his lover Cardinal Alfonso Petrucci killed after an alleged attempt to assassinate him, and Pope Julius III, who reportedly slept in the same bed with his lover, Innocenzo Ciocchi Del Monte.

Another thing is that gay men (there are no women in the Holy See), are the ones who are hypocritically renouncing homosexuality and fiercely fighting against same-sex marriage. The "Vatileaks" scandal was allegedly one of the reasons for Pope Emeritus Benedict's shocking resignation. Many said the "gay lobby" had forced him out. Naturally, the Vatican said the whole thing was "defamatory, unverified, unverifiable, and completely false." (Was the Vatican lying again?)

The gay community, however, considered the entire matter insensitive and homophobic. According to Franco Grillini, president of Gaynet Rights Group, "That priests have sex with other men doesn't authorize anyone to speak about a gay lobby, because we're not talking about a group that represents the interests of the homosexual community, but rather a group that is an integral part of a power structure." (*In other words, don't put us in that mess at the Vatican.*)

And just who do these pompous, arrogant, so-called world spiritual leaders and heavenly aristocrats think they are? These grandiose, self-righteous, egotists. Pope Francis has urged Church leaders to *"avoid behaving as if they were in a royal court."* He said that "the bishops, cardinals and the pope need to be good servants of God, not good bosses of God's people. Stop being arrogant, egotistical, petty and nasty." Some experts say that Siricius was the first bishop to call himself "pope," while others say it was Damasus I, around 366. And Leo I, a lawyer-pope, was only the second to call himself "the Great," insisting that as pope, he was the only guardian of what the church sanctioned. (*A lawyer-pope saying, "Just trust me." It figures.*)

By the way, it's the 21st Century and Pope Francis, the oldest of five children, is a trained chemical technician (scientist), with a master's degree in chemistry from the University of Buenos Aires. Earlier as a janitor he swept floors, then worked for a while as a bouncer at a nightclub in Buenos Aires. (The pope threw drunks and troublemakers out of bars but became Time Magazine's Man Of The Year for 2013, and Esquire Magazine's best dressed). Pope Francis also made the cover of Rolling Stone Magazine, and there's even a mural of him as a flying superhero painted on the side of a building near the Vatican.

It is alleged that in 2012 Pope John Paul II elevated "Opus Dei" to the first and only personal prelature which is not linked to any church, except where they live. It is a self-organized power, and most prelates live in Rome. Opus Dei is frequently thought of as a secretive cult of the Catholic Church with a jurisdiction and bishops of its own, elected by specific members who are appointed by the pope. (*More secret above-the-law stuff.*)

Theirs is an ancient world of existentialism and pageantry, not at all like the modern, real world the rest of us are living in. Especially the pope who sits on the throne of St. Peter as a king. Not just any king, but literally king of the world, who rules over everybody else. *The Pope is the only man alive who is not subject to any authority on earth.* And, of course, none of the Catholic hierarchy are married or have any children of their own. That is, unless they were previously Lutheran or Anglican priests who were already married with families, like the 80 to 120 Anglican priests who have recently been ordained Catholic priests, and thousands of others who quietly go about their duties. Typically married priests inconspicuously work as seminary teachers or chancery workers without parishes. All it takes is a dispensation from the Pope and you're "good to go." In the Byzantine, Ukrainian, Russian and Greek Catholic churches priests can be married, but bishops must remain celibate.

Incredibly, it means that today there are Catholic priests who are indeed married. In 2009, Pope Benedict XVI declared that the new policy was acceptable, making it official. But actually, there has never been any apostolic or theological reason why priests couldn't be married all along. Just as there has never been any reason why women couldn't be priests. In fact, during Jesus' time, rabbis were expected to be married. In 1975 there were about 59,000 Catholic priests in America; today there are only 39,000. Allowing priests to be married now may not be theological or apostolic at all, but necessary. Many parishes have no full-time resident priest, and in the U.S. half of the priests are planning to retire by 2019. In Brazil, for example, there are 50,000 parishes served by only 17,000 priests.

Latin America is home to 39 percent of the world's Catholics. At one time Catholics represented 99 percent of the Brazilian population, while today they are only 57 percent, having lost ground to evangelical (prosperity ministry) Protestants. Much of the loss can be attributed to allegations of corruption and child sex abuse.

But the Catholic Church is far from being alone when it comes to sex abuse scandals. In the May/June 2014 issue of *The American Prospect,* Boz Tchividjian, the late Billy Graham's grandson believes that the Protestants' response to sexual abuse has been worse. A former prosecuter who teaches law at Jerry Falwell's Liberty University in Lynchburg, Virginia, he says that Churches are havens for abusers. *93 percent of convicted sex offenders describe themselves as religious.* Offenders who report strong church ties also abuse more often, with younger victims. In the article, *"By Grace alone",* Kathryn Joyce tells how Tchividjian is on a mission to persuade Protestant churches to come clean.

For example during a *20/20* report in 2011 it was revealed that 15-year-old Tina Anderson, who lived in New Hampshire was raped and impregnated by one of the church deacons while working as a babysitter. Her parents told their pastor, who had the teenager stand in front of the congregation while he read a confession about her pregnancy. Tina was then sent away to have the baby, who was put up for adoption. Her rapist, a registered sex offender, confessed as well—but to adultery, not rape. After his confession he was still permitted to remain with the church.

At a Pentacostal church two sisters, 8 years old and 12 years old, were allegedly being abused by their Sunday School volunteer, a convicted sex offender. The girls told their parents, and when the father approached the pastor, he advised a sit-down with the volunteer.

Tchividjian said during the meeting "the perp did what perps usually do: cry and ask for forgiveness, so happy he was caught." Naturally, the pastor thought that was repentence enough, and the accused could prove it by staying active in the church. *Reporting the incidents to the authorities wouldn't be necessary.* The father agreed, if that's what God wanted them to do. Six years later the victims' family was asked to leave the church, with no consideration for what had happened to the two girls. Tchividjian says that he had seen the same thing happen many times before.

He said that even when there's a trial pastors would come to court supporting the perpetrator, not the victim. "Church people—always looking to see the best in people, to welcome converts, to save sinful souls—are easy to fool." When something does surface, all too often the leadership quiets it down because they're concerned about reputation. "This could harm the name of Jesus, so let's just take care of it internally." Religion can be used to sweep abuse under the rug. After years of investigating abuse cases Tchividjian says "we spend our days swimming in Christian cesspools."

Another problem for the Catholic Church in Latin American countries is its birth control policy. The average Brazilian mother has lots of children. But is the church's policy deliberately designed not to prevent unwanted birth, but to maximize potential births? (Create more little Catholics.) One Brazilian woman named all fifteen of her children Walter, after her husband. And a ninety-year-old Brazilian man who fathered at least fifty children must be the Catholic Church's all-time favorite daddy. He doesn't even know all their names.

Pope Francis' humility stands in stark contrast to Benedict's aristocratic elitism. In Brazil, Francis wasn't surrounded by a host of bodyguards, carried his own bags onto the plane, and rode around Rio in a Fiat. Even on the plane he was like any other passenger, laid-back as he casually talked to reporters. Benedict wanted questions ahead of time, and the Vatican would decide which ones he would answer. (Even though Pope Francis is a regular guy, his 53 million-dollar visit did piss off a lot of poor Brazilians.) The 2014 World Cup set them back another 14.5 billion dollars.

With all the problems the Catholic Church is having, nobody knows where it is headed, and even the number of marriages and baptisms (and maybe money) is down. Some parishes won't be having daily masses or masses every Sunday (a big problem for the Catholic Church). In northern France one priest serves twenty-seven parishes. *Twenty years from now there won't be any priests left.* (Manpower problems). And like everybody else, today Catholic families are also having fewer children, which means fewer priests. (Because of the acute shortage you can now access a priest through Rent-A-Priest, by calling 1-800-Priest-9, by going to the website www.rentapriest.com, e-mailing rentapriest@aol.com, or just writing them.)

Incidentally, for centuries the Catholic Church's policy has been that when a pope dies his chamberlain approaches him asking "Are you dead?" When there is no reply the chamberlain picks up a silver hammer and strikes the Pope on the head, repeating the question. "Are you dead?" The Pope's name is called out three times, and when there is still no response, the chamberlain declares him dead. (But suppose the Pope hasn't died but is only in a coma?) I guess officially he's still dead.

Pope Stephen VII was so crazy that he had the corpse of his immediate predecessor Formosus, who had been dead for nine days, brought into the council chamber and put on trial, with his lawyer present. Screaming like a madman throughout the proceedings, Pope Stephen then had the corpse's clothes removed and his fingers cut off, before dragging the body through the Palace and thrown off a balcony. Pope Stephen himself ended up being strangled to death.

CHAPTER 5

Scandals & Constantine's Consolidation

As previously stated, for twenty-five years Joseph Ratzinger led the office for investigating allegations of sex abuse by priests, the "Congregation For The Dictum Of The Faith." In 2001, every serious Catholic sex abuse case involving minors went to him. Not some, but all. He knew more about acts of sexual immorality, perversion, and pedophilia within the Catholic Church than anyone else on earth. Records of child sex abuse by priests had been recorded as far back as the fourth century.

In 2014 the United Nations convened a panel to investigate tens of thousands of child sex abuse cases. They wanted detailed records on all alleged incidents committed by clergy, brothers and nuns. Including compensation, confidentiality, and the names of priests who were transferred, further endangering unsuspecting children. One committee has already accused the Catholic Church of protecting itself instead of the victims, saying that priests who have been abusers should be removed immediately.

Many of those children have been scarred for life. Awash in feelings of guilt and shame, they fail both in school and later in life. In response the U.N. wants any clergy suspected of child sex abuse reported to law enforcement authorities, not recycled and moved to other parishes and even other countries. Many want Vatican records opened so abusers and their protectors can finally be punished. The Vatican calls that *interference in its affairs. It says that dealing with sexual abuse by priests is nobody else's business.* But how is sexual violence against anyone not everybody's business, especially in church? Nobody expects Jewish Rabbis or Protestant preachers to get away with rape. Why should Catholic priests be able to do it? Not in Rome at the Vatican, but anywhere around the world. In Australia 7% of Catholic priests abuse children.

Archbishop Silvano Tomasi, the Vatican Representative in Geneva, found himself at odds in trying to convince the Committee Against Torture that the Holy See is responsible only for the actions of those inside the Vatican City State, less than 1,000 people. According to Tomasi, the Vatican, the world's smallest country, is actually separate from the Catholic Church. In fact guidelines issued by a panel of bishops explicitly states that they are not required to inform law enforcement authorities if they suspect a child has been sexually assaulted.

There was even an attempt to have Pope Benedict XVI and Vatican Cardinals investigated for possible crimes against humanity, but the court based in the Hague rejected the request. Pope Francis said he takes personal responsibility for the "evil" of clergy sex abuse, and sought forgiveness from victims.

Pope Francis himself formed an advisory board called the Pontifical Commission for the Protection of Minors, to approve accountability in dealing with abuse allegations. It consists of three clergy and five laypeople, including Boston's Cardinal Sean O'Malley, the same O'Malley who wasn't fair with the nuns. Even though the Pope apologized and insisted that those who are guilty will be held accountable, critics say that's not enough. They say that "Saying and doing are different things. All they do is talk!"

Pope Francis even fired Paraguayan Bishop Rogelio Ricardo Livieres Plano, who refused to resign after being accused of protecting pediphiles like Argentine priest the Rev. Carlos Urrutigoity. Urrutigoity was serving in Scranton, Pennsylvania, and even received a promotion to deputy bishop. He and Eric Ensey, another priest, were accused of molesting children at St. Gregory's Academy. Naturally, Urrutigoity was kicked out of his number two position. Bishop Plano's response "Pope Francis will have to answer to God not to him". In addition to cover-ups Plano was also accused of embezzlement. But who's to say? Maybe embezzlement is as widespread in the Catholic Church as sex abuse is.

Former Archbishop Jozef Wesolowski, Vatican Ambassador in the Dominican Republic was arrested and placed under house arrest. He faced up to twelve years in prison after being accused of paying for sex with children. Wesolowski's trial was the first ever held inside the Vatican for sexual abuse.

The Catholic Church has lost trust. Barbara Blain, president of the Survivors Network, said "Pope Francis and the bishops are not taking action that would protect children." According to the panel on torture, sexual violence and rape fall well within its definition. *Children are being tortured!* Under international law, there is no statute of limitations for torture, so somebody should definitely be going to jail. The Catholic Church could also be forced into facing lawsuits dating back decades. Under international law—in addition to prosecutions—accountability may finally be coming. (That's why Tomasi wants Vatican City kept separate from the Catholic Church). Nevertheless, the Vatican still has one more card to play. In its arrogance there is no guarantee that U.S. courts would agree with the U.N. committee, even when it comes to protecting innocent children. (*POLITICS*)!

In Boston, Cardinal John Law was involved in a cover-up that cost the church tens of millions of dollars. Instead of being fired, he was merely moved to Rome and given a palace to live in. Irish priest Tony Walsh, an Elvis impersonator known as "the singing priest," was Ireland's most notorious pedophile, abusing more than 200 children by his own account. The archdiocese of Dublin knew about his activities for more than twenty years, never informing parents or the police. Involved parents reported assaults to the archdiocese, but the church didn't punish the priest or support the victims for over ten years, allowing him to continue to abuse vulnerable, helpless children. Priests and the Vatican permitted the abuse to go on, dissuading victims from talking and alerting suspected priests. Walsh was finally convicted of sex abuse in 1995.

Los Angeles Cardinal Roger Mahoney was implicated in a child abuse scandal, and Father Marcial Maciel, founder of the Legion of Christ in 1941, with an annual budget of six hundred and fifty million dollars, has been labeled both a pedophile and a psychopath. Father Maciel, who was the Catholic Church's greatest fund raiser, has been called the devil in disguise, and was also accused of being a morphine addict and a ruthless sex criminal. He abused legionaries too, ordering them to masturbate him and participate in other sexual acts. Father Maciel has also had at least two mistresses and fathered four children, but according to Pope John Paul II, Father Maciel was a holy man and a visionary. Maciel told the boys he abused that if they told anybody their families would burn in hell. After abusing them he gave them absolution, forgiving them for sinning. Everyone involved had to swear that they would never say anything bad about Father Maciel.

Among those he abused were his own two sons. Raul Gonzales described how Maciel, his father, had ordered him to pull his pants down to show him how he wanted to be kissed (sucked), and then assaulted him. Maciel, who never wore his clergy attire, had successfully convinced his family in Monterrey, Mexico, that he was away from home so much because he worked for the CIA. In seventeen years they had never seen him dressed as a priest. They didn't know it until they saw his picture on the cover of a magazine tied to a church sex abuse scandal, and even then he denied that it was him. Father Maciel died in 2008 without ever going on trial . . . *still a priest*. Maciel, the pedophile, was also the grandnephew of Bishop Rafael Guizar Valencia, another Catholic saint. One of Maciel's uncles was successful in ordaining him a priest even after he was expelled from two seminaries. Upon Maciel's death it was announced that he was already in heaven.

At St. John's School For The Deaf, in Milwaukee, Wisconsin, Father Lawrence Murphy abused deaf children for years, children who had difficulty telling. In the confessional, Father Murphy would ask questions like "Have you been with other boys?" or "Do you play with yourself?" and then watch the boys masturbate and ejaculate after ordering them to pull down their pants. [Yet priests can forgive sins . . . How?]

Father Murphy then decided to move the confessional to a second-story closet where he continued his molestation. (Where were the nuns?)

Richard Sipe studied the phenomenon of celibacy in the priesthood for twenty-five years, and says that at any one time no more than 50 percent of Roman Catholic priests were practicing celibacy. Sipe says the hierarchy knows that celibacy is not being practiced, but acquiesced as long as it was kept secret (like the U.S. military's policy of don't ask, don't tell). "Noble cause corruption" was the justification (excuse), that good intentions purify bad behavior.

Father Murphy also enlisted older boys he had already abused to molest others with oral sex, breaking them in for him. During the summer, he would take some of the youngsters to his summer home where one of them was required to sleep with him, molesting the child almost every night.

According to Patrick J. Wall, a former Benedictine monk, there was a pattern of misuse, with treatment centers around the world for priests who abuse and sodomize children. Priests were removed and sent somewhere else, and Wall was authorized to pay up to $250,000 compensation to settle, provided there was a court order ensuring confidentiality.

In 1995, the budget to settle Catholic childhood sexual abuse cases was seven million dollars. The cases were never to be reported, but squelched. Father Murphy left St. John's for "health reasons" just before being publicly exposed. (Everybody leaves for health reasons.)

The Order of the Paraclete was opened by Father Fitzgerald to help priests who were sexual predators and alcoholics. He proposed buying an island in the Caribbean with a $5,000 down payment, but the idea was rejected by hierarchy. *From 1950 to 1990, the church spent eighty million dollars to treat more than 2,000 priests.* [Apparently vows of celibacy don't work].

The First Order of Secrecy was issued by the Vatican and since that time, the Catholic Church has spent an estimated three billion dollars. (The Catholic Church is really, really rich, even though Jesus reserved harsh criticism for rich people.) The problem for designated Pope Emeritus, Ratzinger, is that he was right smack-dab in the middle of it, and now he says he will never speak publicly again *(I'm not talkin'....! I ain't sayin' nothin' to nobody)*, except Francis I who is clueless. Before he stopped, however, as Pope Benedict he spoke about *filth* being inside the church. Remember, for twenty-five years before becoming pope, Cardinal Ratzinger headed the office called "Congregatio Pro Doctrina Fidei" or "Congregation For The Doctrine Of The Faith," the same office as the old Inquisition, which tortured and murdered tens of thousands who had been labeled heretics.

Under canon law, the law of the Roman Catholic Church, details of crimes were to be hidden behind church walls and never talked about publicly. Victims were sworn to absolute secrecy. That goes for the accused, the accuser, and even witnesses, as ordered by the Vatican. They will never reveal any details for fear of excommunication (blackmail)! Also under canon law, the pope cannot be judged by civil or religious authority. THE POPE REALLY IS ABOVE THE LAW! ANY LAW! Yet, he is only human like the rest of us. How can nearly 300 men, including murderers and perverts, be above the law simply by making up laws of their own and calling them *"Canon Law"*? *The Pope is not God, and it does not say that he is in any creed or catechism.* The pope can't create his own doctrine or speak for God. Remember, there was a debate about whether or not Jesus was even God. But unlike Jesus, popes are absolutely 100% human, they catch colds and have diarrhea. So, why should any pope be accorded the highest moral voice in the world, and considered the closest we will ever come to God? ... Almost all white men! In the 13th Century Boniface VIII declared that the pope was superior to a prince, a king, or an emperor. Even pronouncing who goes to heaven.

Much of the information, relative to child sex abuse and the Vatican, can be seen in the HBO documentary *Mea Maxima Culpa, Silence in the House of God.* Curiously, the Protestant church's position is almost the same. *No questions!* Moreover, the Vatican says it doesn't have the authority to sanction priests around the world, ascribing that responsibility to the Bishops. (But keep sending those checks.)

Curiously, in Ganswein's case, he was charged with crimes against the state, not by the Italian government, but by the Vatican. It's also curious that while a medieval lord lived in a castle surrounded by peasants, the pope lives in a palace in absolute splendor, surrounded by other palaces with magnificent gardens and priceless works of art, with an annual budget estimated at three hundred and ten million dollars. Money that could be used to help feed and clothe the poor. (The new pope "the Father of Kings and Princes, the Pastor of the Universe, and the Vicar on Earth of Our Lord Jesus Christ," was chosen, not by God but by men, and like Emperor Constantine the Great, because of a few sweetheart deals.) And did God make the pope, who has no children, the Father of Kings and Princes and Pastor of the Universe? I didn't see that in any of the Bibles I consulted either. Maybe I wasn't being thorough enough. And what about Jesus? Was he the Father of Kings and Princes and Pastor of the Universe too, like the Pope? Who thinks of that kind of foolishness anyway? Pastor of the Universe? I guess that includes the sun and the moon. It's the biggest job in the cosmos. Maybe popes should start taking on names like Pope Jupiter or Pope Apollo.

The Pope also presides over high-level meetings at the Vatican. Infallible, he exercises supreme authority in teaching and speaks for Jesus until his death or retirement. Obedience to the Pope is a Cardinal Rule. Papal Supremacy began around 606 and infallibility around 1076. *The pope is never wrong and never makes mistakes (maybe they should rename them "God II, God III, and the like," since they're already acting for God). But what about Pope Julius II who said black people didn't have souls, and Pope Pius XI who sided with Mussolini after World War I, and then Hitler?* Certainly Jesus would not have picked Rome, especially an opulent Vatican City as his base of operations. (With all that the Romans have done to Christians for centuries, why is the Vatican in Rome and run by Romans instead of Capernaum, where Jesus had many followers, or someplace he liked? And why is Jesus' church now the Roman Catholic Church?) Maybe politics, power, money, and too many Italians for Pope Francis. There is now a movement afoot to have the Vatican city-state status rescinded.

If the Church of England has no real authority outside of the UK today, why does the Roman Catholic Church enjoy such privileges outside of Rome? The Famiglia, chief laymen at the Vatican, come from the oldest

Roman families, but what the hell does Rome have to do with America? During the second century it was Tertullian, a prominent church father, who asked almost the same question. *"What has Athens [Greece] to do with Jerusalem?"* I like the Tertullian reference, and I think it makes a lot of sense. It was Tertullian, writing in Latin rather than Greek, who originated much of the terminology that influenced early Christian and Western theology. For Tertullian, it didn't make sense that Greece should have so much influence in Jerusalem, just as it doesn't make sense for Rome to have so much authority in New Orleans or in New York City today. *Why are Americans being told what to do by a few puffed-up, out-of-touch white men in Vatican City?*

At the Vatican and later at the Basilica of the Sagrada Familia in Barcelona, my wife and I literally witnessed tens of thousands of tourists and crowded tour buses, plus store owners, and vendors on street corners selling everything from smiling pictures of Pope Francis waving, to hot dogs and cold sodas. Everybody was eager to see the Vatican and the Basilica of the Sagrada Familia, and to experience their unique splendor. What they saw and experienced were thousands of others who were casually dressed like themselves, using smartphones to take pictures too, of graven images like those denounced in Exodus 20.

There were thousands upon thousands of pilgrims and tourists. Interestingly, I have seen it written somewhere that all Christians are not Catholics, and that most Catholics aren't real Christians because they have fallen into idolatry (like kneeling and kissing the pope's ring, or kissing a porcelain doll representing Jesus, a doll that somebody made and then painted). And Catholic dogma means nothing. In Acts 10: 25-26, *when Cornelius, the Roman centurion fell to his knees to worship Peter, Peter told him to get up. Peter (the first Pope) said "stand up; I myself also am a man"*. Other pagan practices included the lighting of candles, beginning in 320 A. D., the worship of saints around 375, the wearing of distinctive robes by priests in 500, and kissing the Pope's foot in 709. Holy water was invented in 850, prayer beads were introduced in 1090, indulgences were first sold in 1190, and confessions began in 1215. The

key point is that all of these traditions were invented or thought-up by somebody, especially indulgences, which was a lucrative way of making money. Today's Vatican "saints factory" sells sainthood. (Just think about this. *Jesus never tasted any holy water, carried prayer beads, or confessed his sins to any human being.*) Where does *holy water* come from anyway? Just about everything concerning religion is man made! *Made up!*

Seeing all those "holy-commercial" excesses, I'm sure Jesus would have gone, not just postal, but ballistic. Jesus probably had one pair of shoes, walked thousands of miles or rode on a donkey, and never owned his own house. When the donkey died, he walked. An ancient itinerant preacher, Jesus spent most of his time with poor people, living as they did. In fact, Jesus probably never traveled more than 100 miles away from his own village. As pope, Benedict rode in a $120,000-dollar-modified M Class Mercedes SUV Popemobile, flew in a private helicopter, and lived in a pseudo-utopian paradise.

For the record, however, Pope Francis saw all the fancy cars priests and nuns were riding around in and said it hurt his heart thinking about so many children in the world who are hungry. (My thought exactly.) His car of choice is a donated, used, white, 1984 Renault with 190,000 miles on it. *Pope Francis says that a shepherd for the faithful must smell like his sheep.* As pope for the forgotten and the forsaken, that also means no palace. Instead, Francis resides in the Vatican guest house where he entertains and holds meetings. Having lived in the real world as a young man, the pope realizes that clergy can be tempted and corrupted by power, and fears that some have become "wolves and not shepherds." In fact, it's been said that the only thing worse than a wolf in sheep's clothing is a wolf in shepherd's clothing.

As leader of the world's Catholics, Pope Francis said that he is the bishop of Rome, and not the entire planet. (Like I said, it's a big job.) *Being a Jesuit and an intellectual, and coming from a tradition of social*

awareness and poverty, the pope says he wants a poor church for poor people . . . (good luck with that). In the twelfth Century the original St. Francis was rich, but gave up everything, including his clothes. It was also St. Francis who said, "God make me an instrument of thy peace." During a visit to Assisi, Italy, St. Francis' hometown, Pope Francis even ate at a soup kitchen with everyday, ordinary people.

In Matthew 19:21, *when the rich young man asks Jesus what he needs to do to be perfect, Jesus tells him to "go sell your possessions and give your money to the poor."* The account in Mark 10:21 has Jesus telling him to *"sell what you own and give the money to the poor."* (Maybe the Vatican and the Protestant church should do the same thing. Sell everything to help the poor.) By the way, even though Pope Francis I was born Jorge Mario Bergoglio, in Argentina, his father, Mario Jose Bergoglio, was born in Italy, and his mother, Regina Maria Sivori, was born in Buenos Aires of Italian parents. In fact Fascism was the reason why Pope Francis' father, an accountant, moved from Italy to Argentina in the first place. So, basically, Francis I is still an Italian. (Damn those Italians!) Sneaky. But Francis is touted as the first non-Italian pope in centuries, the first pope from South America, and the first non-European pope since Gregory III centuries ago. (More public relations.)

During the third century, Cyprian, somebody we would know today as a lawyer, gave up his practice and sold everything he had to help poor Christians. Cyprian, who didn't like rich people very much because of what he called the "insecurity of riches," was actually the first person to call himself a "born-again Christian."

Another reason why Christianity survived was Roman Emperor Constantine the Great, a pagan, who as previously mentioned, also cut a few sweet deals for himself. In 325 AD at the Council of Nicea, Constantine, who financed the first Bible, and whose mother Saint Helena was a devout Christian, had the final say-so as to how Christianity would or would not be practiced. *Emperor Constantine, like the Apostle Paul, was deciding who God was.* Before he took charge, Christianity, a relatively unimportant sect, was small and not well organized at all, with most people thinking Christians were either insane or drunkards. To most people the early Christian church was a joke. (Remember Noah, the first drunk in the bible, Lot – Abraham's nephew, and those other guys with their vino, who talked to God in their sleep.)

Organized Christians who were mostly illiterate gave Emperor Constantine complete control. During the Fourth Century AD, Constantine decided that some of the ancient gospels such as the Gospel of Judas, discovered in 2006, the Gospel of Mary, the Gospel of Phillip, the Gospel of Thomas, and nearly fifty other gospels and writings were not to be included in the sacred book so *Jesus would appear to be less human and more supernatural in the books that did get into the Bible.* To make Jesus more God like. (LIKE PAUL, CONSTANTINE MADE JESUS "BIGGER THAN LIFE.") He decided which books would get in, and which ones would not. *And like Don Corleone in Mario Puzo's "The Godfather", Constantine made both the Christians and the people of Rome an offer they couldn't refuse.* He also made his family offers they couldn't refuse, boiling his wife alive and having his son executed.

Constantine decided to protect the Christian religion, tearing down unbelievers' houses of worship and giving the grounds to the Catholic Church. It all started with a vision Constantine had of a Christian cross just before going to war, and winning. From that point on, believing in the power of Christianity, he converted.

There are experts however, who say that Constantine never had that dream, and that Bishop Eusebius, the man who baptized Constantine, rewrote the events of the "Battle of the Milvian Bridge", including the dream, 13 years after the event. Eusebius, a distant relative of Constantine, was an ambitious wheeler-dealer, authenticating the dream to make Constantine appear to be divinely inspired. Eusebius was also an unorthodox scholar who probably helped Constantine in orchestrating his plan, declaring him the first Christian Bishop. *But was Constantine only pretending to be a Christian who worshiped Jesus, and was his goal to actually sabotage Jesus' message and to replace him?* CONSTANTINE TRANSFORMED JESUS, THE PASSIONATE

REVOLUTIONARY INTO A PEACE-LOVING FLOWER CHILD WHO WAS DIVINE, GOD'S SON...AND GOD!

Emperor Domitian, Titus Flavius Domitianus, one of Constantine's heroes, was a ruthless autocrat, the last of the Flavian dynasty, who hated Jews and Christians. He was assassinated in a conspiracy which included his wife Domitia in 96 A.D. Domitian administered a totalitarian government, seeing himself as the man to guide both private and public morals, as Constantine later would.

Domitian firmly believed in the traditional Roman religion and revered Jupiter. He fiercely persecuted Jews and Christians, and considered Christians either Jews or atheists. He was the first Roman Emperor to be called *"dominus et deus" or Lord of God.* (Sounds like Catholicism. Again, was Constantine, who was an adherent of Domitian, only practicing *"if you can't beat 'em join 'em?" But not really).* Constantine's full name was Flavius Valerius Aurelius Constantinus Augustus, and throughout his life he made sacrifices to gods like Apollo, Hercules and Diana. *Was Constantine scamming Christians, who were a threat to Rome, only saying he believed in God and Jesus to gain their support?* POLITICS!

Constantine built magnificent churches for his co-conspirator Catholic friends, giving them judicial power and actually making some of them judges. In fact, before the scheme was uncovered in the 1400s, it was commonly believed that Constantine had handed over to Pope Sylvester and the Catholic Church dominion over his entire empire in perpetuity, including the city of Rome. In their secular role popes ruled most of Italy for over 1,000 years, supported by their own army. For the Catholic Church that was one brilliant scam to make the church even wealthier. Forever! It was a forgery called the "Donation of Constantine," and it was attributed to the fact that Constantine was so grateful to Pope Sylvester for curing him of leprosy that he wanted the church to have almost everything. Cunningly, the whole thing was a lie concocted in the Curia. (Lies and forgery by the Catholic Church almost 2,000 years ago, and even Pope Gregory VII was said to be a master forger.) Later, under the "Donation of Pepin," even more territory was claimed.

At the Council of Nicea the hierarchy of bishops was established and the long line of "papal royalty" began. The Vatican started as a glorified library. The pope commissioned that all papal documents and books be brought to Rome. *The question remains as to why they wanted everything else destroyed. Remember, history is written by winners. White history!!!*

Constantine's motive for consolidating Christianity (making up the rules), was not spiritual but political, to unify the church and the state in Rome, with both entities serving him. Constantine ruled supreme. There would be no dividing line between religion and politics. The tenants of Christianity were instituted and placed under the control of the emperor. Himself. With the Edict of Milan in 313 Christianity was legalized, becoming the official state religion and exported. For world domination the Roman Empire helped the spread of Christianity. No more Gnosticism. Before that there were too many people, 75% of them in Rome slaves, following different religions. Constantine realized that Christianity could pull everything together. And since Paul had written that leaders received God's blessings, rebelling against Constantine would essentially be rebelling against God.

For followers Jesus was the "sun of God", the light, wisdom and essence of God. Not a human son. To convert Romans to Christianity, Constantine proclaimed Jesus as the "son of God", the same as Mithra.

Small family-based secret meetings, held at believers' houses to talk about Jesus and discuss problems were prohibited, with lowly community priests being elevated to leadership positions, and paid. The ruling class mentality of the Romans was transferred to the church, mirroring Roman imperial court ceremonies, with kneeling, priestly robes, statues, strict formal mass, and paying no taxes. Obsessed with status, political power became consolidated in a male hierarchy controlled by Constantine's ruling class, and moved away from the average person. (The invention of the Catholic Church.)

Because of Emperor Constantine the Great everybody had to worship the same God. Christians were also no longer to fight and kill each other. Archbishop Anastasius issued the decree that only officially sanctioned books were to be read, and all others were to be destroyed. Alternative views were not to be made public. It was then that Constantine's Bible was created, 50 parchment copies. For political reasons. If God inspired the gospels, Constantine, the first Roman Emperor to become a Christian inspired the Bible using money. *Don't read any other books. Don't copy any other books. And burn everything else.* Later, competing Bibles such as the Wycliffe Bible, the Tyndale Bible, and the Geneva Bible would be outlawed.

For 1700 years Catholics were not allowed to read bibles, relying solely on the priests explanations of Latin translations. During that time a fictitious devil was conveniently dreamed-up to take the rap for all of the world's problems. Afterall, it was only human nature to blame something or somebody else for whatever was going wrong in their lives.

The devil was the perfect fall-guy. Priests then vilified him to intimidate believers, thereby insuring their own job security. As for human beings, are God and the devil merely superstitious prattle or coping devices that provide a calming, finite sense of closure? When I die I already know I'm going home to glory! To the spirit in the sky. *Hope for heaven, fear of hell.* Filled with contradictions however, reading the bible may actually leave you more confused and insecure.

There was generally a lack of any original corroborating evidence outside of Christian beliefs. Because ancient manuscripts were copied by hand there were often changes, some accidental while other were deliberate, which I'll discuss later. Similar to Christian documentation, manuscripts by early historians like Josephus, Herodotus, Origen and Eusebius cannot definitively be authenticated either.

CHAPTER 6

Reason's for Christianity's Survival

William Tyndale's (1494–1536) Bible, the number one reason, was the first to be translated into English from Hebrew (the Old Testament) and Greek (the New Testament). It was the first Bible to be mass produced for the common man. This, at a time when the Bible was a "forbidden book" only to be read by clergymen. For Tyndale the church was the believers, not the Catholic Church structure which he and other early reformers considered unnecessary. *Scripture alone was important, not a visible, systematized institution but the people themselves.* They considered lay members and clergy equal, with the clergy not being of a higher order than ordinary Christians. *Elders, selected by the people, could take the place of priests.* Some reformers believed every Christian was a priest who could read and interpret the Scriptures, and that *power should belong to the people.* Tyndale stated that his purpose was "to cause a boy that driveth the plough to know more Scripture" than clergy who were typically illiterate. (Everybody should be able to read the Bible for themselves). He was strangled to death and burned at the stake. (Never cross the Catholic Church.) Tyndale's Bible, in English, influenced 90 percent of the Authorized King James Version of the Bible, helping to shape civilizations throughout the world.

John Wycliffe (1330–1384) was an English philosopher, theologian, translator and preacher, who was one of the first to challenge the teachings of the Roman Catholic Church. At a time when few people could read, Wycliffe was the first person to do a complete English translation of the Bible, handwritten, before the printing press was invented. He said that "it helpeth Christian men to study the gospel in that tongue in which they know best Christ's sentence." (If it was printed in English everybody could read their own Bible.)

Wycliffe also argued that monasticism (organized religion) was corrupt, and that the priests were unworthy. Wycliffe charged that there was a big difference between what the church should have been doing and what it was actually doing. He too believed that the church should be poor, as Jesus and the disciples were. *He also said that no pope can say that he is the head of the church. (If it is God's church, how could the pope be its head? As of today, 266 of them throughout history.)* After he died, Pope Martin V ordered Wycliffe's body dug up, burned, then thrown in the River Swift. (Nuts ... Now that's evil. And the pope did it!)

If you were caught reading any other version of the Bible than the Authorized King James Version, you could be arrested or killed. Because of Constantine and his cronies, other ancient writings had to be hidden, and it is those recently discovered books that are giving us a clearer picture of Jesus and the world he lived in.

As emperor, with wealthy, powerful priests in his back pocket, there was no stopping Constantine when it came to making himself top man of both the church and the state. Like Emperor Domitian, who considered himself God, even though he had murdered his own brother, Constantine also had delusions of being divine.

Constantine, whom the Catholic Church now regards as a saint, had his oldest son Crispus poisoned, and his wife, the Empress Fausta, boiled to death at his mother, Saint Helena's orders. Emperor Constantine, the man most responsible for the Holy Scriptures and Holy Bible had no problem killing his next of kin.

At the Council of Nicea he provided food, drinks, and other goodies to make sure the bishops were kept happy and on his side. Much like today, Constantine, the crooked politician, knew what it took to bribe the corrupt holy men. Anyone declared a heretic was punished and *their writings destroyed* as well. And under Constantine, anybody insulting a priest could be killed. (Don Carleone's kind of protection for priests.) Constantine, the man who helped shape and spread Christianity, was also thought to be an evil fanatic who skillfully used religion to suit his own ends, believing that whatever happened was God's will, no matter how cruel or inhumane, or it never would have happened. (If God didn't approve he wouldn't have gotten away with it.)

Emperor Constantine, the supposed benevolent Christian, was not a very nice man at all. He was in fact a brutal dictator who was manipulative and depraved. Constantine's consolidation of Christianity actually had little to do with God or Jesus; yet it was he who decided which type of Jesus and religious ideology Christians would follow. Put bluntly, *Constantine (inspired by his own obsession with power) designed Christianity. Not God, but Emperor Constantine,* who is now considered a saint, along with his mother the Empress Helena, even though he converted to Christianity only on his deathbed. Constantine had become very ill, promising that if he lived he would be a better Christian. As previously stated, some experts believe Constantine never became a Christian. That was a lie too, and merely another dying man's promise to do better.

Empress Helena, born into poverty, actually helped poor people, having many of them released from prison. But two millennia later we have corrupt, child-molesting priests and preachers being sanctified and living high on the hog, and most people still too lazy to do any real thinking for themselves. Many are living in poverty, with children who are unfortunately doomed to live empty lives. (In America priests and pastors have their own caste system.)

It is important to remember that just as the nature of God is questioned today, so it was 2,000 years ago. For example, "Who made God?" and "In the beginning were there others besides Adam and Eve?" Naturally, there were questions too about whether God was real or not thousands of years ago. Such questions just couldn't be asked openly.

In his massive 799-page book, *Pagans and Christians,* published in 1986, Robin Fox Lane speaks about life during Constantine's time. He says:

> *Christianity had never preached an outright social revolution.* There was no "liberation theology," no sanction

for a direct assault on the forms of social dependence and slavery ... Distinctions of rank and degree multiplied and the inequalities of property widened. [Christianity did nothing to help the poor and oppressed, while the rich got richer, but thanks to ministers and congregations of the 60s and 70s liberation theology is a reality today, critically supporting important social issues.]

While Christians have aggressively condemned so-called pagans as being primitive compared to monotheistic Christianity with its one God, under paganism there were many gods, cults, mysteries and philosophies to choose from. According to Lane, *"Paganism, a made-up Christian word, helped people to explain their misfortune in external terms, by errors, not by sin.* Pagans might be neglecting one angry divinity among many, whose mood accounted for their hardship." *In other words, no sin was committed; you just pissed-off the wrong god.* Likewise, there was "no one" or "no thing" to have faith in, knowing nothing about Judeo-Christianity or sinning.. *Today there are secular observers who simply say "shit happens."*

Robin Lane also says that because of prophecies and magical feats, people were relying less on common sense, and that *it was Christianity's good fortune that it came along at a time when people would believe anything.* (Many people, being irrational, naïve and gullible still believe anything.)

Today, there are people much like myself who wonder what the world might look like if a philosopher and thinker like Marcus Aurelius had been emperor during Jesus' time. As a stoic who repressed his feelings and was indifferent to pleasure and pain, a man dedicated to understanding, fate, and reason, he was the opposite of Constantine, the superstitious, consummately self-absorbed opportunist. Marcus Aurelius was highly educated, relatively fair-minded and honest. By contrast, Constantine was neither a good man nor the sharpest tool in the box. Marcus Aurelius was not a man driven by superstition or emotion. He was staunchly anti-Christian, but still took care of orphans, freed slaves, and unlike Constantine, didn't even persecute people who joked about him or criticized him. People Constantine (the Christian sympathizer) would have had chopped into little pieces.

As fair-minded as Marcus Aurelius was with his own people, emperor from 161 to 180 AD, he thoroughly disliked Christians. He had Christians tortured, even after they had already been beaten, making them walk barefooted on nails and sharp shells, then continued to have the skin beaten off of them until their veins could be seen. Marcus Aurelius was perfectly sane . . . until it came to Christians.

The point is that just as it is today, there were people who were smart and generally reasonable, who were not manipulated and misdirected by religion, superstition, or anything else that was fallacious and illogical. What if a thinker rather than a so-called Christian had been in charge and calling all the shots? What if the same were true today? Constantine actually believed the same ugly things about Jesus that Marcus Aurelius did, but pretending to be a Christian was critical in achieving his goal.

Unlike Constantine however, if Marcus Aurelius had been emperor during Jesus' time, there would have been no deal struck with corrupt, self-serving priests. *There would have been a greater emphasis on common sense, knowledge, and understanding, rather than ignorance and superstition disguised as faith.* Without the foreshadowing and the ethnocentrism of religion, man might truly have evolved and lived up to his intrinsic potential, as he clearly has not. According to Marcus Aurelius, "everything we hear is an opinion, not a fact. Everything we see is a perspective, not a truth." He also said, "*It is not death that a man should fear, but he should fear never beginning to live.*" (Great advice!) But Constantine had something else in mind: ignorance and superstition which continue to this day, leaving believers in the dark. Plus dominance and subordination.

Marcus Aurelius was succeeded by his son Commodus, one of the most evil Roman emperors who ever lived. Like others during that time, Commodus was one of the world's very first sex addicts, if there is such a thing, surrounding himself with 300 women. And boys. Commodus, who was definitely a few nuggets short of a happy meal, even called himself Hercules, competing in the arena and fighting both humans and animals before he was assassinated. And yes, he always won. For Commodus, life was one big happy orgy. Every day was sex, drugs, and "rock and roll."

Another opponent of Christianity around Jesus' time was the Greek Celsus, an intellectual like Marcus Aurelius, who also had a knowledge of other religions and mythologies. *Celsus, who lived during the Second Century, accepted the fact that Jesus was the natural son of Mary and Joseph, but found it contradictory that he was God's son since Jesus' own friends and countrymen, the people who had known him as a child obviously didn't believe it.* (Would you believe that somebody you know is God's son? If some poor, uneducated fourteen-year-old teenager living in Harlem or Memphis told you an angel said that she was going to have God's baby would you believe her?) Likewise, if someone can have a baby for God or his sons, could somebody else have had a baby for the devil, as in the movies, *"The Omen"* and *"Damien: Omen II"*?

Celsus didn't believe God had placed man above any other animal. What he did believe however, was that Jesus' miracles, like the resurrection, were lies made up by his disciples. He didn't like the fact that Christians believed according to blind faith instead of reason. *Celsus also felt that only women and ignorant men were choosing to be Christians.* Unlike Marcus Aurelius or the Romans, it wasn't that Celsus hated Christians, he just didn't believe them or trust them.

Celsus also didn't believe there existed something called a devil who was powerful enough to challenge God, and that that kind of thinking in itself was blasphemy. In today's Bahá'í faith Satan is not an independent evil power either, but rather a metaphor representing man's ego or his lower human nature.

It was Celsus who said Jesus' father was a Roman soldier named Panthera, who either seduced or raped Mary, and that *Jesus' miracles were sorcery, just like tricks performed by magicians.* Celsus tried to understand how somebody could "conclude from the same works that the one is of God and the other sorcery." *Celsus wanted to know how Jesus could say that the magicians' tricks (human sorcery) were not godly (magic), but his miracles were from God. (That's the same question any reasonable person would be asking today.)*

Celsus said Jesus invented his own virgin birth and that his disgraced mother, Mary, was a poor woman who had committed adultery and been kicked to the curb by her husband. Before coming back to Galilee from Egypt and declaring himself God's son, Celsus said Jesus just drifted from place to place. And he was only one of the many respected citizens who had questions and doubts about Jesus. Including his own family. In *Caesar's Messiah* author Joseph Atwill says the Romans invented a docile Jesus to pacify hostile Christians through mind control. (The reinvented Jesus used by American slave owners.)

This may be an unpopular view and hard to imagine now, but the real Jesus was actually an illiterate homeless drifter who called himself the messiah. (Not the sexy Jesus we see in Hollywood movies). Today there is a provocative life-size bronze statue *Jesus the Homeless*, by Canadian sculptor Timothy Schmalz, a devout Catholic, depicting Jesus as a homeless man sleeping on a park bench. It was inspired by Matthew 25: 35-46. The sculpture is outside St. Alban's Episcopal Church in Davidson, North Carolina, in the middle of an upscale neighborhood. Reverend Dr. David E. Buck, the rector says "we're reminded of what our ultimate call is as Christians," bringing church members closer to God when they sit on the bench beside the statue. As a homeless person Jesus is needy too. The sculpture is of Jesus hidden under a blanket. The only thing that tells you who it is are the crucifixion wounds on his uncovered, shoeless feet. Driving by for the first time one woman, thinking it was a real hobo, did indeed call the police. Schmalz says "It's meant to challenge people."

In November of 2013 Schmalz traveled to the Vatican, where he presented a miniature to Pope Francis himself. Pope Francis touched the knee of *Jesus the Homeless*, and closed his eyes and prayed. (Most people today could never accept the idea of Jesus, God's son being homeless.)

Centuries ago, at the Council of Nicea, Arius, the father of Arianism, believed that Jesus Christ wasn't one substance with God, rejecting that he had no beginning and no end the same as God. *"Jesus wasn't God."* Begotten by God, he was subordinate to God. Arius believed Jesus was a good man created by God for a particular purpose, but he shouldn't be worshiped. People were listening. Remember, many early Christians never believed Jesus was God anyway.

The question of Jesus' nature continues to this day. Arius, who died of poisoning, even believed that Jesus had free will and could do either good or evil, like anybody else. He was human, flesh and blood. *Jesus wasn't divine.* By extrapolation, Emperor Constantine the Great may have arrived at the conclusion that people might start thinking he wasn't divine either. Before being murdered, Arius was banished and excommunicated and *his writings destroyed. Burning everything else ultimately meant a "hail Mary" pass for Christianity and the Catholic Church.* (Getting rid of the competition.)

The very last thing Constantine wanted people to believe was that Jesus was human, a mere mortal like every other human being. CONSTANTINE CONFIRMED JESUS AS GOD'S SON, and in 380 AD Emperor Theodosius the Great made believing any other gospel heresy and a crime against the state. For the monophytes of Egypt, Palestine, and Syria, the opposite was believed and established beyond a doubt. Jesus Christ was absolutely God rather than man.

Two more reasons for Christianity's survival would be King James, who consolidated the Bible into the Old and New Testaments, and the invention of the Gutenberg printing press in 1436. That meant mass production of its first publication, the Bible, our very first literary masterpiece. *Quoting the great American philosopher George Santayana, "The Bible is literature not dogma."* True, simply because the church says it's true. *In my opinion the Bible is also propaganda.*

The King James Version however, was not actually the first Bible, but a revision of the Bishop's Bible of 1568, which in turn was a revision of the Great Bible of 1539. It all began with "textus receptus", work previously painstakingly collected by Desideratus Erasmus, a homosexual Christian monk. *Another reason why King James may have decided to produce the Bible was that he was an insecure cripple who stuttered.* (King James had problems.) He spoke several languages and loved reading. Believe it or not, today there is a *Queen James Bible* for homosexuals, edited to exclude homophobic misrepresentations about God's word.

There are accounts stating that King James was so vicious that he would make Adolf Hitler, who was raised Catholic like most Nazis, look like Santa Claus. Hitler, who Germans considered a gift from God once said, "Hence today I believe I am acting in accordance with the will of the Almighty Creator: by defending myself against the Jews, I am fighting for the work of the Lord." *So, King James, the man whose Bible most people read, like Constantine and Adolph Hitler, who also followed Christ, wasn't a very nice man either.* He was corrupt, manipulative, and vicious. The same King James Christians love to love.

The authorized King James Version of the Bible was published for the first time in 1611, and at that time there were strict restrictions on who could read it without being fined or put in jail. For example, women of high social status were allowed to read it, while commoners couldn't. And from that time forward, by order of the Church of England, it was the only Bible that was to be read. *Among the scholars who wrote the King James Version of the Bible was William Shakespeare, who had been instructed by the king not to let anybody know about his involvement.* Unlike the Gnostic scrolls which were much more primitive, the Bible was poetic and flowery because the English translation was written by professionals. King James's best. *So, was the Bible inspired or engineered?*

The men who translated the Bible in 1611 were the finest scholars and intellectuals in England at that time. While Shakespeare helped because he was an accomplished actor and playwright, he was not a linguist or a literary scholar as the others were. King James appointed fifty-four men, but only forty-seven worked until the end. The men working on the Bible were divided into six groups by Richard Bancroft, the bishop in charge of the project. Each man was responsible for translating a section, then passing it on to the others to review. There were seven men in each group. The versions were combined, then reviewed by everybody. After that, two men from each group made up a committee to review the entire translation. The final editing was done by Miles Smith and Thomas Bilson.

Among the scholars who edited the Bible were Lancelot Andrews, a master of fifteen languages, who learned a new language every summer,

John Bois, who had read the entire Hebrew Bible by the age of five, and Mark Smith, who spoke Hebrew, Chaldee, Syriac, and Arabic. Smith was called "a very walking library." As I said, King James' best edited the Bible. *Not inspired men. But geniuses who never knew Jesus.*

The next reason for Christianity's survival is the most compelling. Murder! Being killed by the church, and by Christians who went from being the hunted to being the hunter. Christians who were not being very Christ-like at all, sometimes like Moses, being mass murderers, practicing genocide and killing thousands. After Joshua won the Battle of Jericho he had everybody killed except Rahab, the prostitute his two spies had spent the night with, and her "peeps." *Kill everything that moves—all the men, women, children, old people, cows, sheep, and even the donkeys.* But remember to bring the silver, gold, bronze, and iron to me so I can give it all to God. Then burn everything else to the ground. Samuel became angry with King Saul because he didn't kill everybody as he said God had instructed. *Were early Christians actually terrorists?* David chopped off Goliath's head. Why didn't Saul obey Samuel? Did he think the old man was lying when he said God wanted everybody slaughtered, or did Saul think that Samuel was a fanatical, genocidal maniac? Throughout holy wars known as the Crusades, Christians murdered thousands of Muslims. During the Spanish Inquisition 200,000 people were arrested, tortured, or murdered by the Church. *Catholic Butchers!*

In Psalm 137, the Jews had fun slaughtering their enemies' children. Verse 8 reads, "O daughter of Babylon, you devastator! *Happy shall they be who pay you back for what you have done to us."* Verse 9 reads, *"Happy shall they be who take your little ones and dash them against the rock!"*

For Jesus' apostles after his death, continuing to preach was one way to make sure the cash kept coming in. And like today's priests and preachers, you could get paid big bucks for talking without ever breaking a sweat. Being a preacher was usually a pretty easy gig too, even back then. Admittedly, there was a downside: *torture and murder.*

A "Perfect Storm" of elements were in place for Christianity's continued survival, but there are still a few more reasons why it thrives.

Children, laziness, and finally sex. People generally feel that it's a good idea for their kids to receive the kind of discipline and moral instruction provided by the Church. And rather than finding their own answers, it's easier to just "go with the flow." My friend Blaine is a Catholic who sends his children to Catholic schools for precisely those reasons. I remember him telling me, "it's not so much I believe all that stuff. I mostly go because of my wife and my kids. But you've got to live with people; you know how it is . . ." *"Going along to get along!"*

For many blacks (and some whites) in America, I believe what Blaine said is true. There is certainly a very special reason for pretending to follow the tenants of Christianity and Jesus. Fear. Not the fear of being lynched or beaten, but fear of being ostracized or turned on by others who claim to be believers. Being dissed or bullied and finding yourself on the outside looking in. Many Christians attend church, not so much because they are believers, but because of tradition. *Habit!* Their parents and grandparents went to church so they go too. Because of a preacher who was crucified 2,000 years ago. *People are genuinely afraid to admit that they are not believers and have doubts . . . which is considered a sin.*

Another possible reason why Christianity may have survived is dopamine, the hormone that gives people a euphoric feeling when they are in love or high on crack, that makes believers feel ecstatic too; when they are emotionally stimulated and experiencing histrionics. Psychedelics also played a role. Like love, believing in Jesus may also be sentimental.

Today, 84% of women believe in God; 73% of men. And 91% of African Americans believe in God, compared to 81% of Hispanics and 78% of whites, even though blacks comprise only 13% of the national population. *Black people need Jesus!*

Unlike whites who are typically unfamiliar with threats and being punished or pushed around, having inherited a long legacy of freedom and of thinking and behaving independently, for blacks the experience has been quite the opposite. Most of us are personally all too familiar with coercion, intimidation, and aggrieved suppression. Rugged individualism, which has seemingly worked for white people, has typically been MIA (missing in action) for black people. *The fact is that blacks have advanced and survived as a group, due in large part to the belief in a God who loves and protects them.* In many ways Christianity was like the "placebo effect" (sugar pill). Just believing helped. *Miracles!* For at least three centuries slaves had nothing else. Even now, what is the fate of any black person who does not believe in God or who is not a loyal Democrat? We already know the short answer. *They're not black enough!*

Some of us truly are afraid of the unknown. Suppose God is real and I piss him off by denying him. What if I steal a Rolex or hook up with my co-worker this weekend while her husband goes fishing? Is God going to punish me? Will I go straight to hell for stealing and cheating? Sixty-year-old adults are as frightened as five-year-old children are, and they're all afraid of the same thing: the dark; *the great unknown.*

Many blacks do indeed live in a constant state of fear; fear of being mugged, fear of being racially profiled by the police, fear of losing a child, a job, or a home, and on and on, including the fear of God. (Fear that has been thrust upon them since childhood.) You know, *"Screw up and God, the great enforcer, is gonna' gitcha'!"* Black fear is real for them!

Like deer caught in the headlights of an oncoming car, black people have been debilitated and paralyzed by slavery's crippling legacy. They received no debriefing. Carrying their own baggage, the slave owners' descendants are facing their own demons, but it's still much more difficult for blacks to live in this country. Free-thinkers like Dr. Claude Anderson, the author of *"Powernomics"* and I argued that as a white woman President Hillary Clinton could do more for minorities than President Barack Obama, who seldom discussed race, but few listened.

CHAPTER 7

Who Was the Real Jesus?

Most people don't realize that Jesus' name is not *Jesus Christ*. Again, *Jesus* means "savior," the same way *messiah* means "chosen one or deliverer." Early on, the Greek word *Christ*, which was added, did not mean "a divine being" or "anointed one, chosen by God" as it later did, especially during the first century when Jesus lived. *Messiah*, or "anointed one" meant "king," and had no religious connotation. Jesus would simply become ruler of the Jews like any other king. Not as a Christian or the son of God. "Lord" (ruler) wasn't religious either.

Growing up Jesus was ordinary. Nobody special. He didn't get a second look. No one in Nazareth knew about his miraculous birth in Bethlehem. *Miracles didn't happen.* As a Jew, Jesus didn't consider himself divine. Jews didn't believe in supernatural beings. Christ was simply a title acknowledged as "Jesus, the Christ" or "Iesous Christos" in Greek, King Jesus. Jesus referred to himself as the *"son of Man"*, Aramaic for a "person" or a "human being". In John 6:38, Jesus said, "For I have come down from heaven" as a spokesman for God. (Did Jesus really say it?) Remember, it was Paul who first preached that Jesus was king of the Jews and of the world, but he wasn't really interested in anything Jesus had to say. Paul had a different agenda.

I'm reasonably sure Jesus was never called Christ as a boy either, which one might wrongly assume today. He was like any other little kid who played outside and got dirty. Jesus wasn't God's son, and he wasn't going to save the neighborhood or clean-up corruption. He was the same as any other little boy . . . with no daddy. *So, Jesus wasn't always known as Jesus Christ, the same way Barack Obama wasn't always President Obama, and definitely not when he was only six or seven years old.* Just think about that for a minute!... Let it really sink in. Jesus wasn't always Jesus Christ! He probably would have been referred to as Jesus of Nazareth, which we already know, or "Yeshua bar Yosef," Jesus, the son of Joseph, like a thousand other males in Jerusalem, the center of the world at that time. WRONG! There is no Jesus name in Hebrew. There is no "j" sound in either Aramaic (Jesus' 2,000 year old language), Hebrew or Latin.

Mark 6:3 identifies Jesus as the carpenter, the son of Mary, Yeshua bar Maryam, implying that Jesus' father was either unknown or not Jewish. Not naming Joseph was highly irregular and disrespectful. But Jesus absolutely would have been called Yeshua or Yoshua. Here again, we worship somebody without even knowing what his real name was, or why. God, Yahweh, was said to be named "Jealous" in Exodus 34:14. *Do you really believe God would have given himself such a ridiculous name?*

During ancient times a name had meaning. It described that individual. For example, Mary, Maryam in Aramaic, and Miriam in Hebrew, like Moses' sister, probably meant "wished for child." Some Hebrew sources maintain that Mary means "female rebel", "bitter" or "weeping". The first to speak Aramaic were Aramean desert nomads.

Before being translated by the Greeks from the Hebrew Bible, the name Jesus didn't exist in the Greek language. Jesus' name is a Greek creation. Because of different sounds, English speakers mispronounced Hebrew words. We know one Jesus, but the name Jesus, or more accurately Yeshua, was one of the most popular names back then, just as John and William are today. *There were Jesuses, or rather Yeshuas all over the place, and even another prominent holy Jew, a farmer named "Yeshua ben Ananias," or Jesus son of Ananias.* It was the same way with crucifixions. There were hundreds of thousands executed and at least 10,000 people crucified on crosses by the Romans the same way Jesus was, including 6000 of Spartacus' rebel slaves. Jesus and the two thieves who died with him were only three out of thousands. Crucifixion was entertainment, fun, like lynchings would become centuries later in America. The Romans crucified thousands of enemies of the state, not just Jesus. But because of its barbarity, Roman citizens were never to be crucified.

And by the way, how big a man was Jesus? And how tall (long), and how heavy was the solid wooden cross he supposedly dragged around all by himself after being brutalized and nearly beaten to death by the Romans? Did Jesus really carry that cross or was it merely another graphic, colorful story made up to support his divinity?

The Romans intended to break Jesus' legs when he was crucified, which was normal procedure, but then realized he was already dead. (For Jews, Jesus the sacrificial lamb could have no broken bones.) One of the soldiers pierced Jesus' side with a lance to make sure. The lance, known as the "Spear of Destiny," was seized by Hitler's S.S. at the beginning of World War II. Hitler, who believed God was on his side, was obsessed with the occult and thought the spear that wounded Jesus would give him supernatural powers. According to the legend, its possessor would rule the world, but if he lost the spear he would die immediately.

Some believe that even if Jesus had indeed survived 39 lashes from a whip embedded with pieces of metal and glass, or small metal balls tied to the end of leather straps, plus crucifixion, he definitely couldn't have lasted very long. Just as painful was the crown of thorns cutting into his scalp and the holes in his hands and feet from the nails.

The Romans found creative ways of persecuting Christians. Sewing them up in animal skins with vicious dogs sicced on them. Dressing them in shirts made of stiff wax, tying them to axletrees and lighting them like candles. Flaying them (skinning them alive), and even boiling them. They hanged them, burned them alive, beheaded them and drowned them. The most symbolic way of eliminating Christians, however, was to force sharp thorns on their heads, then run them through with a spear, the same thing they did to Jesus.

As a small boy and as a teenager, I listened to my minister enthusiastically preaching about Simon-Peter, Jesus' first disciple. What I now know, however, is that like the name Jesus, there was no Simon-Peter either. Simon was actually "Shimon" in Hebrew and Aramaic. Jesus called him Peter, *kephas* in Aramaic, *petros* in Greek, or rock. So, Simon-Peter would've been called Shimon Bar-Jonah. Remember, even Mary Jesus' mother would not have been Mary, but Maryam in Aramaic.

If Peter, Jesus' first apostle had not become a disciple and Jesus not said "upon this rock I will build my church" (in this world), the Catholic Church and Christianity might not exist today. On some levels that is certainly true. But how do we know that Jesus actually said those words to Peter? And was Peter himself the rock, or was the rock actually his faith in God? With Peter as the rock however, other popes would continue to have jobs and the Catholic Church would live on. *But it was Jesus himself who was the real rock.* According to some Bible scholars, nowhere in the New Testament does it say that Peter ever went to Rome. So, where did the Catholic Church dig that up? Maybe the same place they found the lie about Constantine giving them dominion over Rome forever. And remember, any questions and you were dead. *Questioning any part of Catholicism was considered heresy.*

It was conniving Constantine the opportunist who decided to build a basilica over the spot where Peter was supposedly buried, and Adam and Eve were created, at the Vatican (one heck of a coincidence). Peter was jealous, insecure, and denied Jesus three times. It was Peter who told the guards, "I don't know him, never saw him." At times Peter was a bumbling coward, but according to the Catholic Church Jesus still picked him to be his successor. Why? *And even if Jesus himself had picked Peter to be the first bishop* (pope), *we know for a fact that he never picked any of the other 265 popes who claimed to speak for him and for God.*

Although some of the disciples might have been a little flakey from time to time while Jesus was alive, after his resurrection they sometimes became more self-assured *(found bigger balls)*. This, in spite of the fact that Christians were being demonized after Jesus' crucifixion and even hiding out to avoid the same fate. Their leader was dead and nothing happened. Was Jesus a false messiah? Peter was even crucified upside down because he didn't think he was worthy of being crucified the same way Jesus was. Peter's death devastated Jesus' followers.

Like others, I discovered that what I learned in the Bible was incorrect. How could Peter, *a Jew*, become the first Catholic pope, supposedly commissioned by Jesus Christ himself. And before becoming pope, or rather bishop, because the word pope didn't exist yet, Peter gave up everything except his wife and family to follow Jesus. *Yes, the first pope had a wife and children, as did subsequent leaders and other popes.* A mother-in-law with fever that Jesus healed, and maybe a dog. Like other disciples Peter's wife traveled with him when he preached. Their daughter became Saint Petronilla. In 1 Corinthians 9: 4-6, Paul talked about the disciples "believing wives", like Phillip's.

Some of the other popes who were married before taking office included Pope Hormisdas, who was Pope Silverius' father; Pope Adrian II, whose wife Stephania and daughter lived with him in the Lateran Palace before they were murdered by the Church's chief librarian; Pope John XVII, who had three sons who became priests; and Clement IV, who had two daughters who were nuns.

Marriage was "honorable in all", and certainly *Jesus never told Peter or any of the apostles they couldn't be married. Disgraced, an unmarried man wasn't a real man.* Brazilian Cardinal Claudio Hummes, Pope Francis' close friend said "celibacy is a discipline, not a dogma of the church." (Who was married and who wasn't was the last thing on Jesus' mind.)

The first thirty-nine popes were married, and the Catholic Church was a thousand years old before priests were forbidden from doing so. While wives were often by their sides, others had concubines. "Shacking-up." In 1074 Pope Gregory VII said "priest must first escape from the clutches of their wives" and take a vow of celibacy.

With the exception of Paul (who wasn't married, according to Tertullian, St. Jerome, and St. Augustine), most of the early apostles were married. But Clement of Alexandria and St Ignatius of Antioch said that Paul was indeed married. Which proves one thing. *(We don't know a damn thing about anything)*. And incidentally, early on God had already told Abraham to leave his tribesmen behind, so he could go out and handle his business, not for Christianity's sake, because Abraham was a Hebrew before Christianity existed, but to "get paid," becoming rich and famous (Genesis 12:1–3). Tertullian, St. Augustine, Clement of Alexandria, Cyprian and Origen were supposedly people of color.

In addition to the money, don't forget the prophecy about one of Abraham's descendants inheriting God's blessing. With that kind of persistent brainwashing, it was only a matter of time before Jesus too would break. While it may be true that Jesus and his family believed in God (Yehweh), in addition to rich Great-Uncle Abraham, it was also said that God promised King David a great dynasty that would never end. Remember, God promised Abraham that "everyone on earth would be blessed because of him and his descendants." Only Abraham, Isaac and Jacob heard God making that deal with their family. It took a little while, but Jesus was that man, that blessing, that spiritual king. Jacob, Isaac's son and Abraham's grandson, had twelve sons who became the heads of the twelve tribes, now Israel. The rest is history. Or rather now. William Faulkner once said "the past is never dead. It's not even past."

Was there actually a scheme in place all along to capture that long foretold rich and powerful dynasty? Nobody ever begs to be poor, and all Jesus and John the Baptist had to do was look across the Sea of Galilee from Capernaum to see the beautiful city of Tiberius on the other side, built by Antipas for the Romans and his rich Jewish friends, to know how wealthy the Romans were at their expense. Like seeing Tiberius for the first time, Jesus was blown away when he saw Jerusalem. Like a country boy going to Las Vegas, New York or New Orleans for the first time. *Poor Jews, many of them day laborers, were getting screwed and they knew it.* They saw it every time they traveled four miles from Nazareth to Greek speaking Sepphoris, the nearest big city to find work.

For the average person life was very difficult, filled with disease and hardship. During good times there was olive oil, milk, and cheese, but even then poor Hebrews barely ate wholesome meals or ever had meat. When the elements were harsh, like extended droughts, there was famine, malnutrition and frequently death. The few hundred people living in Nazareth needed each other to survive, and intermarriage was often necessary. Family support was essential, so why did Jesus just decide to pack up and leave, living like a drifter? *"Taking a hike?"* Was Jesus simply living his own life? Following his dream and saying God ordered him to do it? (Maybe Jesus just didn't want to be a carpenter or a mason like Joseph.) Or, was he possibly an undiagnosed victim of Post-Traumatic Stress Disorder? Remember, the priests wanted to run him out of the synagogue because they thought he was nuts. People in Nazareth thought Jesus had a few loose screws too.

Jews had long awaited a political messiah and an earthly king sent by God to save them. The disciples were convinced that Jesus would be king, wearing a golden crown, and they would be the new rulers, defeating Herod and the Romans. No more abuse or unjust Roman taxes and laws. This time the Hebrews would be on top. John and James actually pissed the other apostles off. Each of the twelve expected thrones (seats), to rule the twelve tribes, but John and James wanted theirs right next to Jesus in his new government once they took over. *On earth in Palestine, not in heaven.* ON EARTH! Luke 17:21 "the kingdom of God is within you." The disciples indeed wanted to kill their arch-enemies the Samaritans, never speaking to one.

The kingdom of God referred to ending Babylonian exile and Roman oppression <u>in the land. Israel! (Jeremiah 23:5).</u> Not heaven. God would <u>soon</u> reveal himself and rescue his people. "End of the world" didn't literally mean the world would explode with believers going to heaven. It meant a "turning point." A drastic change for Judaism.

Even though most of Jesus' followers were poor, *"Jesus wasn't promisin' 'em nothin' until after they were dead."* At least not anything tangible. According to the Bible, he actually convinced the poor people he lived among that suffering, being down and out and being brutalized was a good thing. Matthew 5:5, the meek shall inherit the earth. When? IN ADDITION TO BEING A SUPERSTAR, JESUS WAS A SUPERSALESMAN TOO! Joel Osteen for the 1st Century.

Was Jesus really the blond-haired, blue-eyed character we have been taught to know and love (Raphael, Leonardo Da Vinci, Michelangelo, and Rembrandt's celestial white male painted between the fourteenth and seventeenth centuries)? Those were the images Europeans were familiar with and naturally leaned toward, images ordered by the Roman church to be created. Michelangelo's cousin may have been the model for paintings of Jesus, while his aunt and uncle posed for Adam and Eve.

Because painting a picture of someone like a messiah was considered offensive, like photographing an Indian chief during America's early frontier days, only the Carpocratians, who were considered heretics, had paintings of Jesus on the walls of house churches run by women. The Carpocratians were said to have an actual painting of Jesus made during his lifetime, commissioned by Pilate himself. Remember, Jews believed death was the penalty for looking upon God with mortal eyes, and even today they are forbidden to pronounce the sacred name of God.

The Gnostic Carpocratians did not believe Jesus was divine, but that his soul was pure (similar to Arius' beliefs). He also didn't die on the cross but survived. Jesus was simply a good man and nothing more. Ownership of property was unnatural and both property and women were for all. *The Carpocratians were not bound by Mosaic law or any other morality, which they believed was only a human opinion.* There was no such thing as good or evil, and Jesus was not a redeemer. A person would receive salvation by being like Jesus, not by simply being one of his followers. Angels created the world and used magic to help Jesus.

The Carpocratians did it all, including wild sex. (Christians having orgies.) To leave this world people's imprisoned souls, which lived forever, must pass through every earthly experience, so that when they died there was no reason to be reincarnated. No rewards or punishment. (No coming back). They went straight to God. The body was merely a shell. At their Christian gatherings they had sex where they wanted (free love), with whomever they wanted (like the Vikings). Unlike believers with their sexual hang-ups, Carpocratians and heathens were having all the fun. The Carpocratians practiced magic.

Today, not only is Jesus white, blond-haired and blue-eyed, he's also looking more and more like an American, teaching America's brand of Christianity to the whole world. Naturally, on the recent 10-hour History Channel production, *The Bible*, Sampson (Delilah's boyfriend), and his mother may have been black, but we know that Jesus, the star (king), was always going to be white. Not only was Jesus white, he was a long-haired, straight-nosed English speaking American. The Jesus we see in movies is never a Jew, but always a handsome white Christian. (No wonder we're all "f'ed-up".) The producers Roma Downy and Mark Burnett claimed authenticity. From books and paintings to television and films Blacks and other minorities are demeaned and excluded. In Russell Crowe's movie *Noah*, damn near everybody appeared to be white too ... Blacks and Latinos weren't even around to drown.

Was the opposite in fact true in real life? *Was Jesus actually a poor man of color, a black Jew who could identify with black slavery, persecution, suffering and white racism?* Again, nobody really knows, but typically people subjected to the blistering heat in the region of Palestine near Nazareth where Jesus lived did not have fair skin, blond hair or blue eyes. They were olive complexioned, sun-bronzed by the scorching sun. *(Were Jesus, Mary, and Joseph the only white people around?)*

Revelation 1:14–15; Revelation 2:18
His hair was white like wool. His feet like unto fine brass.

Daniel 7:9 also speaks about a vision he had of God, saying that "the hair of his head was like pure wool."

So, tell me. When was the last time you saw straight wool or white brass? Don't forget that Jesus' lineage was from Jacob's son Judah, who was married to a Canaanite, or "woman of color." Even the name Adam (Adamha), as in Adam and Eve, means "red dirt," like soil or clay, and dirt definitely *ain't* white. Adam also stands for both the first man and mankind. (Much of this information can be found in an excellent book by William Gilbert Emanuel called *People of Color in the Bible* or *The Black Presence in the Lands of the Bible* by David Malik Watts.)

In their comedy *Black Jesus*, Aaron McGruder and Mike Clattenberg showcase a black Jesus Christ living in a broken down, illegally parked van in "the hood" in Compton, California. This shabby black Jesus is hanging out with his homies, a group of poverty struck hood rats. What else would Jesus be doing today, and who would he be doing it with?... Definitely not some stuck up bishop and his crew...In the series Jesus is smokin' and cussin', but that's what it might take to finally get people's attention and wake them up ... Maybe what they should really be fired-up about is not Black Jesus, but all those other Jesuses we've been watching for decades.

And incidentally, in Luke 3:38, the Bible speaks about Adam "which is the son of God." So, was Eve Adam's sister or his wife, and were Adam and Eve Jesus' brother and sister, or at least Adam his brother, since the Bible expressly says Adam was God's son too? *And were the only two children God ever had two white guys named Adam and Jesus?* No daughters, just two white sons. One married with billions of kids; the other single. And a virgin.

Remember that experts and scholars can't even agree on whether James was Jesus' brother or not, and nobody ever talked about what he looked like or anybody else in Jesus' family. Were James, Joseph, Simon, Judah, and their sisters related to Jesus by birth (meaning Mary), or through Joseph's previous marriage? Speaking of Joseph again, what became of him after Jesus turned twelve and he disappeared?

A young Jewish male, was Jesus ever betrothed or married, which would have been the case at that time? That was the custom and the culture for boys who had attained manhood at thirteen. There is no Hebrew word for bachelor. Being fruitful and multiplying was a religious obligation. There were exceptions, especially for Essenes who practiced celibacy, believing the body was corrupt and unclean. In the orthodox Christian tradition, nothing is known about Jesus from age twelve to age thirty, from adolescence to late adulthood, until he showed up to be baptized. Some believe Jesus was actually married to Mary Magdalene, the woman accused of being a prostitute and having a son with Jesus named Bar-Abbas. In the 2007 documentary, *The Lost Tomb of Jesus*, Jesus' son Judah is supposedly buried in an ossuary (a small box, vault, or urn) in Jerusalem. If Jesus was actually married that means we never truly knew him at all. (Obviously, being married or having a girlfriend and being worldly would have weakened claims of his divinity.) Did Jesus ever say he was God's "only begotten" son, or God?

In *Did Jesus Exist?* Bart Ehrman reminds us that it was Jesus of Nazareth, not of Nashville or of New York. Jesus was a first-century Palestinian Jew, not a 21st Century American. He wasn't like us. According to Ehrman "there's not a church in North America that Jesus could go into and recognize himself, and he never wanted to start a new religion, let alone a religion based on his death and resurrection," being idolized. (Jesus wouldn't have a clue.) Ehrman says Jesus gets used by everybody who claim to be Christians for their own purposes, calling it an abuse of Jesus, not respecting what he stood for. *But Jesus, a homeless drifter, did think he would become king.* According to Ehrman, "Christians did not invent Jesus, they invented the idea of a suffering messiah" by hijacking the Israelite god "Yehweh, I am," named by Moses, and Yehweh's son Yeshua, *Jesus*. "There is no physical or archeological evidence that Jesus ever existed, and everything we know about him was written by people who believed in him." *A Jesus cult.* The Romans (who documented everything) never wrote about Jesus.

Mr. Ehrman certainly does an excellent job when it comes to providing information, especially since peasants left no archaeological footprints. In *How Jesus Became God* he writes about the baby who was born of a virgin. The mother had visitors from heaven before he was born, telling her that her son would be divine, "with the unusual divine signs from heaven." As an adult the young man became a traveling preacher, with followers who were convinced that he was the son of God. As proof: "he did miracles, could heal the sick, cast out demons, and raise the dead." He was put on trial by the Romans, suffered and died as Isaiah had prophesied, "ascended to heaven and continues to live there till this day." He appeared again to at least one of his doubting followers. Later other followers wrote books about him, and we can still read about him today.

Jesus, right? Wrong!

Mr. Ehrman is not talking about Jesus of Nazareth, but about Apollonius of Tyana, a polytheistic Greek philosopher who worshipped many gods. He was a real person who lived during the 1st Century when Jesus did, and their followers actually competed with each other. Jesus' followers claimed that Apollonius was a charlatan and a fraud; Apollonius' followers claimed that Jesus was the impostor. While the Romans persecuted Jesus and his followers, they gladly listened to Apollonius. Some pundits believe that Jesus' life, crafted by Paul, was fictionally based on Apollonius' life as the son of Zeus. But Apollonius' miracles were credited to his genius, not tricks or sorcery. Most of us basically know nothing about religion unless it involves Christianity. And even then we know very little, especially about Jesus.

CHAPTER 8

Mary Magdalene

⸻

Early Mormons were convinced that Jesus was polygamous (had many wives), attributing the idea to Celsus. They believed that Elizabeth, Mary, and the other women who followed Jesus were all his wives. On the other hand, there are those who fiercely disagree. Jesus, some say, had a big job to do and therefore no time for a wife and kids.

In *The Holy Blood and the Holy Grail* by Michael Baigent, Richard Leigh and Henry Lincoln, Jesus and Mary Magdalene's bloodline is hypothesized. What is important is that God, being incarnate in Jesus, wanted to know firsthand (for himself) what human beings experienced. *How could God fully understand what being human meant without sex and without children?* Naturally, that position was antithetical for the puritanical Western world that saw sex as dirty, nasty and sinful. *The concept of an "Immaculate Conception" was the early church's way of not dealing with sex as it fulfilled ancient prophecy.*

The Bible never says Mary Magdalene was a woman of ill-repute. Calling her a loose woman, Pope Gregory the Great started the 1,400-year-old lie attacking her character in 591 AD, perhaps precipitated by his own pious nature as a monk. He didn't appreciate her independence. Mary Magdalene was self-sufficient enough to take care of Jesus by being in the fishing business. Other women, *witches*, made mind-altering psychoactive wine or brewed beer, psychedelically spiked with potent roots, herbs, and fungi, sacred plant medicine "evil drugs", used in secret house churches to find God. (Not cooking Hansel and Gretel). Today Gregory, an aristocratic sexist from a wealthy family is a saint. No matter how rich any family was, the church was the largest land owner. Now one of the largest financial institutions.

Even though she was no easy target, Mary Magdalene still had another big red bull's-eye painted on her back. Some of Jesus' fine disciples were jealous of his affection for her. Especially Peter, who bristled at the fact that Jesus would talk to a woman about spiritual matters. What that means is that some of the disciples, Christianity's heroes, were also petty and insecure. A chief disciple, the first bishop who later became the first pope was jealous of a woman. They may have been called apostles or disciples, but they were still ordinary men with human weaknesses. In the Gnostic Gospel of Mary Magdalene (Mary), discovered in 1896, Mary Magdalene wasn't a repentant prostitute but a beloved disciple. She was powerful in a time when the world was dominated by men. (Today's Hillary Clinton, Nancy Pelosi and Supreme Court Justice Ruth Bader Ginsburg). Magdalene means tower in Hebrew.

In the Gnostic Gospels of Thomas, Phillip, and Mary, Jesus sided with Mary Magdalene against Peter when he demanded that she be sent away. A disciple named Levi tells Peter, "if the Savior made her worthy, who are you to reject her? Certainly the Savior knows her very well. That is why he loved her more than us." Those gospels were never canonized.

In Gnosticism there were things Jesus only told Mary Magdalene, and whether disciples or priests, men didn't like the idea of women having power. Mary Magdalene was the only one in his inner circle that Jesus told about the spiritual journey of the soul, a Gnostic concept dealing with the afterlife, angels and demons, secret teachings and symbols to access the unknown. Mary Magdalene may have been the only one who truly understood what made Jesus tick. *She was his soul mate!* But because of Constantine, Christianity was in and Gnosticism was out, along with Mary Magdalene. Like Marcus Aurelius, if the Gnostics had won today's world would be very different. The church certainly would have been different, focusing more on insight and understanding than hierarchy and materialism (preachers, priests, and money).

Like ancient Jews who had different beliefs, ancient Christians had different beliefs too. Some Christians believed in more than one God, and different communities even read other scriptures and gospels. From dissimilar perspectives also came different practices. Gnostics believed anyone with divine knowledge or supernatural powers was a son or daughter of God. *Jesus was really having a hard time convincing people that he alone was God's son, or that he was even God's son.*

Gnostic gospels claimed that Jesus wasn't resurrected at all, and that the real Christ wasn't the Jesus who died on the cross. Remember, there were different kinds of believers during Jesus' time. Gnostics who knew him, didn't believe Jesus was supernatural, had supernatural powers, could perform miracles, or was the messiah they had been waiting for. Like others, he was simply a guide. *The Gnostic Gospel of Thomas only contained sayings of Jesus, with no miracles or fantastic feats.*

For Gnostics Jesus' birth and other events were not to be taken literally. Gnostic means "one who knows," just as shaman does, and they believed in a mystical inner sense, a secret knowledge, understanding the nature of who God is, and understanding the nature of who man is. Understanding this revealed truth could save you. The invisible would become visible. Another big problem the Gnostics presented was that before 300 AD they believed God was within, a personal connection. *Truly knowing yourself was to know God*. Gnostics didn't need priests or bishops (no bosses) or a church. They also didn't believe in being baptized. Priests and bishops who naturally objected would have been unemployed, the same as John the Baptist's plan would have done. And we know what happened to him. The only reason Pope Francis I, the 116 cardinals, the bishops, priests and everybody else working for the Church have clerical jobs today is because of Emperor Constantine. In fact, Catholics are now a minority in the United States.

There was something else about Gnostics that was especially problematic, angering the holy men. The Gnostics believed in the Great Mother or goddess of heaven, who was both male and female. While Christians hated the thought of women with power, Gnostics were open to the idea, in fact endorsing it. (Women and blacks being prominent in the Bible would have changed history.) For that reason the priestly hierarchy were fearful of the implication that priests could also be male or female. (No woman or black heathen is taking my spot!) For my wife and I, the most astounding thing we saw when we visited the Vatican were the thousands and thousands of paintings, tapestries, relics and sculptures ... And almost all of them white people ... *Even Jesus was one of them!*

Gnostics believed that only the soul was resurrected after death (as many believers do now), and humans were created by the same beings who created the earth. (Aliens? Were the wise men following a UFO?) Gnostics also believed that man once crawled like a worm until the Supreme Power gave him life. (Evolution, like the Biblical story of Adam and Eve emerging from dirt.) Perhaps dusty dirt people. *Nomads!*

Speaking of aliens, let's not forget about the isolated Dogon tribe of West Africa who say they were created by the Nommos who came to earth from the Sirian star system, six trillion miles away 5,000 years ago. Flying in a jet today it would take about 200,000 years to get there. According to Ogotemmeli, the tribe's oral historian, the Nommos, space aliens resembling serpents, lizards, chameleons and fish, landed with *"great noise and wind"* in a three-legged spacecraft. The problem is that the Dogons have been pointing to Serius B, a smaller star for centuries, but astronomers didn't discover it until they started using the Hubble Space Telescope exactly where the Dogons said it was. *How did the Dogons know?* You can see a car or a bus traveling at a distance, but a spacecraft disappears out of sight. Who told the Dogons where to look or where they came from?

In September of 2012, Dr. Karen King of Harvard University, one of the world's foremost authorities on Coptic scholarship, uncovered a papyrus gospel fragment the size of a credit card which she calls *"The Gospel of Jesus' Wife."* On it, written in the ancient Coptic language, Jesus is quoted as saying "my wife." Naturally, critics immediately denounced it as a fraud, but of course, why wouldn't the so-called experts? Anything new challenges what has already been established and accepted, what they have always touted, and something that could possibly reverse the previously held role of women. Then again, what do experts know?

While Mary Magdalene was damned for being immoral, the Bible does not condemn men for having sex with prostitutes. But under

Christianity, the female prostitutes, if discovered, were to be stoned and burned at the stake. (Murder the women, but according to the Bible the men walk away.) The exception was Temple prostitutes, where Baal and Asherah were worshiped in fertility rites. Kind of like it is today. *The prostitute goes to jail; the john gets to fool around another day.*

In 464 BC Xenophon dedicated 100 girls to the Greek Temple in Corinth, and at one time there were more than 1,000 slave-prostitutes. *Prostitution in Rome was both legal and highly profitable.* There was believed to be a connection between humans having sex and rain (God's seed, heavenly sperm) watering the earth to grow crops. In Deuteronomy 25:17-19 Moses wrote about male and female prostitutes. In fact, the Bible says little about punishing men who screw around, with the possible exceptions of Jesus' Sermon on the Mount and Matthew speaking on adultery. If the wife cheats, however, she is the one committing adultery. And don't forget, even a little incest (Lot), and an occasional rape now and then were alright too, as long as you were on the right team. Just as it is today, the Catholic Church (the Roman church) was biased and sexist, and women were to have no prominent roles or equity back then either, especially around misogynistic Pope Gregory.

Galatians 3:28
There is neither Jew nor Greek, *slave nor free, male nor female,* for you are all one in Christ Jesus.

Maybe the Catholic Church and Christian men just didn't like that part about slaves and women being equals, even though it says so in the Holy Book God gave them. Other religions certainly had both gods and goddesses. (Two thousand years later we still don't know the names of Jesus' sisters.)

But the Bible doesn't say that Jesus wasn't married, although some claimed that he was married to the church. Being half God and half human, Christians generally focus on Jesus' divinity, often denying his human side, but Jesus was indeed human. (Remember, even as a human Jesus could certainly have been too busy for a wife and kids.)

Matthew 11:18–19

18For John came neither eating nor drinking, and they say, "He has a demon." 19The Son of Man came eating and drinking, and they say, "Here is a glutton and a drunkard, a friend of tax collectors and sinners."

Remember, Jesus' first miracle was turning water into wine. (Six jars of 20 to 30 gallons each, 1000 bottles. Because Joseph was a good teacher Jesus made the good stuff.) Today Calvary Lutheran Church in Dallas–Fort Worth, has what is called "Church in a Pub", where the congregation enjoys the service while sipping their favorite brew. In Oregon, members of "First Christian Church of Portland, Christian Church Disciples of Christ" have what they call "Beer and Hymns". Singing, praying and drinking. Creative ways to increase membership. Matthew 26:29 even says there will be wine in heaven. *Just don't get wasted up there, and make sure you know where the restroom is.*

Living in Galilee, wine country, Jesus enjoyed drinking, and perhaps women. Maybe he was being attacked for being human. Psalm 104:14–15 talks about food from the earth and wine to gladden the human heart. Proverbs 31:7 says "let them drink and forget their poverty, and remember their misery no more." Wine made men glad, and some may have even got drunk during the Lord's Supper, later institutionalized as "communion." No communion (spiked psychedelic wine), no Christianity. *(Jesus and his disciples were all human and a few drinks sometimes was a good thing.)* Believers were real people, neither angels nor something piously called a saint. Don't forget about Noah being naked and plastered, even though God drowned everybody who wasn't righteous, including thousands of giants. How about Lot, "knocked out," with his two innocent daughters in a cave. The Bible says alcoholics cannot go to heaven.

Hard liquor as we know it today, 40 to 50 percent alcohol, that really wipes you out and leads to alcoholism, is produced by distilling things like grain-based mash. Nothing that strong existed during Jesus' time, so they sucked up a lot of whatever they were drinking to get tanked. What about that sacred wine, and spiked beer?

Jesus told his disciples not to drink too much because it showed a lack of judgment and control. Nobody representing God could be a sloppy, violent, woman-chasing alcoholic jerk. The Bible tells that drunkards will not enter the Kingdom, and Isaiah 19:14 says that drunk men stagger in their own vomit. Proverbs 23:20-21 goes even further, saying that you should stay away from both alcoholics and glutton eaters of meat (greedy fat people), because if all you do is drink, eat, and sleep you'll end up wearing rags. *(Broke). So, what about people like Moses, Noah and the popes who got drunk? Matthew 11:19 includes Jesus.*

Terrence McKenna, in his book *Food of the Gods*, suggests that Psilocybin mushrooms (psychedelic mushrooms), also known as magic mushrooms or shrooms, could've been favorites of Bible characters like Abraham, Moses, and even Jesus. Containing psychedelic compounds like psilocybin and psilocin, wild mushrooms were often used as an ancient recreational drug or in religious rites and ceremonies to communicate with God. They changed the sense of time, produced visual illusions like Moses burning bush, shimmering, enhanced colors, created a "halo" around light sources, distorted sounds, and altered thinking processes to produce a sense of euphoria. *(Got them high!)* Many ancients were free-wheelin' 1st Century hippies, Timothy Leary's 20th Century LSD users.

Bible characters also "tripped" on infamous white-topped Amanita muscari mushrooms, eating and drinking the juice. Spiritual food from heaven, appearing in the morning dew (mushrooms) manna was bread "flesh of the gods" or "blood of the gods". Similar to what Jesus said about himself at the *visionary* Last Supper. Were the Bible, the Koran and the Torah actually psychedelically induced? The mushrooms were so potent that men drank each other's urine or deer urine for a fix. In the 1100s Pope Innocent III initiated *Transubstantiation, making ordinary bread and wine the body and blood of Jesus by saying a few magic words.*

In the Dead Sea Scrolls, discovered in a cave in Nag Hammadi, Egypt in 1947, Jesus is said to have kissed Mary Magdalene often, and it was she, with others, who were at his side when he was crucified, refusing to betray him by running away as the men did. Well-to-do Mary

Magdalene and a few generous women traveled with Jesus and paid the bills, remember. Some think she led the movement, not Jesus. She was the real messiah. In the Gnostic Gospel of Mary and the Acts of Philip, Mary Magdalene is even referred to as Jesus' companion and apostle to the apostles. He empowered women. *As Jesus' favorite, Mary Magdalene may have been more of a fighter than the men were. Were Mary (Jesus' mom) and Mary Magdalene (his lady friend) both female revolutionaries? Freedom fighters!*

What happened to Mary Magdalene after Jesus was crucified and she was first to witness his resurrection? Some believe she was pregnant with Jesus' baby and moved to France, where her descendants founded the Merovingian line of kings. She left 250,000 people in jam-packed Jerusalem with Jesus' mother.

At the seventh century Monastery of Sainte Maria de Oia, in the Cistercian church (the region of northern Spain and southern France), there is a painting showing Mary Magdalene as the central figure, surrounded by the apostles, with the dove representing the Holy Spirit descending. At another Cistercian monastery, the Royal Monastery of the Holy Cross, *Mary Magdalene is depicted pregnant at Jesus' crucifixion*, with the Virgin Mary and the apostle John nearby. In yet another picture, Mary Magdalene is carrying one child and holding the other one's hand. (In America we only see reproductions of Jesus, Mary, and Joseph, egotistically assumed to be historically accurate.)

It was Mary Magdalene and another woman named Mary, probably Mary's sister-in-law, Jesus' aunt, or Mary, Jesus' mother, and Salome, Jesus' aunt, also called Mary, who discovered the stone rolled away from the entrance of the tomb on Easter Sunday following Jesus' crucifixion. It was then that Mary Magdalene saw two angels wearing bright robes. (So she said. Remember, Jewish prophecy had to be fulfilled, and people were getting just a little bit antsy.) But who told Mary Magdalene they were angels? And why were the angels wearing bright robes? Of what fabric were those robes made? And who would've made them? (A heavenly seamstress perhaps?) *Even the yet innocent Adam and Eve wore leaves, and not white robes.* Were the two angels black or white, or perhaps one white and one black, and let's not forget they also spoke. (Aramaic, the ancient Semitic language, or Hebrew, but definitely not English as we see in movies).

There were other explanations for what had happened. Some believed Jesus hadn't really died. That he had only fainted. (But if somebody who was crucified wasn't actually dead, or was switched, the soldier guarding him would be crucified himself, so the guards definitely made sure Jesus was dead.) Others thought the women went to the wrong tomb, or by the time they arrived Jesus' body had already been removed for anointing and reburial. Then there were those who believed Jesus' resurrection was symbolic or spiritual, and not physical.

Some scholars feel that allegations about Jesus being married to Mary Magdalene are way off base. This is true for certain members of the gay community who insist that the only reason why Christians miss signs of Jesus himself being gay is their own heterosexuality. Because Luke traveled with Paul and Mark was Peter's companion, some people say the disciples were gay too. Their argument—that Jesus was thirty years old, unmarried, and always hanging out with twelve other men. *Jesus had no girlfriends, no kids, and John was referred to as the disciple Jesus loved, depicted with his head on Jesus' chest at the Last Supper.* That plus the fact that thirty years of his life are unaccounted for? Was being gay why Jesus left home? Straight Christians say the opposite is true. Because homosexuals are out of the closet they want Jesus outed.

It was the British homosexual advocate Peter Tatchell who said:

> We don't know for sure whether Jesus was straight, gay, bisexual or celibate. There is certainly no evidence for the Church's presumption that he was heterosexual. Nothing in the Bible points to him having desires or relationships with women. The possibility of a gay Christ cannot be ruled out [again, what was Jesus doing for thirty years, and why doesn't he have a "sex life"?].

In 1973 Morton Smith, a professor of ancient history at Columbia University, claimed to have found a letter from Clement of Alexandria, a second-century church father to a follower named Theodore. The gospel was given by the Carpocratians. Clement writes about Jesus:

> And they come into Bethany. And a certain woman whose brother had died was there. And, coming, she prostrated herself before Jesus and says to him, "Son of David, have mercy on me." But the disciples rebuked her. And Jesus, being angered, went off with her into the garden where the tomb was, and straightaway a great cry was heard from the tomb.
>
> And going near Jesus rolled away the stone from the door of the tomb. And straightaway, going in where the youth was, he stretched forth his hand and raised him, seizing his hand. But the youth, looking upon him, loved him and began to beseech him that he might be with him. And going out of the tomb they came into the house of the youth, for he was rich. And after six days Jesus told him what to do and in the evening the youth comes to him, wearing a linen cloth *over his naked body*. And he remained with him that night, for Jesus taught him the mystery of the Kingdom of God. And thence, arising he returned to the other side of the Jordan....
>
> And the sister of the youth whom Jesus loved and his mother and Salome were there, and Jesus did not receive them. [What was meant by *"whom Jesus loved"*?]

Naturally there were those who believed that Secret Mark, an expanded version of the canonical Gospel of Mark, only to be read to an inner circle of initiates was a forgery. In Mark 14:51–52, a young man escapes during Jesus' arrest. (51) a certain young man was following him, wearing nothing but a linen cloth. They caught hold of him; (52) but he left the linen cloth and *ran off naked*. (*Was there some connection between the two naked boys and Jesus?*) In the Gospel of Barnabas it is the Apostle John (whom Jesus loved), who is wrapped in a linen cloth, who runs off naked when a soldier grabs him. Others believe the boy was Mark.

Obviously there were other explanations to prove there was no homosexuality and that Jesus was not gay. If Jesus had been gay that would have meant serious problems for the church, and nobody would have followed him. Jesus probably would have been stoned and burned to death. But like men today who are on the "down low," he certainly could have married Mary Magdalene to cover it up.

When Mary Magdalene told the disciples about Jesus' resurrection, even they thought she was lying. This time it was the disciples who were blown away. Especially Thomas, who didn't believe Mary was a virgin, or that Jesus had risen from the dead until he saw him and touched his wounds. Being a woman what did Mary Magdalene know? Jesus coming back to life was the very last thing anybody expected to hear. That itself is surprising, because in Matthew 16:21, Jesus tells his disciples that he must go to Jerusalem and undergo great suffering at the hands of the elders and chief priests and scribes, be killed, and on the third day be raised. Why were they surprised? *Jesus himself told them he was going to die and then be resurrected.* Did the disciples not believe the prophecies of Isaiah and Zechariah, oral traditions (stories), and their own messiah? *As loyal Jews like Jesus, is it also possible that they never believed Jesus was actually God's son either?* Illiterate rebels, they did not expect Jesus to die, but instead to massacre the Romans so they could take over, like Moses defying the Egyptians. Their messiah was to be a conqueror, another David, a champion, not a sacrificial lamb, and none of the disciples believed Jesus was going to *"cash in"* so their sins would be forgiven. (The apocalyptic disciples knew what they were fighting for, while the Bible is simply a fictitious invention that came along much later.)

After his crucifixion Mary Magdalene didn't recognize Jesus at first, asking him where Jesus' body was. She thought he was a gardener until he spoke her name. Raised from the dead, Jesus went forty miles from Jerusalem to Galilee and appeared to Simon Peter and fellow disciples who were fishing with him at the Sea of Tiberias, but they too didn't recognize him. And on the road to Emmaus, disciples who were walking with Jesus didn't know it was him either. Not until he blessed their bread as he had done many times before. Why didn't Jesus' companions realize who he was? Were the stories true, hallucinations, or convenient legends in the ancient Greek and Roman traditions of "gods in disguise?"

Pagans had visions of people who were dead coming back, but Jesus was more than a mirage for Christians. He was the real deal. Not just some spirit or ghost. Remember, at the tomb the women held Jesus' feet. Jesus also asked his believers to feel him and poke their fingers into his wounds. He even cooked for them. Broiled fish. Jesus did something else no pagan had ever done before. Transfiguration. Going from human to supernatural, then back to human again. *It took forty days to convince his disciples that he was still alive.* But where did Jesus go after that and where is he now? Catholics believe Mary came back already.

Jesus is supposed to be God, and as you see, a number of people claimed to have seen Jesus (God) again after his crucifixion. But Exodus 33:20 clearly states that "You cannot see my face, for no one may see me and live." (No exceptions!) If no one can see God are claims to have heard him equally untrue? *Is Jesus both God and the son of God?*

Jacob said he saw God face to face; so did Abraham and Moses. Moses, Aaron and 70 other people were eating and drinking (partying) when God showed up. Abraham was also lucky enough to see him travelling incognito with two angels. Perhaps Enoch, Noah, Abraham and Zacharias never walked with God either because they couldn't see him. What about Jesus walking through locked doors and disappearing? Walking with God was a metaphor, a figure of speech, just as seeing him was because God is invisible and beyond comprehension.

Somewhat contradictory, Revelations 1:13-15 says that at the "end times", Jesus, the incarnation of God has white hair like wool, with arms, legs and feet like burnished bronze (imagine a tanned body builder), and eyes like flames of fire. God is riding a white horse and wearing a long white linen robe with a gold sash across his chest. In addition to God's flaming eyes, there's also a fiery red dragon with seven heads in Revelations 12:3.

Speaking of riding animals, forget about the white horse God rides. What about the talking donkey in Numbers 22 (or that talking snake in Genesis).

The Bible says that Balaam, a magician, riding his faithful donkey, has been summoned by Balak, the king of Moab. Fearing that the Israelites will attack his kingdom, Balak wants a curse put on them. Meanwhile, God sends an angel to stop Balaam. On their way his donkey sees an angel wielding a flaming sword and tries to get around him. With nowhere to run the donkey lies down in the middle of the road.

Balaam beats the donkey three times, trying to get her to move when God opens the donkey's mouth and it asks "What have I done to you, that you struck me these three times? Haven't I always been your faithful donkey? Have I ever served you poorly?" (Remember Mr. Ed, TV's talking horse.) Then God opened Balaam's eyes so he could see the angel too. At that point the angel tells Balaam that if it had not been for the donkey, he would already have killed him three times. Like others who were seeing things, had Balaam nodded off too, perhaps because of a little spiked vino, some hashish, or a few psychedelic mushrooms?

In the non-canonical gospel *The Acts of Peter*, a talking dog bravely confronts Simon Magnus the sorcerer, accusing him of being afraid to face Peter. After delivering his message the dog went back to Peter, telling him what he had said to Magnus, who was called a master of delusion. Were Peter and Jesus also masters of delusion; not miracle workers? Was Jonah's survival inside the belly of a fish a miracle, a mushroom-inspired delusion or perhaps a myth? *A fishy tale!* The name Jonah means dove. *Was Jonah actually flying high as a kite <u>outside</u> of the fish's belly?*

CHAPTER 9

Jesus' Divinity or Not

In the Old Testament there was no heaven or hell. Before Jesus came along God only appeared in dreams, clouds, clouds of smoke, burning bushes, or heavenly noises such as voices, thunder and the like. In the Jewish tradition there was always a historical connection, like some ancient prophecy. (Non-human appearances happened for a reason.) *It was only in the New Testament, after Jesus arrived, that deities like God and angels actually started showing up in person.* Why? What had changed? Well, maybe in addition to props like burning bushes and thunder, Christianity, which was new and different needed real "front men", actual people who could be seen and heard. And touched. The gospels do say that Jesus appeared in several forms. But if he appeared in several forms, how could anyone be certain it was Jesus? Epiphany, gods appearing in human form, or as a friend for special people, was also a common occurrence in the pagan world long before Christianity. *Let's not forget that during ancient times people in the Middle East either smoked, chewed, or drank a lot of hashish, a powerful narcotic made from the cannabis plant, a hallucinogen that would have you seeing and hearing all kinds of things, just as the Indians (Native Americans) smoked peyote in their peace pipes to talk to their gods.* With that in mind, why is the Christians' God any more real than the Native Americans' gods? Many spiritual frontier Indians hated Christians.

Today we know about marijuana, crack, cocaine, crystal meth, plus powerful prescription drugs, to name a few, and I'm sure drugs and alcohol have quite a few people seeing and talking to God. At least today when we hear thunder we know about electricity, and that it's not God talking to us. And if it's raining and the sun is shining it's not the devil beating his wife. I'm sure some people still believe that.

Something most people don't realize is that President Thomas Jefferson also published a Bible, with no miracles. Jefferson's Bible, *The Life and Morals of Jesus of Nazareth*, an 84-page volume written in 1820, was constructed by taking scissors, a razor and glue, then removing passages about anything supernatural or Jesus being divine. Like Jesus feeding the multitude with only two fish and five loaves of bread. *Jefferson said he wanted to leave out all the gimmicks the priests used to make themselves rich and only focus on Jesus' doctrine. He called the miracles nonsense.* That taking out all the crap was like separating diamonds from a dunghill (shit hill). But Jefferson never actually called his work a Bible, and he didn't believe in a creator. He, too, believed in Jesus' teachings, but disagreed with many of the interpretations. Jefferson didn't trust the interpreters and interpretations, which he called "the corruption of schematizing followers." George Washington, who owned over 300 slaves, also believed Jesus was a myth.

Thomas Paine, the Founding Father who named the United States of America, was the genius who wrote *The Age of Reason*, challenging organized religion. It was his declaration of war against religious dogmatism that had squashed individual liberties over the centuries. Paine called Christianity a fable. He denied "that the Almighty ever did communicate anything to man, by speech, language, or vision."

Paine wrote, "I do not believe in the creed professed by the Jewish church, by the Roman church, by the Greek church, by the Turkish church, nor by any church I know of. My own mind is my church. *All national institutions of churches . . . appear to me no other than human inventions, set up to terrify and enslave mankind, and monopolize power and profit.*" Paine hated religious tyranny. In his opinion, organized religion turned the divine mystery into "bad mythology." The above was taken from *50 Things You're Not Supposed To Know* by Daniele Bolelli. (It was also Thomas Paine who said "We have it within our power to begin the world all over again," but nothing ever really changes does it?

Phillip Patterson, a New Yorker, finished writing the entire King James Version of the Bible, by hand word for word. It took him four years to write 2,400 pages, sometimes writing fourteen hours a day. When asked if he thought Jesus was divine or was God's son, Patterson answered that he wasn't sure about any of that. But Jesus is his messiah because he has definitely changed the world.

In *The Jesus Family Tomb* by Simcha Jacobovici and Charles Pellegrino, Jacobovici also talks about ancient Jews who lived where Jesus lived, while he lived. Jesus didn't just walk around bragging about being God's son and everybody quietly lined up behind him. Remember, the Ebionites were Jews who believed Jesus was the messiah while rejecting his divinity. The Nazarenes, however, accepted everything about Christianity, including Jesus' virgin birth . . . *After his death.*

In Matthew 28:11–15, when the priests paid the guards to say Jesus' disciples had stolen his body during the night, many, like the Ebionites, would have believed them. That Jesus' body was moved and he was never resurrected! Afterall, God had not saved either Jesus or John the Baptist. The Nazarenes accepted Mary Magdalene's account of Jesus' resurrection, even though she, as both a follower and Jesus' companion and best friend, would have had good reason to lie. Still, if Jesus had not risen from the grave, Mary Magdalene and the others would have looked like fools, accusations already made, probably signaling the end of their sect. Paul said Jesus became the son of God upon his resurrection. Matthew and Luke disagreed, saying at conception. *Jesus' resurrection vindicated them, and Christianity.*

Crucifixion without resurrection would have been meaningless. *Jesus was the Hebrew messiah and his memory had to be kept alive!* By any means necessary. *Jesus' birth and death had to be spectacular.* The bottom line was Christianity's survival. Hence, creation of the sacred books. Without men like Henry Ford, Karl Benz (Mercedes Benz), and R. E. Olds (Oldsmobile), we would still have cars because other men were working on the same problem in different places. And without the Wright brothers we would still have airplanes today for the same reason, other men working on the same problem. But Christianity is different. Without Jesus there is no Christianity. Prophecies foretold his death and execution. If Jesus is not God then there is no Christianity. *Jesus is Christianity. Christianity is Jesus. Jesus is God.* Christianity comes from Christ, specifically referring to Jesus of Nazareth. Is Jesus Christ really the world's only manifestation of God? Nathaniel, a disciple asked "Can anything good come from Nazareth?" Why would God's son live in a place like that? Maybe mind-altering drugged wine, nectar of the gods.

In their controversial narrative, Jacobovici and Pellegrino suggest that Jesus' mysterious family tomb, the Talpiot Tomb, was excavated in Israel in 1980. It contained the remains of Jesus, Mary, Mary Magdalene, and even a son of Jesus, "Yehuda bar Yeshua," Judah, son of Jesus. (The family had to be buried somewhere.) The Ark of the Covenant, containing Moses' Ten Commandments, is said to be in the town of Aksum, Ethiopia, guarded by one single person, appointed for life, who has no contact at all with the outside world. Nobody else sees the Ark.

Now there's a new twist. It's just been revealed by the Catholic Church that the Holy Grail Jesus used to drink from at the Last Supper has been in a church in Spain for the last 1,000 years. The cup, encrusted with beautiful jewels, is magnificent. How would Jesus and the apostles have had access to anything that lavish? *Rich women!*

Jews who knew Jesus were dumbfounded. Who did he think he was? Remember, people were saying Jesus was beside himself; possessed by demons. *Everybody thought he had lost his mind. That he was homeless and insane, including his family, dragging him away from Peter's house in Mark 3:21.* How could Jesus have been God's son when he was born, but a psychotic "mad man," a "crackpot" when he said so as an adult? *(If he ever said it at all).* Keeping that in mind, why is anyone who questions Jesus' divinity today, 2,000 years later, considered either a sinner or a moron by so-called believers? To this day Jews believe the real messiah is yet to come (so they're still waiting). *Remember, many of the people of Nazareth where Jesus grew up as a child, with playmates, didn't know he was God's son (blasphemy, according to the Torah).* They were shocked by what Jesus was saying. A troublesome agitator, he was not the messiah they expected. During the Jewish Feast of Tabernacles, his brothers tried to coax him into going to Judea to perform some feat that would prove who he was, but Jesus didn't oblige them. *(He wasn't feelin' it.)*

> John 7:2–5
> But when the Jewish Feast of Tabernacles was near, Jesus' brothers said to him, "You ought to leave here and go to Judea, so that your disciples may see the miracles you do. No one who wants to become a public figure acts in secret. Since you are doing these things, show yourself to the world. *For even his own brothers did not believe him." [And why did they accuse Jesus of wanting to be a public figure?]* Maybe because he desired very much to be a public figure. *King!*

Jesus' own brothers misunderstood him and didn't believe he was God's son. If they really believed their mother Mary was a virgin when Jesus was born, why not accept the claim that their brother was God's son? No, they were daring him, calling his bluff, but the Bible says that Jesus couldn't always perform miracles, especially when people were not true believers. Kind of like a hypnotist who can't hypnotize someone because they don't believe in hypnotism. Jesus refused to perform miracles to prove who he was. When he started preaching, his family didn't follow his example or become part of his movement, never during his lifetime. Jesus was embarrassing them. *Some followers had started seeing him as a common criminal, and maybe a con man, like other preachers and drug dealing healers who prayed on the weak.* Neighbors who didn't accept Jesus as the messiah actually wanted to run him out of town before he got himself, and them killed. He was putting their village in grave danger and they were furious. Anyone against Jesus was an enemy who would pay dearly.

Jews believed there was only one God, he was beyond their comprehension, and that Jesus was a troublemaker who would be dealt with by the Romans. It was heresy for anybody but the Emperor to claim to be divine, God's son. For Jews there was no hell because God didn't make a place just to punish them, and no devil. Their Hebrew messiah would be a natural human being, not someone whose mother was a virgin. Jesus felt the same way. *Remember, Jesus of Nazareth being God's son was Paul's idea, along with whoever had helped Mary out when she became pregnant.* Jews also believed that any Jew could be saved if he lived morally and righteously. Like ancient Catholics, many rejected a fire and brimstone hell.

For Jews today, Jesus still cannot be the messiah because he didn't fulfill the messianic prophecies. Jesus did not build the Third Temple. He did not gather all Jews back to Israel. He did not usher in world peace. And he has not united humanity as one by spreading universal knowledge of the God of Israel, recreating David's kingdom on earth.

Although Jesus' brothers were not followers in the early days, after his crucifixion there was much infighting going on. Even between disciples. (No, not the disciples fighting!) Competing to see who would take Jesus' place (be the new boss, taking over Jesus' spot). That had become more important to them than Jesus' mission. Who was going to be "top dog"? *On earth, in Palestine!* In the end, however, it was his brother James who won. *Jesus' brother became the new leader of his church.*

Like Jesus' family, the disciples, uneducated peasants never really understood his message or what Jesus was actually talking about. They just didn't get it when he said that his kingdom was not of this world.

I need to make another observation here. Remember Peter, the man who became the first pope, abandoned his kinsmen and then Jesus. And Paul, the spokesman who never met Jesus was an opportunist. Between his trial and his death, almost all of the disciples abandoned Jesus. Terrified, everybody ran for their lives leaving him behind, except John. Jesus felt abandoned by God, on the ground begging not to die. According to David Leafe, after Jesus died there was the same power struggle just mentioned, to see who would take Jesus' place. Even though the gospels say Jesus wanted Peter, at least four different documents suggest that Jesus wanted his brother James to take his place. (Maybe the reason the governing authorities wanted Peter was precisely because he was impulsive and could be easily manipulated.)

According to the writings of Hegesippus, an early Christian historian who lived between 110 AD and 180 AD, *"The succession of the church passed to James, the brother of the Lord."* He said, *"As the first bishop of Jerusalem, James had an arch-rival in the apostle Paul, whose teachings were different from his in one key respect: the issue of whether Jesus really was the son of God."* Josephus, who lived during that time, also said that Jesus' brother James became the leader of the church after Jesus was crucified.

"*Like Jesus, James was a Jew, and in line with Old Testament prophecies, he believed that Jesus was an ordinary man chosen by God to lead his people.* [But not God's son.] This was very different from the ideas championed by Paul that Jesus was divine, being born of God himself." (*Again, the original idea of Jesus being God's son was Paul's, Mary's handlers, and Constantine.*) *Jesus never heard things Paul later preached.*

It's intriguing too, that the letter of James, Jesus' brother, was not included in the Scriptures, although James didn't personally write it. *The letter deals with what James learned from Jesus.* But it was dangerous because it said that *Jesus was master, but not divine. That Jesus was blessed by God, but not his Son. It contains teachings of Jesus, but not about Jesus* (like Thomas Jefferson's Bible). In James's letter, Jesus was simply a human being blessed by God. *Jesus was Lord, but not the Lord God. And Jesus wasn't the son of God but a servant of God.* There is no theology about Jesus, no cross of Christ, no blood of Jesus, and no forgiving our sins by our Heavenly Father. *Jesus' own brother, who took his place after his crucifixion, said Jesus wasn't God's son.* Josephus didn't believe it either.

The Didikai, written during the 1st Century, also tells about the early Christians. There was no virgin birth, no Jesus as Lord, and no resurrection. The Didikai provided practical advice for early Christians, giving them structure, telling them how to work, pray, and even baptize. It explained what was sacred Scripture and what was heresy.

At one point, contained in one of the earliest Bibles which exists today in Palestine, Jude, Jesus' other brother, speaks out about people who are among them who are not to be trusted. People perverting family traditions. Could Paul the latecomer have been one such person?

The Gentiles, outsiders recruited by Paul, soon outnumbered their competition, James' Jewish-Christians. The Jewish high priests had James stoned to death and in 70 A. D. when the Romans captured Jerusalem and destroyed the Great Temple, James's followers had nowhere else to go. *Eventually Constantine totally obscured (erased) James and the others, and Paul's teachings became the official doctrine we follow today.* The myth gained traction, Jesus became divine, and James' message about serving God in our everyday actions (liberation theology) got lost. (Later the rich or those who were brutal could be saved without changing by purchasing their salvation from the church.) Did Peter, Paul, and the Orthodox church hijack Christianity? The evidence appears to speak for itself. Or does it? Did Paul steal Christianity or actually save it?

Remember, not only had Paul never met Jesus, he never thought Jesus could pull it all together. He had little respect for the original twelve nor they for him. In spite of that, Paul saw himself as being the man who would take Jesus' place, claiming that since Jesus had personally talked to him after his crucifixion and resurrection, he was obviously Jesus' choice and his closest apostle. But was Paul calculating again, and lying about talking to Jesus after he was crucified? (*Or maybe smoking a little something, eating a few mushrooms and then seeing Jesus?*)

Both Jesus and Paul were tribalist who only supported Jews. As previously stated, Paul changed, befriending Gentiles, while Jesus remained staunchly separatist. Both men believed God loved Hebrews alone, that others were of no value, and salvation was solely for Jews. It was wrong to go to a Gentiles' house, intermarry, or eat their food. *Racial segregation.* A Shammaite, Paul believed having money meant God's approval, being poor was a curse, and that only rich, responsible people should be taught Scripture.

For whatever reason, Paul ended up going to the Hillel school where he learned the virtues of charity, humility, patience and piety. He had a master teacher, Gamaliel of Jerusalem, Hillel's grandson. Hillels believed Jews were God's special people, and any Jew who turned away from idolatry and outdated Jewish laws was welcomed. Hillels and Shammaites were complete opposites. For example, while Shammaites felt that healing somebody on the Sabbath was work, Hillels like Paul considered it a good deed. Shammaites killed many Hillels.

In contrast, some of Hillel's teachings were similar to Jesus'. But while Jesus only focused on (all nations) of Jews, Paul expanded Hillel's message to include anybody and everybody. *The foundation of Christianity, having almost nothing to do with Jesus or his teachings.*

Don't forget, the aristocratic Sadducees believed doctrines like the resurrection of the dead, the existence of angels and spirits, and the idea of punishment or rewards after death were not based on written laws, but Zoroastrianism. *Jesus wasn't coming back.*

Again, during Christianity's early days there were different sects. Some believed Jesus was God incarnate. For others, he was a mystic, somebody dealing in secret rites or the occult. *Magic.* Then there were those who saw Jesus as a simple prophet or preacher. The Nazarenes thought he had been crucified, resurrected, and gone to heaven already. They were only waiting for him to come back. Right back. (Jesus preached that the end-times and the Kingdom of God were near, right around the corner, and he was talking about back then, not in 2019, 2020, or somewhere far out there in never-never land.) Jesus was wrong!

Even today, for us thinking about what's going to happen in the next 2,000 years is incomprehensible. It's too much to wrap our tiny brains around. In Jesus' little village there was only primitive technology, like wheels and early tools. They didn't even think of thinking about the next 20 years, let alone 2,000 years. No. *Jesus, their fearless messiah was coming right back. He wasn't dead and soon he was going to show up again.* Jesus was never a Christian or a Catholic and neither were the twelve apostles. He would not have wanted to be one! He was born a Jew and died a Jew! The end-times didn't come and Jesus never became the messiah (king of Israel), as they expected. He failed!

During Jesus' time, believers, humble peasants, only needed to have faith, be obedient and dedicated, and do good works. Remember, before Jesus' followers were called Christians they were known as Nazarenes, even though they always thought of themselves as Jews. "True Jews"! Early

Christians actually lived as practicing Jews. The more rational Ebionites thought no such thing about only needing faith. For them questions were both necessary and reasonable, and not simply following orders. (Today, Episcopalians might be more like Ebionites while Baptists, Catholics, and Evangelicals are similar to Nazarenes.)

In his book *The Jesus Dynasty*, Professor James Tabor takes a new look at the messiah. The following is taken from *U.S. News and World Report*'s "Secrets of Christianity."

> "According to Tabor, *Jesus, in partnership with his cousin John the Baptizer, saw himself as the founder not of a new religion but of a worldly royal dynasty.* Fulfilling ancient prophecies, the dynasty, descended from King David, was to restore Israel through an apocalyptic upheaval culminating in the Kingdom of God on Earth, not in some distant or metaphorical future, but in the very time in which they lived . . . Tabor says, Jesus had established a provisional government with 12 tribal officials." (Jesus, God, was already on earth.)
>
> "In discussing the Gospel of Matthew's claim that Jesus' virgin birth was the fulfillment of Isaiah's prophecy, Tabor explains that the Hebrew word that Matthew translates as 'virgin' means a 'young woman' or 'maiden' and carries no miraculous implications." It's an interesting hypothesis, as I stated earlier.
>
> Also, in *Secrets of Christianity*, "Albert Schweitzer concluded that all his major predecessors tended to find a Jesus who suited their own personal and ideological needs."

The most important distinction I can make is that Jesus preached about the "Kingdom of God" established on earth, ruled by God, governed by Jewish law under a Davidic king, while Matthew's phrase "Kingdom of Heaven" and Levi's vision of a heavenly temple where God lives have totally confused and distorted Jesus' message and purpose.

What I find intriguing is that I, like others, was led to believe that John the Baptist was this wise, old prophet who announced to the world that Jesus was the messiah, and then baptized him. Again, that John the Baptist would baptize the anointed one was foretold by Isaiah, who preceded him, also fulfilling Jewish prophecy. When Jesus showed up at the Jordan River to be baptized and John told everybody who he was, John, who played with Jesus as a child in Jerusalem, and who was actually only a few months older than Jesus, failed to mention that Jesus, who appeared to be a stranger, was really his first cousin. (No, "hey, y'all, I want you to meet my cuz" moment. John the Baptist was probably thinking, "Hey, cuz, whatcha' doin'?" or "Hey, cuz, we doin' this?")

In fact, in the Gospel of John, 1:30-34, John the Baptist actually said that he did not know Jesus, the cousin he grew up playing with.

> John 1:30-34
>
> 30 This is he of whom I said, after me comes a man who ranks ahead of me because he was before me. 31 *I myself did not know him*, but I came baptizing with water for this reason, that he might be revealed to Israel. 32 And John testified, " I saw the Spirit descending from heaven like a dove, and it remained on him 33 *I myself did not know him*, but the one who sent me to baptize with water said to me, 'He on whom you see the Holy Spirit descend and remain is the one who baptizes with the Holy Spirit." 34 And I myself have seen and have testified that this is God's Chosen One." (The leader, not God's son.)

Was John the Baptist lying? How could he not have known Jesus, the cousin who had grown up as God's son, according to his mother Elizabeth, by his virgin aunt Mary? When Jesus showed up to be baptized and John announced that he was the messiah, he already knew Jesus was to be the messiah. *He knew him! That's why he asked Jesus to baptize him first.* Even eighteen years later Jesus hadn't changed that much.

When the symbolic dove landed on Jesus, John the Baptist was convinced that he was the messiah. In John's Gospel the dove lands before Jesus is baptized; Matthew, Mark, and Luke have the bird showing up after his baptisim. They're called synoptic gospels because they tell the same stories, copying Mark, even using the same words, verbatim. The reason John "the dipper" believed he was the man who would proclaim the messiah was because his own father, Zechariah, a priest at the Temple in Jerusalem had told him so. (What good son wouldn't believe his own "dear old dad," a well-known, highly respected priest with money and power?) *Jesus' uncle.* So, Jesus' cousin conveniently told everybody how great this stranger was, but not that he was God's son!

John the Baptist, however, as a devoted Jew, probably never said Jesus was God's son, although it says just that in many bible translations.

Mark 1:7–8
He [John] proclaimed, "The one who is more powerful than I is coming after me; I am not worthy to stoop down and untie the thong of his sandals."

Matthew later adds John acknowledging Jesus as the one coming after me. Like the talking snake that tempted Eve in the Garden of Eden, this time in Matthew, after the dove shows up, the voice in the sky says, "You are my Son; the Beloved. In you I am well pleased." (Was the heavenly voice speaking Aramaic or Hebrew?) And had John the Baptist, who was never a Christian, drank, chewed or smoked anything?

God himself was supposedly speaking to his son Jesus, the messiah. Even before Jesus' followers were called Nazarenes or Ebionites, early Christians were members of an illegal cult known as "The Way". Jesus taught them that the only way to God was through him. Not following Jesus made you an outcast. He alone was "the way", which was blasphemy for orthodox Jews. To be blessed you had to accept him first. While others like Moses and Elijah, who lived centuries before Jesus were "way-showers" giving directions, Jesus was saying the buck stops with me. END OF STORY!

Don't forget that Ebionites knew nothing about Jesus' divinity, his virgin birth, or that he was God's son. Nobody knew about it because Mary was terrified and didn't tell anybody. And in the shame/honor Middle Eastern culture she was living in, being pregnant would have destroyed her, literally, the opposite of the warm, fuzzy, loving manger scene we know. How could a sweet, innocent girl like Mary, who was so devoted to God be pregnant? Her parents may have known, and Elizabeth probably told Zacharias, her rich priest husband, but who else knew? Wearing loose baggy clothes, maybe going to Bethlehem to pay taxes or for a census was an excuse to get away from Nazareth for Jesus' birth. Remember, Jesus grew up as the carpenter's son, not God's son. Why did it take thirty years for people to find that out? Why did Jesus wait thirty years to perform miracles and to start helping people? Remember, for Ebionites Jesus was a teacher and prophet who was human like everybody else. He was a servant of the Jewish God, just as James' letter stated. Quoting Jesus in Matthew 5:17 during the Sermon on the Mount, "Think not that I am come to destroy the Law or the Prophets. I am not come to destroy, but to fulfil." Jesus and his disciples were born into Jewish families, raised in Jewish towns and reared according to Jewish law.

Again, neither Jesus, Paul nor "The Twelve" were ever Christians, but instead loyal leaders of "The Way", with the exception of Paul. Another surprise is that like Paul, who spoke fluent Greek, Jesus spoke Greek too, as a second language, which would have been helpful in finding work. Greek was the everyday language in Israel after Alexander the Great's conquest in 323 B.C. Jesus and the apostles probably spoke Aramaic, Hebrew and Greek, especially Matthew, collecting Roman taxes.

CHAPTER 10

Did Moses Borrow from Ancient Wisdom?

―──

Gabriel, the angel who told Mary about Jesus, told Elizabeth what the plan was. *"Prophecy was going down."* Remember, Elizabeth, 60 to 80 years old, was supposed to be barren when Mary visited her, comparing (coordinating) messages from Gabriel, who was one very busy angel. Were both women already pregnant or was it all a lie? There hadn't been a miracle or a message from God or an angel in over 400 years, not since Gabriel shocked Daniel. Gabriel also dropped by to see Zechariah to give him the news, but he wasn't buyin' it either. Elizabeth stayed secluded for five months, until she was showing, so people wouldn't think she was nuts. And by the way, who named the angel Gabriel, God or Gabriel's angel parents? Was there an *"angels' names list"* in heaven that was strikingly similar to human names on earth? Why didn't Gabriel have some weird alien name, like Alf or Mork?

Not only was Elizabeth, John the Baptist's mom married to a priest, she was also a descendant of Aaron, Moses' brother, a chief priest of Israel with a dynasty of priests lasting for over 1,000 years (money and power, definitely middle and upper class, respected, lots of pretty things, a nice house in a good neighborhood). Appointed for life by Moses, only Aaron or his sons could offer animal sacrifices, incense, or carry the Ark of the Covenant. Almost everybody in Jesus' family was a priest, and both Zechariah and his wife Elizabeth were descendants of hierarchy dating back to the time before King David. Unlike ordinary priests, high priests had to be born into the right wealthy family, serving from 25 to 50 years old. They all had money. Sometimes there was even bidding for the position. Family members also "traded places" and "took turns" being the high priest. (Everybody was related just like the shamans. It also sounds like the Curia and the Catholic Church.) In Jewish law the priesthood was passed on by blood relatives of Sadducees who ran the Temple. Under the Old Covenant priests were to be married and to have children who would become priests. (During Jesus' time there were about 7,000 priests in Palestine.)

Once a year, on Yom Kippur, the high priest was allowed to enter The Holy of Holies, that special part of the Temple where God was, behind a huge curtain. Anyone entering whose heart wasn't pure died immediately. A rope was tied to the high priest's leg so he could be pulled out if anything went wrong. (Another theatrical con.)

An interesting piece of gossip is that Miriam's, Moses' and Aaron's father Amram was married to their Aunt Jochebed, his daddy's sister, making the three of them products of incest. To produce children for herding and farming, marrying kinsmen within the clan wasn't sinful but necessary. As Levi's daughter, Jochebed was Amram's wife and aunt. So historically all these men were related and married, but way, way down the line, somewhere in the 12th century at the First Lateran Council, the Catholic Church decided that clerical marriages were invalid, and that priests should remain celibate. (Divorce would mean alimony, child support, and health care for the wife and kids one day. And suppose there's a second divorce with even more children and more child support?) But Eastern Orthodox clergy are not permitted to remarry if they become widowed. On the negative side, a single priest who is dating and trying to find Miss Right might just give the wrong impression.

That's why Jesus couldn't set a precedent of having been married with a family. All those dependents, plus financial settlements, how to pass on property (inheritance), and pensions? (Talk about complicated). Sooner or later the Catholic Church would have to come up with some big, big bucks, and we know for sure that that wasn't going to happen. It would have been like today's child sex abuse pay-offs.

Priests and bishops had power and controlled land that might someday go to their heirs. Land that meant wealth and even more power. And some scheming priests did actually will land they were responsible for to family members. So the Church truly had reason to worry.

Naturally, Popes like Gregory VII, who formalized the celibacy doctrine, and Calixtus II, who saw the Vatican as his own private gold mine, didn't want any of those heirs getting their grubby little hands on Church property. For that reason celibacy is the subject of Canon Law 247 which derails such shenanigans. But Canon Law is only a man-made rule or a regulation that can change, while dogma (true beliefs) is not. In other words Canon Law is not set in stone. As a matter of fact the Pope can change one whenever he feels like it, just like the President of the United States signing an "executive order", with a simple stroke of his pen. *Celibacy is simply another rule created by human beings to maintain power and control over others by attributing it to God.* Pretending that rules like celibacy came from God also prevent them from being challenged or changed (just as the Bible and religion do).

Canon Law also forbids popes from publicly recognizing children. The pope is God on earth, just like Jesus. No kids, even if they're alive and walking around. The same way an annulment erases a marriage. *Maybe Jesus and Mary Magdalene were the Catholic Church's first annulment.* Their relationship was deemed invalid, then rescinded. And certainly as God's son, Jesus could not be perceived as ever getting pussy or recognizing any children in public. *(God's grandchildren).*

Canon Law 290 is very interesting. Once a priest has been ordained, ordination can never be invalidated or revoked. (A marriage and children can be invalidated but not a priest.) *"Once a priest, always a priest"* including priests who are serial pedophiles. Except for laicization.

The Church's argument in support of celibacy was that sexual abstinence would increase priests purity (making them more like Jesus). Unmarried priests could focus all their attention on God, and be continuously available for service. In Corinthians 7:32-34 Paul says

> 32 I want you to be free from anxieties. The unmarried man is anxious about the affairs of the Lord, how to please the Lord; 33 but the married man is anxious about the affairs of the world, how to please his wife 34 and his interest are divided.

But God didn't say that. Paul said it (maybe). Because somewhat contradictory, in writing to Timothy Paul said that "a bishop should be married but once." And speaking about affairs of the world, married priests were even to abstain from having sex with their wives for a certain period of time before administering the Eucharist, the body and blood of Christ. A full 24 hours. Denying the urges of the body to reach the divine. *Acting as a priest meant not behaving like a man.* Like an animal! Now that's deep. (No nookie tonight!) And no sex on Noah's ark.

Paul pissed married men off, telling wives to refuse husbands. In the Old Testament Jewish priests were to abstain when serving in the Temple for spiritual reasons, but since Catholic priests serve everyday, that means no sex at all. Period! No poontang ever! NEVER!

During ancient times rules about sexual abstinence grew out of a belief that sexual intercourse made a person unclean because women were viewed as being less moral and less worthy than men. (And remember women menstruate). *Sexual intercourse with a woman would therefore make the man unclean too.* Under Pope Innocent VIII women were even accused of witchcraft because the pope said they were more interested in the flesh (sex), and he used that as an excuse to seize their property, in addition to burning them alive.

Throughout the Middle Ages many scholars and theologians of that time did not believe witches were real, or were a threat to Christianity. To foster his own agenda, however, Pope Innocent used a book which he commissioned called "The Malleus Maleficarum" (The Witches Hammer). During the Inquisition it was a guide to be used by witch hunters and proof that witches really existed. Pope Innocent even said that witches could fly, change shape, and have sex with the devil.

For nearly 250 years anywhere from 600,000 to nine million people were hanged or burned at the stake by the Catholic Church, and their property seized, especially noble women with money. Sometimes hundreds were burned at one time and tens of thousands were brutally tortured. Midwives, herb gatherers, Jews, widows and spinsters who were not under the authority of a man were especially suspect. Sometimes even illness was considered the result of magic, witchcraft or devil worship, severely affecting the lives of hundreds of thousands of men and children. A child could accuse somebody like an old person, a loner, or someone who was mentally ill of being a witch. All with the blessings of Pope Innocent VIII and other Popes who were always looking for new ways to get their hands on *quick cash*, or to hold on to whatever they already had. Women in general were of little value, less than cattle.

In 1139 at the Second Lateran Council mandatory celibacy for all priests became law, and even a priest who was already married had to leave his wife and family. Popes' marriages retroactively became invalid upon ordination, spouses were demoted to concubines. Pope Urban II even had priests' wives sold into slavery, leaving their children behind, abandoned. Naturally, some holy men refused, and during the Reformation other priests rebelled, marrying nuns. Under the Church's anti-marriage mandates, the spiritual was pure, the material fleeting and corruptible. In the fifth-century St. Augustine said "Nothing is more powerful in drawing the spirit of a man downwards as the caresses of a woman."

Today one of the problems the Catholic Church still faces is trying to figure out how much to pay priests who are married with families. The average salary for an unmarried priest is $20,000.00, plus digs at the rectory. Married, that same priest would need a bigger place for his wife and their little crumb-pickers, plus even more cash for insurance, groceries, a second car, and probably tuition.

At the same time the priest's family is expected to behave like angels. The priest, of course, can't be in two places at once, so somebody's got to lose. Either he's there for his family, or he's not there because he's out somewhere working for God. Whatever Moses might have believed or whatever Paul might have believed, in Matthew 22:23-30, *Jesus said that nobody in heaven will be married.* When asked which one of the seven brothers the widow who had successively married each one from the oldest to the youngest would belong to in heaven, Jesus' answer was nobody. Nobody.

Does that mean that in heaven your beloved sweetie won't be your wife anymore? And what about your kids, the little knuckleheads? Who will they be in heaven, and how will you recognize each other, or even find each other among the billions of others who might make it up above the clouds to deep space? How old will you be up there?

Recently, on a Christian radio broadcast I heard one little girl ask a pastor "When a baby dies is it still going to be a baby in heaven?" The preacher's answer was no. He told the little girl, who sounded about five years old, that "in heaven it (the baby) would be the perfect age." Excuse me, but what the hell does that mean, the perfect age? *No babies born in heaven. Wow! And let's not forget that babies are born sinners too, from the moment they draw their first breath.* No exceptions.

No marriage or falling in love in heaven. Who woulda' thought. Perhaps family isn't as important as we may think it is? Is anything in heaven actually going to be the way we think it will be? Maybe instead of a giant reunion with friends and loved ones, everybody in heaven is just going to love everybody else. One big heavenly commune.

Some believe Jesus wasn't saying nobody will be married in heaven, but nobody will get married in heaven. If you're already married you'll still be married. Since nobody in heaven ever dies you won't have to remarry. If a Christian who has been granted eternal life dies is his or her mate forbidden to remarry because that person hasn't really died? Will single people be single forever?

In Matthew 22:30 Moses said *"in the resurrection they neither marry nor are given in marriage, but are like angels in heaven."* How would Moses know that? And do angels have sex in heaven? Let's not forget the Bible does say that the sons of God came to earth and knocked boots. So they had the necessary equipment, including a sex drive. (But Jesus said angels never got married or had children, so where did angels come from)? And do they still have wings for flying around?

In ancient times women were often treated like property, and given in marriage could mean sold. Did the statement actually mean that in heaven women wouldn't be treated like property anymore? And what would Solomon do with his 700 wives and 300 concubines? Will there even be different genders, male and female, men and women in heaven? Is a carnal act like sex even allowed, especially since there are no babies born up there? Remember, rules are different in heaven *(absolutely no screwing around because your new body may not have any equipment).*

Since there are no babies born in heaven there will be no need for sexual differences. Don't forget that the most important commandment is to "love God with all your heart, and with all your soul, and with all your mind." Not the wife and kids you may not have in heaven, but God. (Obviously this explanation goes contrary to the sons of God claim.) But besides all that did Moses ever really know what he was talking about anyway? Or did he just realize that as the Israelite leader he had to say something? *...Anything!*

Aaron and Miriam even challenged Moses' right to speak for God. Moses' own brother, a priest, and his sister didn't believe what he was saying. Remember, Jesus' brothers didn't believe him either. Aaron and Miriam also didn't like the fact that Moses was married to Jethro's daughter, Zipporah, an Ethiopian, a foreigner. God told Moses to put his hand into his cloak, it came out white. Because of her prejudice, Miriam was struck with leprosy and turned white as snow. Were Moses, Aaron and Miriam people of color? (Just as it is today with distinctions between dark skinned blacks and light complexioned Creoles and mulattoes, there were different classifications and distinctions in ancient times too, not necessarily based on color, but rather the region a person was descended from, their tribe or nationality.)

Aaron and Miriam knew Moses was smart and educated, and that he could put anything over on the ignorant, superstitious Israelites, like coming down from Mount Sinai with The Ten Commandments, then saying Jehovah had given them to him. Moses also said he saw God and talked to him. So, Moses was still seeing and hearing things up there on the mountain all by his lonesome. Nobody but him and maybe a little something to smoke, and probably a little vino to wash it down. Was he lying? Keep in mind that Moses, the first man to ever meet God, may have been a heavy drinker. The reason he might have been drinking was because he didn't think anybody would believe him, especially about a talking, burning bush. (Say whaaatt!) It took God seven days to convince Moses to make a move, and he even wanted God to send somebody else. God was so angry with Moses that he made it impossible for him to speak. *Like Abraham and Melchizedek, there is no proof that Moses ever existed either, or Jesus.* Physical or archaeological. Similar to other Bible stories like Noah and his ark, Moses' story mirrors earlier Mesopotamian and Egyptian myths about a baby being discovered in some reeds.

Moses was no "spring chicken". Imagine climbing up that mountain seven or eight times, probably without lunch, and staying up there forty days and forty nights with nobody to talk to and no sleep, while God, using his finger, inscribed the tablets on both sides. Moses had to be exhausted. So did he actually experience Jehovah, or was he hallucinating? Hey, maybe after a few puffs he really was convinced that God talked to him.

Aaron and Miriam also knew that Moses was aware of the Babylonian culture, the Sumerian religion, the worship of Marduk, *magic ceremonies,* the cult of Anu- the heaven god, and animism, which profoundly influenced both the Old and New Testaments. He also would have learned how important location (the Promised Land—a gift from

God), politics, and spirituality were to each other. Moses would have known about Inanna, the virgin heaven goddess, *Mama, the goddess who created man from clay, about Hammurabi - the wise king, and about the cuneiform tablets containing all human knowledge before the flood.* Even more important, *Moses would've learned about monotheism, which evolved, and one God.*

The Enuma Elish is the Babylonian creation myth that was written on seven clay tablets, explaining the world, man's place in it, and the gods. *It resembles Genesis, written or perhaps edited by Moses from earlier accounts, and many believe that Genesis was a rewrite of the Enuma Elish.* Others argue that the Enuma Elish was a rewrite of Genesis, even though the Enuma Elish preceded Genesis by several hundred years. However, unlike superstitious Christians, Babylonians understood that myths were not reality. The first six lines of the Enuma Elish are as follows:

> When the skies above were not yet named
> Nor earth below pronounced by name,
> Apsu, the first one, their begetter, [male]
> And maker Tiamat, who bore them all [female]
> Had mixed their waters together,
> But had not formed pastures, nor discovered reed-beds;
> [creation of the oceans, the sky, and the earth]

Marduk was called Lord, becoming Lord of the gods of heaven and earth. Everything owed its existence to Marduk, the Lord, who made humanity. *Marduk, the Lord, created man.*

Being aware of Babylonian science and astronomy, Moses would also have understood what eclipses were and that they were predictable and affected the tides, and he would have known that when he miraculously parted the Red Sea. Maybe Moses was using science and not invoking God as he professed. Or maybe he felt that God had shown science to him. Once again, we'll never know. It was later revealed that Greeks who studied astronomy in Egypt and understood eclipses took particular interest in the one that happened during Jesus' crucifixion. (Educated people understood eclipses, even back then.)

Beginning in BC 1722, it was King Hammurabi who established the government in Babylon, making it the most political and intellectual center in the region, building cities, canals, and churches long before Christianity. And again, Hammurabi was responsible for creating the laws of the kingdom, the Code of Hammurabi that was etched into huge columns. They were reminiscent of Moses' Ten Commandments, before the Egyptians invented paper (papyrus). The columns were seven and a half feet tall, written in a common language (so everybody could read and understand them), and placed where everybody could see them. King Hammurabi said he was called by the gods Anu and Bel to cause justice to prevail in the land, *to destroy the wicked, to prevent the strong from oppressing the weak, to go forth like the sun over the black-faced race,* to enlighten the land, and to further the welfare of the people. There were 282 separate laws.

In Babylonian religion, another key figure was Eridu, the water god, and the Babylonians believed that *all things were created by the "word".* (Sound familiar), a*lmost 2,000 years before Christianity.* Of course, in Christianity there was a concept called "fiat." God just said "Let it be," "the word," and it happened. Mind over matter. Miracles. As the Babylonian account goes, *it was the priests who named everything, like cows, cats, and horses* (sound familiar too?). In the Bible that was Adam's job.

Religion in Babylon was spread through written language. Like the time of Christianity, many average citizens didn't believe in gods of fate who determined a person's destiny. They didn't believe in signs or mystical powers either. Through the "Dialogue of Pessimism," the Babylonians questioned how gods who controlled all things and who were fair and just could allow the righteous to suffer. (Why did the gods let bad things happen to good people?) Doesn't that also sound familiar, but from Babylon 4,000 years ago?

Still, there were others in Babylon who didn't believe that being pious paid off at all. Eventually, for believers the idea of rewards after death became popular, but unlike Christianity nobody was ever punished for not believing.

As I said, Hammurabi, the man from whom Moses may have borrowed a few ideas was very wise. It's one thing to say it, yet another to document it. The following are just a few of the Babylonian laws regarding marriage and family four millennia ago, 2,000 years before Christianity. HAMMURABI'S LAWS WERE BASED ON AN EYE FOR AN EYE AND THE PRESUMPTION OF INNOCENCE.

- Marriage was by purchase, arranged between the respective parents, the bridegroom's father providing the bride-price.
- The dowry might be real property, but was generally personal effects or household furniture. It remained the wife's for life, descending to her children, if any.
- The couple formed a unit, especially for debt, the man being responsible for his wife's debts, even those contracted before marriage.
- A man might divorce his wife at will, but he had to restore the dowry, and she held the custody of her children. Suitable alimony had to be provided, which the wife shared equally with the children.
- If she had been a bad wife, however, he might divorce her while keeping the children and the dowry, or he might reduce her to bare maintenance as a slave in his house.
- If it was proved that the fault was upon her side she was to be drowned. If left in her husband's absence without maintenance she might cohabit with another man but must go back to her husband on his return, but if she had maintenance, cohabitation would be adultery.
- A childless wife might give her husband a maid to bear him children, who were reckoned hers.

- A concubine was free and a wife, though of inferior rank to the first.
- A father had complete control over his children until their marriage, to dispose of their labour, and even of their persons for his profit.
- All legitimate children shared equally in the father's estate at death.

Before Moses and Hammurabi, The Code of Ur-Nammu, the oldest tablet of laws, was written in Sumerian on tablets 300 years before Hammurabi. The Ur-Nammu Codes even considered compensation for bodily injury, but murder, robbery, adultery, and rape were capital offenses. There were between forty-two and fifty-seven laws. E.g.:

- If a man commits a murder, that man must be killed
- If a man commits a robbery, he will be killed.
- If a slave marries a slave, and that slave is set free, he does not leave the household.
- If a man violates the right of another and deflowers the virgin wife of a young man, they shall kill that male.
- If a man knocks out the tooth of another man, he shall pay two shekels of silver.

As you can readily see, people had strict laws long before Jesus, Moses, and Hammurabi came along. The Ten Commandments originally came from the "42 Negative Confessions of Black Egyptians." Civil societies already existed prior to Christianity and racism raising their ugly heads. While the Babylonians had the written word to spread religion, Christianity had Roman roads and trade routes instead, making travel from place to place with the "Good News" possible. "That Christians no longer needed to be intimidated by fear, hypocrisy, and hatred." In Babylon, there was knowledge, enlightenment, and justice. Today, still immersed in our own egotistical arrogance and dismissing justice and enlightenment, we turn our heads and look the other way when we see something that is wrong (child sex abuse, income inequality, and racism), failing to admit what we know is true because we are afraid of the consequences. *Many Christians stand divided and driven by sinister political and religious schemes orchestrated thousands of years ago that continue to profit a few at the expense of many.*

Hammurabi, a brilliant strategist, was also wise enough to take the smartest and most talented minds back to Babylon with him after a victory. By incorporating them into his society and exploiting their abilities, he was guaranteeing an advanced civilization (just as the U.S. today seeks mathematicians, engineers, and scientists from countries like India to exploit their potential). Hammurabi also knew that he didn't want to leave talented people like that behind, an oversight that might cost him later. (Unfortunately, the United States, wanting to remain predominantly white and Christian, would reject or overlook people Hammurabi would have gladly accepted.) Hammurabi's numerous contributions are a matter of record.

While the Babylonians had their huge cuneiform tablets and Moses his Ten Commandments, according to The Banned *Book of Jubilees*, Enoch, an Ethiopian, was the first man who learned to write, and he was taught to do so by angels, watchers – the sons of God who took him to heaven in a fiery chariot. The watchers, giant angels, allegedly lived in heaven and looked like human beings. While they were told to watch humans they were not to become involved as they did in Genesis with earth's women. As punishment for his wickedness before the Flood (screwing around), in Genesis 6:3-4 God declared that man's life shall last for no longer than 120 years. This, in spite of the Bible's exceedingly long lifespans for people like Adam, Methuselah, Enoch, Noah, and Lamech, who almost lived to be 1000 years old. Only men! And can human organs and skin even last for hundreds of years? Remember, the average lifespan for people who lived 2000 years ago was 15 to 30 years old. The Book of Enoch suggests that dating between angels and humans might have been easy too because Hebrew was the language spoken in heaven. Did the angels teach the Hebrews their language? What else did they teach them?

CHAPTER 11

Church Politicking

We will never know whether all the great acts credited to Moses, a descendant of Hebrews who immigrated from Canaan were true or not, but we are told that his own brother and sister didn't trust him. At the time Aaron went up the mountain with Moses he was 123 years old. (Kind of old for mountain climbing, don't you think?)

Poor cousin John the Baptist, while he was in jail for a couple of years waiting to have his head cut off, like Jesus' brothers, had doubts about Jesus being the messiah too. So John sent two of his disciples to talk to Jesus. (Yes, John the Baptist had disciples too.) Just about everybody did. A disciple is simply a follower who believes, a learner, while an apostle is a leader sent on a mission. *"Disciple" and "apostle" are only titles and nothing more, just like messiah and pope are.* (There is nothing spiritual or miraculous about a title or a word.) Again, John the Baptist, the man some suspected of being the messiah, wasn't sure about Jesus, his own cousin being the messiah either, even though some of his own loyal disciples, including Andrew and another of the original 12, left John's ministry to follow Jesus. And what about the voice of God in the clouds that John the Baptist heard saying "this is my son, whom I love; with him I am well pleased." Was John lying again?

If John the Baptist believed Jesus was the messiah, why didn't he stop preaching to follow Jesus too, after baptizing him, instead of continuing to preach on his own accord? John the Baptist, the greatest prophet who ever lived until then, already had throngs of people flocking to him out in the desert. (Like today's preachers, John wasn't goin' nowhere or givin' up nothin', especially to some new kid on the block. Even his own cousin.) Remember, many considered him the messiah, not Jesus. John's disciples were rivals of Jesus' disciples. Jesus' apostles rivaled each other.

157

Luke 7:20
So the men came to Jesus and said, John the Baptist sent us to you to ask, Are you the one who is to come, or shall we [continue to] look for another?

John the Baptist said he wasn't fit to untie Jesus' sandals, but later he didn't have confidence in him or follow him. Even John the Baptist had doubts about Jesus. Think about what that implies! *John never baptized anybody who wasn't a Jew. Jesus never baptized anybody.*

Many had questions, but there was a lot of political maneuvering going on. Is it possible that as an eight-year-old, an eighteen-year-old and in his early twenties, Jesus too had doubts about who he really was? A devoted Jew, he might indeed have been skeptical, certainly about something as controversial as seeing himself as God or his son, especially during his childhood. How would Jesus have known he was God's son if someone had not told him so? Matthew 16:16 quotes Peter; "You are the messiah, the son of the living God." Remember, messiah means king, not son. Translation, *"You are the king, the son of the living God!"*

Is it possible that by the time he turned thirty Jesus had matured and finally stepped forward to reclaim David's throne? To save his people and preserve their identity, not the whole world. Was Jesus spiritual, political, or perhaps both? Did he ever have a girlfriend, or like his mother Mary was he possibly a virgin all his life too, like the apostle John, and perhaps his brother James? *But if Jesus was in fact with Mary Magdalene, that whole virginity story goes down the drain. SUPPOSE JESUS HAD SEX!* And what about the rest of the family? With the exception of Jesus being at the Temple when he was twelve years old, where were Joseph, Mary, and the other children for those eighteen missing years?

Another thing that might have confused quite a few citizens after Jesus was crucified were dead people coming back to life on their own and walking into Jerusalem, not to mention Lazarus who had already been dead for four days when Jesus brought him back to life.

> Matthew 27:51–52
> At that moment the curtain of the temple was torn in two from top to bottom. The earth shook and the rocks split. The tombs broke open and the bodies of many holy people who had died were raised to life. They came out of the tombs, and after Jesus' resurrection they went into the holy city and appeared to many people.

The curtain torn, God was then approachable for all believers. Were the dead people still wearing their white burial clothes? Had their bodies decomposed? Did they stink like Lazarus did? Did they stay alive for a couple of weeks and then go back to being dead again? Or were they dead all along and just visiting Jerusalem? Today we would call dead people walking into town ZOMBIES, as in the popular AMC series *The Walking Dead*. So, is the Bible saying that zombies are real? Or is there some other way to logically explain something like this being written? Perhaps Isaiah 26:19, your dead shall live, their corpses shall rise.

One thing is true, however; centuries of images and pictures of a white Jesus, married or not, undoubtedly made white people feel empowered and good about themselves, while making black people feel impotent and inferior, standing unenlightened and dumbfounded on the sidelines. Confused and suffering from low self-esteem. *Europeans love feeling superior, and it doesn't get any better than saying that you've been chosen by God and created in his image.* (Jesus was one of us.) Likewise, a black Jesus and a black God would have helped black people feel good about themselves in the same way. *In-group-favoritism.*

Naturally, for whites there is only one way of seeing things, including God, and that's their way. But how can any one group possibly believe that they alone truly know God and understand what his plans are for everybody else on this planet? In the meantime, *blacks are still symbolically sitting in the back pews of the church, while whites proudly sit up front eagerly listening to lies, exaggerations, and unfathomable distortions about their own incredible ancestors, steeped in racial prejudice. Like they are gods too.*

In a world populated by millions of black people at the time, why was their presence so conspicuously absent from the Bible? Even in the "Song of Solomon," most people don't really get it when the Shulamite woman says, "Dark am I, yet lovely." She was saying that she was a person of color! And it was Job who said, "My skin is black upon me, and my bones are burned with heat." Job was another person of color.

Many Bible characters were people of color, Goliath, Abraham, Noah, King Solomon, and Paul who was so dark that he was mistaken for an Egyptian. People of color in the Bible ranged in complexion from light to dark, with straight, curly, and even nappy hair. Many Israelites married black women, figures like Abraham, Moses, Joseph, Judah, King David, King Solomon and even Sampson. Solomon's wife, the Queen of Sheba, and Cleopatra were black. Quite a few "brothers and sisters" were running around in the Old and New Testament days with hair like wool and feet like brass cast and presumed to be white, even though the evidence supports a different conclusion.

Minister Louis Farrakhan, leader of the Nation of Islam, went so far as to call the worship of a blond-haired, blue-eyed Jesus idolatrous, incarnating white identity and values. Absolutely, there were no blond, blue-eyed Jews in ancient Palestine. Mormons, Muslims, and many Catholics freely concede that Christianity is a white man's religion. Recently Reverend Farrakhan has aligned himself with L. Ron Hubbard's Church of Scientology, saying he is "seeking truth." This, even though most black people have never heard of scientology and the truth it espouses. Virtually, the only thing a few black people know about it is that Tom Cruise, the actor who jumped up and down on Oprah's sofa is a leading scientologist, and that Scientology rakes in the "big bucks".

Before 1978 blacks could not become Mormon priests. Brigham Young, the Mormon founder is to have said, "Shall I tell you the law of God in regard to the African race? If the white man who belongs to the *chosen* seed mixes his blood with the seed of Cain, the penalty, under the law of God is death. This will always be so." (Death for being interracial. Now *that's* deep!) How could the church condone killing two people because they were sexually involved and not the same race? Mormons were like the KKK. Shortly after the Civil Rights Act passed Mormons suddenly realized that black people were not animals. Are human beings biologically hardwired from infancy to be tribal? *Us vs. them!*

My friend Noah, no, not *that* Noah, sometimes tells the story about a wedding he once attended. On the wall behind the pulpit was a huge picture of a blond, blue-eyed Jesus with young black children, starry eyed and tugging at his garment. Noah stood up, turned around, and walked out of the church before the ceremony even began.

In 2005, two men from completely different backgrounds came together to write a fascinating little book called *The Church Enslaved*. Michael Battle, an African American and an ordained Baptist minister, grew up middle class in Raleigh, North Carolina, where he attended integrated schools, ultimately becoming Episcopalian and eventually an Anglican priest. He was educated at Notre Dame, Duke, Princeton Theological Seminary, and Yale, later living in Cape Town, South Africa, with Archbishop Desmond Tutu.

Tony Campolo, an Italian, and of course white, grew up in West Philly, in a white neighborhood that eventually turned into a black neighborhood. He became a sociologist, an evangelical minister, and a member of a black Baptist church. Ironically, the church he grew up going to was segregated and wouldn't accept black people as members of the congregation.

Battle and Campolo believe that *"if racism, America's first sin is not faced head-on, it will lead to our destruction and the ultimate destruction of America."* They believe that the church has been complicit in fostering racism through practices like institutional segregation and encouraging and supporting a culture of white superiority and black inferiority.

According to Battle and Campolo, modern racism manifests itself in two ways. The first is that people in powerful positions negatively impact the lives of people of color, keeping them down. The second is that people who try to "do the right thing" still end up actually perpetuating "old-fashioned racism." White privilege, white supremacy and class warfare.

In *The Church Enslaved,* Valerie Batts, a multiculturalism consultant, also discusses modern racism and five dominant behaviors of white people.

1. Dysfunctional rescuing—Blacks need help because they can't help themselves.
2. Blaming the victim—It's the black person's fault if he has problems and not the culture or the system.
3. Avoiding contact—Whites keep their distance from blacks and do not try to understand them.
4. Denying cultural differences—White people minimize the physical, cultural, or behavioral difference of blacks.
5. Denying the political significance of differences—Minimizing the differing influence that social, political, economic, historical, and psychological realities have on blacks and whites.

According to Batts, blacks practice internalized racism as well, then she lists five behaviors they typically employ.

1. Beating the system—Blacks try to take advantage or get over.
2. Blaming the system—When blacks fail by not being prepared instead of taking responsibility for failure.
3. Avoiding contact—Distrusting and avoiding whites and even blacks who are not black enough.
4. Denying cultural heritage—When people of color show a preference for whites, not trusting their own people or thinking that whites may know more or be in a better position to help them.
5. Lack of understanding or minimization of the political significance of racial oppression—Discriminating against other less powerful persons of color, being harder on them or preferential toward whites.

Battle and Campolo say that, "*there is really no unity in Christ, only convenient alliances between Christians.*" Is the church enslaved by the white, European perspective? The slave had no choice in the matter. Even though he understood that Christianity was oppressive and supported his enslavement, he had to accept his white masters' depraved and perverted version. Slaves pretended to forget, realizing full-well the value of their own memories. (Even without books, the Internet, and Black History Month, slaves knew something just didn't smell right.)

While George Bernard Shaw, economist and writer, humorously said that "*God created us in his image, and we decided to return the favor,*" creating him in our image, it was French sociologist, philosopher, and anthropologist Emile Durkheim (1858–1917) who believed in "collective consciousness." *That values and beliefs held by a society or culture direct its behavior even though its members do not realize it.* (In America and elsewhere, religion and entitlement also make some of us behave a certain way without realizing it.) Three words that immediately come to mind are racism, discrimination, and ethnocentrism. For those who may not be familiar with the term ethnocentrism, *The World Book Dictionary* defines it as follows: the emotional attitude that regards one's own group or culture as superior, and is contemptuous of other groups and cultures. (Is this attitude not reflected in the example of the black couple who were not allowed to be married in a white church recently, and the Mississippi high school students who, heretofore, were not allowed to attend an interracial senior high school prom together?)

Durkheim simply states that totem worship representing the tribe eventually becomes the god, and religion becomes no more than a group worshiping itself (*like statues, icons, and pictures of a white Jesus and white saints prescribed by white Europeans and white people in America representing Christianity becomes nothing more than whites worshiping themselves*). Hence, "white people believing they've been chosen by God!" So, coincidentally, God is white. It's that simple. Jesus was white. Adam and Eve were white. Columbus was white too, even though he didn't discover America or ever set foot on the North American continent. In fact, Columbus himself never even claimed to have discovered America as history books tell us, but then America invents its own heroes, doesn't it? Superman, Batman, Santa Claus, Uncle Sam, Tarzan, The Lone Ranger and even "The Duke" John Wayne, all are white. Images that reinforce bigotry. The Lone Ranger's horse "Silver" was white.

If race and color aren't important why are all of American's heroes white? (Except for the Reverend Doctor Martin Luther King, Jr., maybe. One black hero.) Blacks are accused of being lazy and inferior. Mexicans are drunkards. Indians are savages, but it's not important, right? Right! You know, the only good Indian (Native American—they were here first) I've ever seen in movies or on television was Tonto, the Lone Ranger's sidekick. And even then, the name "Tonto" meant silly or stupid in Spanish. Of course, white people don't have such issues and never did. *From this country's earliest days, an attitude of Caucasian racial pride was leading to an alleged American national character that was white.* And it stuck because efforts to keep it that way were brutal. But seriously, why is America's God who lives in heaven white too? Why are all of the Catholic churches' icons white in America and most of them at the Vatican? (I suppose if God is invisible and colorblind, which would probably be the case, there wouldn't be anything to sell, black or white.)

People of color were marginalized and made to seem insignificant, cleverly and deliberately, beginning with the Bible. *And while it's easy for white people to ask why color should matter, it always seems to matter to them . . . in just about everything.* Many say they've never thought about God having a color. That's probably because it was always a given and they didn't have to think about it. *God is white.* As long as black people were powerless and not learned scholars, there were no questions from them either, and no problems. But what they say really is proving to be true, that "Knowledge Is Power." It's now obvious that color certainly does matter. *Another truth is that the Roman Catholic Church and mainline Protestant denominations are racist, and that most white people, no matter what the truth is, "ain't changin'."*

Dr. Martin Luther King, Jr. once said, "It is appalling that the most segregated hour of Christian America is eleven o'clock on Sunday morning." And again, the more things change, the more they stay the same. Religion is the trusted cornerstone of hatred and bigotry.

For many years I remember saying black people and white people aren't generally real friends. We may work together, and even work-out together, but we don't often visit each other's houses or eat barbeque together on the Fourth of July or Labor Day, refusing to leave our comfort zones. That trend is reflected in church attendance. No matter what we profess, we don't truly see ourselves as brothers and sisters in Christ. *Do black people and white people even have the same concept of God and worship the same God?* (Positively, God has never been black for most white people and predictably never will be.) Religion, Christianity, hasn't melded many of us together at all has it? Dividing us instead.

A new Reuters Poll shows that about 40 percent of white Americans and about 25 percent of non-white Americans are surrounded exclusively by friends of their own race. Thirty percent aren't even mixing at work, where workplace relationships sometimes lead to friendship relationships. Many white people have never been to a black person's house and vice versa. By contrast, 50 percent of Hispanics are married to, or are in relationships with non-Hispanics. For young adults, one in three Americans under thirty has a spouse or partner who is of a different race, while only 13 percent of those over forty have a spouse or partner of a different race. Which shows that "times they are a changin'!" Slowly.

As I said earlier, the people in Alabama were great to my wife and I after Hurricane Katrina. They were courteous, compassionate, and helpful. However, in two years of living in Birmingham, I had normal, extended conversations with only two white people. (Two people in two years). Blacks generally associated with other blacks, while whites typically identified with other whites. Separate but Equal still appears to be, if not the law of the land, at least its spirit. People may be courteous and friendly, but they're definitely not friends, with the possible exception of occasional small groups, a few church members and sometimes young people. It has even been reported that at the University of Alabama in Birmingham 12% of Greek sororities are still segregated. Social segregation reigns supreme, in spite of the fact that Alabama is in the heart of the so-called Bible Belt. *After 400 years, blacks and whites are still strangers living with contempt, indifference, and suspicion. Some have gone even farther, saying that America itself is a nation of strangers. Others!*

Rev. Frederick K. C. Price once told *Emerge Magazine* that "the problem with the church is not the Bible. It's those who have interpreted it, or more accurately, misinterpreted." Dr. Price also said "*White folks always want to forget the past, but you can't forget the past because the present is always the result of the past.* It's such interpretations, such actions, that are costing the Christian community," Price said. "I'm concerned because the racism in the church and in this nation historically has turned a lot of black men sour on Christianity. So they are leaving and have left Christianity because they perceive Christianity as the white man's religion." Beginning with Indian-killing, slave-holding Pilgrims.

According to Ted Stepien, owner of the Cleveland Cavaliers in 1982, "I think people are afraid to speak out on the subject. *White people have to have white heroes.* I myself cannot equate to black heroes. I'll be truthful. I respect them, but *I need white people.* It's in me, and I think the Cavaliers have too many blacks." There are always too many blacks, even in decaying black schools and black neighborhoods, that are now gentrified because of income, and increasingly more segregated and tribal.

Battle and Campolo maintain that "becoming a Christian was the same as becoming westernized," part of a colonial empire or having white values. And Christianity is the only religion that promotes such a fundamental change. *Whether Indian, African or Chinese, everybody falls in line and subscribes to white values after accepting Christianity.* Foreigners are even encouraged to learn to speak English, and it was actually illegal for Native Americans to speak in their own cultural tongue. *If God and Jesus are white, then white really must be right!* If, by becoming a Christian, people thought about eating soul food, nobody but black people would be in line. *As Christians everybody has to identify with whiteness.*

In his masterful book, *Black Theology and Black Power*, distinguished scholar James H. Cone stated:

Unfortunately, Christianity came to the black man through white oppressors who demanded that he reject his concern for this world as well as his blackness and affirm the next world and whiteness. *The black intellectual community, however, with its emphasis on black identity, is becoming increasingly suspicious of Christianity because the oppressor has used it as a means of stifling the oppressed' concern for present inequities.* Naturally, as the slave questions his existence as a slave, he also questions the religion of the enslaver. "We must," writes Maulan Ron Karenga, "concern ourselves more with this life which has its own problems. For the next life across Jordan is much further away from the growl of dogs and policemen and the pains of hunger and disease."

"Therefore, it is appropriate to ask: Is it possible for men to be really black and still feel any identity with the biblical tradition expressed in the Old and the New Testaments? Is it possible to strip the gospel as it has been interpreted of its "whiteness," so that its real message will become a live option for radical advocates of black consciousness? Is there any relationship at all between the work of God and the activity of the ghetto? *Must black people be forced to deny their identity in order to embrace the Christian faith?*"

Dr. Cone went further, "*God cannot be for us and for whites at the same time. Either God is for blacks in their fight for liberation from white oppressors, or he is not.*" Cone acknowledges that there are white people suffering, and focuses on the liberation of all humankind from the forces of oppression. Dr. Cone states that, "the problem for whites is that black theology appears to be a rejection of whiteness."

For Cornel West, "*Liberation theology at its best is a worldly theology—a theology that not only opens our eyes to the social misery of the world but also teaches us to understand it better and transform it.*" For Pablo Richard and Raul Vidales, leaders in the field of Latin Liberation theology, "there is a deepening in theory within the practice of liberation, wherein believers seek to live, communicate, express, celebrate, and reflect on their faith, hope, and love." Do all Christians share the same values?

In *The Ideological Weapons Of Death,* Dr. Franz Hinkelammert describes what he calls a fetish, the spirit of an institution saying that "it does not arise out of nothing, nor does it fall from heaven, but it exists in linkage to a particular form of social organization" (the people of a church, their religion and their culture.) "Contra-wise, the material relationship between things is experienced as a social relationship between living subjects. *The belief system of churches becomes a tangible thing, and the thing gains power over the person as they intermingle." (The person becomes powerless to an idea.)* RELIGION OVERPOWERS AND CONSUMES US.

Contemporary legislation has determined that a corporation is a person, and likewise is this the domain of the church, being the same as a corporation or a person, a person who has the power to determine what you can and cannot do, as well as what the consequences for your life will be if you do not comply? *But in a real sense, beyond theology and beyond demagoguery, in the real world of real people, how and why is what you do or what you don't do any of your church's business?*

Eventually the product, Christianity, which becomes the same as a person, gets beyond control of the people (its producers). The believers. (People become slaves to religion, an idea.) The idea of orthodox Christianity grew out of insecurity and domination, the insecurity of believers who were afraid of reprisals, and the domination of the clergy who wanted to hold on to power, money, and the status quo.

According to Dr. Hinkelammert, the link between real life and the religious world is the commodity seen as a person. "Religion becomes the form of social consciousness . . . in which persons have delegated decision making power over life and death to a commodity mechanism for whose results they have relinquished responsibility." *In other words, the individual is no longer the decision maker. Religion controls your life, telling you what is right or wrong, for example, abortion and gay rights, and not only what the consequences will be after you die, but the consequences you'll suffer while you are alive as well.* Like going to prison.

Again, the above was taken from *The Ideological Weapons Of Death*, by Dr. Franz Hinkelammert, world-renowned economist and theologian. Dr. Hinkelammert also believes that *Christianity should be reread from the perspective of the oppressed,* and that people should be liberated from material deprivation. (Maybe oppressed people should have written the first Bible and our Constitution as well). In liberation theology—and Black Liberation Theology in particular, *it is critical that blacks do not lose their identity to the church and many of its false beliefs.* (Unfortunately, many already have.) It's too late.

James Cone, the father of Black Liberation Theology, says "white racist theologians are in charge of defining the nature of the gospel. *God does not do theology. Human beings do theology.* Who can pray when all hell has broken loose and human existence is being trampled underfoot by evil forces? Who can thank God for food when we know that our brothers and sisters are starving as we dine like kings? *Prayer is not kneeling morning, noon, and evening. Prayer is the spirit that is evident in all oppressed communities when they know that they have a job to do."* (Prayer is about handling your business.) Cone says:

> "It is not God who does all this talking, it is human beings who do it. It is human beings who write books, do theology, and do biblical and scientific work. And we know that human beings are not perfect; therefore, they need to be challenged, and they need to be challenged with evidence."

Dr. Cone also said, "because of the unchristian behavior of persons who say they are Christians, 'church' in America may very well refer to respectable murderers who destroy human dignity while 'worshipping' God and feeling no guilt about it. *They equate things as if they are with*

God's will," (*the same way Constantine did when he slaughtered thousands of people*). If something happens (tornadoes, bombings, cancer, slavery, and discrimination), it's alright because God wanted it to happen…*I don't think so!*

Dr. Cone adds, "To think of the church in this society is to visualize buildings with crosses and signs designating Sunday morning worship. It is to think of pious white oppressors gathering on Sunday, singing hymns and praying to God, while their preachers talk endlessly about some white cat who died on a cross." (Remember, John the Baptist, St. Stephen, and the Gnostics didn't believe in dogma and church buildings.)

Continuing, "Unfortunately black churches are also guilty of prostituting the name of God's church. The black denominational churches seem to be content with things as they are, getting fat on the misery of their sisters and brothers [chasing those dollars]. Although possessing the greatest potentiality for black revolution, *the black churches satisfy themselves with white solutions to earthly injustice.* That is why persons interested in justice in this world so often scorn the black church, saying that it is nothing but a second-rate oppressor. The truly Christian response to earthly problems is doing what one must do because it is the *human* thing to do."

"*For blacks death is not really a future reality; it is a part of their everyday existence. They stake their whole existence [life] on heaven. [Dying and going there someday].* We know all about pearly gates, golden streets, and long white robes. We have sung songs about heaven until we were hoarse, but it did not change the present state or ease the pain. To be sure, we may 'walk in Jerusalem jus' like John' and 'there may be a great camp meeting in the Promised Land,' but we want to walk in *this* land—'the land of the free and the home of the brave.' We want to know why Harlem cannot become Jerusalem, and Chicago the Promised Land? *What good are golden crowns, slippers, white robes or even eternal life, if it means that we have to turn our backs on the pain and suffering of our own children?*"

Here, I have yet another question, which I believe is germane. *Is it more important that your child have a healthy breakfast and get a good education today, or see Moses in heaven in eighty years, or a million years from now?* And by the way, those who said they died and went to the "other side" talked about seeing a bright light, and maybe a familiar friend or relative, but few have said anything about seeing Jesus or Moses. Surely, Jesus and Moses must be there too, and Peter, and Paul, and Mary, and Mary Magdalene. You get the idea.

Frank, an 81 year old retired longshoreman joked that he's never known anybody who came back talking about how wonderful it is up there in heaven. *And neither have I.* He said he's living his life now, every day, and not wasting one minute thinking about any golden streets. He also told me if the gospel is free, as Jesus said, why should he give 10% of his retirement savings to a church? *10% is the ultimate Ponzi scheme, but you only get to collect after you make it to heaven. If you make it! And even then you can't spend it. Is 10% a fee, dues, or a tax?*

Dr. Cone said, "*White missionaries have always encouraged blacks to forget about present injustice and look forward to heavenly justice.* But black theology says no, insisting that we either put new meaning into Christian hope by relating it to our liberation or drop it altogether."

"Black theology believes that emphasis on heaven in black churches was due to white slave masters whose intention was to transfer slaves' loyalties from earthly reality to heavenly reality. In that way, *masters could do what they willed about this world, knowing that their slaves were content with a better life in the next world. Heaven cannot mean accepting injustice of the present because we know we have a home over yonder.*" (Slaves' songs about freedom, sung every Sunday, say nothing to whites who were never oppressed.) 'Swing Low Sweet Chariot', about Elijah and his son Elisha going up to heaven in a chariot, is meaningless to white people who will never truly be 'one in Christ Jesus' with oppressed black people. 'Steal Away' was a code for secret religious meetings, which were illegal, only applying to slaves. *White religion is not black religion because our histories and our experiences are so different: that of the black slave and the white slave master.* One knows subservience and the other dominance. One hopelessness, the other hopefulness." (Ironically, Sir John Newton, the man who wrote "Amazing Grace" was a Christian who sold slaves. Christians were eagerly selling slaves to other Christians.) Even The Star-Spangled Banner's aristocratic Francis Scott Key, a rich slave owning lawyer from Maryland.

"To speak of God and God's participation in the liberation of the oppressed of the land is a risky venture in any society. But if the society is racist and also uses God-language [Republicans and Christian conservatives] as an instrument to further the cause of human humiliation, then the task of authentic theological speech is even more dangerous and difficult. All national institutions represent the interest of society as a whole. *We live in a nation which is committed to the perpetuation of white supremacy, and it will try to exterminate all who fail to support this ideal.*"

Dr. Cone continues, "When George Washington, Thomas Jefferson, Lyndon Johnson, Richard Nixon [Ronald Reagan, Bush I and Bush II, Sarah Palin, Rick Perry, Mike Pence] and other 'great' Americans can invoke the name of God at the same time they are shaping a society for whites only, then black theology knows it cannot approach the God-question casually. It must ask, '*How can we speak of God without being associated with oppressors?*' White racism is so pervasive that oppressors can destroy the revolutionary mood along with the oppressed by introducing a complacent (loving) white God into the black community, thereby quelling the spirit of freedom." (If God is laid-back and forgiving, his followers are too laid-back and too forgiving).

"*Reacting to the ungodly behavior of white churches and the timid, Uncle Tom approach of black churches, many black militants have no time for God and the deadly prattle about loving your enemies and turning the other cheek.* Christianity, they argue, participates in the enslavement of black Americans. Therefore an emancipation from white oppression also means liberation from the ungodly influences of white religion."

As for loving your enemies and turning the other cheek, the ancient Jews were not literally speaking about the enemies you are at war with (such as Americans loving Nazis or vice versa). Their reference was more like forgiving a neighbor you had some disagreement with. "A fellow

Jew." *Reyacha* in Hebrew. Jews were nationalists who supported other Jews. Only. *Loving someone who is trying to annihilate you would obviously be insane.* (Like the Bible saying that as Jesus was being crucified he said "Father, forgive them for they know not what they do.") They knew what they were doing alright, getting rid of him. (And did Jesus, a rebellious freedom fighter, really ask God to forgive the people who had nailed him to a cross, with blood pouring out of his wounds, or does the Bible just say that he said it in order to pacify the rest of us?) The sheep. (And as a contradiction Jesus says it in Luke's Gospel but not in Mark's.)

An ardent nativist, Jesus never thought about saving anybody but Jews, especially not his murderers. Saving fellow Jews was his mission as messiah. Even the apostles only preached to their own people, calling Gentiles dogs. Christianity's brotherly love was a myth. Another fairy tale.

"Black theology affirms that there is nothing special about the English word 'God' in itself. Black theology asks whether the word 'God' has lost its liberating power." (Does it still stand for the spiritual Father of all mankind, or only for whites?)

"Oppressed and oppressors [helpless people and powerful people] cannot possibly mean the same thing when they speak of God. The God of the oppressed is a God of revolution who breaks the chains of slavery. The oppressors' God is a God of slavery and must be destroyed along with the interpretations and sentiments. *The question then, as black theology sees it, is not whether blacks believe in God, but whose God?*" Again, was the Hebrews tough "eye for an eye" God the same as the Christians' loving, merciful God?

It is truly amazing to hear Conservatives like Rush Limbaugh and Sean Hannity venomously denounce people like Reverend Jeremiah Wright and Black Liberation Theology, when even the slave realized that taking a similar view was in his best interest, and that sermons taken from the Bible were a deliberate distortion.

Limbaugh said *"this white guilt, it's time for all this white guilt to end. If any race of people should not have guilt about slavery (legal human plunder),* it's Caucasians." Rush says that *"white people in America didn't have slaves nearly as long as everybody else."* (Whatever he's been smoking, I want some too.) Limbaugh seems to be overlooking murder, torture, rape, mutilation, Jim Crow - lasting until 1965, and the racism which prevails today in the form of corrupt social institutions and unjust laws, like the George Zimmerman verdict. We know Rush, and we know he'll say anything to keep his people hyped up and listening to him!

In the 1800s slavery was perfectly normal, America's first business model. Frederick Douglass, the former slave and black abolitionist, often wondered how, after all the suffering and abuse, freed slaves could believe in their tormentors' religion, actually drawing a distinction between "slaveholding religion" and Christianity. Frederick Douglass wrote:

> Were I again to be reduced to the chains of slavery, next to the enslavement, I should regard being the slave of a religious master the greatest calamity that could befall me. For of all slaveholders with whom I have ever met, religious slaveholders are the worst.

Frederick Douglass also said:
> The cow skin makes as deep a gash in my flesh, when wielded by a professed saint, as it does when wielded by an open sinner. [Many white Christians were brutal.]

He couldn't understand how somebody who prayed with them on Sunday then beat them on Monday was a Christian. And while slave owners used religion to control slaves, Frederick Douglass believed God would eventually save them.

As further testimony to the inhumanity of Christian practitioners, the following examples of senseless cruelty are taken from *Narrative of the Life of Frederick Douglass, an American Slave (Written by Himself)*.

> The overseer's name was Plummer. Mr. Plummer was a miserable drunkard, a profane swearer, and a savage

monster. He always went armed with a cowskin and a heavy cudgel. I have known him to cut and slash the women's heads so horribly, that even master would be enraged at his cruelty, and would threaten to whip him if he did not mind himself. Master, however, was not a humane slaveholder. It required extraordinary barbarity on the part of an overseer to affect him. He was a cruel man, hardened by a long life of slaveholding. He would at times seem to take great pleasure in whipping a slave. I have often been awaked at the dawn of day by the most heart-rending shrieks of an own aunt of mine, whom he used to tie up to a joist, and whip upon her naked back till she was literally covered with blood. No words, no tears, no prayers, from his gory victim, seemed to move his iron heart from its bloody purpose. The louder she screamed, the harder he whipped; and where the blood ran fastest, there he whipped longest. He would whip her to make her scream, and whip her to make her hush; and not until overcome by fatigue, would he cease to swing the blood-clotted cowskin. [The white Christian overseer unmercifully beat the black slave woman for having sex with a black man behind his back. For cheating on him.]

And

I have said my master found religious sanction for his cruelty. As an example, I will state one of many facts going to prove the charge. I have seen him tie up a lame young woman, and whip her with a heavy cowskin upon her naked shoulders, causing the warm red blood to drip; and, in justification of the bloody deed, he would quote this passage of Scripture—"He that knoweth his master's will, and doeth it not, shall be beaten with many stripes." Master would keep this lacerated young woman tied up in this horrid situation four or five hours at a time. I have known him to tie her up early in the morning, and whip her before breakfast; leave her, go to his store, return at dinner, and whip her again, cutting her in the places already made raw with his cruel lash. The secret of master's cruelty toward "Henny" is found in the fact of her being almost helpless. When quite a child, she fell into the fire, and burnt herself horribly. Her hands were so burnt that she never got the use of them. [He was a sadistic, Christian sonofabitch!]

What Frederick Douglass may or may not have understood was that even Jesus appreciated what would happen to slaves who didn't cooperate or do as they were told.

Luke 12:47
That servant who knows his master's will and does not get ready or does not do what his master wants will be beaten with many blows.

The following is an account from *Slave Testimony* by John W. Blassingame. They are the words of Henry Baker, a former slave who was interviewed in Alabama in 1938 at the age of 83. Mr. Baker is talking about two paddy rollers (runaway slave patrollers) killed during the Civil War.

Henry Baker (slave)
Ben Williams en John Williams who wuz patterrollers dey went tuh de war when de war broke out en John, he got killed in the fust battle en Ben went through de second battle en den he got killed en Jim Coleman he got killed in de second battle too. *De white folks wuz talkin' tuh me one day 'bout bein' chose in Christ 'fore de world begin en I sed, I didn't b'lieve it.* Dey sed, "Now Henry, yuh Dady is a

hard shell Baptist en yuh don' bel'eve it." *I sed No I didn't bel'eve it.* Dey sed, "Well here, John Williams got killed in de fust battle. Ben Williams got killed in de second. Tom Williams went through six different fights en nevah got a pin scratch en yuh say yuh don't bel'eve God chose de people." Jeff Coleman wuz a patterroller en so he went tuh war en when de news come back dat he wuz killed de "niggers" jes shouted en shouted, dey wuz so glad he wuz dead cause he wuz so mean tuh dem.

<u>Coase es a rule people don't bel'eve in de Bible</u>. I wuz talkin tuh er white man tuther day en he sed people is done lef Jesus Christ. Yuh know de Bible says dat yuh is saved in Christ 'fore de World began. People in muh section uv de country don't bel'eve dat. [So, contrary to contemporary belief, all slaves weren't on their knees praying. Many didn't believe in the Bible, or that white people were God's chosen people and made in his image, often criticizing and challenging interpretations whites used to keep them enslaved.]

Charles Colcock Jones, a slave-owning evangelical missionary, felt that more should be done to Christianize slaves. Jones said, "It is true they [slaves] have access to the house of God on the Sabbath; but it is also true that even where the privilege is within their reach, a minority only, [and frequently a very small one] embrace it." *Slaves weren't breaking their necks to become Christians or to worship a white God.*

In an 1898 speech, Henry McNeal Turner, a Negro said "we have as much right biblically and otherwise to believe that God is a Negro." It was Langston Hughes, the famous Negro writer whose poem started with *"Christ is a nigger, Beaten and black, Oh, bear your back!"* Because of their suffering, many blacks saw themselves in Jesus, and see themselves in Jesus today, especially when he is viewed as a black man.

The great W.E.B. Du Bois, African-American sociologist, historian, and Civil Rights Activist, who was generally thought to be an agnostic (believing that you can never truly know God), had his own ideas about Jesus. Even though he didn't believe in organized religion, Du Bois did read the Bible analytically, was a man of deep spiritual conviction, and was convinced that Jesus would have identified with poor people. He wrote:

> ...Jesus Christ was a laborer and black men are laborers; He was poor and we are poor; He was despised of his fellow men and we are despised; He was persecuted and crucified, and we are mobbed and lynched. If Jesus Christ came to America He would associate with Negroes and Italians and working people; He would eat and pray with them, and He would seldom see the interior of the Cathedral of Saint John the Divine.

Could Jesus be black? Josephus said he was dark, with little hair. Depictions of *The Black Madonna of Czestochowa*, a painting revered by Polish Pope John Paul II, *The Black Madonna of Spain*, known as "The Queen of the Pyrenees," Spain's *Black Madonna at Montserrat*, and Russia's most famous icon, *The Virgin of Kazan* are most certainly black. There is also *Our Lady of Guadalupe* in Spain, *Our Lady of Koden* in Poland, over 300 depictions of Black Madonnas in France, and others in Belgium and Germany. Why would white Europeans who lived centuries ago have steeped so much adoration in sacred relics of the black mother and child if they did not love and believe in them? Was Mary black? Representations of a black madonna actually predate those of a white one. As for Jesus, was he simply a brave black freedom fighter defying the white Roman power structure? A black messiah!

In *The Story of Civilization*, Will Durant writes that "Statues of Isis, and Horus - the Egyptian sky-god, were renamed Mary and Jesus." In 1979, *The Washington Post* reported "Many of the madonnas painted in the earliest centuries of Christendom were black, according to historians, and it wasn't until the Renaissance [rebirth of European consciousness] that it became popular to give the Mother of Christ the features of a Florentine maiden [a white woman]." The Madonna and Child became Mary and Jesus, turning white (or rather, were turned white). And yes, maybe the devil did make somebody do it. Having turned white, Mary and Jesus made their way across the Atlantic Ocean from Europe to America to live on happily ever after. (In whiteness.) America's "one drop" rule automatically makes Jesus black. *A person of color.*

Was Jesus of Nazareth selflessly devoted to others? I think not. The following is taken from Matthew 10:5-6. "These twelve Jesus sent out with the following: Go nowhere among the Gentiles, and enter no town of the [mixed race] Samaritans. But go rather to the lost sheep of the House of Israel", untainted, uncontaminated Jews. Jesus was a staunch separatist, a tribalist who was implicitly biased, instinctively identifying with others like himself, never preaching to a Samaritan or a Gentile. *A card-carrying narcissist.* In Matthew 15:21-28 Jesus calls the Canaanite woman whose daughter is possessed by demons a dog because both sexism and racism (tribalism), were integral to Jewish culture, with Jews always feeling superior, especially men.

In the 1960s Malcolm X declared that "Christianity was an oppressive religion," that "Christianity is the white man's religion that was forced on negro slaves." American Christianity and slavery began in the four original New England States; Rhode Island, Connecticut, New York, and Massachusetts. According to Malcolm:

> Brothers and sisters, the white man has brainwashed us black people to fasten our gaze upon a blond-haired, blue-eyed Jesus! We're worshiping a Jesus that doesn't even look like us! Oh, yes! . . . Now just think of this. The blond-haired, blue-eyed white man has taught you and me to worship a white Jesus, and to shout and sing and pray to this God that's his God, the white man's God. *The white man has taught us to shout and sing and pray until we die, to*

> *wait until death, for some dreamy heaven-in-the-hereafter, when we're dead, while this white man has his milk and honey in the streets paved with golden dollars here on this earth!*

I believe in a religion that believes in freedom. Anytime I have to accept a religion that won't let me fight a battle for my people, I say to hell with that religion. [Do you really believe that a man like Malcolm X would go straight to hell simply because he wasn't a Christian?]

Malcolm X also said that black people were being lulled to sleep by being told "bedtime stories." And it was Chairman Bobby Seale, the infamous Black Panther leader who pronounced that *"Black people will never accomplish anything until they get off their knees."*

Remember, Peter told Cornelius to get off his knees, because he (Peter) was only a man. As commander of 100 occupying Roman troops in Palestine, Cornelius understood that Jews considered him the enemy. He felt the same way about them. It was unlawful for a Jew to visit someone from another nation, and Jews were to avoid all contact with Gentiles. Instead of following the rules, Peter decided to bring God's word to Cornelius, accepting the Centurion as a God-fearing man of prayer.

Long before both Malcolm and Bobby, it was Nietzsche who said that *"so-called Christian morality made sheep out of people"*, and that *"what passes for Christian morality is, in truth, motivated as much by the drive for personal power and control as it is by selfless devotion to others."* (Religious leaders are looking out for number one.) Friedrich Nietzsche's first intended vocation was to be a pastor.

CHAPTER 12

Magic?

Before becoming disenchanted with the church, I myself had often thought that religion was oppressive, subordinating, and anti-intellectual. That it kept people controlled, backward, and uninformed. *(Dumbed down)*. I was young then and didn't know any better, but what else should I have expected from black preachers who had been validated in some seminary where they spent years being brainwashed and learning white theology from biased white theologians? As Cone said, at the same time they were learning nothing about racism, white supremacy and white authoritarianism, or the exploitation of black people. The prospective black ministers also didn't want to come across as being too militant or racist themselves. With preachers being influenced so greatly by that kind of indoctrination, my advice to you is to remember to think first, and for yourself, especially before turning that other cheek. Charlie, a conservative Republican friend from the gym really nailed it when he laughed, *"the thing I like the most about black religion is that it keeps them [blacks] about fifty years behind us [whites], just like rednecks."*

To better understand the implications and the impact of Christianity in today's world, I turned to a little book by Kelly Brown Douglass, *The Black Christ*. According to Reverend Douglass, for the slave-owning Christian there was of course, no doubt. Jesus was white and anybody questioning that fact was obviously a heretic (and in big trouble). Ever since America's colonization by English Pilgrims at Plymouth in 1620, there was the well-established belief that Jesus and God were white and esteemed, just as the term "white" had always been synonymous with goodness and righteousness while black was the opposite, namely, bad and malevolent. Benjamin Rush, an eighteenth-century physician, actually believed the Negro's dark complexion was a disease, while there were others who thought that when slaves ran away it was a disease too. Drapetomania. Even today there are those who loathe so-called ugly black skin, but what they think black people are running away from now is hard work and responsibility.

White slave owners absolutely believed they were Christians, no matter how cruelly they behaved (like many of today's Evangelical Christians). Murder, torture, raping women and children, buying and selling them—nothing mattered as long as he or she had accepted God and Jesus as his son. *Theodore Roosevelt himself justified lynching black men by saying that rape by black men was even worse than murder . . . although white men continued to rape black women, and to murder them legally.* In white minds, masters were still guaranteed a place in heaven. But maybe instead of following Jesus and God they should have been paying attention to Confucius' golden rule, *"Never impose on others what you would not choose for yourself."* In Matthew (7:12), Jesus taught, *"Do unto others as you would have them do unto you," . . . 600 years after Confucius.*

In *The Black Christ* Reverend Douglass wrote, "That God became human is the essential fact in what it means for Jesus to be the Christ." *What Jesus did on earth has little, if anything, to do with what it means for him to be the Christ . . . Simply doing good deeds doesn't make somebody God's son.* Jesus was never the only miracle worker either, and healing was a part of everyday life during his time. For example, the Bible says God also gave Paul and Barnabas the power to work miracles and wonders. Before Jesus there was "Honi the Circledrawer," who drew a circle and stood in the center until it rained, and afterward came the poor mystic "Hanina ben Dosa," plus many others. There was also a Jewish magician known as "the Egyptian" (probably black) who also said he was king of the Jews, and that he would bring down the walls of Jerusalem just as Joshua had done at Jericho.

Remember, Egyptians had their magicians too. For example, the time Aaron turned his staff into a snake to scare Pharaoh, and Pharaoh's magicians did the same trick. (Egyptians didn't call their rulers Pharaohs.

Pharaoh is a Hebrew word.) Like Jesus, Elisha, and the prophet Elijah who brought the widow's son back from the dead, Spyridon-Bishop of Cyprus could raise the dead. In Acts 9:36-40, Peter brings Dorcas (Tabitha in Greek) back to life. In Acts 8:18–20, after seeing John and Peter laying on hands and the power of the Holy Spirit, Simon Magnus, the magician who was said to have been a disciple of Phillip, offered them cash to teach him the new trick. *Laying on hands*. Magnus was hoping they would help him become a better magician. *Even the world's most famous magician at that time thought John and Peter were magicians too.* It was Paul who brought Eutychus back to life. So, even being dead and coming back was no big deal. Peter even walked on water like Jesus. But were the stories actually supposed to be true, or like mythology and fables, understood to be symbolic?

Although a Samarian Jew, Simon Magnus, who considered himself a god in the flesh, was also the leader of the Gnostics. As you already know, the Gnostics were rivals of the Christians, competing against Jesus and his followers. Remember, Gnosticism was based on something within. And it seems only natural to me, that since their leader was openly known to be a magician, Gnosticism was steeped in magic too.

There's a legend about Simon Magnus' death in the Acts of St. Peter. After being embarrassed by Peter and John, Simon, angry, wanted to impress Nero. He summoned demons who helped him, and he flew over their heads (a flying man-who could become invisible). Peter and Paul prayed and caused Magnus to fall from the sky, then stoned by an angry crowd, he soon died. Some scholars believe Paul made Simon Magnus up. Just as he may have invented stories about Jesus' life.

Belief in Christianity was based on supernatural deeds, deeds that, as Celsus suggested, were called miracles instead of magic. We would never have heard of Moses had God not talked to him from the burning bush (that didn't burn), or if he had not parted the Red Sea. In Matthew 14:13–21 *when Jesus fed 5,000 hungry people with five loves and only two measly fish, could that not have been considered magic, or in today's world, at least a mass hallucination or mass hypnosis?* Or maybe it never happened.

According to Peter, the difference was that magicians and miracle workers expected to get paid while Aaron, Moses and Jesus worked for free. The process was the same. When Pharaoh's magicians' snakes were eaten by Aaron's snake nobody who saw that thought it was a miracle. It was only magic and Aaron's magic was just stronger than Pharaoh's magicians' magic. (It was always about the magic.) It was about the most powerful gods too. And because Jesus' God was the strongest and had the most powerful magic, Jesus' followers took it all the way to the top. They hit the ball clean out of the ball park by saying that Jesus was the one and only son of the most powerful God. (Bet you can't touch that!)

During my nightclub days we had a promotion called "Potluck," and every Thursday night there was a surprise entertainment feature. You never knew what you were going to see until the show started. It might be a mime, a ventriloquist, an animal act or even break-dancers.

My favorite was a master magician named Joe Harrison. He was perfect. A short, slightly stocky, rosy-cheeked white guy with a thin, well-trimmed mustache, Joe was always dressed in a black tuxedo and had tons of personality. Naturally, his Girl-Friday was perfect too.

With his assistant's help, Joe performed what was called "The Hindu Basket." The assistant would bring out a covered straw basket about two feet deep with a diameter (the distance across) of about three feet. She placed the basket in the center of the floor, our floor, surrounded by 500 curious viewers, and then climbed into it and lay on the bottom. Joe quickly draped it with a cover, and then covered it with the straw top. Next, he stuck about nine steel swords (that we checked to make sure were steel), through various openings, including right through the center of the top. (Ouch!)

He said a few magic words, removed the swords, removed the top, then stepped into the basket and walked around in it, not being raised one inch from the level floor. (Where did the girl disappear to?) He stepped back out of the basket, re-covered it with the straw top, said a few more magic words, removed the top and the drape, and the girl stood up in the basket again. A *different* girl. How in the hell did he do it? And what happened to the first girl? I know for a fact that there was no trap door or secret hole in the floor because it was our floor, the same floor 500 people had started dancing on again.

Like today's magicians it took years to develop those tricks. *Suppose that Jesus the rabbi, in addition to being dedicated to his faith, also practiced the art of sorcery as some believed.* There are still those eighteen years missing from the pages of his biography. (How could eighteen years be unaccounted for unless it was deliberate?) How can we think we know Jesus when so much about him has been mysteriously hidden? Houdini was an excellent magician for his time, as is our own David Blaine. Today, some of these guys can make an entire 747 disappear, then reappear, but it's only magic. Or maybe mass hallucinations. It took discipline, study, and a lot of practice to develop and perfect those tricks. It didn't happen overnight. If David Blaine told you he is the messiah or God's son simply because he did a couple of great magic tricks, would you believe him? I should hope not ... They didn't believe Jesus either.

The same thing was true during Jesus' day. He performed excellent feats, but people didn't think that proved he was their messiah or God's son. *Great tricks didn't really prove anything, or Pharaoh's magicians could have said the same thing, that they were messiahs and God's sons too.* Moses and Jesus just happened to be two of the best, along with Merlin, the Welsh mystic or magician who even appears in today's cartoons, movies and children's books. *Aaron's snake was not a miracle, but magic, just as Pharaoh's magicians' snakes were magic and not miracles.* And again, what was Jesus doing for those missing eighteen years? If he was studying magic that certainly would not have been advertised. It would have been kept on the down low. "TOP SECRET!" (Just as religion is still steeped in mystery and secrecy behind close doors).

In *The Testament of Solomon*, Solomon is called the *Master of Demons*, after conjuring up an army of evil spirits. And while performing an exorcism, Jesus actually compared himself to Solomon, saying that he was "greater than Solomon," who had a magic flying carpet. Was Jesus a magician too? *Was there any real difference between magic and miracles?* Is there a difference? Are some of today's scientific and medical successes merely "old-fashioned miracles" or "old-fashioned magic?"

For the Romans and some of Jesus' fellow Jews there was no doubt. *Jesus used magic.* In Mark 7:31–35 Jesus cures a deaf man, taking him away from the crowd, putting his finger into the man's ear, spitting, touching the man's tongue, then looking up to heaven and saying "*Ephphatha*," meaning "Be open." Jesus told people who witnessed the feat not to tell anybody what he had done. Nobody listened. In Matthew 16:16 he warns the disciples not to tell anybody who he is.

In Mark 8:22–26 Jesus cures a blind man, taking him away, putting saliva on the man's eyes, laying hands on him, and asking "Can you see anything?" The man answered, "I can see people but they look like trees walking." Jesus laid his hands on again and the man was healed. In the Infancy Gospel of Thomas, as a child, what about the clay sparrows Jesus made fly, or the playmate he raised from the dead?

Did Moses just wake up one day and realize he had a magic staff, and that he could part the Red Sea with it? Like Elijah parting the Jordan River with his cloak? I don't think it works like that unless you're on something really strong, if you know what I mean. There are people today who believe they can fly, and we know what gives them their hallucinations.

What most of us don't generally realize is that in addition to the Five Books of Moses, "The Pentateuch," there are also reported to be a Sixth and a Seventh. The Sixth and Seventh Books are said to be lost or hidden—like so many other things that have been mysteriously lost or hidden. The lost books deal with magic spells, incantations, and seals (drawings and spells used to perform miracles, control weather, and contact the dead. Harry Potter stuff). In 1963, the Jamaican group Maytals released a song called "Six and Seven Books of Moses." In Christianity, would an angel not be considered a spirit? Many of the miracles performed could have been considered wizardry. Were Moses, Aaron, and some of the others actually wizards or magicians?

CHAPTER 13

Leaning, Leaning...

During slavery in America masters didn't need magic. They focused on God instead of Jesus' good works, while the slaves looked to Jesus' good works as a guide to get closer to God. Perhaps that principle holds true for blacks and whites today and explains the huge disparity in how we go about living our lives. Black people often speak about being more like Jesus, going to church five or six times a week, while white people enjoy "the good life" every day, playing golf, boating and traveling. Blacks go to church, where they are told how to live and behave, and what they can and cannot do. Whites, on the other hand, choose how and where to live and do whatever they feel like doing. (There are, of course, poor whites who are as limited as blacks.) But that sounds about right. And this is a critically important distinction. Wade, a neighbor of mine, grew up in one of the notoriously dilapidated, *de facto* black housing projects in New Orleans. He says that one of the things he will never forget about his poor mother is that she was always *"prayin' and waitin' on Jesus."* Hoping to go home to glory. Heaven.

Greg, another lifelong friend said that his grandmother Miss Louise died at 116 years old, broke. His mother Clara died at ninety-one, broke. *Both his mother and his grandmother lived their entire lives prayin' and waitin' on Jesus, then died broke.* Greg said if he hadn't seen the light he would probably leave here the same way. *On his knees and broke.*

Slaves naturally had a different perspective from their white masters. Slaves couldn't possibly understand how some people could consider themselves Christians after all of the savage atrocities they had committed. It was also easy for whites to say that they were God's chosen people and made in his image because they were never the ones being lynched and tortured. One ex-slave is to have said, "I'd rather live with a card player or with a drunkard than with a Christian."

As another example of cruelty, in one particularly unsettling account Mr. Johnson, a former slave, spoke about a barbaric incident he personally witnessed on a plantation.

> One day my master was dining with a gentleman who had a wife as black as dat hat. A young colored woman, as likely for her color as any lady in dis assembly (a laugh), waited on table. She happened to spill a little gravy on the gown of her mistress. The gentleman took his carving-knife, dragged her out to wood pile, and cut her head off; den wash his hands, come in and finish his dinner like nothing had happened! Do you call dat a Christian country? I never saw the like in Africa. My master dropped his knife and fork, and eat no more. [Christian slave owners, both male and female were brutal, including preachers.]

While whites had only to believe, blacks were told that they had to behave a certain way. (Be more like Jesus.) The slave had to be virtuous to receive God's blessings ... Even when mistreated they were still expected to do the right thing. The usual control tactics were employed, and the slave was told those instructions came directly from the Bible and God ... Remember, slaves couldn't read ... "Obey your master. Don't break his tools. And don't lie and steal." Those who were brainwashed believed their masters' lies about a benevolent (white) Jesus who would protect them and prepare a place for them in heaven someday. The suffering would end and they would be "washed in the blood of the Lamb" and redeemed. *God was going to make a way out of no way ... someday!*

In spite of the fact that they couldn't read, many of the slaves realized they were being bamboozled. Some of them believed that being disobedient and even trying to escape were not sins that would keep them from going to heaven, but a good thing. *(How could trying to escape rape and torture possibly be a sin?)* Quite the contrary, instead of waiting until after they were dead, Jesus would save them while they were still alive. (They had their own brand of liberation theology.) That Jesus was born poor, suffered as they did and was courageous was endearing, inspiring them to seek their own salvation.

Another suffering connection slaves might have felt toward Jesus was his paternity. Being illegitimate, he too would have been heckled, bullied, and gossiped about. Today we know that Jesus was ridiculed and laughed at as *Mary's son*, because their neighbors suspected that he was born out of wedlock. *Imagine the humiliation.* And even though he was part of a large extended family, Jesus still might have experienced loneliness. Deep in their hearts, slaves felt that he knew the black man's pain and was one of them because Jesus had been wronged too. And like themselves, Jesus shouldn't have suffered either, and would have felt empathy for them. In their grief and suffering his story was appealing and irresistible. *Having endured so much pain and sorrow, many of the slaves needed somebody to lean on, and that somebody was a kind and loving Jesus.* One of their favorite hymns goes . . . "Leaning, leaning, leaning on the everlasting arm."

In the 1960s, it was Bill Withers who sang "Lean On Me", one of his biggest hits. And early in his own career, Academy Award winning actor Morgan Freeman starred in *Lean On Me*. Highly successful, it was one of the very first contemporary movies dealing with difficulties in an urban inner-city school . . . but as they so often say today, don't get it twisted (by romanticizing what leaning is).

What about that other leaning thing blacks get accused of doing? You know, the one they say we do all the time because we're too lazy to work. (Remember, Drapetomania.) Leaning against walls, telephone poles, fences, or whatever would hold us up because we're supposed to be too worthless to go out and get a job. *Ignored is the reality that stolen black labor made America great. In fact, if there really is "American Exceptionalism," it is due in large measure to over 300 years of free slave labor.* White people kept all the money for almost four centuries, while unpaid workers enhanced productivity by providing them with time and resources to pursue and develop innovation, ultimately leading to a higher standard of living and that American greatness which allowed this country to excel. (Suppose other countries had also had slavery for 300 years, which would have enabled them to be productive and competitive?) AMERICAN GREATNESS IS BASED ON EXPLOITATION AND PREDATORY CAPITALISM! Especially slavery. That, plus stealing land, minerals, and resources that belonged to somebody else all over the globe. Europeans have savagely exploited people around the world as they attempted to dominate through brutality and racism. Today in America for every dollar held by whites, blacks have 6¢ and Latinos 7¢. GREED AND RACISM, ENDORSED BY CHRISTIANITY, PRODUCED CAPITALISM IN AMERICA!

In 1861 slavery was essential for progress in the South. *Without slave labor to produce cheap crops, the Southern states could never have attained or maintained the high profits that helped to create their social and cultural way of life. (Laissez-faire, rich, white gentry and pathetic black work animals.)* One out of every three people was a black slave, worth more than the farmland they were forced to plow, about three billion dollars today. Unlike the other animals slaves could think for themselves. *Christianity was an indispensable tool for influencing and controlling them.* Slavery was the business model for the Industrial Revolution. Industrial slavery was the leasing or selling of black convicts (factory slaves), mainly guilty of no crimes, to private corporations like U.S. Steel and others to companies like the Georgia Pacific Railroad. Christianity was America's cattle prod moving black people aimlessly along, going nowhere!

Presently, there may be only one thing I personally agree with when it comes to Republicans and political conservatives like John Boehner, Paul Ryan, Ted Cruz, and Mitch McConnell, and that's the need for personal responsibility and self-reliance. *(The opposite of leaning).* Of course, whites have always had their own affirmative action, leaning on mommy and daddy, and grandma and granddad through generational wealth (land, houses, cars, stocks and bonds, college tuition, inheritance and cash in the bank). Their success wasn't due to the fact that they were smarter, more self-reliant, or even worked harder. It was primarily a matter of exploitation, skin color, opportunity and possibly luck.

In an Associated Press Release Bernard Condon, Josh Boak and Christopher S. Rugaber report that in the future "Hard work will matter less, inherited wealth more. The fortunes of the few will unsettle the foundations of democracy. By its nature, capitalism fuels inequality and can destabilize democracies." In 2012 the top 1% of US households received 22.5% of the nation's income. They didn't make it on their own.

The top 1% pocketed almost one quarter of this country's income, and the 400 richest people owned more than everybody in the bottom 50% combined. It's one of the reasons why poor people are complacent, have no ambition or turn to a life of crime. From everything they've seen average and poor people already know the deck is neatly stacked against them. *They'll never make it!*

According to NPR's John Ydstie, in his best-seller *Capital in the Twenty First Century*, French economist Thomas Piketty warns that inequality is likely to grow because "capitalism tends to reward the owners of capital with a greater and greater share of the economy's output, while wage-earners get a smaller and smaller share." *Wall Street vs. Main Street.* "The elites start dominating the political discourse and even political decision-making [the infamous billionaire Koch Brothers or Donald Trump]. Then they reinforce their own authoritarian privileges." The rich celebrate, the poor cry.

The people in the middle and at the bottom eventually give up because there's no light at the end of the tunnel no matter how hard they work. Consequently, the world we all live in ends up going to hell in the proverbial hand basket. Capitalism, beginning with enslaving Native Americans for labor, only works for those with money.

Billionaire Sam Zell naturally had a vastly different opinion. Zell says the 1% work harder, but Tom Perkins, his friend and fellow billionaire, goes even farther, saying that the left's treatment of the 1% is comparable to the way Nazis persecuted Jews. (They've got to be kidding). Do the top 1% really do any work anyway? It's more likely that they buy their way up there, having become even richer because of a rigged system. Are today's billionaire's yesterday's ruthless robber barons?

Absolutely!—Black people in America have been shafted! (With giant phalluses and *no* Vaseline.) Today, slavery is nonchalantly dismissed as if it were only an insignificant blip on the screen of America's past, and the slave owner a caring, misunderstood gentleman farmer with a compassionate heart. Which, as we all know—*is bullshit*.

Since the slave couldn't testify against him, the white master could kill one of his niggers without fear of being punished, certainly not by his neighbors, or even the law. (It was not illegal to murder black people or Indians.) There was absolutely nobody the slave could actually complain to. His master may have been an active, sadistic pedophile who sexually abused young girls (perhaps boys as well for gay masters), and helpless women. Black males were poster children for castrations and other forms of sexual sadism. The slave master serially cheated on his wife by exploiting BLACK SEX SLAVES. Literally, FREE PUSSY! Pussy, on his property, that he legally owned and could abuse any way he wanted to. Criminologists today call it "sex on the shelf." (He didn't even own his wife's genitalia but he literally owned the black slave woman's.) I'm sure the woman felt just the opposite, that her private parts were hers, and not his. After a long, hard day out in the hot fields, he could just pick out a slave as if he was doing little more than taking one of his hunting dogs for a walk. Pull out his penis, use him or her, then go about his business. On the Alford Plantation, all of my grandmother's playmates were abused, except her.

If the woman master was raping became pregnant, that meant more *FREE LABOR,* his own child. (I can see them now, a group of white men standing around bragging and joking about their sexual escapades with their slaves.) Who knows? Maybe one day somebody will be able to help me understand how anybody can think that they have the right to own other human beings, or be able to separately ride in the front of the bus, drink from a certain water fountain, or live exclusively in a particular neighborhood. It takes a really sick mind to come up with something like that. Segregation, jail, or lynching. Great choices for black people while white people continue to feel exceptional, privileged and entitled. Slavery created southern wealth while black people, starting from scratch, had 0 net worth at Emancipation.

I remember my dear friend, Dr. Rosie Milligan, who grew up on her father's farm in Como, Mississippi, talking about something he had witnessed as a young man with his own eyes. One of the sharecroppers was sitting on his front porch in the quarters when the plantation owner's son walked up, spoke to the man who remained outside, then went inside and was alone with the man's wife. When the white man came back outside, chewing tobacco, he tapped the black farmer on the shoulder, telling him "that's some good pussy." Then he just stepped off the porch and coolly walked down the dirt road. White boys first sexual experiences were with female slaves. Imagine the fighting that would've broken out if white men had to give that up? It was called "The Civil War," and it was only over after 600,000 men had lost their lives.

But as they say, payback really is a motherfucker. While master was busy doing his thing, sleeping with his black wenches, many white women got busy too, with black male slaves, experiencing bucks and doing the unspeakable. For the white man his woman was too pure and too perfect

for sex, while God had created the black woman to be a sexual animal. All this while the Christian church preached against fornication. It was the hypocritical flouting of St. Paul's *"Let every man have his own wife and every woman her own husband."*

Whites, who are so proud of "American Exceptionalism" and their accomplishments as a race need to face the facts. Great-grandpa, and maybe even great-grandma, were some mean, sick, sadistic sociopaths. There was so much screwing around going on that the following quotation was made by a group of white South Carolina ministers in 1837. It was taken from *"Long Memory"* by Mary Frances Berry and John W. Blassingame.

> The influence of the negroes upon the moral and religious interests of the whites is destructive in the extreme ... We are chained to a putrid carcass; it sickens and destroys us. We have a millstone hanging about the neck of our society, to sink us deep in the sea of vice. [Having sex and mixing with blacks was a boomerang that would ultimately destroy America.]

SLAVERY WAS AMERICA'S SECOND ACT OF DOMESTIC TERRORISM, INSTIGATED BY AMERICANS ON AMERICAN SOIL, EXCEEDED ONLY BY WHAT WAS DONE PREVIOUSLY TO NATIVE AMERICANS. TAKING LAND IN TEXAS AND CALIFORNIA THAT WAS ONE-HALF OF MEXICO AND DRIVING OUT MEXICANS WAS LAGNIAPPE, SOMETHING EXTRA. Europeans destroyed every society they invaded, *taking treasures and leaving Bibles.* Turning the naïve and unsuspecting into powerless whimps. What about Chinese, abused in California to build railroads? The greatest crimes ever committed against humanity should never be set aside, but it really is time to move on. Not to forget about the past, and certainly not to excuse or to forgive any misdeeds. How can we? What happened yesterday and last week absolutely affects us today, and will tomorrow. But it really is time to move ahead ... Forward. Because we've been going down this same road for far too long. It hasn't worked, and we actually appear to be going backwards.

We shouldn't allow anybody or anything to hold us back. Especially excuses. It's time to handle our own business because we've been letting somebody else do it instead of doing it ourselves with devastating consequences. Politicians and preachers in particular. We should vehemently demand justice, but tough times are going to get even tougher, and people who aren't suffering themselves are definitely less likely to be sympathetic to somebody else's needs. Especially white people who have no idea about how much black people have suffered. All they know is *"You can't blame me. I never owned slaves. I didn't do anything to you."* (Remember, after a while people stopped caring about Hurricane Katrina and survivors in New Orleans.) The time for leaning is over. Standing up straight makes much more sense; walking, and maybe you can even start running like Sylvester Stallone did in *Rocky*. While you're at it, you might as well buy a punching bag and get some real exercise.

White people and other ethnicities who are suffering like you are won't give a damn either. They'll be too busy fighting their own battles. So, the 1% will just lay back and enjoy the ride while the rest of us annihilate each other for whatever they leave behind.

There have always been strong willed black people who didn't believe in leaning on anybody or anything. Instead of leaning, they learned to support and rely on each other. As best they could, they handled their own affairs behind their master's back. *It was a brand of Christianity that didn't allow them to give up, to wait, or to submit* ... And as for salvation, their philosophy was *"reward me now!"* Heaven can take care of itself. A militant Frederick Douglass also said:

> If there is no struggle, there is no progress. Those who profess to favor freedom, and yet depreciate agitation, are men who want crops without plowing up the ground. They want rain without thunder and lightning ... This

struggle may be a moral one; or it may be a physical one; or it may be both moral and physical; but there must be a struggle.

One hundred and fifty years later, Dr. Martin Luther King, Jr., the staunch proponent for nonviolence would earnestly say, *"If a man hasn't discovered something he will die for he isn't fit to live."* (Dr. Martin Luther King, Jr. was ready to throw down!) Still, Jesus resurrected inspires many blacks today as they continue to see him and the church as towering beacons of hope. Surely, their Lord and Savior will pull them through one more time, when they're the ones who should be busy fighting to save themselves. The leaners, sitters, and yes even the kneelers.

A former slave, abused, berated and beaten, Frederick Douglass lived in hell right here on earth. He lived the reality that merely complaining about discrimination and injustice accomplishes absolutely nothing. And remember that in America the Bible is arguably the white man's book of religion when it states that slavery was ordained by God. I'm sure many of today's Christian, conservative, Republican capitalists would have agreed, as well as some Democrats.

<u>Jesus never preached against slavery.</u> The son of God, how could he believe that violence and abuse were acceptable? Paul even sent Philemon, a runaway slave back to his Christian master. These days protest marches, "sit down talks" or humble *"thoughts and prayers"*, words, will not effectively change anything or erase America's racial divide. Any effort taken must be accompanied by action and commitment. "Power" wrote Frederick Douglass, "concedes nothing without a demand. It never did. It never will." Quoting Socrates, who was possibly black, "Let him who would move the world first move himself." Power, wealth and privilege that are constant forces throughout our lives, make people feel omnipotent, and even lead good people to do bad things, or nothing. The only way to change things is to stop sitting on your behind. *Do something!*

W.E.B. DuBois, author of *The Souls of Black Folk*, published in 1903, eloquently stated that "the problem of the twentieth century is the problem of the color-line." Du Bois created the term *"double consciousness"*, which means that black people must have two fields of vision at all times. They must be conscious of how they view themselves, as well as how the world views them.

Double consciousness reveals the psycho-social divisions of a white racist American society, and the challenges faced by African Americans who are always seeing themselves through the eyes of others who look upon them with amused contempt and pity. Quoting Shirley Chisholm once more "We must reject not only the stereotypes that others hold on us, but also the stereotypes that we hold on ourselves." According to Du Bois black people are both black and American, two waring ideals in one body. That's especially true for accomplished black people.

Tennis great Serena Williams was accused of cheating by an umpire during the US Open. Blasting her sexist, racist mistreatment and throwing her racket down (white male players did far worse), Serena called the umpire a "liar" and "thief". She was ridiculed and characterized as an angry black ape. Is Serena, a famous black female athlete never to react?

Many African Americans buy into the stereotypical negative image the world has of them, living their entire lives in a kind of suspended purgatory *"hell-hole on earth"*, as second-class citizens with few rights. Having more, and feeling that they are better, white people have created their own equally flawed double conscious world view of themselves, being both white and Americans. Narcissistic recipients of exclusive and all rights as *"The American People"*. As always *"America First!"*

I frankly believe that many of the mass shootings we see in America are the negative result of "white double consciousness". Those attacks are being committed by angry white males, presumed winners because of their privileged ethnic heritage, who realize in their own hearts and minds that they are losers who will never live up to imbedded social and tribal expectations, failing their group and themselves. Expectations that are artificially based on white superiority. My fear, is what fate awaits America and the world, as xenophobic white people who must win at all costs, fall victim to white double consciousness, losing status, identity, and security?

CHAPTER 14

The Role of the Benjamins

I was being trained too, to think in a kind of CONDITIONED FATALISM. I remember sermons about how much Jesus had suffered and how we needed to be more like him, turning the other cheek. Like a trained flea I was being schooled, groomed not to jump out of the jar. You know how it works. You put the flea into the jar, then screw the lid on. The flea keeps jumping up to get out, knocking his head against the top over and over again. He jumps a little bit lower, then a little lower, and a little bit lower after that. Finally the flea gives up and you don't need the top anymore because he's stopped trying to get out. That's what religion and racism do to some black people. It keeps them from trying to get out

or ever getting ahead. *It's the twenty-first century, and they're still waitin' and prayin' for God to bring them up to heaven.* A far cry from the '50s and the '60s when people were willing to fight for freedom and equality, like early Christians. *Whenever the waiters and prayers need something it's always "The Lord will provide";* when they don't get it they say, *"The Lord knows what's best"* or *"It must be the Lord's will."* Whatever happens, *"God did it."* But is it *really* God's will or is something else going on? Like no will and probably no direction. Nietzsche said that "human beings have a natural drive to impose their will and power on others," a drive to condition them to be *TRAINED FLEAS*. Are you a trained flea too, or just another powerless Twenty-first-Century slave who doesn't realize it, conditioned like Ivan Pavlov's dog?

In spite of life's harsh realities: racial profiling, poverty, single-parent households, etc., many black people are still praying to the same white God and white Jesus their forefathers prayed to four centuries ago on the plantation. Others endure hardship as they continue to supplicate to a black Jesus for some of the same blessings. *God freed their ancestors from bondage, then mercifully sent Dr. Martin Luther King Jr. (Michael King Jr.), to secure their civil rights. Barack Obama (their black messiah) would finally deliver them, making a way out of no way.* Racism will be obliterated.

Really?

An Associated Press poll showed that racial prejudice has actually increased exponentially since Obama was elected. Something any thinking person knew would happen before his nomination. Quoting columnist A. Peter Bailey "It is very disturbing that an educated Black person could believe that a Black president, no matter what he said during his campaign, could bring about meaningful change in a society where race *really* matters. This is a society that has never, in its entire history, voluntarily given Black people anything. Every move forward in a struggle for equal rights, equal opportunity and equal justice came about after many of our people paid the ultimate sacrifice with their lives," still valued less than white lives after 500 years.

Since Barack Obama's election there has been much discussion about the post racial society we are living in in America. Decisions have consequences. Until recent police shootings middle-class blacks' fears were generally not life-threatening, but watching black men being murdered, the world now realizes that racial healing was just another myth and more propaganda. Can the idea of race ever be separated from the reality of color, "skin color"? Is a post racial society a pipe dream?

Was Barack Obama, from a historical perspective our first black president, or simply our first "not too black president?" What about Lincoln, Jefferson, Jackson and Harding, with black ancestry? A political novice, was Barack ahead of his time? Years ago my sister accepted an executive position with a major hotel chain in Dallas, Texas. When she arrived and met her new supervisor for the first time, a white Texan, he told her that "he was happy she wasn't too dark." Was that the case with President Obama and his family? *They weren't too black... But just black enough!!*

The venomous Tea Party originated because Barack Obama became the first black President of the United States. Conservative Republicans were frantic about having a black president living in the White House with what they saw as his little pickaninny family. A top House GOP leader told President Obama "I cannot even stand to look at you," arguably the most disrespectful comment ever made to a sitting American President. Remember George Santayana's quotation, "Those who cannot remember the past are doomed to repeat it." RACISM NEVER LOSES!

One of the reasons for so much praying going on is because of single-parent, female-headed households. Women who need help, especially with sons, who turn to the church for comfort and support and usually don't get it. Prayers help, but it's important to operate from a position of strength... not weakness. Typically, that was the man's role, but today that man is missing, mostly through no fault of his own. The same was true during slavery. *The black male was missing and the women were on their knees with their children praying.*

Mark 3:27
But no one can enter a strong man's house and plunder his goods, unless he first binds the strong man, then indeed he may plunder his house.

Are strong black men missing and imprisoned (1.5 million), to deny them and their families security and prosperity, plundered like slaves? Being unemployed or locked up in overcrowded American prisons they are not able to protect their families. Someone can also be missing and imprisoned mentally, emotionally and psychologically, especially when they are powerless. Was that the plan all along? Just as white settlers thought the only good Indian was a dead Indian during frontier days, is the only good black man helpless and emasculated? Why is the black male, no matter how powerful or responsible he is, cast as being weak, while the black female is always stronger or more popular (Michelle Obama)? The answer goes back to slavery and pillow talk. While master owned her and since she posed no real threat, black women ran the "big house" the way they now run the house and the office. *She* became the "bread winner" while *he* hopelessly hung out on street corners. <u>With no more cotton to pick, what would America do with 40 million black people?</u>

The blame for the black man's failure has always unfairly rested on the black man himself. Because he was not there to take care of the children he made he was especially suspect. Although he fathered them, he was not creating and nurturing a normal family. In my book *In Search of Goodpussy*, I used the analogy of an Arizona rancher who wanted to build up his herd of horses. He mates a stallion with five different mares every year. At the end of five years, this stallion has had 25 mates and at least 25 offspring. How could he head all 25 families at one time? And how could he keep up with the offspring of his offspring, the second generation of ponies? *Displaced grandkids with no daddy or granddaddy.* Was the fact that he was forced to breed actually his fault at all, except for being properly equipped and good at what he did?

Some black men had similar experiences during slavery. Like the stallion, they produced many offspring, but couldn't be in 25 places at one time. Not only could they not keep up with their 25 families, they couldn't clone themselves to even catch up. Twenty-four families, but it's the slaves' fault for not being there. *"More Bullshit!"* I think it's somebody else's fault for using them like prized studs. Black men didn't load themselves in shackles onto filthy slave ships so they could leisurely cruise to America and become overworked farm animals. Black men are more VICTIMS than PERPETRATORS? *Conditions in America today are a result of pathology and unbridled greed.*

In Richard Pryor's 1976 LP *Bicentennial Nigger* he said

> He has that lovely white folks expression, but he is happy. He is happy 'cause he been here four hundred years
> And I am so glad you white folks took me out of dark Africa. Ha, Ha, Ha! I used to live to be a hundred and fifty, now I die with high blood pressure by the time I's fifty-two. Ha, Ha, Ha.
> And that just thrills me to death. I am just so pleased to be in America! They brought me over here on a boat. It was four hundred of us come over here. Three hundred of us died on the way over here. Ha, Ha, Ha!
> I just love that! Ha, Ha, Ha! That just thrills me so! *You white folks are just so good to us.* Got over here another twenty of us died from disease, Ha, Ha, Ha, but you didn't have any doctors to take care of us. I am so sorry you didn't. Upset you all some too. Didn't it? Ha, Ha, Ha. Split all of us up; took my mama over this way; took my kids off yonder. Ha, Ha. I just so happy. Ha, Ha. I am just so happy. Ha, Ha! I don't know what to do if I don't get two hundred more years of this! Ha, Ha, Ha, Ha. Lord a mercy! Yessiree, I don't know where my old mama is now. *She up yonder in that white folks heaven in the sky.* Ha, Ha, Ha, Ha. You probably done forgot about it, but I'll never forget it!

While slaves believed that God and Jesus were against slavery and would save them, most Southerns and many Northerns, embracing white supremacy, felt just the opposite. Black people were already saved and should've been grateful. *Slaves were obviously better off because they were owned by Christian masters who were introducing them to Jesus and the wonderful gospels.* As Richard Pryor noted sarcastically, Christianity and slavery were just so good for their niggers. God himself ordained slavery, giving masters the right to have slaves forever. Slavery was a good thing. The church preached it. The Holy Bible wisely approved, and good white Christians could prove it. Ephesians 6:5 says, "Slaves be obedient to them that are your masters . . . as unto Christ." Slavery was also a way to pay a debt. Early in the Bible it says . . .

Genesis 9:25
"Cursed be Canaan! The lowest of slaves will he be to his brothers."

It was final. The Scriptures were against them too. *The Bible was clearly stating that Negroes were inferior and not equal to white people, even in the eyes of God.* The curse came from Noah's generation to Canaan, a son of Ham, father of the Hamites, the black race. Because of the curse Noah pronounced, Ham was to have turned black, and all of his descendants would have kinky, twisted hair, red eyes, and thick lips. The males would also have large penises. Even God was against the Canaanites, black party people, ordering the Israelites to slaughter them.

All the way back to Abraham's time we know that Canaanites were vilified (implicit bias), which is one helluva long time for black people to be put down. Abraham, the Bill Gates of ancient times, insisted that God told him to take the Promised Land from the heathen blacks (his outcast relatives). And what about Abraham the Hebrew and his many slaves? (God did give the OK for slavery, didn't he?) We know that slaves during that time, Ethiopians, were black. Greeks like Homer (850 BC) and Herodotus (450 BC) referred to blacks as "Ethiopian," derived from

Aetiop, meaning burnt face. Herodotus said black people always lived in Mesopotamia, India, and Egypt. Tropical man was never white.

The justification for slavery was undeniable: profit, making money. It was all about the Benjamins. The role of Christianity was to render the transported captives powerless. In his book *From the Browder File*, author Anthony T. Browder states that "In 1411 AD, *Portuguese slave traders presented the first slaves to the pope [Pope Julius II of Rome], who deemed the Africans to be soulless individuals.*" This dictum by Pope Julius II became the sanctioned justification for the Atlantic slave trade. *Slavery was official and authorized by the Catholic Church.* Under Pope Innocent VIII, by supporting the slave trade of Spain and Portugal the Catholic Church received a share of the profits. During his last year as pope, Innocent even gave members of the Curia and his friends 100 of the finest Moorish slaves as gifts. Browder asks, *"Is it a coincidence that the same mentality that created organized crime, the Mafia, also created organized religion and sanctioned the beginning of the slave trade?"* Both the Catholic Church and the mafia's traditions are about making money. Coincidentally, the second ship to transport slaves from Africa to America was named *The Jesus*.

Remember, at the Vatican there were relatively few black sculptures, paintings, or black relics—even though such artifacts were prominent elsewhere, including other parts of Europe. I suppose that goes back to Pope Julius' comments about black people not having souls. And are there few black writings in the Vatican library either, for the same reason? To the Catholic Church black people weren't human, not until they had enough money for the collection plate.

Another reason why black people are sparsely depicted at the Vatican may be the age-old perception of whiteness being beautiful and blackness being ugly. Rome is synonymous with culture, beauty, and fine works of art that black people supposedly could never produce. White people are even said to have *fair* skin (and can be trusted), while black people have dark skin and are not trustworthy.

For centuries belief in a white European God and a white European Jesus supported the notion that white people are superior and made in God's image, with white supremacy and white privilege becoming the order-of-the-day. Early democracies thrived because of slavery. Is the segregationist "Old South" being reincarnated as the United States of America? Supporting slavery, is the Holy Bible which preceded the repugnant Confederate flag also a symbol of brainwashing, white supremacy and racism? The proslavery Southern Baptist Convention began in 1845.

The Bible inspired Confederate leaders like President Jefferson Davis to believe that slavery, the cause rebels were fighting for was ordered by God in The Holy Scriptures. As God's "chosen people" Confederates were the superior race and God was on the white man's side. Don't forget that American racism began with Christianity.

The white church has always been racist; the southern church the backbone of the Confederacy. Whiteness signified purity; one drop of black blood meant contamination. Whiteness was identified with freedom, while blackness was associated with slavery. Race has no scientific basis, and to this day the Supreme Court has still not provided a definition of what constitutes "white." Barack Obama candidly remarked that "Racism, we are not cured of it". And we never will be!

Would white people even be Christians these days if Jesus wasn't white? In a non-scientific survey I conducted the white response to that question ran the full gamut from "it wouldn't matter" to "probably not" and finally to "absolutely not!" Christianity is over. Done!

What would white people in America, who became white through mutation and adaptation, do without Christianity, which along with skin color binds them together, giving them a sense of unity, identity and entitlement? By professing to be "good Christians," do white people validate themselves as fellow Americans, a tribe who embody ethics and good character? Who would white people be without Christianity? Who would black people, who need God and Jesus of Nazareth be?

CHAPTER 15

Past and Present Examples of Lynchings

Italians had seen black people before, when Hannibal, the great Nubian (black) military commander came from Africa, marched his elephants over the Pyrenees and the Alps, and kicked Rome's behind. Emperor Napoleon Bonaparte called Hannibal a great military strategist. Today some scholars are claiming that Hannibal wasn't black, that he was a dark-skinned white guy from Northern Africa. (Hannibal was a white man because there were no black people in North Africa, even though the Berbers, who were indigenes of North Africa were black.) No great black people. What about Ludwig Van Beethoven, and Alexandre Dumas, author of *The Three Musketeers?* Both presumed white.

As you might expect, the usual questions arise. Like Jesus, why is Hannibal's racial identity important? Because he was one hell of a commander, and he was a full blooded black man, that's why. Hannibal was one of those heroes who wasn't supposed to have existed. The coins engraved with his image clearly depict a black man with kinky, cornrowed hair, a broad nose and thick lips. But all heroes are white, aren't they?

According to Browder, "Africans were the first people on this planet to develop a system of religious beliefs. Their temples were repositories for knowledge pertaining to themselves and their Creator. Thousands of years after these religious beliefs had been developed and implemented, they were stolen by foreigners and used as the foundation for the development of new religious systems which spread throughout the world. One such system was the Europeans' brand of Christianity which destroyed other cultures, colonizing information about the world, and colonizing images of themselves being God's chosen people and made in his image. Even Herodotus said that the Negro race, black Egyptians, were the originators of the arts and sciences.

Adding fuel to the fires of racism was the Council of Cardinals, held in Holland in 1457, approving "the enslavement of Africans for the purpose of their conversion to Christianity, and to be exploited in the labor market as chattel property." Before that, in 1455, the pope had already authorized Spain and Portugal to enslave infidels, meaning Africans and Asians, which began the African slave trade. *Using the Bible as cover, with images of themselves as God's chosen people, Europeans saw everybody else as inferior.* And remember, giving others the Caucasian religion also meant giving them Caucasian values.

The following observations are from the American historian Dr. John Henrik Clarke, and may be found in *The Iceman Inheritance*, published in 1978, where Canadian author Michael Bradley looks at such influences, as well as the way Father Bartolomé de las Casas, an eyewitness who traveled with Columbus on his third voyage, describes mass murder and annihilation in Haiti by Spaniards. (Secretly Jewish, Columbus hoped to find a new Promised Land.) Geography and water were always critical.

> All the land so far discovered is a beehive of people; it is as though God had crowded into these islands the great majority of mankind. And of all the infinite universe of humanity these people are the most guileless, the most devoid of wickedness and duplicity, the most obedient and faithful to their native masters and to the Spanish Christians whom they serve. They are by nature the most humble, patient, and peaceable, holding no grudges, free from embroilments, neither excitable nor quarrelsome. These people are the most devoid of rancor, hatreds, or desire for vengeance of any people in the world. And because they are so weak and complaisant, they are less able to endure heavy labor and soon die of no matter what malady. The sons of nobles among us, brought up in the enjoyments of life's refinements, are no more delicate than are these Indians, even those among them who are

of the lowest rank of laborer. They are also poor people, for they not only possess little but have no desire to possess worldly goods. For this reason they are not arrogant, embittered, or greedy.

And

They were very clean in their persons, with alert, intelligent minds, docile and open to doctrine, very apt to receive our holy Catholic faith, to be endowed with virtuous customs, and to behave in a godly fashion . . .

Yet into this sheepfold, into this land of weak outcasts there came some Spaniards who immediately behaved like ravening wild beasts, wolves, tigers, or lions that had been starved for many days. And Spaniards have behaved in no other way during the past forty years, down to the present time, for they are still acting like ravening beasts, killing, terrorizing, afflicting, torturing and destroying the native peoples, doing all this with the strangest and most varied new methods of cruelty, never seen or heard of before, and to such a degree that this Island of Hispaniola, once so populous (having a population that I estimated to be more than three million), has now a population of barely two hundred persons. [From a priest traveling with Columbus who was an eyewitness. In spite of the brutality, Europeans still considered themselves civilized Christians who were made in God's image.] The Spaniards were genocidal butchers. Terrorists!

According to Dr. Clarke, *"the ghastly traffic in human misery was given the cloak of respectability and anointed with the oil of pontifical righteousness in Jesus' name."* We know now that Dr. W.E.B. Dubois was right when he said, "The problem of the twentieth century is the problem of the color line." DuBois said that "Negro suffrage ended a Civil War by beginning a race feud." The Catholic Church helped to institute racism, spreading and facilitating it through unsuspecting Christian missionaries. *Brainwashing the world.* What possible justification could the Catholic Church, and more specifically the pope, God's intercessor, have had for the enslavement of human beings? Did God just give a thumbs-up? His stamp of approval.

Noted historian Lerone Bennett Jr. once wrote, "the whites have always been an unjust, jealous, unmerciful, avaricious, bloodthirsty set of beings, always seeking after power and authority."

In American slavery, whites may or may not have agreed with Christianizing slaves, believing that if the slaves found out too much about Jesus they might want more. Something called freedom, and being treated like human beings instead of dumb animals. Freedom, and maybe justice too! Baptizing them could make it harder to keep them as slaves. Christianity might ruin them, making slaves think they were equal to white people, or embarrass other whites into not treating their new Christian brothers as slaves any longer. White children might lose everything; their inheritance, land and slaves their parents owned. *One Southern woman was afraid she might see black slaves in heaven. While slaves were told if they were good they would go to heaven, it was also made clear that even in heaven they wouldn't be close to their masters and mistresses.*

Thomas Holt Jr. wrote that "Whites felt that blacks who could read would be led to read the Scriptures and would become 'infected' by their explicit and implicit teachings on human equality and liberation. Once those held as slaves could read, then who could keep them from writing? The ability to write would open up channels of communication that could result in insurrections." (No reading, and especially no writing, but today blacks are chastised because of illiteracy and called dumb by whites who never wanted to see them educated or have a level playing field). And remember what Marcus Garvey, one of the greatest black visionaries of our time had to say over 100 years ago, before crack, cocaine, the hand gun explosion, and Black-on- Black crime: *That 'having had the wrong kind of education, the Negro has become his own greatest enemy'.*

In *The Cross And The Lynching Tree,* James Cone says the following. (I'm basically quoting but occasionally paraphrasing Dr. Cone because I couldn't have said the things he said any better.)

> The cross and the lynching tree are separated by nearly 2,000 years. One is the universal symbol of Christian faith; the other is the quintessential symbol of black oppression in America. Though both are symbols of death, one represents a message of hope and salvation, while the other signifies the negation of that message by white supremacy. Lynching was a public spectacle, often announced in advance in newspapers and over radios attracting crowds of up to 20,000 people.
>
> But as with the evils of chattel slavery and Jim Crow segregation, blacks and whites and other Americans who want to understand the true meaning of the American experience need to remember lynching. While the lynching tree is seldom discussed or depicted, the cross is one of the most visible symbols of America's Christian origins. The cross is the great symbol of the Christian narrative of salvation, detached from any reference to the ongoing suffering and oppression of human beings, "the crucified people of history." [Nearly 5,000 African Americans.] The cross has been transformed into a harmless non-offensive ornament that Christians wear around their necks.
>
> Until we can see the cross and the lynching tree together, until we can identify Christ with a "recrucified" black body hanging from a lynching tree, there can be no genuine

understanding of Christian identity in America. White people were virtually free to do anything to blacks with impunity. The violent crosses of the Ku Klux Klan were a familiar reality, and white racists preached a dehumanizing segregated gospel in the name of Jesus' cross every Sunday. How could whites confess and live the Christian faith and also impose three-and-a-half centuries of slavery and segregation upon black people? Self-interest and power corrupted their understanding of the Christian gospel. If white Americans could look at the terror they inflicted on their own black population, slavery, segregation, and lynching then they might be able to understand what is coming at them from others.

Lynching as primarily mob violence and torture directed against blacks began to increase after the Civil War and the end of slavery. The people of the South didn't think any more of killing the black fellows than you would think of killing a flea. It was like killing a chicken or a snake. (Jesus hung on a cross, white people hanged niggers.)

Cole Blease, the two-time governor and U.S. senator from South Carolina, proclaimed that lynching is a "divine right of the Caucasian race to dispose of the offending blackamoor with the benefit of jury." *Lynching was the white community's way of forcibly reminding black people of their inferiority and powerlessness.* [But blacks could never lynch whites.] Blacks had no rights which the white man was bound to respect. Whites could kill blacks, knowing that a jury of their peers would free them but would convict and execute any black who dared to challenge the white way of life. White juries, judges, and lawyers kept America "safe from the threat of the black community." The crucifixion of Jesus by the Romans in Jerusalem and the lynching of blacks by whites in the United States are so amazingly similar that one wonders what blocks the American

Christian imagination from seeing the connection. (Black Christians and white Christians will never fully understand each other.)

One modern day example of lynching, witnessed by the entire world, occurred during the George Zimmerman trial when white defense attorney Mark O'Mara pummeled high school senior Rachel Jeantel on the witness stand. As you remember, lynching was the white community's way of forcibly reminding blacks of their inferiority and powerlessness, with or without a rope. *Just like the old slavery and Jim Crow days, whites act as a mob or a gang. They think and behave the same way, sticking together to maintain control and order (the rule of law), with themselves on top.* That's the case, whether it's a deserted cotton field in Tuskegee, a state of the art newsroom in Atlanta or a crowded, hushed, courtroom in Florida. *White anger and intimidation, based on fear!*

Living the American dream, middle and upper class whites are still always right as they continue to control the social, political, and economic life of black people, brown people, and everybody else. Just ask Rush Limbaugh. Even New York City's powerful former mayor, Michael Bloomberg, has gone on record saying that too many white people in his city are being stopped and frisked. Profiled, the same way blacks and Latinos are being racially profiled. Anybody making furtive (sneaky) moves could be stopped as long as they were not white. Plus the cops got points for assailing people. New York City is literally becoming a police state for some people. A black bus driver, standing outside his own home a 1:00 a.m. in the morning, talking to a friend, was even arrested and charged with impeding pedestrian traffic. *Which happens a lot in New York, in the middle of the night.* But Mayor Bloomberg still said it's not fair to profile white people, because they're not the criminals. The mayor said, "*It's not fair!*" I want some of whatever he's been smoking too! What about black people murdered by the police?

In New York, the police department's stop-and-frisk policy (racial profiling) has been deemed unconstitutional because it unlawfully and unfairly targeted blacks and Latinos for over a decade. The police

have systematically stopped innocent people without evidence of their having committed any crime. The policy violates the Fourth Amendment right barring unreasonable searches and the Fourteenth Amendment right guaranteeing equal protection. In her ruling, Federal Judge Shira Scheindlin wrote, "No one should live in fear of being stopped whenever he leaves his home to go about the activities of daily life." Naturally, Mayor Bloomberg said that nothing would change overnight. (Welcome to America and more lynchings without a rope.)

Needless to say Mayor Bloomberg did not address high-end stores like Barneys and Macy's "shop and frisk" policies, where Blacks and Latinos are racially profiled and detained by police after legally purchasing expensive items and producing receipts.

Kayla Phillips, a Brooklyn nursing student was stopped after buying a $2,500.00 Celine handbag from Barneys. And 19 year old Trayon Christian, an engineering student from Queens, New York, was held by police after he legally purchased a $349.00 Ferragamo belt at Barneys. Stopping him a block from the store, two undercover cops wanted to know "How could you afford a belt like this?" Trayon had a very simple explanation. His paycheck was direct deposited into his Chase Bank account, so he used his Chase debit card and signed his name. Kayla and Trayon were accused of debit card fraud. So now even buying a belt or a handbag in New York can get an innocent minority targeted and arrested while white people continue to move about freely.

The crime of "shopping while Black". They were being followed while shopping strictly because of skin color and the fact that they were of a minority race. Blacks and Latinos have to fear both the cops and the robbers in The Big Apple. The stores blamed the police, and the police blamed the stores. I suppose the Mayor thinks that pointing the finger at each other is unfair too. Naturally, an internal investigation by Barney's found no wrong doing.

In Florida, Rachel Jeantel was the last person Trayvon Martin spoke to using his cell phone, and she too was profiled—as surely as Trayvon was—by both the defense attorney and the jury. The young high school student was cast as a dummy who was less than human simply because of her skin color and the way she spoke. The problem with that argument is that most white Americans don't speak the King's English either. Their speech is bastardized too. White people in America don't even speak "good English," but they still find ways to criticize everybody else, saying, "It's not the same."

All the while, it was the white attorney himself who didn't recognize his own ineptitude. Rachel was indeed credible and sincere, facing the trauma of having lost her best friend to a senseless, indefensible homicide. Because of his own ethnocentric insensitivity, O'Mara didn't appreciate something most black people in this country could clearly see. He was being a typical white man demonizing another innocent black victim. A mature white, adult male (lawyer) lynching an eighteen-year-old (powerless) black female teenager. Like many whites, O'Mara was willing to do whatever he had to, to maintain the perception of dominance and superiority, even in the sanctity of a courtroom where justice should prevail.

Asking why she or Trayvon didn't call the police was a dumb question, because anybody black (and most white people), already knew that the Sanford police might have shown up and actually shot Trayvon, a black teenage male fighting a white man. By accident, of course. If the situation was reversed and Trayvon Martin was a black man who had murdered Zimmerman, a white teenager, do you really believe there would have been any debate about who was on top or who the aggressor was? Hell no! Trayvon Martin would already be headed to death row because he was a nigger who used a gun to shoot an unarmed white teenager. Legally registered or not. If he was still alive.

Others who criticized Rachel were equally guilty of being jackasses. Any fool knows that "a creepy-ass cracker" has no real racial significance compared to the evil and the historical narrative surrounding the word "nigger," a word that has been used over and over again to dehumanize and even to kill, recreating violent images of lynchings and beatings. "Kill that nigger!" Context absolutely impacts meaning, then there's always the debate about who gets to say "*nigger!*" In 2007 the Detroit Chapter of the N.A.A.C.P. even held a funeral for the word. Ironically, most of the people using "nigger" in an inflammatory manner, both then and now, call themselves Christians.

But Trayvon has been buried, and the prosecutor, the witnesses, the judge, and the jury have moved on. Supporters have prayed, marched and ranted. As Kojo Livingston would say, *"We've done our mandatory two weeks of protesting. Now what?"*

In a strange twist, Michael Dunn, 47, was not found guilty of first degree murder in the shooting of 17 year old Jordan Davis, another unarmed black teenager, also shot dead in Florida, outside a Jacksonville convenience store. Dunn, who is white, showed no remorse, describing himself as *the fucking victim!* He said he approached the red Dodge Durango the four black teenagers were riding in to complain about the "loud thug music" they were playing. An argument broke out with Davis threatening him, and that's when Dunn said he saw the barrel of a shotgun pointed at him through the SUV's window.

Grabbing his semi-automatic from his glove compartment, Dunn said he fired in self-defense, ten times. Shooting the car up, Davis died on the scene, with no evidence that there was ever any gun. Dunn left the scene with his girlfriend who had gone inside to buy snacks, never calling the police or reporting the incident, even after watching the news that night and learning that someone had died. Dunn and his companion went back to the motel where they were staying, ordered a pizza and went to sleep. The next day they drove back home, two hundred miles away. The police were able to track him down because a witness memorized his license plate number. And Dunn only turned himself in after talking to a friend in law enforcement.

While in jail awaiting trial he wrote letters. In one Dunn complained that "jails are full of blacks." He said that "if more people would arm themselves and kill these *fucking idiots* when they're threatening you, eventually they may take the hint and change their behavior."

Dunn has been convicted however, by a mostly white jury, of attempted murder and firing into an occupied vehicle, showing no emotion as the verdict was read, with a sentence of sixty years. Looking at his parents he raised his hands in disbelief, obviously feeling that the *assassination* of young black males is justifiable. After the fact of his committing murder, Dunn was not found guilty, and I'm sure most of the people in court that day considered themselves Christians, starting with Holy Bibles and sworn oaths. But where was *Christian* justice? Ironically Dunn's trial was prosecuted by the same State Attorney's Office that handled Zimmerman's case.

Eric Garner, a 43-year-old asthmatic who was the father of six children, died of a chokehold that was administered while he was being restrained by several New York City police officers. Like Trayvon Martin, he too was unarmed. His crime: selling onezies, single cigarettes, which is illegal in New York. Garner can be heard on videos saying "I can't breathe" as the officers smothered him to death.

John Crawford was in a Wal-Mart store in Ohio with his girlfriend when his cellphone rang. While talking to his mother, he had innocently picked up a BB gun, for sale in the store, and ended up shot twice in the chest, in the same Wal-Mart by overzealous police officers.

Of course, we all know what happened to Michael Brown, the unarmed teenager in Ferguson, Missouri. But there are always at least two different stories. Those of eyewitnesses, those of the assailant, and sometimes those of family members and friends.

What's the real issue? LYNCHING! The white community's way of forcibly reminding blacks of their inferiority and powerlessness. Praying, marching, and singing aren't as effective, so the "Rambo" styled police officers, dressed like the paramilitary in a war zone, are again treating citizens like enemy combatants. Demanding IDs, modern police replaced overseers and paddy rollers who demanded passes. Christianity is no longer an effective deterrent in maintaining order, so authorities returned to a policy of intimidation and violence. Like Michal J. Fox's movie, it's *"Back to The Future."* SELLING HEAVEN IS DYING OUT!

Another *Back to the Future* element exists in the stereotypical perception of young black males. All the way back in 1915 and the first movie, D.W. Griffith's *Birth of a Nation*, the image of the black male was cast as *"the brutal black buck who was unintelligent and aggressive toward white women"*. (On Hollywood screens, exaggerating white supremacy there were five character types for blacks; Toms, Coons, Mulattoes, Mammies and Bucks.) Plus King Kong in 1933. The KKK used *Birth of a Nation* as a recruiting tool and it was the first film ever shown at the White House by President Woodrow Wilson, an outspoken racist.

In the movie, based on *The Clansman* by Rev. Thomas Dixon, the black male was a lecherous wild animal, crazed by his desire to rape a helpless white woman. Strong and murderous, he was a menace to society. (We're still afraid of him today.) He's a dangerous animal with a big penis and he's out of control. There's only one way for a normal human being to deal with such a beast, and that's with a weapon. But shoot to kill and make sure he's dead! (Because any wild black brut can be a threat!) Is anti-black bias the real reason why black males are so often victims of lethal force, especially by the police?

At one point the media was ablaze with debate about Minnesota Viking's star running back Adrian Peterson abusing two of his children, and Baltimore Ravens player Ray Rice's assault on his wife. Most of the people leading the discussion were ultra-moral white men and white women in the media. (Violent acts involving black males are always winners in the ratings battle.)

Whites in the media were acting as both judge and jury, as usual. They accused Peterson and Rice of being superstars who play by their own rules, but acting as prosecutors, the critics were guilty of playing by their own rules too (guilty until proven innocent). Implicit bias! *But white people in America have always operated by different rules. And nothing can make or force men respect each other.*

Just as star athletes may believe that they are better than everybody else because of a lifetime of preferential treatment, many whites feel that they too are better, because of their own history of preferential treatment, programs like the GI Bill. Skin color most often signals the line of demarcation. Racism begins at home, at school, and in church.

As basketball great Charles Barkley said, "Our cultures are different" and "parents should be able to discipline their own children." Barkley said that as a child he was spanked with a switch (just as I was), and that by today's standards our own parents and grandparents would have ended up behind bars.

Adrian Peterson was quoted as saying "I am, without a doubt, not a child abuser." He was simply disciplining his child the same way he was disciplined. (Corporal punishment is still legal in 49 out of 50 states.) Peterson continued "Deep in my heart I have always believed I could have been one of those kids that was lost in the streets [or murdered], without the discipline (obeying the rules), instilled in me by my parents and other relatives. I have always believed that the way my parents disciplined me has a great deal to do with the success I have enjoyed as a man." Spankings and strict supervision may have saved his life.

Once, as a child, my buddies and my two brothers and I were in our back yard throwing rocks at an abandoned house next door. My mother made me go cut a switch, myself, and then she proceeded to spank all seven of us. Like Adrian, we grew up with "spare the rod, spoil the child" and I, too, thank my parents.

Time and time again after some black teenager has been murdered by white police officers the dialogue about never having the conversation about race in America begins anew. Now another dimension has been added. "How do we talk to our black sons who are most often the tragic victims?" Bad things *do* happen, and all any parent wants is for their child to be safe. That means staying alert.

Historically, black parents and grandparents have always had that *non-verbal* conversation. *It was called a spanking, with a switch.* They fully realized that any misconduct on the part of their youngsters could prove tragic. It was no laughing matter; stern discipline might save their child's life someday. Remember that black people know more about being on the receiving end of beatings than white people do, including white psychologists. For much of this country's history black women were the ones rearing and disciplining white children. Including spankings.

Today many black parents understand that there is no "*time out*" in America for their youngsters. *Time out* may work for Ethan and Zoey, but not for Daquain and Sheenequa. Time out, however, can also be abusive, especially if you don't feed your isolated child anything but bread and water for two or three days. But once again concerned, responsible black parents are being put on public display as brutes. Some even suggest that this newest form of lynching is simply the white community's latest way of reminding high profile blacks that "*I made you and I can break you.*" You may have escaped the ghetto with its crime and poverty, but I can always send you back. *CHARACTER ASSASSINATIONS!*

In his *Washington Post* Article, Pulitzer Prize-winning columnist Eugene Robinson wrote the following "Hopelessness grew in the ghetto while dreams were made in the suburbs. Millions of black children are being raised in circumstances of limited opportunity, crushing poverty and a lack of socialization. For those left behind, the prospect of a decent education leading to a decent job leading to a decent livelihood, the prospects are fewer, there are no role models left to look up to for guidance, and the families that have been crushed by the burdens they face are incapable of breaking the cycle of despair."

Mr. Robinson, author of *Disintegration: The Splintering of Black America* continued: "The market creates winners and losers, but the system must be altered so that the winners do not win so big and the losers do not lose everything. Consumers (ordinary people) must of necessity be able to buy things, pay bills and meet other needs."

Like everything else, however, I think that there are many reasons why incidents such as Ferguson appear to be on the rise. For one thing times are getting even tougher for poor people. Food prices are skyrocketing and there are no jobs. And let's not forget that the "middle class" is getting its ass kicked too. Another thing is that we always seem to be fighting wars somewhere, and now we're even facing threats of terrorists aggression right here on our own soil. That fear is creating feelings of helplessness, hopelessness, and even more stress and anxiety. Thanks to corporate greed, technology, robotics, globalization, and a global population explosion, things are going to get even worse, in every way imaginable. The genie will never go back into the bottle.

Black people now realize something. Like the 40 acres and the mule their forefathers never received, they won't get anything either. White people who moved to the suburbs, allowing cities to crumble, are moving back. Including young people who moved to the city for college, leaving mom and dad alone in big empty houses that were once surrounded by bustling businesses that are moving back too. Through gentrification white people are reclaiming what black people have worked hard to rehab, maintain and hold on to. Inner city ghettos legislated and engineered by decades of federal, state and local governmental neglect are now prime real estate. Segregated public housing prompted racial segregation, white flight, and today's wealth gap. The 1862 Homestead Act gave two million acres of Indian land to white settlers. The 1935 Social Security Act excluded black domestic and agriculture workers. Exclusive "whites only" affirmative action.

The GI Bill guaranteeing a chance to get an education and buy a house (become middle class), was specifically designed for white veterans from a segregated military to accommodate the Jim Crow South. It created immense resources and generational wealth for white families. Today it would take a black family 228 years to catch up.

Like coyotes and alligators in the Florida swamps that have lost their habitat to humans, where will black people go next? Where can they go? For people of color the cavalry never showed up and it won't be coming. Not one hero. African Americans continue to be "locked out" of home ownership at rates lower than the 1930s, as they are denied equal access to mainstream mortgage credit that could build wealth. America is still white, Christian, mostly straight and male-dominated.

President Obama's election was tragically Black America's first and last shot. What happened to "change we can believe in?" As Eugene Robinson said, black people feel abandoned and left behind. With forces deliberately put in place to hold them back, like inferior schools and teachers, uninformed parents and depressed red-lined communities with few jobs and services, should they have expected anything else? Parents who are uneducated and unemployed, who don't know very much and haven't seen very much probably can't teach their children very much. White people will continue to feel entitled and empowered, while black people forsakenly throw in the towel.

White people, on the other hand have their own frustrations. By 2042 they will no longer be the majority in this country, as white males continue to lose leadership roles, both at home and at the workplace, and in general. They're desperately doing all they can to hold on to power, including lynching (without a rope), and acting as a gang. *Uncertainty is exacerbating insecurity for everybody. Including white people.*

Most troubling for me is the fact that people continue to live their lives based on unrealistic expectations and something as ethereal as heaven. *Dying and going there someday.* Putting up with anything now for a final reward later. What we need to be doing right now is to face the facts, and seriously look for solutions to problems that aren't going to just disappear or go away. Do you honestly believe that you will live forever, happily ever after in a paradise called heaven? And even if you do believe it, what are you doing about the life you're living now?

African Americans have a long standing tradition of not wanting to air their dirty laundry in public. They mostly keep their mouths shut while masking their frustrations. (They also don't want to expose weaknesses.) Given their history in America as an abused race, blacks are obviously facing quite a few serious issues of their own. In *"In Search of GoodPussy"* I maintain that black people are pretending to be normal in an abnormal environment. Others are trying to convince themselves that they are like everybody else ... *Living in denial!*

What we are now beginning to see, however, is the cumulative effect of all that abuse and pretending, again, like the rioting in Ferguson, Missouri. Blacks are snapping and beginning to reach a breaking point, finally realizing that they have been scammed and bamboozled by almost everybody. From African chiefs who sold their ancestors to slave traders, to politicians and religious leaders who are exploiting and making suckers of them today. Most African Americans, including the middle class, are still powerless and broken. With nobody doing anything to fix them. Undiagnosed victims of Post-Traumatic Stress Disorder.

Centuries of listening to preachers and about 50 years of taking the advice of politicians has barely advanced black causes, to everyone's apparent detriment. *God has not delivered them, and the probability appears bleak. Without stable jobs and families they'll die in jail or poor.*

Dr. Anthea Butler, associate professor of religious studies and Africana studies at the University of Pennsylvania says that *"most Americans worship a white racist god with a problem, who is carrying a gun and stalking young black men."* Dr. Butler believes that God is omnipotent and almighty, but in contrast there is "America's God," who is the cause of the racial disparity we see in the legal, judicial, social, economic and political systems.

According to Dr. Butler, *"God ain't good all the time."* In fact, *"sometimes God is not for us. He is a white racist God with a problem. I know that this American God ain't my God."* Dr. Butler maintains that "stand your ground justifies the use of deadly force when a person suspects their life is in danger and that laws have been misapplied, misused and abused against blacks to justify unjust killings. When you take race out of the picture, it's as if it doesn't exist. Like everybody is equal and equally protected. And blacks are left to respect laws that destroy us." BAD LAWS, that white people created, mostly applying to unprotected minorities.

Whites, and Christian conservatives in particular, always stand strong defending laws and the Constitution, even "Bad Laws" like slavery and Jim Crow, as long as those laws benefit them. But as soon as those same Christians see a law they don't like, they change it. It becomes a bad law, and soon it's no longer the law. Prohibition, for example, and now legalizing marijuana in some states, because their kids smoke too. According to the Constitution, America always pays its bills, but in 2013 during the "debt ceiling debacle" to increase U.S. spending limits, Tea Party Republicans said no. Once again conservative Christian law makers were ignoring a law they didn't like. But never forget that what is legal is not always right, and what is right is not always legal.

It is illegal to deport children back to their homeland when their lives are in imminent danger. That policy was established during George W. Bush's presidency. The William Wilberforce Trafficking Victims' Protection Reauthorization Act of 2008 gave protection to children who came to America alone from Mexico or Canada. But conservatives want to ignore the law when it comes to children traveling alone from Central American countries like Honduras, Ecuador, and Guatemala, even though their lives were in imminent danger. They expect countries like Jordan to deal with the crisis in Syria, but want America to turn its back and look the other way when it comes to Latinos. Recent statistics show that in New York City there is a 1 in 25,000 chance you'll be murdered. In Honduras it's 1 in 14. In the good ole' U.S.A. Native American tribes have nearly been exterminated, 10 to 30 million killed. Today helpless Hispanic children are being deported, with resentful Caucasians (many of them Christians), still claiming this land belongs to them, alone. It's the law.

Rev. Ishakamusa Barashango, author of *God, The Bible and the Black Man's Destiny*, writes, "*The God we serve should be one who works in our behalf, not to the benefit of those who seek to destroy us.* Our concepts of him must be rooted in the history of our people and he must look like us. This is the way of an intelligent, civilized people such as we once were, and will be again."

Reverend Barashango also said, "In order to survive, you must know your enemy. To know your enemy is to know that you cannot depend on him to do for you that which you must do for yourself. *We must struggle for freedom. No one will give it to us.*"

It was the humanist philosopher Robert G. Ingersoll, 1833–1899, who said "*Religion can never reform mankind because religion is slavery. The real oppressor, enslaver and corrupter of the people is the Bible.*" And while some feared that religion might make controlling Negroes more difficult, others thought that Christianizing them might have the opposite effect. Christianity would remind them of their duty to their masters. "*Christianity would make blacks better slaves!*" Certainly, whatever the slave master did was never in the best interest of the slave, including instituting *his* religion. Ingersol called Christianity superstitious mythology.

Black people are repeatedly told to get over the past! Quoting the author and social critic James Baldwin; "History, as no one seems to know, is not merely something to be read. And it does not refer merely, or even principally to the past. On the contrary, the great force of history comes from the fact that we carry it within us, are unconsciously controlled by it in many ways, and history is literally present in all that we do."

In *100 Years of Lynchings,* published in 1988, freelance journalist Ralph Ginzburg references lynchings recorded in newspapers across the United States. Tuskegee Institute documented 4,749 known lynchings between 1862 and 1968. One every two or three days.

New York Age
April 30, 1914

WAS POWERLESS TO AID SISTER WHO WAS RAPED AND LYNCHED

CLOVIS, N. M., Apr. 27 – The brother of the young colored girl who was lynched by a mob of white ruffians near Wagner, Okla., a few weeks ago, passed through this town on his way to Mexico. He gave a pathetic account of the lynching to colored citizens here.

The young man's sister was but 17 years old and of respectable parents. Two half-drunken white men walked into their home during the absence of the mother and found the girl dressing, locked themselves into her room and criminally assaulted her. Her screams for help were heard by her brother, who, kicking down the door, went to her rescue. In defending his sister, he shot one of the brutes. The other escaped.

Later in the evening the local authorities, failing to find the brother, arrested the sister, who was taken from jail by a mob at 4 o'clock in the morning and lynched. From his hiding place the brother, who is 21 years old, could hear his sister's cries for help, but he was powerless to aid her.

MACON (GEORGIA) TELEGRAPH
October 26, 1934
BIG PREPARATION MADE FOR LYNCHING TONIGHT

GREEN, Fla., Oct. 26—Local citizens have been preparing all day for the lynching of a negro scheduled to take place here tonight. This morning a mob seized Claude Neal, 23, from a jail in Brewton, Ala., where he had been held in connection with the murder of a white girl which took place here several days ago.

At noon, a "Committee of Six" representing the mob announced a timetable for the lynching which was given in newspapers and over the radio as follows:

At sundown the negro will be taken to the farm two miles from here where Miss Lola Cannidy, the murder victim, lived. There he will be mutilated by the girl's father.

Then he will be brought to a pig-pen in the middle of a cotton field nearby, where the girl's body was found, and killed.

Finally his body will be brought to Marianna, the county seat, nine miles from here, and hung in the court house square for all to see.

The negro is presently being held at an undisclosed location in a swamp along the Chattahoochee River, not far from the Cannidy farm.

"All white folks are invited to the party," said the announcement issued by the mob's Committee of Six.

As a result, thousands of citizens have been congregating all afternoon at the Cannidy farm. Bonfires have been started, piles of sharp sticks have been prepared, knives have been sharpened and one woman has displayed a curry-comb with which she promises to torture the negro.

The crowd is said to have been addressed by a member of the Florida State Legislature who, in a humorous vein, promised that no one would be disappointed if the crowd maintained decorum.

Some misgivings are said to have been expressed by the Committee over the fact that the crowd is heavily armed and highly intoxicated. It is feared that shots aimed at the negro may go astray and injure innocent bystanders, who include some women with babes in arms.

During the early afternoon a party of men broke off from the crowd at the Cannidy farm and paid a visit to the cabin where Neal's family lives and burned it to the ground.

In New York, Walter White, Secretary of the National Association for the Advancement of Colored People, sent a telegram to Florida Governor David Sholtz urging him to "take immediate steps" to protect Neal. J. P. Newell, the Governor's Executive Secretary at Tallahassee, has replied that the Governor is "out of the capital" and can not be reached.

BIRMINGHAM (ALABAMA) POST
October 27, 1934
LYNCHING CARRIED OFF ALMOST AS ADVERTISED

MARIANNA, Fla., Oct. 27—The body of Claude Neal, 23, negro, confessed attacker and slayer of a white girl, swung from a tree on the courthouse lawn here today, victim of an enraged mob's vengeance.

A crowd of 100 men, women and children silently gazed at the body, nude except for a sack reaching from waist to knee. The negro had been shot at least 50 times, burned with red hot irons and dragged through the streets behind an automobile.

An eye-witness to the lynching, which took place yesterday, said that Neal had been forced to mutilate himself before he died. The eye-witness gave the following account of the event which took place in a swamp beside the Chattahoochee River:

"Due to the large number of people who wanted to lynch the nigger, it was decided to do away with him first and then bring him to the Cannidy house dead.

"First they cut off his penis. He was made to eat it. Then they cut off his testicles and made him eat them and say he liked it.

"Then they sliced his sides and stomach with knives and every now and then somebody would cut off a finger or toe. Red hot irons were used on the nigger to burn him from top to bottom. From time to time during the torture a rope would be tied around Neal's neck and he was pulled up over a limb and held there until he almost choked to death, when he would be let down and the torture begun all over again. After several hours of this punishment, they decided just to kill him.

"Neal's body was tied to a rope on the rear of an automobile and dragged over the highway to the Cannidy home. Here a mob estimated to number somewhere between 3,000 and 7,000 people from eleven southern states was excitedly waiting his arrival. When the car which was dragging Neal's body came in front of the Cannidy home, a man who was riding the rear bumper cut the rope.

"A woman came out of the Cannidy house and drove a butcher knife into his heart. Then the crowd came by and some kicked him and some drove their cars over him."

What remained of the body was brought by the mob to Marianna where it is now hanging from a tree on the northeast corner of the courthouse square.

Photographers say they will soon have pictures of the body for sale at fifty cents each. Fingers and toes from Neal's body are freely exhibited on street-corners here.

Neal is said to have confessed to attacking and killing the while girl when he was first brought to the jail for safe-keeping.

NEW YORK TIMES
July 27, 1946
GEORGIA MOB MASSACRES TWO NEGROES AND WIVES

MONROE, Ga., July 26—Two young Negroes, one a veteran just returned from the war, and their wives were lined up last night near a secluded road and shot dead by an unmasked band of twenty white men.

The ghastly details of the multiple lynching were told today by Loy Harrison, a well-to-do white farmer who had just hired the Negroes to

work on his farm. Harrison was bringing the Negroes to his farm when his car was waylaid by the mob eight miles from Monroe. Questioning of one of the Negroes by the mob indicated, Harrison said, that he was suspected of having stabbed his former employer, a white man. The Negroes, Roger Malcolm and George Dorsey, both 27, were removed from the car and led down a side road.

The women, who were sisters and who had just recently married Malcolm and Dorsey, began to scream. Then a mob member said that one of the women had recognized him.

"Get those damned women, too," the mob leader shouted.

Several of the men then came back and dragged the shrieking women from the automobile. A few moments later Mr. Harrison heard the shots—many of them and the mob dispersed.

The grotesquely sprawled bodies were found in a clump of bushes beside a little-used sideroad, the upper parts of the bodies scarcely recognizable from the mass of bullet holes.

Dorsey's mother, Monia Williams, said that her son had just been discharged after five years in the Army and that she had received his discharge button in the mail just this week.

The lynching was the first in the nation in nearly a year and was the first multiple lynching since two 14-year-old Negro boys were hanged by a Mississippi mob in October, 1942. For Georgia it was the first lynching of more than one person since 1918 when ten Negroes were lynched in Brooks County.

NEW YORK WORLD-TELEGRAM
December 8, 1933
HEART AND GENITALS CARVED
FROM LYNCHED NEGRO'S CORPSE

KOUNTZE, Tex., Dec. 8—David Gregory, a Negro ex-convict accused of attacking and slaying a white woman, was shot to death when he was said to have resisted arrest by a posse and his body later mutilated and burned by a mob which dragged it to a pyre in the Negro section of Kountze early today.

Officers and incensed citizens had been searching for the Negro since Mrs. Nellie Williams Brockman, 30, wife of a farmer, was found dead on a highway near here last Saturday.

Last night a posse trailed the Negro to his hiding place in the belfry of a Negro church at Voth, a town between Kountze and Beaumont. There he was shot and wounded when officers said he drew a pistol and resisted arrest.

The wounded Negro, unconscious, was taken to a hospital at Beaumont, but when officers received information a mob was forming at Kountze and starting toward Beaumont, they took the Negro away in an automobile, trying to protect him.

Without regaining consciousness or being able to make any statement as to his guilt or innocence, the Negro died as the car bearing him sped toward Vidor, six miles east of Beaumont.

The body was taken to Silsbee, another small town in the vicinity by Sheriff Miles Jordan of Hardin County.

On learning of these developments, the mob, slowly increasing in size, trailed the sheriff to Silsbee, took the body from him, tied it behind an automobile with chains, and dragged it for thirty-five minutes through the Negro section of Kountze to terrorize the negro population. Members of the mob of approximately 300, cut out the Negro's heart and sexual organs before casting it to the flames.

Many thousands of other black people were brutally executed, including Nat Turner, the rebel leading preacher who was skinned alive, beheaded, cut to pieces and his body made into soap.

How could anyone who participated, driving from miles away to take pictures and buy souvenirs, possibly have seen themselves as Christians who were made in God's image? And furthermore, how could the Bible tell people who had been terrorized and so viciously brutalized to simply turn the other cheek, to love their enemies, and to not seek reprisal? That they would be rewarded over yonder after flying off to heaven, "In The Sweet By-and-By". Especially since Exodus 15:3 tells that "the Lord is a warrior against those who commit evil deeds." Jesus himself said "greater love hath no man than this. That a man lay down his life for his friend." *(Jesus still wasn't joking around.)*

After the Nat Turner and Denmark Vesey revolts, one loyal slave minister tried to calm his white masters' fears. He told them *"If you will give us the gospel [Christianity], it will do more for the obedience of servants and the peace of the community than all your guards and guns, and bayonets."* [They would be better slaves.] *As the slave minister suggested, are the gospels (and prisons) being used now instead of guns and bayonets for the peace of the community? Are today's prisons in fact yesterday's plantations and chain gangs?* The following is taken from *White Over Black*, written by Winthrop Jordan concerning Christianity and controlling slaves.

> By embracing the Gospel, then, the Negro was to obtain protection from his own "Lusts" and "Inordinate Desires," though not, as the good bishop made evident, from the white man's. *These clergymen had been forced by the circumstance of racial slavery in America into propagating the Gospel by presenting it as an attractive device for slave control.* As the Reverend Hugh Jones of Virginia put it, *"Christianity encourages and orders them to become more humble and better servants, and not worse, than when they were heathens."* The Reverend Thomas Bacon felt no hesitation in telling slaves that they must obey their masters in all things, even when cruelly abused: "Your Masters and Mistresses," he explained glowingly, "are God's Overseers." [Even being Christianized, black slaves were never to see themselves equal to white people.]

Throughout history white people helped black people. Today however, we are aware of a concept called moral self-licensing. Past good deeds which make people feel moral and good about themselves can justify or balance out future bad deeds. "I'm white but I voted for Barack Obama, so I can't be a racist, even if I never do anything for another black person." Being a Christian also gives moral license, and helps white people feel innocent and comfortable with white supremacy and racism. Lessons taught by mom and dad, friends, family, teachers and preachers, insulating them from guilt. Nobody talks about slavery or Jim Crow, that Nazis even studied.

Another thing that wasn't written or talked about was The Greenwood Massacre, "Black Wall Street Massacre" of 1921. In the Greenwood District of Tulsa, Oklahoma, the heart of "The Bible Belt," because of oil money and segregation, 35 square city blocks of 600 successful black businesses thrived. They included hotels, theaters, restaurants, schools, 2 black banks, 2 hospitals, 2 black newspapers and even a black bus line. Black millionaires owned their own airplanes. Following World War I envious white supremacist, including the KKK in "God's country" nicknamed Greenwood "Little Africa."

Because of Jim Crow laws black people were not permitted to go to other parts of the city except for working in a white business of for a white family, with strict curfew laws. Forced to patronize their own businesses became Greenwood's source of wealth. Diamond Dick Rowland, a black teenage shoe shiner who worked in a segregated white building was accused of attacking Sarah Page, a white elevator operator. Getting into the elevator to go to a nearby "colored restroom" Roland tripped, grabbing the operator's arm and was accused of sexual assault when she screamed. Ten white people and two black people died in a shootout at the courthouse, swirling around rumors that Roland was to be lynched. An angry mob of white rioters, including police and the Oklahoma National Guard, committed to a belief that blacks were inferior attacked, looted and obliterated homes and businesses over a period of 18 hours.

Rampaging, they dropped turpentine fireballs from airplanes, with a machine gun firing on Greenwood Ave. from a rooftop. At least 300 black people were murdered, 800 injured, 10,000 homeless survived, but 1,200 homes were destroyed with no compensation. Firefighters were forced to leave and not one lawbreaker was ever arrested or jailed, although 6,000 black Tulsans were confined. *White privilege!*

During Louisiana's slave revolt of 1811, up to 500 escaped slaves marched from plantation to plantation toward New Orleans, armed with hand tools, burning plantations and crops. A white militia was formed, killing 40 to 45 slaves, while only two white men died. Other apprehended slaves were killed by firing squads or hanged, their heads mounted on poles, by Christians.

CHAPTER 16

Will the Real Jesus Please Stand Up

⟿

In the '60s, like just about everybody else, I found myself sitting in church too, the church I had gone to since childhood. It was the same church that had taught me how to be a Christian. And being a good Christian meant being obedient, submissive, and yes, being a good little Negro boy who was more acceptable for good colored folks and white people. I was being prepped (trained like a new puppy or our friend the flea) to become a perfect little gentleman in this laughable dog and pony show called civilization. Hair combed. Teeth brushed. Shoes polished. What I was really being groomed for was to be anything but my own man. Like Hitler's youth squad on religious steroids. (Nazis and German troops were hooked on crystal meth.) I was being brainwashed, but in the opposite direction. I was being programmed to turn that other cheek. To go sit in a corner and be quiet. Surrounded by people I had known and trusted all my life, I eventually realized that I didn't know what to believe anymore.

There were many black churches that still depicted the same white Christ whose picture always hung on the wall behind the pulpit, along with white angels and white disciples at the Last Supper (no women or black people). God was always a serious old grey-haired white guy with attitude. Other more contemporary congregations featured the new and improved version. (The idea of God has always meant different things to different groups and none of those ideas are objective. Each group and each generation has its own ideas about who God and Jesus are.) Some of the images of the new black Jesus attempted to be inspiring and were very ethnic in appearance, with curly hair and even sideburns, a really cool-looking beard, or sometimes even a goatee. Not to mention preachers wearing Nehru suits, colorful Afrocentric dashikis, platform shoes, and three-inch Afros (which were both a fashion statement and one helluva' distraction). But it made the reverend look like he was really cool and on top of his game.

Unremarkably, something absolutely remarkable was taking place. Jesus and God, uncontested constants in our lives, were no longer absolutes and personal confidants. A new Jesus was being smuggled in, and we were looking straight at him. We had a choice. We could believe . . . or else. But what we were actually being presented with was a more user-friendly way of not burning in hell! In an instant, right there in front of us, was this new guy in our old, trusted friend's place. (Like going to class, your favorite teacher won't be back, and there's a new permanent substitute in his or her place.) . . . Like switching Jesuses was as easy as changing shirts or dashikis.

This dark-skinned stranger, a man we had never seen before, was now supposed to save us from the devil and deliver us from the demons and ravages of hell. Well, whatever happened to the first Jesus? Did he just pack up and move somewhere else without telling us? Did he simply vanish into thin air, or did he decide to retire or resign, just as Pope Benedict XVI did? No, the white Jesus is still around. He mostly hangs out at white churches saving white people these days, leaving black people behind to do their own thing or be saved by the other guy. The white Jesus still has his old job.

I suppose that means there are two Jesuses then, one for white people and one for black people, and maybe two Gods as well. But what about the Chinese and their Jesus, and Eskimos, and where did those Jesuses grow up? Was there a Chinese God and a Chinese Jesus too? And an Eskimo God and an Eskimo Jesus? I do know one thing. *"It's gettin' crowded up in here."* And what happens in integrated congregations? Is it majority rule? *Do* they flip a coin, or use their imaginations? *Just kidding . . .* They do nothing. They never talk about it. On the other hand, maybe Jesus was part white and part black, half and half. But it is interesting, to say the least, that whiteness is still always good while blackness is irrefutably evil. Perhaps like the pagans' gods, the white God and the white Jesus are just stronger than the black God and the black Jesus. Since Caucasians always seem to come out on top.

Holistically speaking, from a compassionate or spiritual perspective, is it truly any more important that Jesus or God be white, Chinese, Black, or Eskimo? *Should Christian love, if there is such a thing, not be colorless or at least color blind?* Ideally, of course. Because obviously, we're not living in a perfect world. Anything but.

As William Howell, the American anthropologist so eloquently stated, "that man, unlike other animals, is the creature who comprehends things he cannot see and believes in things he cannot comprehend." It truly does seem to be a part of our DNA to want to do the impossible, like walking on the moon or performing heart transplants, or to believe in a God whose complexity we cannot possibly understand or ever begin to appreciate. Being human, most of us have to believe in something. Leaving the church of my youth meant walking away from something I believed in and missing the great music, the delicious food and my homies. What else could I do? There were too many unanswered questions. Some of my friends are still at that church. An entire lifetime spent in the same place, singing the same old, tired songs, and seeing the same aging faces every seven days. Are you blessed and highly favored too, giving your life to Jesus? Is a punishing God scaring you straight?

I'm reasonably sure white people, seeing a black Jesus for the first time must have really been messed up too *(or another "up" proceeded by the "f" word)*, or maybe they were just angry or placidly amused. "Hey, look at that new cool-looking Jesus the black people have." Or, "Who the hell do these Negroes think they are? First, they wanted to vote; now, they think Jesus is a god damn spook too. Damn niggers are dumber than we thought. Shoulda' left their black asses back there in Africa where they belong anyway." Or, from the upper class, "It's absurd! Jesus simply cannot be black!" Well, whatever. For most white people he definitely *ain't* black. But Filipinos celebrate the Black Nazarene; Panamanians venerate Cristo Negro.

IF JESUS WAS BLACK, IT MEANS THAT HE WAS THE OPPOSITE, NOT ONLY PHYSICALLY, BUT EMOTIONALLY, PSYCHOLOGICALLY AND SPIRITUALLY OF WHAT WE ALL BELIEVE. *Because of black skin, Jesus might possibly have experienced even more hatred and been affected by it just as people of color are today.* Things like insecurity, self-hatred, low self-esteem and confusion. *Jesus!* (I need a job. The Romans want to throw me in jail, or kill me.) And if it is people of color who are indeed made in God's image, whose image are white people made in? Afterall, there were no white people in the Jewish Holy Scriptures. Jesus never saw a Caucasian.

In *The Black Messiah*, Reverend Albert Cleage, Jr. writes that *"Jesus was black and he was speaking to a black Nation.* He was always telling black people how to fight white people, so there wasn't any way in the world the whites could read Jesus and know what he was talking about today." Cleage said, *"We must realize that talking about love doesn't change our problems.* You can sing *'We Shall Overcome'* and you can talk about Redemption Suffering, but neither of these will change your earthly condition. *We have to concern ourselves with justice, not love."*

Reverend Cleage, who was born in 1911 and died in 2000, also said that Jesus Christ was a zealot and a revolutionary black leader. According to him, "<u>Black people cannot build dignity on their knees worshiping a white Christ</u>. We must put down this white Jesus which the white man gave us in slavery, which has been tearing us to pieces." And again, Reverend Cleage said Jesus was a black zealot (extremist) way back in the early 1900s. Modern school lessons now contradict old Sunday School lessons.

Dr. Cleage went on; *"We have been taught what someone else wanted us to know. What we have been taught about Christianity is what white people wanted us to believe, and used to keep black men enslaved."* He insisted that "Jesus was a black messiah who came to free a Black people [black Hebrews, God's chosen people] from the oppression of the white gentiles. We have accepted the white man's interpretation of our Christian faith because we had no alternative."

Reverend Cleage also said, "For nearly 500 years the illusion that Jesus was white dominated the world only because white Europeans dominated the world. Now, with the emergence of the nationalist movements of the world's colored majority, the historic truth is finally beginning to emerge—that Jesus was the non-white leader of a non-white people struggling for national liberation against the rule of a white nation, Rome."

"We no longer feel helpless as black people. We do not feel that we must sit and wait for God [who is supposedly white], to intervene and settle our problems for us. We waited 400 years and he didn't do much of anything, so for the next 400 years we're going to be fighting to change conditions for ourselves." Reverend Cleage said that almost 100 years ago. And when white domination ends does white Jesus also end?

After Jesus' time on earth during the first century nobody actually saw him again. We imagined what he must have looked like . . . But then here we were being told to picture him looking like something else . . . And equally important, somebody else. Voltaire, the 18th century anti-Christian French Deist (from the Enlightenment Period) who often ended up in the Bastille (prison), once wrote, *"If God did not exist it would be necessary to invent him."* Have we invented God? Have we invented notions of God and Jesus we feel comfortable with? Abraham, Buddha, Confucius, Moses, Muhammad, Zoroaster and most recently Baha'u'llah are also considered messengers from God. So, Jesus has plenty of company. In a 2008 Pew Forum survey, 52 percent of American Christians interviewed believe that following other faiths can lead to eternal life. Jesus then, isn't even alone when it comes to granting salvation. Only 46 percent of one group surveyed in this country believe in Creationism. That a supernatural being created everything— life, earth, and the universe as we know it.

I am reminded of a quiz show that aired in the late fifties and early sixties called *To Tell The Truth*. The host, Garry Moore (white, of course), would have three contestants on, identifying themselves by the same name. Number one, "I'm Hilton Hunter." Number two, "I'm Hilton Hunter." Number three, "I'm Hilton Hunter." Garry would then read a story about something that person had done (like being broke and winning a 50 million-dollar lottery), and three celebrity panelists guessed which one was telling the truth. Gary would then say, "Will the real Hilton Hunter please stand up." Hilton would stand, then the other two contestants would identify themselves as a plumber and a cabdriver. The idea was to trick the panelists into picking the wrong people. Maybe that's the way religion works too. WILL THE REAL JESUS CHRIST PLEASE STAND UP!

LIKEWISE, WILL THE REAL CHRISTIANITY PLEASE STAND UP! It was the late Dr. Paul Hutchinson, distinguished

Methodist minister and editor of the *Christian Century Magazine* who said, "To be sure, these living religions in which we can see our fellows seeking contact with the infinite did not materialize suddenly without ancestry. Sometimes their followers speak of them as unique, so utterly set apart from other faiths—past and present—as to be a spontaneous and self-contained spiritual manifestation, something akin to the biblical figure Melchizedek, 'without father, without mother, without descent, having neither beginning of days, nor end of life." Hutchinson says that "religions have their genealogy." *Religion came from somewhere. Christianity didn't just spontaneously materialize.* No faith ever uniquely existed in a vacuum. Whether it was magic, myths, or fertility rites, Christianity didn't just start in an instant with one big bang.

No matter how original or how unique we think it is, Christianity comes from a succession of other beliefs or religions. Tim C. Leedom, editor of *The Book Your Church Doesn't Want You To Read*, says that Zoroastrianism, an ancient Persian religion, was the blueprint for Christianity and Judaism. It was Zoroaster (628–511 BC) who first made man aware of the constant battle between good (Spenta Mainyu) and evil (Angra Mainyu, the devil), paradise, the last judgment, and the resurrection of the dead. *Zarathustra, Zoroaster, was sent by God, one God not many gods, an omniscient and loving Father to save his children.*

Jesus, like Zoroaster, was not the only god-man who died around Easter. *Attis, Dionysus, and Osiris, like Jesus and Zoroaster, were resurrected after three days as well. Zoroaster also used the exact same words Jesus did when he reportedly said, "I am the Way, the Truth, and the Light."* The language and the stories are almost identical, but Zoroaster was here over 600 years before Jesus arrived on the scene. So, did Zoroaster repeat what Jesus said and did, or was it Jesus who copied Zoroaster? But Buddha said it too, also centuries before Jesus.

According to William Lewis Edelen, in sixth-century BC Mithraism, *Mithra was known as "the way," "the truth," "the light," "the word," "the son of God," and "the good shepherd."* He was believed to have been born of a virgin, the shepherds were there, and Sunday was "The Lord's Day." Mithra's birthday was celebrated on December 25th, when he was wrapped in swaddling clothes and placed in a manger. Mithra had 12 companions (equal to 12 Zodiac signs), performed miracles, and his religion had a Lord's supper. Mithra was called *"Theos ek Petras"*, meaning *"God from the Rock"* while Peter was the Christian *"Rock."* Commodus, Marcus Aurelius' son, believed in Mithra, as did many Roman soldiers. Mithra's followers were all males, and they held their services in underground caves. Mithra was undeceivable, infallible, eternally watchful and never resting. Mithra was also buried in a tomb and removed three days later. Before Christianity there was Mithraism, superceded by Christianity, in addition to Zoroastrianism and other faiths. Attis was born of a virgin on December 25, crucified and resurrected three days later. Buddha's mother was a virgin named Maya. Ra, the Egyptian sun god's mother was a virgin too. Virgin birth was nothing new. The reason why Jesus' story was different was because unlike the others whose mothers had sex with some god, Mary never had sex with God, but became pregnant by the power of God. The Holy Spirit. *(Was Mary artificially inseminated?)*

In *The Book Your Church Doesn't Want You To Read,* Albert Churchward says that the Egyptian Horus, the revealer of immortality, and the father were one, just as Jesus and God are one. Horus, the son of the Sun God, shared other similarities with Jesus as well.

Horus's birthday is December 25th;
Jesus' birthday, December 25th.

Horus was baptized with water by Anup;
Jesus was baptized with water by John.
There were seven on board the boat with Horus;
There were seven fishers on board the boat with Jesus.

Horus was called the Lamb;
Jesus was called the Lamb.

Horus was a man of thirty years at his baptism;
Jesus was thirty years old at his baptism.

Horus was called the Krst;
Jesus was called the Christ.
The star was the announcer of the child Horus;

The star in the east indicated Jesus' birth place.
Three kings or Magi brought gifts to Horus;
Three wise men or Magi brought gifts to Jesus.

These are similarities Jesus shared with Horus and other spiritual leaders who lived long before he did. Noah's flood traces back 4,000 years to the ancient Babylonian Gilgamesh epic. It described the covered ark, rain, the dove, and the ark landing on a mountain 1000 years before Noah's boat, when Utnapishtim took his family and all species on a giant ship. Trees Noah used for wood hadn't even begun to grow yet, and building the ark took 120 years.

The idea of a messiah being born of a virgin was neither unique nor original. And contrary to what we may believe today, Jesus wasn't the only savior. There were many claiming to be prophets or messiahs, like Menahem, a power-hungry Jewish rebel who was also murdered. It was Menahem who famously recaptured Masada from the Romans. Simon son of Giora was another messiah, leading thousands of men in fighting the Roman Empire, killing upper-class Jews and freeing their slaves.

Before Jesus, even Abraham, the founder of three faiths—Christianity, Islam and Judaism paid tithes to Melchizedek, the high priest of the place we now know as Jerusalem, Shalem, before <u>the Greeks, who used a mind altering magic sacrament</u> renamed it. Melchizedek, as previously stated, unlike Jesus who succeeded him, was created without a father, without a mother, with no beginning, no relatives, and no end. So, this guy with no mom and no dad was once the king of Palestine, the Promised Land. (It's another one of those little things somebody wrote about that can't be explained, like the "walking dead people.")

Hebrews 7:1–3

This "King Melchizedek of Salem, priest of the Most High God, met Abraham as he was returning from defeating the kings and blessed him"; and to him Abraham apportioned "one-tenth of everything." His name, in the first place, means "king of righteousness"; next he is also king of Salem that is, "king of peace." *Without father, without mother, without genealogy, having neither beginning of days nor end of life,* but resembling the Son of God, he remains a priest forever. *(Nor end of life. Melchizedek's not dead yet.)*

Just as facts surrounding Melchizedek's birth are difficult to explain, so are the issues swirling around the prophet Abraham, a tenth-generation descendant of Noah. Jesus was at least considered to be a real person, but there is no actual proof that Abraham (father love), the Jewish patriarch God promised land to in Genesis ever lived. Or Moses either. Some scholars believe Abraham might have been a mercenary and traveling chieftain. *According to Rabbi Menachem Froman, "For me, Abraham is philosophy, Abraham is culture. Abraham may or may not be historical.* Abraham is a message of loving kindness. Abraham is an idea. Abraham is everything. *I don't need flesh and blood."* (Abraham wasn't a real person after all.) And that's coming from a highly respected Jewish rabbi. Docetics were gnostics who believed Jesus' body was an illusion that only appeared to be a man, spiritual, not physical. Then there were those who believed Jesus was a real man, made mythical.

In high school physics classes we learned that "matter can neither be created nor destroyed". You cannot create something from nothing. Don't forget, if there was no Abraham, there was no Jesus and no "Promised Land". Is the Bible about God or was it part of an elaborate scheme to acquire land and cattle that meant everything? *Follow the money!*

Before the 60s one thing most of us did actually believe was that God and Jesus were white, and living in heaven. These days, however, if Jesus was ever proven to be a person of color with non-white descendants, and God's lineage being black, Christianity would probably implode. Likewise, would a non-white Pope also mark the end of Catholicism? Is that the real reason why Jesus is almost always depicted as white? Does the myth of white supremacy actually begin with God?

CHAPTER 17

Abraham's Story

The name Abraham (formerly Abram, before God gave him a different handle and a new identity), is remarkably similar to the Hindu creator Brahma, with the "a" at the beginning of the name instead of the end, and another "a" in front of the "m." Hinduism, the oldest religion is over 4,000 years old, while Christianity is only 2,000 years old. And who is to say that Abraham wouldn't have changed his name for some other reason. Criminals and people who have something to hide do it all the time.

Remember, according to Jewish Scriptures, the God of Abraham made the Jews his chosen people and told Abraham, in his 70s, that his descendants would become a great nation and he would have plenty of land. That's what the Bible says Abraham said God said. Abraham was also the guy who told Sarah, his good-looking wife, to pretend to be his sister so Pharaoh wouldn't knock him off. Didn't Abraham think God would protect him? (Sarah was actually his half-sister.)

Sarah, Abraham's wife, I mean his biological half-sister, was Pharaoh's mistress until he discovered the truth, that she was Abraham's wife, and Pharaoh's household produced no children. Kicking the two of them out of Egypt with gold, silver and cattle made Abraham, who was already rich, an even richer dirty old man. So, the liar who conned Pharaoh is the same man who said God told him he was going to be rich and the father of a great nation. And we can't overlook the land. (Like one of today's preachers or bishops saying God told him he's getting a mansion in Beverly Hills, a new Bentley and a bank of his very own on Wall Street, after passing his "first lady" off as his sister.)

Israel, Abraham's grandson who changed his name from Jacob, said the same thing dear old granddaddy had said. On his way to Haran to marry a cousin or an aunt, Israel fell asleep using a rock for a pillow. He started dreaming, and in his dream (Jacob's Ladder), angels were climbing up to heaven and back and God was standing at the top. It was then that God promised him and the kids land, money, and power (somebody else's land). The same thing God promised grandpa. This was unusual. In the pagan religions the gods didn't generally get mixed up in other people's business. BUT JACOB WAS DREAMING TOO, JUST LIKE HIS GRANDPAPPY ABRAHAM HAD. And again, what was Jacob (Israel), doing before falling asleep and having visions; seeing things and talking to God? (Today people dream about money and lottery tickets.) One of the reasons why Jacob may have changed his name was because he was on the run for stealing his brother Esau's blessing. His inheritance. Jacob was a liar and a con just like grandpa. Was God's promise of land another scam?

Later, Abraham and Sarah moved to Palestine and told the same lie to King Abimelech, that Sarah was his sister. Abimelech fell for it just as Pharaoh had. (Remember, Sarah was hot.) And Abimelech and his household ended up with the same gynecological issues Pharaoh's household had. Of course, King Abimelech kicked Abraham and Sarah out too, just as Pharaoh had, with even more cattle, slaves and 1,000 pieces of silver. (Abraham really knew how to get paid didn't he?)

Genesis 20:18

> For the Lord had closed fast the wombs of all in Abimelech's household because of Sarah, Abraham's wife.

As Frederick Heese Eaton said in his book *Scandalous Saints*, paid for in his will after his death, "I'll bet you've never heard a preacher talking about any of the characters in the Bible causing women's wombs to be closed." We know female characters were often barren, but what do you think was meant by "a closed womb?" Even though Abraham led Sarah to sleep with other men, since men could have as many wives as they wanted as long as they could afford them, he never committed adultery, but she did. (Now that wasn't very kind of Abraham at all.) According to Eaton, "how could any decent husband have his own wife turning tricks and committing adultery, for any reason?" Especially a holy man like Abraham.

What about Sarah, still childless, telling Abraham to make out with Hagar, their Egyptian slave girl, because she couldn't have any kids. The Bible says that Abraham, who was one hundred years old, fell down laughing when God told him he was going to be a daddy, he and ninety-year-old Sarah. Freaked out, Sarah started laughing too, after overhearing God and two angels discussing her pregnancy as Abraham gave them food. (But why would God and a couple of angels be hungry, and what kind of tasty treats did Abraham feed his heavenly guests?) Nothing but the best, I'm sure.

Abraham and Sarah conspired to get Hagar knocked up, which was an accepted practice at that time, because after twenty-five years the child God promised was still a "no-show." Even though Abraham was God's number-one man, he and Sarah still didn't think God would deliver, just as Moses didn't believe it. Abraham and Sarah didn't believe God would keep his word, even though the Bible calls Abraham *a man of faith.* So Abraham had faith in God when he told him he would be the father of a great nation and have lots of money, but he didn't trust him when it came to being given a child. Can you believe that? (Not Abraham and Sarah!)

Hagar, a much younger woman was still in her prime. I'm reasonably sure she wasn't exactly thrilled at the idea of a wrinkled, shriveled-up, 86 year old man climbing on top of her. And would she be blamed if no child was conceived, or if the baby was a girl? Besides that Abraham was no Brad Pitt or Denzel Washington.

By the time their child Isaac was born, Hagar's son Ishmael (meaning "God has heard" in Hebrew), was already fourteen years old. Sarah, angry that Hagar had flaunted Ishmael, Abraham's first son in front of her, told

Abraham that Hagar and her kid had to go. *(Take your bastard and get the hell out of my house!)* As a matter of fact, because Sarah had not given Abraham an heir, according to Jewish law he could have made her a slave. So, Abraham, the millionaire, threw Hagar and Ishmael out before daybreak without blinking an eye, with nothing but bread and water and the clothes on their backs. (Now, that's cold-blooded even for Abraham.) Some scholars say that it was Sarah who was boss, and that Abraham went along with whatever she wanted. (Sarah was fine, and Abraham was her honey-do, just like Mary and Joseph.) When the bread and water ran out, God heard Ishmael out in the Negev desert, lost, crying and dying, and made Hagar a promise that Ishmael would also become the father of a great nation.

What I don't understand here is that if God is omnipotent and omniscient, all-powerful and all-knowing, how is it that he had to hear Ishmael crying and starving in the desert before realizing there was a problem, just as he didn't know that in addition to having animals in the Garden, Adam needed human companionship too? Hagar's and Ishmael's problems didn't just start out in the middle of the desert either, with no food and no water. There was a serious problem all the way back at the mansion when Abraham threw the two of them out simply because his "old lady," a woman of questionable virtue, was having a bad day. Definitely sounds "henpecked" and "punked" to me. *And if God knows everything, how can there be anything he doesn't know? How can anything surprise God?*

As Isaac (meaning "he who laughs") was growing into manhood, Abraham said he had yet another one of those long talks with God. (Isaac's name meant he who laughs because Abraham and Sarah, who was barren and already past menopause, thought the whole thing had to be a big joke.) Later God told him to sacrifice his son, but then stepped in at the last minute changing his mind. Isaac lived, and Abraham sacrificed a ram instead because God decided that Abraham had proven he could be trusted. (Pity the poor animals.) As you see, Abraham was very busy talking to God, who apparently changed his mind from time to make him happy. Or so Abraham said, maybe after taking a few puffs of hashish, drinking some vino, and having a little nap. In spite of everything Abraham had done (incest, pimping, and adultery), God said, "Abraham obeyed my voice and kept my charge, my commandments, my statutes and my laws," which absolutely shows that you can put a positive spin on anything. Remember, he didn't kill Isaac either, even though child sacrifice was common. *And if God had something important to say to his people, why just tell three people?* (Many clergy these days claim to talk to God, who tells them how to lead their poor sheep, their fleeced flocks.) Born 2000 years after Adam, Abraham allegedly died at 175 years old.

Little is known about Abraham before he was 75 when God appeared to him. Ham's black grandson, Cush's son Nimrod, an astrologer (fortuneteller) was king and the most powerful man in the world. Terah, another astrologer who was Abraham's father was in his court. It was Nimrod who founded Babylon, the first great empire after the Flood, as well as other famous nations and cities. Nimrod also built the Tower of Babel. Terah worshiped idols and twelve major gods, one for each month of the year. (Just as Jesus had 12 apostles that scholars now identify with the 12 signs of the Zodiac.) A member of Babylonian high society, Terah's cash-cow was manufacturing and selling idols and performing sacrifices from home.

Learning that Abraham, a special child would soon be born, Nimrod told Terah to bring the boy to him, strangling him with his own hands and ordering the death of 70,000 others. But Terah had already switched babies with a servant's child born the same day while Emtelia, Abraham's mom secretly delivered him in an empty cave. Forced to leave Abraham behind, the angel Gabriel showed up, feeding Abraham with milk from his finger. At ten days old Abraham was already walking and talking.

Fast forward to Abraham, a teenager breaking Terah's idols with an ax and being brought to Nimrod. Then refusing to worship fire as Nimrod did, and Nimrod baking him in a giant 5000 degree furnace. But like Moses' "burning bush" Abraham didn't incinerate either. Opening the furnace door and seeing Abraham with some angels Nimrod was horrified. *Imagine that!*

CHAPTER 18

Some "Not So Simple" Questions

At the beginning of *Let Us Prey* I posed three questions. Number one, is today's church crippling or helping? Number two, is it a benefit, liability, or even relevant? Number three, has the church retarded personal and societal development? As you see, asking tough questions can be problematic; asking one difficult question can lead to another, and another, and yet another. Dig too deep and you might not like what's been hidden or covered up, but you'll have a chance to find your own answers. Answers that are exactly what you need. LIKE ESTABLISHING REAL DIRECTION IN PLANNING AND LIVING YOUR OWN LIFE. Nietzsche wisely said, "that which does not kill us makes us stronger." KNOWLEDGE IS POWER, AND THE TRUTH, HOWEVER UNPLEASANT, CAN SET YOU FREE!

For me, the idea of there being two Jesuses, one black and one white is intriguing. Such irony, especially since it was the claim of there being two kings of the world, Jesus and Caesar, that got Jesus into trouble and ultimately crucified. The term *Kyrios*, or Lord of the World, used to represent Jesus also applied to Caesar and others. And remember, Caesar, like Christ, is also not a name but a title. I think it's interesting too, that not since ancient times had there been very much discussion about Jesus being black until the 1960s. Was the historical Jesus actually white, black, or possibly ... OTHER?

Whatever your answer, according to Campolo and Battle, *"for now, it suffices to say that while the black church has been grounded in a theology of liberation, its main thrust is still to adapt to the Western world."* As we see everyday, the path black people continue to choose makes them especially susceptible to negative, ruinous consequences.

In *Legacy of Tragedy,* Dr. Elfleda Tate says the following:

> What was selected centuries ago as truth, in spite of the false premises, was passed on to coming generations of Europeans by way of teaching, preaching and inaccurate observation. *These ideas were sold as a package marked Christianity.* What the European called religion was a cover for their lurid economics and policies. [*The behavior of the coming Europeans was barbaric, yet they claimed to be Christians!*]

When reading Western or European accounts, always take care in considering possible hidden agendas and the motivation of the individual or individuals telling any story. As Amiri Baraka, the African American writer said, *"there is no objective anything."* The Bible and Christianity, which are absolutely not objective, have been excellent cover for whites in telling their side, but what have they done for everybody else? As Reverend Cleage said, *"After 400 years of prayin' and waitin' on Jesus for miracles, what do blacks have to show for being good Christians?"* And what about those so-called miracles they pray for? If a man falls off of his roof and breaks his neck, it's bad luck. If he survives it's a miracle. Why couldn't his survival simply have been good luck, the opposite of bad luck, instead of a miracle? Dropping to your knees and calling it a miracle seems like something a backwoods West Virginia hillbilly might have done one or two hundred years ago, or maybe an illiterate sharecropper somewhere deep in Mississippi cotton fields. But that kind of thinking doesn't actually work in today's world because people are generally smarter. *Groveling and kneeling are definitely on their way out.*

When believers die is God going to greet them with open arms, sitting in his big chair somewhere up there in the clouds, with Jesus standing next to him? Is heaven real? Again, here on earth the reality is that many households are headed by single females and living in poverty. Fifty-two percent of black males are not graduating from high school in four years, and many have fathers who are unknown, unemployed, or in jail. Young people who are doing bad have given up because all around them what they see is hopelessness, helplessness, and the absence of any real support or direction.

Past generations found courage and comfort in a Christianity of faith, conviction, and solidarity, while what lingers today are only leftovers that have been hijacked and betrayed by self-serving bishops and CEO-ministers making millions of dollars, strutting around like kings. And like any scavenger, they are busy tearing at the flesh of what remains of the church, getting longer titles, advancing their careers, and getting bigger churches instead of serving the needs of their sometimes desperate, floundering congregations.

THE PREACHER HAS BECOME LORD OVER HIS OWN FIEFDOM. His inner circles are his royal subjects. The deacons are his knights, while ushers serve as his guards along with whatever security team (men in black) he might employ. (Those are the guys who know all "Rev's" tricks and secrets.)

For blacks in America Christianity is like the Democrat Party, a base constituency that can't see the forest for the trees. Christianity and Democracy are only illusions and labels, cruel hoaxes that have been used to miseducate and misdirect clueless, unsuspecting African Americans and others. The real question is can black people still be Christians without a white Jesus and a white God, or if they do not believe that Jesus Christ was God's son? What would the Bible's legacy be if the accounts of Jesus of Nazareth were discovered to be untrue? What would happen if the Bible was exposed as a lie? What would people do? How would they cope? ... What would *you* do if Jesus wasn't what you expected?

In the end, is there really any difference between primitives and ancients who prayed to a water god and a sky god, and people who simply pray to one God in the sky today, who helps them out and covers their backs? In fact, if the ancients could see us going to the moon, flying around in outer space and then coming back, or driving cars 70 miles an hour, wouldn't they think we were gods too? A millennia ago, the word *alien – from another planet*, did not exist, but there was a concept of a god or gods who lived above the earth. Today we know that the word alien means foreign, which is exactly what God or a number of gods who live above earth would be for us, foreign, or different. By that definition and by nature God is an alien. *He is not one of us and we are not clones of him.* God is not daddy! And do we still see God as a Supreme Being, or as an imaginary friend? Our new *Facebook* pal.

Today, we know about DNA, and how to perform heart transplants, eye transplants, liver transplants, etc., miracles by the ancients. In a recent thirteen-hour operation performed by sixteen doctors, twenty-six-year-old Brendan Marrocco, an Afghanistan quadruple amputee injured by a roadside bomb attack, had two arms reattached. Not his own arms, but a donor's arms. *Somebody else's arms.* Some people even consider such an astonishing event a miracle today. Computers will soon be inside our bodies, making us biological hybrids. And what about Thomas Beatie, the first man (transgender) to give birth to three children? Who is to say that many millennium ago there was not some alien with his own supercomputer who simply punched in a few digits, and voilà, here we are? Don't forget, the Bible says that God's sons came from somewhere else. How did an idea like that ever get into the Bible? Could anybody make up an extraordinary tale like that 2,000 years ago of beings from another planet landing on earth? What about Ezikiel's "wheel in a wheel" that roared like great waterfalls, like the noise of a battlefield, Elijah taken up to heaven in a chariot of fire, or the Dead Sea Scrolls flying "Divine Throne Chariot?"

With questions too, sometimes it's just better to know and to be part of the silent majority who understand, than to create unnecessary waves. It's personal and it's your call, but one thing is sure. We're not living in trees and caves anymore. BUT SOME PEOPLE ARE STILL PRAYING FOR MIRACLES, AND PREACHERS ARE BUSY SELLING THEM, ALONG WITH THE AGE-OLD IDEA OF HEAVEN. One hundred years ago poor black farmers sat outside on the front porches of broken down wooden shanties singing hymns and reading from the Bible, if they could read, the only book they owned, praising God. No fine carriages or matched teams of horses. And little or no education. But that era is over.

Today, if you really want to follow the right path, it's time to start thinking in the present, and past the next thing. Most married people are still gossiped about for having a close friend of the opposite sex (outdated Puritan morality). It's time to be rational and reasonable, with the right ideas at the right time. Time to be focused, and to exercise *intelligent faith* instead of *blind faith*. To put it succinctly, "WHEN YOU KNOW BETTER, YOU DO BETTER."

When I talk about thinking in the present I mean the 21st century. My personal best reference is the example of politicians and ministers who claimed that when Hurricane Katrina struck New Orleans the city was doomed, and God was punishing us for our sinful ways; sex, drinking, drugs, and Bourbon Street. Of course, most people immediately realized that any naysayers who could say something that stupid had already lost their minds. Any normal human being understood that God's wrath had nothing to do with what was happening. And I suppose those same naysayers still think thunder is God talking. If the sun's shinning with rain, the devil's beating his wife.

Now that Hurricane Sandy has wreaked havoc on people in New York and in New Jersey, changing lives forever, just like Katrina did to New Orleans, is God punishing them too? Maybe for *Wall Street* and *The Jersey Shore*? What about the people in Moore, Oklahoma, who were hit by a monster tornado, and the devastating tsunamis in Indonesia? It sounds like the naysayers think God is a twisted, sadistic sociopath.

I personally believe one of the reasons why we never appear to be making any progress is because the right questions never seem to get asked. Usually, it's the preacher or the politician, standing at his bully pulpit, both choosing and asking the questions, then answering them himself as he is cheered on by his "amen corner." In the black church, this behavior represents a tradition known as "call and response." It is based on something characterized as resonance, the matching of energy. The preacher gets his congregation excited by telling them something they already know, putting a new spin on it, and turning it into something deliciously unfamiliar. There is no transfer of information, only an emotionally charged, exhilarating feel-good moment without any real substance. Besides feeling good there's nothing else. Except for the fact that your pockets and purses are a bit lighter.

As a teenager, I witnessed something in my church that I still remember to this day. I had volunteered to do some artwork and stumbled upon a group of about seven preachers practicing their sermons for Sunday services. I was caught completely off guard. They were literally practicing, rehearsing, like student actors do for parts in their high school plays, complete with inflections, gestures, histrionics, and even shouting. "Say it like this" and "do it like that." The preachers were sharing each other's moves so they could present more dramatic and more convincing presentations to their unsuspecting congregations. *Remember, Rev's paycheck depends on his performance!* Copper Inuit shamans actually think the tricks they use bring them closer to their gods, and who knows, Rev may think that about his own tricks. God approves.

After the episode I witnessed I was really mixed up. Before that, poor naïve little me, a babe in the woods, had always thought that what I saw on Sunday mornings was spontaneous. Real. You know, inspired by God. Remember, this was a church. They were supposed to be preachers, not actors. Maybe busting them like that explains why I'm so twisted today . . . And that's a good thing. Another good thing is that Jesus really does inspire me, like so many others, to do the right thing and to be a better person. Seeing myself as a deist, much like Thomas Paine and George Washington, I believe that someone or something created all this cosmic order, and appreciate Jesus the Nazarene as a prophet and sage. If Jesus was the perfect son of God I would be sorely disappointed. Somebody who was perfect probably couldn't help me. What I need is real world, hands-on experience.

It would be short-sighted to merely say the Jews killed Jesus. Some believed they had killed God. *Can God die?* That corrupt Jewish priests, conspiring with an equally corrupt Roman authority, supported by an ignorant Jewish following murdered Jesus would be more accurate. Jesus, a Jewish victim of Roman violence was transformed into a Christian victim of Jewish violence. Were Jews unfairly blamed? What goes unrealized is how corrupt the ancient church really was. All anyone needs to do is take a real look at Jesus and his disciples, seriously and critically, according to the accounts, to see that they were single-handedly doing the best they could, fighting for something they believed in.

I have a few more simple questions that you might want to consider. Well, maybe they're not quite so simple. After reading some of the things you've already read and discovering who some of the early Jews and Christians were and what they did, WOULD JESUS HAVE AGREED OR DISAGREED WITH WHAT'S IN THE HOLY BIBLE? WOULD HE APPRECIATE HOW CHRISTIANITY IS BEING PRACTICED TODAY? WOULD JESUS, A LOYAL AND DEVOTED JEW, A TRUE JEW, EVEN BE A CHRISTIAN? WOULD JESUS' CHURCH BE TODAY'S SUPERRICH ROMAN CATHOLIC CHURCH IN ROME, RUN BY ITALIANS AND

THEIR POWERFUL RELATIVES, THE SAME CORRUPT HIERARCHICAL TYPES WHO MURDERED HIM? Remember Pope Francis' words, *"I want a poor church for poor people."* The pope also warned against the dangers of a church that finds its security in resources instead of the free gift of the gospel. *If that old Negro hymn is true, "He's Got the Whole World in His Hands," why are poor people and black people still suffering while the rich and powerful are getting richer and becoming more powerful? If God takes care of the poor and the needy, why then are they still poor and needy?* The preachers say God knows what you need before you do. Again, why hasn't Jesus returned? Or has he?

As Socrates wisely stated, "I know that I know nothing" because "neither of us knows anything that is really worth knowing." Nobody. IT'S ALL AN ILLUSION! Everything is relative. Especially religion and religionists who claim to be wiser by saying they know things they cannot possibly know, especially about God, simply because they read some books in divinity school. Taking a few classes, tacking a PhD after your name and calling yourself doctor isn't knowing God. One must experience God. (Hi, I'm Reverend Jones. That's Dr. Jones, and I'm a doctor of God.) *How does one become a doctor of God anyway?* The same way he becomes a bishop, I suppose. PAY TO PLAY! Go to bishop school and you're a bishop. (And can you flunk out?)

In my opinion today's preachers, priests and bishops are nothing but 21st Century Pharisees. I think that anybody who just wakes up in the morning, puts on a collar and calls himself a preacher or a bishop is illegitimate. Just making up a title with no real authority. They couldn't make it through the front door so they created their own back door. My friend Derek laughingly says "Some are called. Some are sent. And some just went."

Jesus' job was to bring peace, redeeming humanity from injustice and violence, rescuing those who were struggling for real freedom, which clearly has not happened. The world is even more screwed-up now than it was then. Did Jesus actually fail in his mission to save man? And don't forget he never became king of Israel either. "IN THE END, IT'S ALMOST ALWAYS ALL ABOUT THE MONEY AND THE POWER. ESPECIALLY IN THE CHURCH!"

After reading *Let Us Prey*, I'm sure there will be as many questions and answers as there are readers. But I elaborated on many other things too. Like the need to stay focused, and the importance of handling your own business. The Supreme Court recently handed down two groundbreaking decisions. First, key parts of the Voting Rights Act have been struck down. Second, Justices ruled against DOMA, the Defense of Marriage Act.

In the former ruling, black Americans in particular have been broadsided when it comes to participating in the political process, because the court no longer feels that minorities face discrimination in voting. Those who wanted to make sure it is more difficult for blacks and other minorities to be treated fairly have won. Racial discrimination in voting, which may have been somewhat undercover, is open for business again, as we have all observed in recent Republican shenanigans. A Republican Party that nominates candidates whose wealthy fathers run the world does not want the average citizen to have a voice or alter the status quo.

Future generations are now destined to live without a fundamental protection that has been guaranteed since 1965. Nine states, primarily in the South, can now change their election laws without advanced Federal approval (i.e., redistricting or moving polling places). Texas has already announced that a voter identification law that had previously been blocked will now go into effect. For example, someone can vote with a gun permit, but not a college ID. *Voter suppression is supposed to be illegal.* (By the way, I personally believe that the Supreme Court should be renamed the "Supremely Political Court," since all nine justices are alumni of only two law schools, Harvard and Yale, and decisions definitely appear to run along party lines.) Now the Supreme Court has struck down limits on campaign contributions from wealthy donors, which is going to corrupt the system even more in favor of the rich and against the average American citizen. Unsurprisingly the court announced that just as a corporation is a person, money is now the same as free speech. (During slavery laws also favored rich masters, so nothing ever really changes.)

In the latter ruling concerning DOMA, gays who are legally married in states that recognize same-sex marriage are now legally recognized by the United States government. It means that they may now receive the same entitlements as heterosexual couples, such as Social Security and even military benefits.

Why did winners win and losers lose? That's easy. The winners stayed focused, fighting for their cause for over ten years. Distracted, the losers were busy celebrating the election of our first black president, watching *The Real Housewives of Atlanta*, or kissing Rev's ass. They were too jubilant and pride-filled to make even reasonable or modest demands of our new president. *Winners always reward supporters, doing something to alleviate their pain!* <u>*Quid pro quo*</u>. *Something for something.* Minorities, especially our kids will continue to suffer because we dropped the ball, particularly the so-called black leadership and Democratic leadership, while the "white tribe" handled its business, picking judges and getting tax cuts. The chickens hatched then got pulverized! White backlash was imminent. Jim Crow lynchings proved that. Feeling aggrieved and threatened by changing demographics (immigration, globalization and multiculturalism), white people want things the way they used to be, the primacy, freedoms, self esteem, and privileges they used to have. Hence, *"minorities will not replace us!"* <u>Power versus population</u>. *White people will not move to the end of the line or back of the bus. And will Jesus still be white?*

Speaking of money, why do some people give such a big chunk of theirs to somebody who doesn't respect or appreciate them? Are they competing for status? Based on who gives the most, one church has generals. Members should give what they can afford, not what some arrogant, ego-driven preacher orders them to pony up. If you happen to be one of those church groupies, the time is long overdue to take your head out of whatever orifice it may be in.

One of my favorite quotes comes from Mark Twain: *"Life is a competition between you and yourself."* Do your best, be your best! Be ready for whatever comes your way. Not stuck living in the past. Quoting Malcolm X, "Tomorrow belongs to the people who prepare for it today."

CHAPTER 19

The Bible, Adam & Eve

Many of today's Christians believe that the Bible, written by at least forty different writers, including a tax collector and a leather worker, living at different times and in different places, was divinely inspired and is the true story of Jesus. The authors spoke different languages, Hebrew, Aramaic, Latin and Greek, *taking 1,600 years to write the Bible (Holy Scriptures),* over 2,000 years ago. (The Bible was obviously not written at one time.) Another thing most people do not realize is that the New Testament was written many, many years after Jesus died, but it's neither a diary nor a biography. Many historians have thrown in the towel on Jesus.

Mark was written thirty years after Jesus' death, decades after Paul, and like the *Didikai* contained no infancy narrative and no resurrection. Matthew and Luke were written fifteen years later, following Mark's lead but adding contrary infancy narratives and resurrection accounts. John was written sixty years after Jesus died, focusing on his divinity. *The disciples didn't just sit down together to write a book about Jesus because they didn't write the Bible.* Separate stories about Jesus told over and over again, after he was crucified, were finally written down by Greeks who didn't even know him. Matthew, Mark, Luke and John were not written by the disciples themselves, but by followers (their own disciples- secretaries), in their names, in Greek. No one gospel writer gives the whole story. *Nobody who knew Jesus probably ever wrote anything about him.*

Because gospel writers heard different stories, all Bibles are not alike. Some things are omitted in one but included in another. *So there is no "one" word of God, and no one has access to the original text.* Believers claim that the Bible means what it says and says what it means, even though Bibles say different things. What did people think and believe? Do today's words mean the same thing? (In ancient times *world* meant Roman Empire). We see things radically different, like time itself.

The Bible symbolizes the Holy Scripture of Judaism, Jewish people and their ancestors, their world and what they believed, their myths and folklore. Hebrews is undoubtedly about them. The Holy Bible is their history book; much of the Old Testament, which took 1000 years to compile comes from the Jewish Tanakh. The first four books of the New Testament are called the Gospels. The term gospel is Anglo-Saxon, meaning "Good News."

Is the Bible actually based on historical facts, or myths and legends? Are the stories true? According to Bart D. Ehrman, in December 17, 2012's *Newsweek* magazine:

> It is worth considering that much of the "common knowledge" about the babe in Bethlehem cannot be found in any scriptural authority, but is either a modern myth or based on Gospel accounts from outside the sacred bounds of Christian Scripture.
>
> *For many centuries, most Christians garnered their information about the birth of Jesus not from the New Testament, but from popular writings that were not officially considered scripture.* One of the best known of these books is called the "Proto-Gospel of James."
>
> *Christians throughout the Middle Ages were rarely interested in historical accuracy; they loved stories . . .* These are not views of the Bible, but of the Proto-Gospel of James. Luke and Matthew both want to relate Jesus to the ancestral line of the Jewish patriarchs, but neither of them has access to the kind of reliable data they need for the task. So they have provided genealogies that have been invented for the purpose, and as a result, are at odds with each other. (Not factual proof of anything.)
>
> Only in Luke's Gospel do Joseph and Mary make a trip from their home in Nazareth to Bethlehem in order

to register for a census when "the whole world" had to be enrolled under Caesar Augustus. We have good documentation about the reign of Caesar Augustus, and there never was a census of his entire empire. Let alone one in which people had to register in their ancestral home. *In this account Joseph and Mary need to register in Bethlehem (which is why Jesus is supposedly born there) because Joseph is descended from King David, who came from Bethlehem.* But David lived a thousand years earlier. Is everyone in the entire Roman Empire returning to their ancestral home from a thousand years earlier?

This is not a story based on historical fact. *It is a narrative designed to show how Jesus could have been born in Bethlehem—whence the Messiah was to come—when everyone knew, in fact, that he came from Nazareth.*

Christianity is based on the Bible, from the Greek *biblia*, which means "book." It is a collection of sixty-six separate books put into one and divided into two parts, the Old Testament, which deals with the history of the Israelites (Hebrews), or Jewish people (the children of Abraham), and the New Testament, which addresses the life of Jesus Christ. Again, according to the Bible, Jesus Christ, born king of the Jews, was the son of God, born half man and half God, who came down to earth to save mankind. Something you may not realize, however, is that during Jesus' time there was no New Testament. So Jesus used the Old Testament and the unverified Apocrypha, the hidden books, which many of us have never heard of. Tobit, Judith, 1 and 2 Maccabees, Wisdom, Sirach, Baruch, parts of Esther and parts of Daniel. None are Canon Law. He had knowledge of the Five Books of Moses, the Prophets, and Writings like Psalms and Proverbs. Moses' books, meant only for Jews, mattered for 1,400 years. And just as the books of the gospels weren't complete then, the Bible may not be complete today.

The five books of Moses: Genesis, Exodus, Leviticus, Numbers, and Deuteronomy, are collectively known in Hebrew as the Torah, or

Pentateuch in Greek. Fundamentalists believe that God dictated them to Moses word by word. Others believe Moses wrote the books but there was nothing divine about them. *The first five books, plus oral histories, are the written and oral laws, plus the fundamental narrative of the Jews and how their God created them.* REMEMBER, IN THE HOLY BIBLE GOD CREATED THE ISRAELITES, THE JEWISH PEOPLE, MAKING THEM SPECIAL AND NOT LIKE EVERYBODY ELSE!

According to midrash, an ancient commentary or interpretation of part of the Hebrew Scriptures, the Torah was even created before the world was created. Many biblical scholars believe the five books attributed to Moses originated while the Israelites were exiled in Babylon, with its advanced society, ending about 400 years before Jesus arrived on the scene. Today, some scholars are convinced that the Torah was written over centuries by different men, and not by Moses. The Five Books were created around 450 BCE by combining the works of the Jahwist "J," the Elohist "E," the Deuteronomist "D," and the Priestly source "P."

Genesis *Bereshit* means "in the beginning." This is related to primeval history, then Abraham and his descendents and the Promised Land with Jacob's sons leaving Canaan to go to Egypt because of a famine. Exodus *Shemot* means "names," naming the sons of Israel who came out of Egypt. Leviticus, *Vayikra,* means, "and he called," and deals with running the sanctuary and God calling Moses. Numbers, *Bamidbar,* means "in the wilderness," and describes the Israelites' forty years in the desert. Deuteronomy, *Devarim,* means "words," which Moses spoke to the Israelites about their journey. *Moses made Joshua his successor, and then just disappeared with nobody ever seeing him again.* Joseph first disappeared the same way right after Jesus was born. Why?

For centuries scribes meticulously attempted to record the Scriptures letter by letter to preserve their integrity and authenticity. (Some Greek translators deliberately made changes, and forgery was also common.) Much like today, there was money in forgeries, and forgeries were also another way of supporting a particular position, like Christianity, by saying the work was written by an apostle instead of some insignificant nobody people had never heard of before. Individuals credited with writing the Bible didn't. The work was written in their names for status. Brand names make people feel better too, higher self esteem. *Jesus' disciples were unlearned and untrained (Acts 4:13). Nobody could write down what Jesus said to them or what they said to each other.*

Bart Ehrman says that "*many people who wrote the New Testament lied about their identity, claiming to be a famous apostle . . . Peter, Paul, or James . . . knowing full well they were someone else.* In modern parlance that is a lie, and a book written by someone who lies about his identity is a forgery. Lies today are tactfully called pseudepigrapha." As an example, Bible scholars say there is no way 2 Peter was written by Peter himself, and many writings attributed to Paul were not written by him either, like 1 Timothy, written after Paul had already died. In 1 Timothy women were commanded to be silent and submissive (barefoot and pregnant), which was not something Paul, who had female followers, would have said. It was somebody else's position. And, of course, even before the writings and forgeries there were only oral traditions, *including drug secrets.* Those stories became the Old Testament.

In the 4th Century, Jerome, a Christian scholar spent three decades translating the Greek Bible into Latin. (Frankly, I still don't see how somebody who wasn't there would know what God told one person 2,000 years ago out in the desert.)

Is the "Holy Bible" holy? Is it "the word of God?" And can it be disproved? In his book *Deceptions and Myths of the Bible*, Lloyd Graham's answer is "*There is nothing 'holy' about the Bible nor is it the word of God." It was not written by God-inspired saints, but by power-seeking kings and priests, re-editing and retranslating to suit their own purposes.* In addition to the re-editing, retranslating and mistranslating, there were also misinterpretations based on the interpreters own biases and points of view. Remember, most scholarship, even concerning the Bible, was based on the white, male, European model. (What else is new?)

Again, one of the reasons the Gnostic Gospels were excluded from the Bible was their having been considered heresies by the priests who had too much to lose. Even the book of Revelation almost didn't make it into the Bible because the story was unbelievable. Too outrageous!

God's character was personified and never meant to be worshiped. The Bible, the word of God was stolen from pagan sources. Eden, and Adam and Eve were taken from Babylon. Moses is fashioned after the Syrian Mises; its messiah derived from the Egyptian Mahdi (Savior), and certain verses are verbatim Egyptian Scriptures." Don't forget, Moses' Ten Commandments (over 600 do's and do not's meant only for ancient Israelites), came from Hammurabi and the Babylonian tradition. Both reminiscent of "The Golden Rule".

The original first, Graham asserts, or Creation, including God, are personifications written by Jhwhist, a Hebrew mythologist, much like the Greek, Homer. His God, like those of Homer, *were never meant to be worshiped. IN MYTHOLOGY GODS WERE SUPERIOR TO HUMANS BUT NOT SAINTS OR ANGELS.* For their own purposes, the priests turned the personifications into a supernatural version mentioned earlier. (God created everything just by saying "Let It Be"). The creation story was a myth. *Man was now a sinner who needed the priests' help for salvation.* (Priests and preachers were making sure it stayed that way or they would have to go out and find real jobs, working like everybody else, the way preachers used to). Even Paul had a job working as a traveling tentmaker to support his ministry.

Myths taught important lessons, but were never meant to be taken literally, as reality. It was the ancients' way of explaining the unexplainable in a manner they found acceptable and could conceivably live with. Their stories were symbolic reflections of their struggle to find expression in their own existence. Man invented God and the concept of gods who were beyond human comprehension. The ancients believed that instead of being controlled, sometimes they could control their gods.

Pagan gods were more like old friends who also provided protection. (Friends with benefits.) In the Greek tradition gods visited their heroes and favorites (buddies). And only those who were deserving could see them whenever they made an appearance (just as the emperor's new clothes, in the tale by Hans Christian Anderson, were only to be visible to those who were deserving.) Only God's chosen could see him, or see Jesus after his crucifixion. Anybody who couldn't see them wasn't deserving or special enough. *Everybody wants to be a member of God's club, and nobody wants to be kicked out, so the myth lives on.*

Like the child in *"The Emperor's New Clothes"*, someone should have said something about burning bushes that talked, a talking snake, and the walking, talking, cross that came out of the tomb with a giant Jesus and two angels as tall as mountains in the Gospel of Peter. *In paganism even a very beautiful woman or an extremely handsome man could be mistaken for a god or goddess, too perfect to be mere mortals. Superstars (heroes), like LeBron James and Tom Brady gods; Marilyn Monroe and Beyonce goddesses.*

According to Homer, gods and humans hung out and even ate together (like Jesus and the disciples at the Last Supper, a psychoactive sacrament). Like the gods who kept coming back, forty days after his resurrection Jesus spent time with his followers too, appearing in the locked room where they were hiding from the Romans. Jesus reappeared at the Sea of Tiberius, and later before 500 people. Pagan concepts.

Graham adds that "because Western man is incapable of abstract thought, all the metaphysical and cosmological knowledge Western man has came to him from the East. *In his metaphysical incompetency, Western man puts the stamp of his own ego on everything, including the Creator (being made in his image).* That part of him called Christian could not even create a God or religion for himself; he had to borrow stories from Middle Eastern Jews. We had entered a period of materialism and hence spiritual blindness." In 125 A.D., Bishop Irenaeus said "there were a multitude of gospels" but only Matthew, Mark, Luke and John, written in Greek were God's word, not myths. Quoting Graham, *"What remains in our popular King James Version of the Bible are those Gospels that were not destroyed or omitted on purpose."*(And can you imagine a 5,000 page bible? Who would ever read it, or even try to pick it up?)

Although so-called devout Christians claim to live according to the Bible and God's word, many remain fundamentally ignorant of it.

For example, most of them are not familiar with the possibility of two creation stories in the book of Genesis, the first taking place on the sixth day. In the first account, Lilith was seen as a partner, written from a vision given to Moses, not a subordinate like Eve.

Genesis 1:26	Then God said, "Let us make man in our image, in our likeness, and let them rule over the fish of the sea and the birds of the air, over the livestock, over all the earth, and over all the creatures that move along the ground."
1:27	So God created man in his own image, in the image of God he created him; *male and female he created them. (The same day he created animals.)*

AND

Genesis 2:18	The LORD God said, "It is not good for the man to be alone. I will make a helper suitable for him."
2:21	But for Adam no suitable helper was found. So the LORD God caused the man to fall into a deep sleep; and while he was sleeping, he took one of the man's ribs and closed up to the place with flesh. Then the LORD God made a woman from the rib he had taken out of the man, and he brought her to the man.
Genesis 2:23	The man said, "This is now bone of my bones and flesh of my flesh; she shall be called woman." [If God used Adam and his rib as DNA to create Eve, how did other female animals get here?] Did God create male and female animals at the same time, but somehow forget that Adam needed companionship too?

Whenever my friend Fortunata speaks about the magical, talking snake who tempted Adam and Eve in the Garden of Eden, she insists that it was actually Adam's "snake, with a big head," and you can guess what she says it was telling him once he figured out what to do with it. In Greek mythology, Zeus, as a snake, seduced Olympias. Lilith left Adam because he always wanted to be on top when they were doing "the wild thing." Adam really was an animal!

They were created from dirt simultaneously, at the same time, but Adam wanted his partner to be subordinate to him, ordering her to "Lie Beneath Me." Thinking this fool had lost his mind, Lilith wasn't feelin' it. She refused. After pronouncing God's name she became a powerful demon and flew off to heaven. Three angels were sent to bring her back, and she refused. Why should Adam boss her around? Known as the night demon, she was accused of molesting young men who slept alone, the evidence being "wet dreams."

According to the Bible, Adam and Eve knew they were in trouble after eating the fruit (it doesn't say "apple"). In reading the Bible, however, you've got to learn to read between the lines (midrash). *Did Adam and Eve actually realize they didn't have any clothes on because they had eaten a delicious fruit that was innocently dangling from a lovely tree, or was the real truth the fact that they got into trouble for playing with "Adam's snake" all day and half the night?* Not some magical talking snake, but a carnal snake that wouldn't take no for an answer. And as for the so-called "apple" Adam ate, Eve's apple, Fortunata claims that it was probably a different fruit. Eve's *fuzzy* cherry. Imagine yourself in a lush green forest in Hawaii with your significant other, your hormones are racing, and you don't have any clothes on. And Adam was a young man, so you know where his mind was and which *"head"* he was doing his thinking with. Eve could clearly see what he was thinking about too, running around the garden naked. She could feel it too, if he was standing close enough. And don't forget, Adam had experience from his first marriage. He had already learned a thing or two from Lilith.

In Genesis, the creation narrative, when God told Adam and Eve not to eat from the tree, what language did God use? Remember, Adam and

Eve were the only two people on earth, so there was no language yet, not even Aramaic or Hebrew. (Today, there are only 200,000 people in the world who still speak Aramaic. Many live in the suburbs of Chicago.) What language did the snake use in tempting Eve in the Garden? (In the Epic of Gilgamesh a snake steals a plant that gives eternal life.) Either he was very persuasive, like Gabriel, or it must have been a really big, fat, long snake and Eve couldn't help herself. Maybe Eve gave Adam that fruit to take having sex off of his mind!

Like Adam and Eve, God made the snake, so he had to have known what his creation was capable of. And what was the point of the tree in the Garden of Eden in the first place? Was it always God's plan that Eve would allegedly corrupt Adam?

The ancient Romans agreed with Fortunata. Apples had nothing to do with it. Playing with Adam's snake and having sexual intercourse were the real sins, especially for celibate priests who believed that sex for the purpose of producing offspring was appropriate, but sexual intercourse just for fun was a sin. (You know how priests feel about somebody else having a good time.) There are those today who still believe that any position but missionary is wrong, and don't even think about oral or anal sex. (Rev's not one of them. He's at the front of the line when it comes to having a good time.) As a teenager, I recall people talking about how nasty anybody was who performed oral sex (definitely not a black thing, or so they said). One acquaintance of mine, an insurance agent, actually threw his girlfriend out of a second-story window for trying to give him a "head job." The poor woman, who was attractive, educated, and very decent, was only trying to show him how much she loved him. He didn't see it that way.

For committing lascivious sins the ultimate punishment was death, but then every living thing dies and decomposes sooner or later doesn't it? In a male-dominated society, as far as the original sin is concerned, the whole thing was Eve's fault. Adam and his excitable snake were innocent bystanders who were being taken advantage of, just dangling around and minding their own business in the Garden of Eden.

Shame on Eve. She knew God's will, but like any other woman, she did what she wanted to do anyway. Eve made the mistake of hanging around and listening to the lying, talking snake, rather than walking away while she could, before it got too close. (If a good-for-nothing snake is lying to you, shouldn't you be walking away before it bites you too?) The snake was only symbolism for Satan. Not real!

There is still one more twist to the Adam and Eve story. Another pre-Adamite view was that Eve was tempted by a Negro in the Garden of Eden. That meant yet another reason to hate black males, and a double whammy if you think about a big, thick, shiny black snake tempting Eve. That was the curse. A little pale white snake might have been all right.

The Bible says since that time in the Garden when they disobeyed God and ate from the tree of life, man would have to work for his food and women would suffer during childbirth. Adam died at 930 years old, which meant that he was grubbing for food for a long, long time. But Adam wasn't alone in his old age. He and Eve had Seth when he was 130 years old, and he lived another 800 years after that. His son Seth lived 912 years, Enosh, Seth's son, lived 905 years, and Kenan, his son, lived 910 years. Methuselah, Noah's grandfather had Noah's father Lamech at 187 years old and died at 969 years old. Noah had his sons Shem, Ham and Japheth after he was 500 years old. Like I said, there was some serious grubbing going on for a *very long* time. (Exactly when did people start living normal life spans, and why?) Did everybody in the world live to be hundreds of years old or only Israelites? *God's people!*

How old were Adam and Eve when God planted them in his wonderful garden? Were they eight years old, twelve, twenty-one years old? It makes a difference, you know. Imagine infancy (nursing without a mom), childhood, adolescence and puberty. Did they both start off at the same age? Was Adam older or was Eve older? Why did Eve have to listen to Adam? According to the first account in the Bible, God created them at the same time, and called them both "man." (So, Adam was cheeky from day one.) And don't forget about the two cherubim (angels) with four heads (human, eagle, bull, and lion), and four wings, who guarded the Garden of Eden with flaming swords to make sure Adam and Eve didn't go back inside.

Humanist Samuel Clemens, better known as Mark Twain, had his own ideas about Adam and Eve, as revealed in *The Bible According To Mark Twain*, by Howard G. Baetzhold and Joseph B. McCullough. Typical of his style, Mark Twain's observations are filled with blasphemy, sarcasm, and cynicism. This, even though he had read the entire Bible by the time he was fifteen, according to him. For instance, Mark Twain could ask questions like "Did Christ live for thirty-three years in each of the millions and millions of worlds (heavenly bodies) above us, or was it only Earth, our own pigmy little world that was so special to him?" Flying over the Vatican I was thinking the same thing.

Climbing into the heavens I found myself strangely wondering where God was. If he was somewhere around. If God lived in heaven he had to be up there over Rome. *Somewhere, or everywhere!* Even more curious, when astronauts are in outer space is God outside surrounding their space capsule too, but they just can't see him because he's invisible? If he wasn't over the Vatican and he's not in outer space, exactly how far out into the universe would one have to travel before finding God? Just how far up is "up" enough? Did mountain climbing really help Moses find God? I know and you know I'm a little "throwed off".

In *Adam's Diary,* Twain's Adam talks about a new creature with long hair who is always following him around and getting in the way. He wishes "it" would stay with the other animals because he's not used to having company. Adam doesn't get to name anything either because the new creature always beats him to it. And it's always talking, especially about "we," a word he has never heard before. The new creature eats too much fruit too, and it wants to be called Eve. And it says it's not an "it," but a she. (Even in Mark Twain's day, 100 years ago, women liked fruit. How about them apples?)

When he builds a shelter for himself, she goes inside, and when he tries to put her out, water comes out of her face and she wipes it away with the back of her paws, making a distressed animal noise (crying).

Adam has never heard a human voice before, and this one is too close. Right next to him. And if Eve keeps eating all the fruit, they'll run out. Adam escapes, but she hunts him down, making that pitiful noise again, and shedding that water which she calls tears. Adam goes back with her, but the first chance he gets he's running away again. (He can't take it anymore.) Eve tells Adam that she is made from one of his ribs, but he doubts it, since he isn't missing any.

Adam notices that Eve has started hanging around with a snake too, who tells her to eat from the tree that they have been told not to eat from. He cautions her to stay away from it (the snake), but Eve doesn't listen. *(Not a good idea.)* Adam thinks it would have been better if he hadn't said anything at all. *(Women!)* He sees trouble coming and is ready to leave.

He takes off that night on a horse riding as fast he can, and the next morning while riding through a peaceful plain, a thousand animals suddenly started fighting and destroying each other. That can only mean one thing. Death has entered the world because Eve has eaten the forbidden fruit. The tigers even eat his horse. When Eve finds Adam, he is so hungry that he eats some of the apples too. And this time she looks foolish, covered in leaves. Adam tells her to make him some clothes too, out of dead animal skins. (Embarrassed and ashamed at their nakedness.)

While Adam is away at length trapping, Eve catches a creature that they named Cain, believing it to be a fish. But Adam notices that Eve feels closer to it than she does to the other animals, carrying it around in her arms, patting its back and making soothing sounds. Adam also says that he is beginning to have doubts about it being a fish, because he has never seen a fish that laughs before. But it can't be one of them either because it doesn't walk, it's not a bird because it doesn't fly, it's not a frog because it doesn't hop, or a snake because it doesn't crawl. It just lies around on its back with its feet up. Adam says he feels sorry for the poor noisy little animal. He says if it dies he will take it apart to see what it's made of. But they only have one sample. Next he thinks it's a kangaroo, but it has fur on top of its head, just like his. Then he thinks it's a bear. Four months later it is saying *"poppa"* and *"momma."*

Determined to discover what it is, Adam goes off to find his own, but Eve gets lucky again and traps another one while he is gone. Eve calls her new parrot Abel, and Adam wants to stuff one of them for his collection. After ten years, Adam realizes that they are boys.

In *Eve's Diary*, Mark Twain shows us the Garden of Eden from Eve's point of view. Eve wonders who she is, what she is, and where she is. She soon realizes that the other creatures have mates. Eve notices that the animals talk to each other and are friends, but since she doesn't understand what they are saying, they must be smarter than she is.

Eve says she feels like an experiment, that she is tired, and that her feet hurt after that first day, walking to the edge of the circle (the horizon), to try to collect some pretty stars to put into a basket. The next day she follows the other experiment around (Adam), believing it is a man, with frowsy hair and blue eyes, even though she has never seen one. Tracking it as she does makes it nervous and unhappy, and the first time she hears the other experiment speak she doesn't understand the words. Eve says that she loves to talk, even in her sleep. And if the other experiment is a man, it's not an "it," but a "he." He avoids her and doesn't seem to want to talk to her, while Eve says that she was made for company.

She starts using "we" because he seems to enjoy being included. After a while, they are getting along better too, and she's doing everything she can to be a help to him, including naming things because he is so busy. Eve says she just seems to know by its shape what it is. That night she feels lonely, but when she goes to his shelter, he puts her out in the rain. The next morning she is at work improving the estate again, creating fire, smoke, flames, and staying away from him. Fire also creates fear which keeps him away. She hopes that he would praise her for improving the estate, but nothing.

Adam, however, is keeping something to himself. He thinks Eve is beautiful and remarkable in many ways. He also says that it is better to live outside the Garden with her, than inside without her.

Eventually, Eve realizes that she loves Adam too, discovering that it is merely because he is masculine, and hers. And even if he beats and abuses her, she will still love him because of the sex. Even if harm comes to her through pleasing him, she doesn't care.

Adam and Eve are anxious to learn, and one of the first things they discover is that water runs downhill, and not up. Initially, Eve believes that it runs uphill after dark, because the pool it comes from never goes dry, which it would if the water didn't go back at night.

When the Voice speaks to Adam and Eve in the Garden about "good" and "evil," they are perplexed. Good and evil are things they have never seen before. And what about death? They don't know what death is either. They are at the very beginning of things and don't know anything. There is no one to tell them anything either.

In Mark Twain's Bible, once you get to heaven do not speak to Saint Peter, but it's OK to ask for his autograph. Don't overdress. Leave your dog outside, and keep off the grass. It's proper etiquette to bow when you meet angels, and sooner or later you will get your halo. Mark Twain said that God eventually figured out that death was insignificant, that it was a mistake. That's why he invented hell. The Bible also says that God himself orders people killed, even though throughout the Bible it says, "Thou Shall Not Kill."

In Adam's case, Mark Twain said that he had never seen or heard of a dead thing. Twain wrote, "We call him Father," and "in derision, we would detest and denounce any earthly father who should inflict upon his child a thousandth part of the pain and misery and cruelty which our God deals out to his children every day." Even those born before Jesus came along are going to burn in hell. Is that fair?

Mark Twain wanted to know how God could be satisfied with restoring sight to one blind person and not all blind people, curing one cripple instead of all cripples, and feeding 5,000 people instead of the millions who were hungry. If raising dead people was a good thing, why didn't God raise more? According to Mark Twain "There is no evidence that He is just, charitable, kindly, gentle, merciful, and compassionate. *Heaven exists solely upon hearsay evidence, evidence furnished by unknown persons, persons who did not prove that they had ever been there.*" Twain also said that *"Man is not responsible for what he is. He didn't make himself."*

According to Mark Twain:

"God has so contrived him (man), that all his goings out and comings in are beset by traps which he cannot possibly avoid, and which compel him to commit what are called sins—and then God punishes him for doing these very things which from the beginning of time He has always intended that he should do. *Man is a machine, and God made it.* No one would think of such a thing as putting the responsibility upon the machine itself. God, and God alone, is responsible for every act and word of a human being's life between cradle and grave."

Twain made excellent points. How much did primitive man understand before becoming conscious? While Christian conservatives' man has only been around for a few thousand years, evolutionists say Homo Sapiens were here 200,000 years ago. For primitive man there was no language therefore no well-developed voice box. Like other animal vocal sounds, he grunted things like *"fire"* after discovering it.

Man literally had to learn to speak and then to talk, as he evolved to stand up straight (to see farther, freeing his hands for things like cooking), and to walk on two legs. How could God tell Adam and Eve not to eat the apple when they didn't know what an apple was? Or sin.

Note that the same people who believed there were two such people as Adam and Eve, created on the sixth day, also believed God created a world that was flat, and that after Noah's flood all the water just drained over the sides. During the Inquisition, Catholic priests had the astrologer, mathematician, physician and poet Cecco d'Ascoli burned at the stake for claiming that the earth was round. Galileo, the first man to use a telescope to discover that the earth and other planets revolved around the sun, was persecuted for saying the same thing. These were brilliant men, not superstitious egotists, while the priests were the same people who forcefully continued to tell how God had created everything in seven days. (Just as conservative Evangelicals argue today). The holy men knew absolutely nothing about science or natural laws. Whatever happened was happening not because of natural causes, but because of magic, the gods, or God, who even gave Noah calculations for his ark.

Imagine Noah rounding up all those tigers and elephants from India and Africa, kangaroos from Australia, polar bears from Alaska, and male and female rats and roaches, then harvesting enough food to feed all of them for a whole year with almost no help, and keeping it all on his tiny little boat. That's impressive! Hey, maybe Noah had a secret. What really happened to all that water after the Flood? Where did it go? And what about all those animals, like polar bears and penguins? Did they just go back where Noah found them? Is the real truth the fact that Noah never had every possible species on his ark in the first place? If they were on the ark, why isn't every kind of animal still living where the boat landed?

While Noah may have rounded all the animals up and loaded them on to his ark, before that Adam had to name everything, including the tigers from India, giant pandas that only live in Tibet and parts of China, and colossal dinosaurs, even though he had never seen one. *(How does somebody name something they didn't know even existed? Adam had to be a genius too, with a phenomenal vocabulary and memory to make up all those names and words for us.)* Noah's flood was not global, but regional, and

it didn't rain for forty days and forty nights when he was 600 years old. God created Noah's contemporaries who were guilty of sinning, and then drowned them all. As Mark Twain said, didn't God—being omniscient—already realize they were going to sin when he made them? Adam and Eve had already given him a clue. Pre-Adamite racists counted blacks as beasts on Noah's Ark.

In the first account, Genesis 1:27, God created man in his own image, referring to both male and female. Adam, "red dirt," signifies both man and woman, and remember, in the original Hebrew account, God is referred to as *Elohim*, which means "gods," plural. So, the gods, plural, created Adam, the first Hebrew man, and Eve at the same time from dirt. Today, there are those who claim that the plural "Let us make man in our image" is referring to the "Holy Trinity" of the Father, the Son, and the Holy Ghost, but how can that be since the son, or sons, Adam and Jesus, hadn't been born yet? The "Holy Trinity" didn't exist.

Consider this discrepancy in the Story of Creation. In the Book of Genesis God created the sun, the moon, and the stars on the fourth day. But he had already made plants and fruits on the third day. How did vegetation grow without sunlight? Hebrew storytellers didn't have science.

We grew up focusing on Adam and Eve because it was so powerful, theatrical, and majestic. As a writer, I know firsthand that if you want someone to read your work you must capture their attention from the start, and Genesis certainly does that. Like the old days, today's minister gains confidence as he speaks with authority, having been given such an overwhelming topic. We can actually imagine, or even see Eve receiving Adam's rib, especially on gigantic movie screens and in digitized color. It's great, and great entertainment. Goliath got bigger every year. As a public speaker, I also understand that it's important to talk about topics you know something about, and with a captive audience (yelling "Amen!"), it's another guaranteed "slam dunk" for the preacher. He receives the accolades, and a colorful story gets told over and over again.

Remember, according to Jewish legend, found in the Hebrew Scriptures, the first woman God created along with Adam was Lilith.

In the legend she refuses to submit to Adam who always wanted to be on top during intimacy, and when she runs away from him she is turned into a female demon. Adam and his restless snake were the reason Lilith took off in the first place. Enough was enough. She was tired and worn out, and then along comes sweet, little innocent Eve, the virgin. Adam was already hooked and about to hook Eve. In Adam and Lilith's case they did whatever they did together as consenting adults, but only one of them was turned into a demon: the woman.

Many preachers have never heard that account, so it's fascinating to me that people are willing to blindly follow so-called ministers who appear to be no more than "feel good" snake charmers and opportunists who are clueless. Just what are their congregations using for brains, if they do indeed have any? Are their members so sick, so desperate, so ignorant and so needy that they will do and accept almost anything to say that they are a member of some church and somehow closer to God? It seems true enough, especially today, that *the sheep really are sleeping.*

Why does this preacher now call himself bishop? Authority. Theatrics. Like the Bible. The Israelites told great stories just as today's preachers make movies. Bishop sounds better too, more impressive. Bishop... That's cool, and it's sexy. No matter how nerdy he might have been before God called him, brotherman's really got it going on now. Bishop! You can almost hear God saying it (Almost). It's great imagery, and really smart marketing. Just ask the Catholic Church.

Of course, those who were players before being tapped on the shoulder by God get kicked up another woman-chasing, or man-chasing notch, as well. *"Bishop" sounds classy and contemporary, like "Adam and Eve" theatrics for the twenty-first century.* Our man is urbane and sophisticated, not some clumsy hayseed from the back hills. So what if he didn't have shiny new shoes growing up, walking those dirt roads out in the sticks, or running around an inner-city housing project somewhere? He's certainly making up for it now. "Bishop" lets everybody know who's boss and in charge, while "pastor" sounds like somebody seventy years old, driving a banged-up twelve-year-old Dodge pickup truck. *"Bishop" also has the sound and inference of authority and legitimacy, you know, like "pope" or "senator."* And as an added perk, he gets to wear that cool-looking collar... Now, *that's* what I'm talkin' about! Everywhere he goes he holds his head high, because without ever opening his mouth, he tells the world that he is a man of God... A SPECIAL MAN. Ugly, fat, and even funky, he can still attract the ladies.

On the other hand, calling himself bishop may be just the opposite, a way of showing the world he isn't really very special after all. When I want to look cool, I have to wait until winter before I can slip into my black turtleneck. But, hey, maybe I'll beat the bishops to the punch next time... I'll be a SAINT, or maybe a pope, and I'll vote myself in, doing it without the Council of Cardinals or the Curia. I'll just slip into my black suit, grab a Bible and get at it. Then I'll be a *"special man"* too.

CHAPTER 20

Times Have Changed

Prosperity ministries are busy hustling their congregations with "feel-good sermons" and leading their naïve flocks in the wrong direction. If God is real, then the devil and demons are real too. But spending a lot of time talking about devils and demons instead of all the money you are going to receive wouldn't feel very good on Sundays. (No clapping and singing.) Instead of rushing to church with big smiles on their faces, the terrified congregation would be running in the other direction, for a drink and a smoke. Their money would still be in their purses and pockets instead of the collection plate. There's less money if "Rev's" congregation feels depressed rather than uplifted (i.e., lifted up). *It's always about the money.*

The following is also taken from Henry Baker, the bondman in *Slave Testimony*, relative to corruption in the church during the early days of emancipation and freedom.

> *Ef yuh go 'cordin' tuh de Bible dere is very few rail preachers today. Now we got some few good preachers 'mong us but de majority uv dem ain't doin' nuthin' but goin' thru de motions.* Hit don't seem tuh me dat de white preacher takes 'vantage uv his opportunity ter build up rail brotherly love' tween "niggers" en white folks. Yer know de 'postle Paul sed God is no respector uv pussons. *Ef all preachers would think more 'bout de interest uv de people dat dey work wid en not so much 'bout demselves 'ligion would be much better.* We has church meetin's called by de preachers en 'stead er takin' up de livin' conditions uv de people, de widows en dose who is widout means, dose who is

widout homes, *de main think dey discuss is some money fer de preacher en when dey git dat de meetin' is ovah.* De preacher will take up de hour tryin' tuh git er dollar out er de folks. Jesus sed: "Go into all de world en preach de gospel tuh every nation en lo I will be wid yuh to de end." But de preachers jes ain't doin dat. I talks ter de preachers en says dat all 'nominations gotter git togedder en center on one thing en dat is de suffering uv de people, 'gardless uv whuut nomination or whether dey is even in de church. Ef de preacher en muh community (Hickory Grove) has de same idea I has de people would have it, 'cause dey is gonna follow de preacher. In muh co'munity dere is only three "nigger" famblies whut owns deir lan'. *Ef de people would come togedder say now, we get er thousand people en come togedder en say we put up five dollars a year, en eny thousand people could put up dat much money in a yeah's time, which would be five thousand dollars, we could go en buy five thousand dollars worth er lan'.* Hit would be er private enterprise en we could begin settlin' our people on dis lan' en de next yeah raise five thousand dollars agin en in de co'ase uv time all uv de people could be placed on de lan'. Dis would not be a Gov'ment project, hit would be sumpin de Race done fer hitself. We nevah will be 'spected 'til we do sumpin fer ourselves. All dis must be done by honest folks. I 'membah back aftuh surrender, dere wuz sumpin lack dis started, en we got togedder er good deal uv money hopin' tuh buy lan' fer our folks, but hit wuzn't long 'fore de leaders run off wid de money en nobody ain't nevah knowed whut happened tuh hit. Hit is our leaders whut 'stroy de confidences uv de people. [Think of what buying $5,000 a year's worth of real estate would've amounted to by now. But even back then ministers and others didn't practice what they preached, running off with the money. And that was more than 150 years ago.]

Sherman, an astute friend from the political arena, tells this story about three Vietnamese fishermen who wanted to buy fishing boats. All three men worked together to buy one boat the first year, then one boat the second year, and finally one boat the third year. At the end of the third year, all three men proudly owned their own boat. That's what Henry Baker, a former slave proposed after the Civil War for black people, but the men they followed had something else in mind.

With deadly consequences, the image of the devil has been fantasized. His impression has almost become that of a cartoon character, the guy in the red costume with horns, the tail, and a pitchfork, but of course, that's not who the devil is, if he exists as we were told. Satan is not the rubber toy you played with as a child. According to the Bible, Jesus himself healed people who were possessed by demons. (Perhaps mentally ill.)

> Mark 1:23–26
> Suddenly a man with an evil spirit in him entered the meeting place and yelled, "Jesus from Nazareth, what do you want with us? I know who you are! You are God's Holy One."
>
> Jesus told the evil spirit, "Be quiet and come out of the man!" The spirit shook him. Then it gave a loud shout and left. (Was Jesus an exorcist?)

In the Hebrew Bible and in the original Aramaic, Greek, and Hebrew languages, the words used to represent Satan or the devil are understood to mean "accuser" or "adversary." They refer to an antagonist or oppressor. A liar who slanders, obstructs, opposes, or plots against another. It was not the name of a particular character. The devil was not personified as an "evil spirit" or a diabolical demon with wings, a pitchfork, and a tail who defied God and represented sin and evilness until the Second Temple Period. During the sixth century BCE, Hebrew storytellers often made the devil supernatural, but before that he was not the evil demon with horns or the serpent who tempted Eve in the Garden of Eden. Before the sixth century BCE there was no one superdemon. *Satan, the devil, had not been invented yet. Made up.* During Medieval Judaism, rabbis who believed in rational theology even rejected the idea of fallen angels. (And by the way, who sewed Satan's red costume and cape, Mrs. Satan?)

According to believers, the greatest trick the devil ever played was convincing the world that he does not exist. If the devil is real, he or she is probably charming and attractive rather than hideous, repulsive, and offensive. If you want to seduce somebody you've got to use the right bait, and the devil would certainly know that. (Like the exciting lights, sounds, and colors at a casino, sucking you and your money in.) It's tragic that people who should be busy discovering and solidifying their physical and spiritual lives are choosing, instead, to become members of a sacrilegious circus (church), whose ringmaster (pastor) is a blasphemous clown, a pretender and a perpetrator.

If you do believe in God and the devil, do you also believe in heaven and hell? *Do you actually think that when you die you will be removed to a paradise somewhere in the sky where God lives in a big mansion, a place where angels with wings or cherubim with four heads and wings guard huge pearly white gates, where the streets will be paved with gold and your loved ones are happy, feasting, singing, and wearing long white robes?* Who will build God's mansion? What possible reason would there be for paved streets in heaven, and even more fantastic, why would those streets be paved with gold? Why not platinum streets? Is there gold in heaven already, that would have to be mined and processed, or would the new inhabitants bring that from earth too? Like God's mansion, who will pave those golden streets? What tools will they use, will the pavers be trained, and will they have the proper clothing, like heavy steel-toe work boots worn by construction workers on earth? Surely, the people singing and wearing long white robes, tailor made for a perfect fit, won't be doing construction or road work. Besides that, how will those robes and streets be kept clean? We know for sure that holy men and angels won't be doing any hard work. *Like Jerusalem after Jesus' crucifixion, dead people will be walking around again, but this time in heaven, singing, sewing robes, building mansions, paving streets, and panning for gold as trumpets blast. Does God really live in a mega-mansion, in Heaven?*

Just how does one go about getting to heaven? Is there a train or a space shuttle to heaven? Are you beamed up the same way Captain Kirk went back and forth to and from the *Starship Enterprise*? Do you levitate to heaven, or do you just take a very, very long walk on one of those golden streets wearing your new sandals or work boots? After all, you're in no hurry. You've got forever, and you'll be all right as long as you're not afraid of heights. *And don't look down.* But then, why should you be afraid? You're already dead, remember . . .? And when you do get to heaven, WHAT WILL GOD BE DOING? Do you need to make an appointment to see him? Keep in mind that in heaven there are already billions of people in line ahead of you.

Speaking of dead people; in 1 Samuel 28, after Samuel died, Saul, the beloved first king of Israel, disguised as an ordinary soldier, went to see the witch of Endor, asking her to bring Samuel back since God wasn't taking his calls anymore. God had turned his back on Saul because of his sinfulness and lack of repentance, so he dropped by to see the witch. Saul needed a dead man brought back so he could ask him what he was doing wrong, after he, as king of the Israelites, had ordered anybody trying to contact dead people killed. The witch, fearing that it might be a trap hesitated until Saul gave her his promise that nothing would happen to her.

While Samuel was alive Saul never wanted to talk. But the witch did her thing and *shazam*, Samuel's back, after he was already dead and buried. Exodus 22:18 says, "Thou shalt not suffer a witch to live." *Kill the witch!* Samuel's ghost told Saul that God had turned away from him because he hadn't obeyed him, which included killing everybody belonging to an enemy tribe. Samuel also told him that he and his sons would die in battle the very next day. Saul dropped to the floor. The question is, "Is the Bible saying witches are real?" Was the witch of Endor in 1 Samuel: 28:3-25 who brought Samuel back from the dead real? (Is Harry Potter real?) Was Samuel real or a ghost? Did another dead man come back to life? Did the witch use psychoactive drugs to create an illusion? Was she a ventriloquist and Saul saw nothing? Wounded in battle the next day, King Saul killed himself.

The Bible says that Saul was moral, only becoming corrupted by power after Samuel anointed him the first king of Israel. That Saul was "the glory of Israel" who had both good looks and personality.

Since Christianity's beginnings, believers have questioned whether they would have "fleshly pleasure in their own bodies," or would there be no physical bodies and therefore no glorious sex after you die. In ancient times, believers were convinced that virgins would be waiting for them in heaven, just as other faiths did. But how would the virgins get to heaven, or are they already there too, just waiting to have a good time? I guess even in heaven it's every man and his "weenie."

According to empiricist John Derbyshire, in *The American Spectator*, there are two alternatives to heaven: blank extinction (nothing), or an anti-heaven (hell), a place of suffering. Another point Mr. Derbyshire makes is that *our bodies depend on a brain to function, so what would be the function of a brain in heaven beyond being happy, singing, playing harps, sewing, gold mining, and possibly paving roads?* Instead, would people read, use computers, or just enjoy the view and nature? Forever? Are there beautiful forests and lakes in heaven too? Animals? Pets? Will heaven's new inhabitants have the same view of the universe that astronauts have, looking down on the rest of us, from millions of miles or light years away? *On earth, heaven gives us a reason to live, then something to die for.* Heaven is the ultimate and final reward for being good, and one of our greatest fears is not receiving it!

In *Heaven: The Heart's Deepest Longings*, Peter Kreeft says the reasons for believing in heaven are:

> "Philosophical arguments, intuitive wisdom, faith in divine revelation in the Bible and Church, and above all, the resurrection of Jesus."

Derbyshire says such reasoning doesn't prove anything. Atheists simply believe that when you die nothing happens. *"You're dead."* That's it. While most of us do look for some *"feel-good"* reason for living, there are primitive tribes and aborigines who believe much as atheists do. They have never believed in any god, and similarly, don't expect anything to happen when they die. Even when a child dies it's just dead, like a bird or a kitten.

Jonathan Aitken, columnist and author, says that "after citing any number of biblical passages, religious traditions, visions, artworks, experiences, and theological libraries full of 'evidence,' *we are still only guessing about heaven.*" Shmuley Boteach, Jewish rabbi and best-selling author of *Kosher Sex*, says, "as a religious Jew I believe in heaven. It's just that I don't much think about it. *Our objective is not to use heaven as an escape from a world filled with pain, hunger, death, and disappointment; but rather to rid the world of those curses so that the earth itself become more heavenly.*" (Liberation theology).

Aitken says, "Who cares about heaven? I couldn't give one damn where I am going. *Even one moment of thinking about it is a moment taken away from my duties here on earth to clothe the naked, house the homeless, and comfort the bereaved.* Charity and righteousness are not portals through which one ultimately caters to one's own spiritual needs; *and religion dare not become a ticket one purchases for a heavenly lottery. It's time for religion to refocus its efforts on bettering our world rather than getting us into heaven.* We can only start by reversing the idea that life in this world is just a means to an end." Shouldn't loving God and your fellow man be more important than a supernatural reward?

Boteach disagrees with Kreeft's idea that "earth is only the castle's drawbridge, the road to the great hall or the dungeon, upstairs or downstairs."

In matters of eschatology, the branch of theology dealing with "last things," including death, judgment, heaven and hell, James H. Cone, our old friend, the author of *Black Theology and Black Power*, asserts that "*the most corrupting influence among the black churches was their adoption of the 'white lie' that Christianity is primarily concerned with an otherworldly reality.* [Forget about now; heaven is all that matters.] White missionaries persuaded most black religious people that life on earth was insignificant because obedient servants of God could expect a 'reward' in heaven after death. Obedience meant adherence to the laws of their white masters. African slaves believed when they died they would end up with friends and family again in their own homeland. Do African Americans even have a homeland? *What is critical now is getting over the unverified ideas of heaven and Christianity!*

Cone says for black people the name Jesus becomes magical, and that injustice, brutality, and suffering no longer matter. (Suffering in God's name makes them proud.) "Black theology is not eschatological but earthly, not being concerned with last things, but with the present, here and now." *"There is no room in this perspective for an eschatology dealing with a 'reward' in heaven.* Suffering to get to heaven if it is considered the will of God is out of the question, and the idea of heaven is irrelevant. Contemplating the next world is a waste of time." As Cone sees it, *"the free Christian man cannot be concerned about a reward in heaven.* He is a rebel against inhumanity and injustice." (As was Jesus.) I agree with Cone, Boteach, and Aitken, that we need to make things better in *this* life. *We know what is happening on earth now, and really are only guessing about heaven later. Remember Wimpy, from Popeye, "I'll gladly repay you on Tuesday for a hamburger today." The future carries no guarantees. Make things right, now.*

Remember, many people who claim to have gone to the other side said nothing about seeing Jesus or Moses there. And what about the devil? Nobody has ever talked about going to hell and seeing him either.

During the 1800s, Charles Briggs, a scholar and Presbyterian minister basically charged that time and investigation had proven that the Bible and some biblical prophecies contained errors and inconsistencies. He believed that *"preoccupation with the end-time was undermining Christianity,"* insisting that *"all old dead dogmas must be cut away."* It was a new day, and he refused to accept worn-out lies from many centuries ago. In an 1891 speech, Briggs said, "men cannot shut their eyes to truth and facts." (Logic and science.) *He didn't believe in leaving reason (common sense) at the door when you arrive at church.*

A critical thinker and a Historismus, Briggs believed that "all historical phenomena were products of the culture, the time and the place in which they were created." This included Jesus and Christianity in Galilee during the First Century and Catholicism in Rome during ancient times, now world-wide. *By Briggs's account, Biblical texts were no longer seen as the immutable word of God, because what was once considered true may no longer be true. (Man would never fly, but Neil Armstrong and Buzz Aldrin landed on the moon in 1969.)* The ancients' sky god is out of place today, just as Michelangelo's celestial white personalities have become. A modernist, Briggs's faith in God was based on human progress. Progress was God's truth. God was alive, still at work, and flexible. That's how the Bible should be presented and read today. There is much remaining to be discovered, past, present, and future.

As an example of Briggs' insight on time, place, and culture, let's take a look at Leviticus 20:9–22:

> [9] If *there is* anyone who curses his father or his mother, he shall surely be put to death; he has cursed his father or his mother, his bloodguiltiness is upon him. [10] 'If *there is* a man who commits adultery with another man's wife, one who commits adultery with his friend's wife, the adulterer and the adulteress shall surely be put to death. [11] If *there is* a man who lies with his father's wife, he has uncovered his father's nakedness; both of them shall surely be put to death, their bloodguiltiness is upon them. [12] If *there is* a man who lies with his daughter-in-law, both of them shall surely be put to death; they have committed incest, their bloodguiltiness is upon them. [13] If *there is* a man who lies with a male as those who lie with a woman, both of them have committed a detestable act; they shall surely be put to death. Their bloodguiltiness is upon them. [14] If *there is* a man who marries a woman and her mother, it is immorality; both he and they shall be burned with fire, so that there will be no immorality in your midst. [15] If *there is* a man who lies with an animal, he shall surely be put to death; you shall also kill the animal. [16] If *there is* a woman

who approaches any animal to mate with it, you shall kill the woman and the animal; they shall surely be put to death. Their bloodguiltiness is upon them.

¹⁷ If *there is* a man who takes his sister, his father's daughter or his mother's daughter, so that he sees her nakedness and she sees his nakedness, it is a disgrace; and they shall be cut off in the sight of the sons of their people. He has uncovered his sister's nakedness; he bears his guilt. ¹⁸ *If there is a man who lies with a menstruous woman and uncovers her nakedness, he has laid bare her flow, and she has exposed the flow of her blood; thus both of them shall be cut off from among their people.* ¹⁹ You shall also not uncover the nakedness of your mother's sister or of your father's sister, for such a one has made naked his blood relative; they will bear their guilt. ²⁰ If *there is* a man who lies with his uncle's wife, he has uncovered his uncle's nakedness; they will bear their sin. They will die childless. ²¹ If *there is* a man who takes his brother's wife, it is abhorrent; he has uncovered his brother's nakedness. They will be childless.²² 'You are therefore to keep all My statutes and all My ordinances and do them, so that the land to which I am bringing you to live will not spew you out.

The above cited verses show that in ancient times almost anything you did could get you banished, killed, or into some other serious trouble. According to Paul, fornicators, idolaters, male prostitutes, perverts, thieves, the greedy, drunkards, party people and robbers wouldn't be heading to heaven. There were no gray areas. Do wrong and you were history. *A goner.*

Cuss mom or dad out and you're dead. Adultery, dead. Homosexuality, dead. Sleeping with animals, dead (and the animals too). Sleep with your wife while she's having her period, banished (run out of town). And by the way, is a Catholic who eats meat on Friday still committing a sin? As Briggs said, culture, time, and place do matter.

Some of the most important and illuminating comments in *Let Us Prey* come from Karen Armstrong, a former nun and author of *A History of God*. She says almost the same thing Briggs said, that "*each generation has to create the image of God that works for it.*" Miss Armstrong continues:

"The human idea of God has a history, since it has always meant something slightly different to each group of people who have used it at various points of time. *The idea of God formed in one generation by one set of human beings could be meaningless in another.* Had the notion of God not had this flexibility, it would not have survived to become one of the great human ideas. When one conception of God has ceased to have meaning or relevance, it has been quietly discarded and replaced by a new theology.

When people began to devise their myths and worship their gods, they were not seeking a literal explanation for natural phenomena. The symbolic stories, cave paintings and carvings were an attempt to express their wonder and to link this pervasive mystery with their own lives. *These myths [like Christianity] were not intended to be taken literally, but were metaphorical attempts to describe a reality that was too complex and elusive to express in any other way.* These dramatic and evocative stories of gods and goddesses helped people to articulate their sense of the powerful but unseen forces that surrounded them." Framed by storytellers.

Maybe it's time to take a new look at traditional Christianity and what its consequences are for our time. As you have seen in Leviticus, ancient practices that were perfectly acceptable then, are not only unacceptable today, but illegal. *Stoning people and murder are definitely out, as is being run out of town because you "got busy" with your wife during her period. Inappropriate sex with your own spouse!*

The Bible is both patriarchal and misogynistic. Today in 40 percent of American households, women are either the leading, or only breadwinner. *In nearly one out of every four homes (25%), mom is bringing home the bacon.* In 1960, only 4 percent of women made more money than their husbands, but now that number is 23 percent. Although women are now equally educated, they still earn less. Ninety-two percent of all American lesbians, gays, bisexuals, and transgender adults say society has become more accepting of them. But not the Bible, the Protestant Church or the Catholic Church, that remain unapologetic and unrelenting.

In an article "The State of Women," *Time* magazine announced that the gender wars were over, declared a tie, and that it's no longer a man's world. Men and women spend about the same amount of time doing housework, and Gen Y dads (Mr. Moms), are now at home with the kids. Our heroes have changed too. Bruce and Arnold are out while Zac Efron, off the basketball court, performs on *Dancing with the Stars*. Today Liz is the pilot who flies an F-22 fighter jet in the Middle East. And while mom is at war or at work, dad's the one picking up the kids after school and cooking dinner. Today, women, gays, and people of color have choices, and one of those choices may be not to allow themselves to be oppressed and bullied by religion anymore. Has the time finally come to be honest and realistic about what we believe or do not believe, whether it's written in a book called the Holy Bible or not? Things have indeed changed. And remember even Pope Francis says it's time to turn things around.

Our ideas about heaven and hell came from sources like Dante's *Divine Comedy*, Dante's *Inferno*, and John Milton's *Paradise Lost*. Before that there was no "hell." Today we have books, movies, CDs, and the Internet (Google, Skype, and Facebook), and cell phones (texting and Twitter), where all kinds of information is available. Presumably, it's easier to find the truth. In hell the temperature is 50,000 degrees, and grotesque-looking monsters torture and beat you mercilessly for eternity. If you believe in God and the devil and heaven and hell, do you also believe in angels with white feathery wings who are supposed to be something in between man and God? For those who believe, yet another question remains. Are angels among us too, like God's sons in Genesis, who came to earth and snatched up all the prettiest virgins for themselves? If there are virgins in heaven already, why did God's sons come down here to *hook up* and *get busy*? If not, does that mean that the women in heaven have already lost their virginity? Has anybody reported seeing either God's sons, angels, or giants in the last 100 years? (Maybe Yao Ming or Shaquille O'Neal.) Remember, Satan was supposed to be among God's sons too.

If you believe in God and the devil, angels, and heaven and hell, do you likewise believe in Judgment Day and the end of the world? *Do you accept the idea of standing in a very long line with billions and billions of people, everybody who has ever lived (or will live), to see if you're "going up or going down"?* How far down? Or, down to where? *Is hell a pit in the center of the earth? Does the devil really live there?* Does God live in outer space above us, while the devil lives underground below us torturing people. Popes John Paul II and Francis I conceded that hell, with its fire and brimstone is not a real place, but Catholic and Christian iconography and imagery, a metaphor. Sinful souls will simply disappear.

In 1999, 40 percent of American adults believed the world would end in the Battle of Armageddon between Jesus and the Antichrist; 19 percent believed the Antichrist was already here, 18 percent (36 million Americans) believed Jesus would return during their lifetime, 68 percent believed they were going to heaven, and 3 percent said they were going to hell. Quite a few said they had no idea at all.

Two thousand years ago Jesus instructed his disciples to prepare for the end-times, and the apostles, like many others, expected to witness Jesus' return during their own lifetime, including Paul (but nothing earth-shattering happened, and Jesus never showed up and stuck around). People were upset that he wasn't back. *Again, where is Jesus and why hasn't he come back?* In the thirteenth century monks like Joachim of Fiore believed the Antichrist was already on earth.

For religious reformer Martin Luther, the father of Lutheranism, "the Catholic Church itself was the deceiving Antichrist who secretly served Satan." He hated the Pope and what the Catholic Church represented as mediator between God and man. Luther felt that celibacy encouraged masturbation, homosexuality, and illicit fornication. *(One way or another, men were going to "get off".)* Others thought it was the pope himself who was the Antichrist. Joseph Smith, the Mormon patriarch, concluded that *the entire Christian enterprise was a corruption of what used to be.* Today, pandemics, tsunamis, tornadoes, hurricanes like Katrina and Sandy, plus droughts and wars breaking out everywhere have believers convinced that this time the end really is here. More about that can be found in the 1999 issue of *Newsweek*, "Prophecy, What The Bible Says About The End Of The World."

It's curious to me that black people who shout loud and pray so hard (hoopin' and hollerin') which Du Bois called "mad with supernatural joy" and "the frenzy of shouting", know so little about their own religion in this country from its earliest days until now, with the preacher's role being similar to the medicine man's. The Puritans, believers who sailed from Southampton, England, to Plymouth aboard the Mayflower to escape persecution, actually believed in the doctrine of Calvinism and its five principles. John Calvin, a Protestant theologian, influenced the way Puritans felt about community, home, love, and Christianity. He believed that <u>before Adam and Eve, God had already decided who would be saved.</u> (Black people and other minorities weren't on the list.) That's contrary to what Christians believe today about anybody making it to heaven. Heaven was only for a few white people, after Adam gave birth to the white race here on earth. Calvin's five principles are as follows:

1. Total depravity—*Only God, and not a man's actions, will determine whether he is saved or not.* Because of the original sins of Adam and Eve, all men are destined to be sinners. *Good works mean nothing.*

2. Unconditional election—*God selects certain individuals to be saved, and only those.* God chooses people who could not or would not choose him.

3. Limited atonement—*Jesus' sacrifice on the cross was not to redeem everybody, only believers.* God already knows who they are and Jesus died to forgive the sins of the "elect" only, who are predestined, or chosen by God.

4. Irresistible grace—*In spite of their behavior, those who are already chosen will overcome their resistance to the Gospel and be saved.* Man is so corrupt that he will not decide and cannot decide to follow God, so God must intervene through a powerful impulse and the Holy Spirit.

5. Perseverance of the Saints—*"Once saved, always saved,* or eternal salvation." (Nothing would keep you out of heaven.)

The Puritans believed in the Old Testament, and that the Bible was truly the word of God. What they did not teach us in history class is that not everybody aboard the Mayflower for 10 weeks 400 years ago was a believer. Some were headed to the New World to make money. Today's self-indulgent prosperity Christians would have had a real problem with self-sacrificing, Bible-believing Pilgrims. In England, the Puritans wanted to reform the Church of England of rituals and the corruption of the Catholic Church in Rome. (Not corruption in the Catholic Church again!) By English law, however, separating from the church was considered an act of treason.

Sailing to America on board the Arabella, John Winthrop delivered his famous sermon *"A Model of Christian Charity,"* convinced that a harmonious Christian community would be an example to the world. Winthrop believed that *"God has made all men that they are rich, poor, high and eminent and others of lesser character, but also that the rich and mighty should not eat up the poor, nor the poor and despised rise up against their superior and shake off their yoke."* Although 10 to 30 million Indians were killed. Rich people shouldn't step on poor people, and poor people shouldn't yield to anarchy by attacking and harassing rich people. I'm sure Mr. Zell, Mr. Perkins, and the other millionaire and billionaire members of the 1% would agree. *God wants you to stay in your place.*

Just as there are problems of sexual transgressions today, like pornography, so it was in America's early days. In 1642, Thomas Granger, a sixteen or seventeen-year-old boy was convicted of "buggery," having had sex with a mare, a cow, two goats, five sheep, two calves, and a turkey. At first he denied it. He confessed after somebody saw him having sex with a horse. Granger was executed, and as prescribed by the Bible, all of the animals he had been with were destroyed. (Leviticus 20:15, "And if a man lie with a beast, he shall surely be put to death: and ye shall slay the beast.") A big pit was dug and the dead animals thrown into it. Granger was having sex with another boy too, who said that they were told it was done in England all the time, including with animals. It appears that the more things change the more they seem to remain the same. IT SEEMS TRUE THAT THE SAME OPPRESSIVE EXERCISE OF POWER AND ABSOLUTE AUTHORITY THAT THE PILGRIMS WERE ESCAPING FROM, AND SUBSEQUENTLY INSTITUTED, IS REMINISCENT OF THE PSYCHOLOGICAL AND SPIRITUAL CRUELTY BEING PERPETRATED IN TODAY'S CHURCH. CONTROL! CONTROL! CONTROL! EVEN KILLINGS!

In 1636 Roger Williams, a seeker of truth was considered dangerous. In writing "A Letter to the Town of Providence," he was advocating the separation of church and state, defending his ideas of "spirit and religious liberty" or "freedom of conscience," something Englishmen didn't have, and of which Americans would soon be assured in the 1791 Bill of Rights. The governor of Massachusetts tried to banish him back to England. *Williams believed that Puritans should not force people to accept religion or the scriptures as the answer for all civil and political questions.* Civil authorities should be responsible only for civil matters, not religion. Ironically, the Pilgrims' desire for liberty of conscience was why they had journeyed to America, but once they got here they made church attendance mandatory, unauthorized religious assemblies were prohibited, and you could be imprisoned, exiled, or killed if you got caught breaking the rules.

During a period called "The Enlightenment," around the 1700s, thinkers in London and Paris believed that human reason could be used to combat ignorance and superstition to overcome the unjust cruelty and oppression exercised by those in power. This was their solution for building a better world. *Their challenge was to overcome absolutist kings and overbearing dictatorial churches.* (The bottom line is always control and domination, even now.) There's more about this in *The Norton Anthology—American Literature*.

In the Frenchman Michael de Montaigne's "*What Do I Know?*" the author says, "*If we cannot be certain that our values are God-given, then we have no right to impose them or force them on others.*" Montaigne, born in 1533, was considered the father of modern skepticism during the French Renaissance. The enlightened believed that using intelligence and logic could lead to the truth. Monarchs and churches, however, still rigidly insisted that their way was not only the right way, but the only way. Does this not sound like the position held by Tea Party Republicans and Christian conservatives? And were the Neo-cons not trying to exercise absolute authority during George Bush's presidency?

In the seventeenth century, you could be sent to jail for going to the wrong church, or for not going to any church at all. It was also during this time that the church continued to defend slavery. As usual, challenging the church was committing heresy, which could get you locked up or killed. It was very clear that the old way of living and thinking (being controlled by collusion between the church and the state) was wrong. It's still wrong.

From the earliest times, the doctrines of Romanism were effectively being put into place to give the pope supreme authority. The Catholic Church manipulated God's laws and the Scriptures so that Christians could be forced into accepting the pope as its head with absolute rule over bishops and pastors worldwide. He was esteemed as the infallible *"Lord God the Pope,"* Jesus Christ's representative on earth, and all must submit to him, a canon ordered by Pope Pius IX at the First Vatican Council in 1869. *Catholics were forced to look to the pope for salvation instead of God.* But when did God or Jesus ever give such authority? *The Bible says call no man Father, yet the Catholic Church reveres the pope as "The Holy Father."* Where is it written in the Bible or the Scriptures that the pope is God? And again, anybody who disagreed was accused of heresy, tortured, and put to death by the holy man's henchmen. Of course, all records of such cruelty were destroyed by the church. (Possibly another cover-up in a long series of cover-ups.)

The Catholic Church in particular has been instrumental in perpetuating the institution of slavery. The first time the Greek word *catholic,* meaning "universal" (all churches) was even associated with religion was when it was used by the Bishop of Antioch, St. Ignatius. He was also the first to reportedly use the word *Christian.* "Pope," derived from the Greek word *"pappas",* meaning "little father," typically meant some older man, the same way *unc* does today, having had no religious significance at all. Any older man was a pope (*pops*). Many of the early church's popes were Greeks after the Romans. Not only did the church support slavery it owned slaves. Later, *the Catholic Church believed the slave had a soul that was sacred, but his body belonged to his owner.* The Ursuline nuns in New Orleans were major property owners, including two plantations and sixty-one slaves.

In addition to slavery the Catholic Church also supported Magdalene laundries, named after Mary Magdalene, the alleged repentant prostitute. An estimated 30,000 women were incarcerated between 1765 and 1976. So-called "fallen women", prostitutes, unmarried women who were sexually active, and even innocent girls who were still virgins were forced, for their own protection, to wash uniforms for priests and prisoners, cook, scrub floors, and take care of aging nuns. *Without pay! (Slave labor).* The women had to endure long periods of prayer, plus enforced silence for rehabilitation. Unmarried mothers who had illegitimate children were even forced, by the Catholic Church, to give them up. Just as priests had been forced to leave their own families behind.

To make sure the common man remained ignorant of the Scriptures, he was forbidden from reading the Bible or even having one in his house for hundreds of years. As papal power grew, so did ignorance in a period known as the Dark Ages. Monks were used to forge ancient writings and large sums of money (indulgences), could be paid to forgive one's sins, including buying a loved one's way out of purgatory where they waited to be purified before going to heaven. There was even a "layaway plan" for sins that hadn't been committed yet. Adulterous popes lived in luxurious mansions while their followers lived in filth and poverty. (Again, the "holy men" were living the good life.) These accounts, at least most of them, have been taken from *The Great Controversy*, by Mrs. Ellen G. White, published in 1888, and will be revisited shortly.

In the 1800s people like Harriet Beecher Stowe, author of *Uncle Tom's Cabin* disagreed with John Calvin's predestination and strict colonization, sending blacks back to Africa to circumvent racial conflicts that were inevitable. Because black people were unassimilable, primarily due to skin color, many Northerners opposed slavery, but disliked blacks being around even more. They wanted America all-white, overlooking Native Americans. Unsupervised, blacks supposedly created chaos. Calvinists contracted selective memory, forgetting they were actually Europeans, and this was not their country. (America is neither Europe nor a European colony, something that should always be remembered.) White people in America are immigrants too.

The Calvinists' fondest wish would have been for the inferior blacks to die out or disappear, especially since they believed black people were lower than animals and a drain on society. Mixing the races was very dangerous. If white people were behaving badly they said it was because of the Negroes. *(That black people were being terrorized and abused by white people was their own fault.)* After the Civil War, one idea was to move all black people to the Sea Island areas of Georgia and South Carolina. Other states like Indiana and Illinois didn't want black people living there at all, but tolerated all black towns.

According to Whitlow Reid, editor of the *New York Tribune* in the 1850s:

> "Where Negroes reside in any great numbers among the whites, both parties are the worse for it, and it is to the interest of both that a separation should be made as soon as practicable."

There was one very big problem; Negros had fought and died during the Civil War. There was no way to force them out. Harriet Beecher Stowe thought that black people should go back to Africa, not so much because they were hated, but because Africa was the only place where they could thrive and live a reasonable life. She and others felt that black people should be educated in America, then sent back to Africa *after becoming Christians.*

While Calvinism was rigid and cold, people like Stowe believed in romantic racialism. That is, that Anglo-Saxons, Caucasians, were by nature materialistic genocidal conquerors, while the Negro was more like an anti-Caucasian, similar to a good-natured child. *The white man was aggressive, and even vicious, while the black man was meek, docile, and more of a natural Christian.* Stowe felt that black people were the superior race and would be better Christians than Europeans. Brutal whites didn't mind enslaving or even exterminating other people to get what they wanted, and some white people thought there was something innately wrong with the white race because of its history of brutality.

In 1828 the African Repository reported, "the African in this country (America), belongs to the lowest station in society, and from that station he can never rise, be his talent, his enterprise, his virtue what they may." Even freeing slaves would not solve American's problems because slaves would have to be absorbed into a hateful American society. The black man's color would never allow prejudice and his degraded past to die. In 1857 Theodore Parker, a Unitarian minister wrote "In 20 generations Negros will stand just where they are now, if they have not disappeared."

Encouraged early on by what they had seen in England and France, and becoming familiar with the French Enlightenment and its ideas about natural law and inherent freedoms, men like Benjamin Franklin and Thomas Jefferson were guided in their revolutionary thinking. It inspired the American ideal of self-determination, which even transferred to some of the slaves. *Ironically, it was the church that had rigidly maintained such cruelty and domination, now continuing its abhorrent legacy in more subtle ways.*

Churches today not only challenge other religions, they actually challenge each other. Competition keeps everybody on top of their game, and it keeps the dollars rolling in.

> Give me that ole time religion
> Give me that ole time religion
> Give me that ole time religion
> It's good enough for me.

Those are the words of the old Negro hymn, but few people understand what they mean anymore. That "Ole Time Religion" was spiritual, deeply personal, intimate and communal. Too many of today's ministers, morally bankrupt, egotistical, wannabe superstars, have brainwashed themselves, or been brainwashed by the wrong supernatural agents (ego and cash) in their own personal quest for power and fame, egotistically seeing themselves above their members and somehow closer to God.

CHAPTER 21

Church—Big Business

The once beloved leader of the flock was usually a senior, who, because of such great moral responsibility, needed to be wise, trusted, and respected. Today fiery passion and anointing have been replaced by glitter, glamour, and money. Now the elder may even be the twenty-six-year-old son of the current minister who is about to retire, or his wife. They intend to keep all those special goodies in the family treasury. A neophyte, still wet behind the ears, the youngster insists on being addressed as doctor so-and-so, bishop so-and-so, or apostle so-and-so. And I think that daddy, not God, was the one doing the calling, or perhaps cell phoning, e-mailing, or texting. One woman obsessively referred to her pastor as an angel. Not just an angel of a sweet person, but literally one of God's angels, complete with a halo and white feathery wings. In this sister's eyes her hero-preacher could do no wrong.

> Proverbs 19:17
> (paraphrased)

Any story sounds true until someone tells the other side and sets the record straight.

Faster, faster, faster ... That's how we want everything in our lives to be, including church. We want convenience and we want it now. We can satisfy our spiritual conscience and our spiritual commitment for the week in one hour, sometimes less. And if you don't feel like going out, just like ordering a Domino's Pizza, you can worship at home by simply picking up the remote control and clicking your flat screen on.

There are, on the other hand, social as well as spiritual reasons for attending a live service. For the faithful, there's the satisfaction of singing in the choir, serving as an usher or just sharing in the enjoyment of praying and worshiping with others and being among trusted friends. But everyone is not there for the right reason.

For some, church is a fashion show where they can flaunt how successful they are. Driving that new Infinity or their fine Lexus, dressed in Armanis and Rolexes. For others it's a dating game jackpot, with fellow members playing the same games and eager for a new hookup, sometimes openly, most often undercover.

Reuben Armstrong, in his book *Snakes in the Pulpit*, discusses rampant homosexuality in today's church. Reuben said he knew of one pastor who was having sex with the deacons and many others who were sleeping with members of the same sex. Countless members are "living in the closet" or "living on the down low," while others flamboyantly display their mannerisms. The gay members of the congregation are probably the happiest in an environment that is populated by other homosexuals, women, and men who are nonthreatening. And as we well know, many are introduced to homosexuality in church, especially the choir.

Church sometimes offers a singles ministry too, where they will cheerfully hook you up. I'm not sure whether it's pimping or an in-house dating service, but to me something seems to be amiss. I don't believe that feature was offered in any Bible I've ever read. If the member's new mate happens to be an outsider, the church gets to pick yet another pocket. If children enter the picture, they will be dropping envelopes into the collection plates in a few years too, during the "collection parade". One co-pastor/first lady invited me to her church one day, not telling me about the ministry, but rather how many fine, single, good looking women were there. Women with new cars, big houses and money. There are still more singles in black churches than in white churches.

Reverend so-and-so, or bishop so-and-so may even try to regulate your sex life, in spite of the fact that he may be busy trying to "get busy" himself, at every opportunity. Often female members overlook and even try to justify his misconduct, explaining that "he's only a man," that "he's only human." (Well, if he's only a man and he's only human, why isn't he sitting in the pews with the other men instead of preaching and giving orders to everybody else from the pulpit?) Many times it's the sister who is just as guilty as the pastor is, even though they both might be married. It's obvious that a sinful co-conspirator may be a valuable ally. They both get to sin together, conveniently. *In secret.*

Royce, another friend, recently broke up with his Christian fiancée, or rather she broke up with him after accusing him of being a flirt and a cheat. Her own pastor had fathered three illegitimate children, which resulted in his temporary suspension and a simple slap on the wrist by his church association. Predictably, her response, in defense of the whorish preacher was, "he's only a man." She could dismiss the preacher's blatant indiscretions (illegitimate children), but not unsubstantiated suspicions about her own boyfriend, even though the two of them cared for each other very much.

One sister I know actually waited to ambush a visiting pastor who was preaching during a revival. The church's pastor introduced them to each other and from that point on it was "a go." The visiting preacher called the sister at home, told her he needed to talk to her, and when she showed up at his hotel room, he greeted her wearing a shirt and tie, and a pair of boxer shorts. They sat on the bed talking for about half an hour, then stripped and started knocking boots. Rev, who was married, flew her back and forth to Dallas where he lived with the wife and kids, but after a few months, tiring of that arrangement, moved his church mistress to Texas where she now sings in the choir. She lives only a few miles away from the preacher, his spouse, and their two children. Rev's explanation; he's a man who loves pussy.

In the case of Dr. Gloria Milow, she went from being the pastor's mistress to preaching from her own pulpit. Dr. Milow said, "at the age of 17, my pastor would send a limousine to my house to bring me to him at a hotel. He even invited his pastor friends to our room to join in (other preachers). He told them if he ever found out that I was with them in his absence he would kill them." (No cheating behind his back. But sex in front of his face was fine.) The preacher was a *"pulpit pimp"*.

Dr. Milow confessed, "once I did secretly meet with another pastor. He wanted more from me than his money could pay for. He begged me not to tell the other pastor for fear of his life. And I didn't tell, because I really believed the other preacher would have been killed. Sex was wild with them." Dr. Milow tells her story in *Secrets*.

"Another time, the pastor (her sugar daddy), had me bring a woman to The National Baptist Convention for a preacher friend of his. So I brought a girlfriend of mine who was a teacher. They took all sorts of nude pictures. And he promised to send her money every month. When he failed to keep his part of the bargain, she mailed the photos to him at his home. He and his wife divorced as a result of that incident."

Pastor Ronald Harris, Sr. was killed while preaching during a revival service in a Lake Charles, Louisiana church. Harris was shot twice in front of sixty-five people, including his wife and daughter. Woodrow Karey, a former church deacon, walked up to Harris and shot him, and then shot him again on the floor. It was alleged that Karey murdered Harris because the beloved pastor raped his wife. Others said it was a set-up, and that Mrs. Karey was jealous because she found out the preacher was sleeping with seven or eight other women too, while he was keeping her as a "side piece".

Reverand Menard Zvenyika, who was married, committed suicide by drinking poison after allegedly impregnating his housekeeper Rosemary Nyamukachi, four times. She was also married.

Today, even television is getting into the act, like the reality cable show *Preachers of LA*, where the pastor talks about the number of times he has had a venereal disease, and his first lady talks about her days as a crack-smoking prostitute. The wife even talked two other first ladies into going back to the streets she once worked to face her ex-pimp. In a later show, the one-time prostitute has talked the other ministers' wives into going to a club in Las Vegas where she hustles a male customer for drinks, rambunctiously saying she's looking for some naked men and some booty shakin'! *It seems that some Christians (freaks) are losing their minds.*

For a businessman, the church can be the Dow Jones Average, NASDAQ, and his favorite casino all rolled into one. Absolutely, one of the best places for an entrepreneur to network is church, and there are plenty of perks. A successful, respected businessman, the operative words are *business* and *man*, as a financial contributor will surely be recognized as part of the hierarchy, with a steady stream of sisters (both single and married) trying to make him their business.

We're supposed to be discussing the church, but sometimes it's difficult to distinguish a church from a business enterprise. Growing up, I remember what church was like. In the 1960s, New Zion Baptist Church, the church my family attended, was a beautiful new two-story brick building with eight metal and glass doors across the front. (My father, who knew most of the preachers only too well and called them hustlers, never went.) The old decaying wooden structure had been torn down, and the new church erected in the same place. A fairly unkempt apartment building stood next door, and a greasy, Negro-owned cabstand/gas-station was on the corner. A colored-owned drugstore was on the corner across the street from the gas-station, and "Uncle Dan's," a popular diner next to it. It was a real neighborhood, and my church, like the other churches in our neighborhood, was clearly the heart and soul of it all both geographically and spiritually.

I recall stepping out into the street every Sunday as we walked past the gas-station to avoid getting grease on the bottoms of our freshly polished shoes. On Sundays the colored men who worked there were still greasy and grimy from changing oil and fixing flat tires. Even preachers had day jobs. It was a real community, where unlike today, people knew each other and cooperated with each other. They helped each other and even protected one another if it ever came to that. Wherever you turned, there were decent black men and decent black women being productive and raising families.

The central and most accessible place was the church, and each person there recognized everybody else, from the oldest man or woman to the youngest child. At New Zion the sanctuary was upstairs, but my favorite places, the kitchen and dining area were downstairs on the first floor. During the service, older members would be busy in the kitchen cooking fried or stewed chicken dinners with gravy and rice, and potato salad, and baking individual-sized homemade pies, still warm when you bought one. You could smell them baking as soon as your feet touched the front steps. You might see somebody up front wearing a robe and singing with the choir, and half an hour later they were serving you dinner or selling you a 15-cent homemade pie.

We know and love food in New Orleans, and those were absolutely the flakiest and most delicious pies I have ever tasted. I made sure I had 15 cents every Sunday, and sometimes 45 cents, buying a lemon, apple, *and* coconut pie, taking turns as I happily bit into one and then the others. I never liked sweet potatoes. The old people, country cooks (some of them direct descendents of slaves), are gone, and with them those magical recipes.

I can still remember Miss Ellen Bell, the secretary. And no entourage or team of bodyguards for Reverend Davis, who was also New Orleans first black city councilman. Ellen Bell was it, his right-hand man. She paid the bills, in spite of the fact that women weren't considered leaders, and sang in the choir. She was a very large spirit-filled woman with a smooth silky voice, who married one of the male soloists, a well-known gospel singer who was something of a lady's man. They remained together until she died. He married another large but younger member who had taken his wife's place as secretary, who sang in the choir too. There were some "show-offs" and "performers" in our church, competing to make the most women shout, but for the most part everyone was friendly and shared a true belief in God. The wonderful pies are gone, and so is the black church as we knew it. Even the stewed chicken is not the same because the hen that used to run around the yard eating whatever she found is instead a mass-produced springer on a huge factory farm somewhere, with half a million others just like herself, never seeing a real yard for even one day. Filled with hormones to make her grow quickly, in eight weeks she is on your table and ready to eat. She has not truly matured and the taste barely resembles that of an older free-range hen. Like that old-time chicken dinner that wasn't crossbred, most people do not know what that old-time religion was like either.

Is the Black church dead? Eddie Glaude Jr., Ph.D. says that the church "standing at the center of all that takes place in the community is dead in many ways. For most of us life has become much more secular." Glaude adds that "different areas of black life have become more distinct and specialized ... flourishing outside of the bounds and gazes of black churches." Today's black church is "just another facet of people's lives rather than the central organizing principle." The church is also living in a time when it has to compete with sports, the internet and porn for attention.

Huge mega-churches are concentrating on prosperity (money-centered) messages. Focusing on individual success and remaining anti-intellectual, they frequently abandon relevant social issues such as *"African American unemployment, 35% of our children living in poor families, inadequate healthcare, rampant incarceration (racial lynchngs), home foreclosures, and a general sense of helplessness."* Dr. Glaude says that "the prosperity mega church has developed the kind of *winner-take-all* capitalistic attitude Dr. King struggled against." (Me, first. Me, second. And if there's anything left that's for me too.) Because of its overall apathy, today's black church is becoming less relevant. *It is becoming alienated from the moment in which it lives.*

According to Dr. Glaude, another problem is competition with white churches. Many upwardly mobile black people are attending churches pastored by white men like Joel Osteen and Rick Warren, that often "*sound*" a lot like black churches.

Today's church *is* big business, with a corporate headquarters located somewhere downtown in the high-rent business district. (Two of the biggest businesses known to mankind are religion and war.) Some churches have fleets of vans to get you there and huge parking lots that accommodate thousands of cars. At Dr. Frederick Price's Crenshaw Christian Center in Los Angeles there is a parking lot and an elevated parking garage as well, and a shuttle bus to take you to the main sanctuary where the greeters (praise ministry) get you heated up before the service. As they say in Hollywood, "that's entertainment." Many of today's churches are actually arenas where you might need powerful binoculars to get a good look at the preacher, if not for those huge TV screens suspended from the ceiling. (Joel Osteen, T. D. Jakes, etc.) There isn't anything there to remind you that it's a church, even a picture of Jesus (any Jesus). It's not a real church. *It's an arena without beer and popcorn!*

Preachers like T.D. Jakes and Rick Warren are involved in the film industry making movies. Being multimillion-dollar church businesses, they'll need to see your W2 form to make sure you're giving your fair share. And somebody will definitely call or text you if your tithes are late. The Church wants to know how much you make, but do you know how rich your preacher actually is? What's in his bank account, and how did it get there? The Scriptures actually say nothing about tithing 10%, and Jesus himself said that the gift of the gospel is free.

One elderly lady had been a member of a church for sixty years. Like any good Christian, she always paid her tithes religiously. Unfortunately, she died a few months before the year was over. According to the church accountant she still owed $300, and *"Rev wasn't buryin' nobody until that last $300 was paid."* But in Matthew 10:8 Jesus said "you received without payment, give without payment." She was a faithful member of that church for six decades, but instead of grieving, her family members were feverishly running around hustling three hundred extra dollars.

The mother of a friend of mine had had a similar experience. She was on her last leg and dying of cancer, a member of her church for at least fifty years. Mrs. Lewis deeply believed in God and wanted the new preacher to come to her bedside to pray with her just one last time. This special man of the cloth was too busy, telling her grieving son Alvia, no. He wasn't going to any hospital, for any reason. I guess after all those years and all those tithes (she and her family had paid for about 150 years combined), she still wasn't Christian enough, or worthy enough. My own sister, Juanita, had had a confrontation with that preacher at my grandmother Crecia's funeral. The man had entirely too much attitude, demanding a limo that he could ride in alone.

Alone!!!

And why? He was the preacher. Not God. My grandmother, an usher, was a devoted member of that church before he was even born. One thing I really don't understand is why a church somebody has been going to forever charges them $700 for a funeral. Haven't they "paid it forward" already? And what happens to the money? Is that Rev's hustle for the week? His pocket change?

That might also help to explain why Uncle Sam appears to be doing a better job of collecting his fair share these days. If you intend to be a member in good standing you've got to file those taxes on time, and pick up those $39.95 DVDs and CDs. One so-called master prophet wants you to purchase his $120 seed, containing three prosperity CDs and his book. (Seed is the new hustle buzzword.) *AND, YES. PEOPLE REALLY ARE THAT STUPID!* But if the church is truly the moral institution it says it is, as a *silent* corporation, why is it not paying taxes too? Making millions, why is today's church still being protected by the kind of deal Constantine made with corrupt priests 2,000 years ago in Rome (Italy), and Mussolini made almost 70 years ago in Italy? (Those darn Italians again.) But alas, steps are finally being taken to make the Vatican pay up. That probably means your church too.

We can't forget that the good reverend has bills to pay, the mortgage on his mansion, plus his apartment (love nest), furniture bills, restaurant tabs, and with all those expenses the Mrs. (I mean his co-pastor) has, she can't have very much money left in her bank account either. Sending the kids to those exclusive schools in their new cars ... You know, the spoiled, entitlement-driven offspring who already think they're better than you are. (During the early days of Christianity true prophets were to be taken care of by the community, so I guess "Rev" and his clan think that applies to them too.) But there's a big difference between being provided for and being lavished (spoiled to death). "Rev" thinks he's a billion dollar Wall Street CEO. When he steps down his co-pastor wife will take over, or perhaps his entitled, pampered son. As royalty, it's his daddy's church and his inheritance.

You can always count on the city of Atlanta to kick it up another notch. The Catholic archbishop there really knows how to live, building himself a 2.2 million dollar mansion, 6,400 sq. ft., with two dining rooms and a safe room. The money had been donated to be used for charity. All this in Buckhead, Atlanta's finest neighborhood. After being discovered Archbishop Wilton Gregory (who is black) apologized, saying he failed to think about poor people who couldn't pay their mortgages and utility bills, even though he was spending money that rightfully belonged to them. As Archbishop I thought that helping the poor *is* his job. If not what has he been doing with his time besides living like nobility, against Pope Francis' wishes? What about his vow of poverty?

Pope Francis himself denounced the "idolatry of money" and warned against "insidious worldliness" within the church. Especially in light of the clergy's sex abuse scandals and parish churches and schools closing because of Catholics losing faith, and money problems. Archbishop Gregory went on to say that he was disappointed in himself (probably for getting caught).

Never count the Germans out. Pope Francis had to fire Bishop Franz-Peter-Tebartz van Elst who built himself a 43 million dollar mansion. $43 MILLION! And in New Jersey Archbishop John Meyers spent $500,000 to expand his old digs. As I said before the Catholic Church is really, really rich and *pays no taxes*, while Jesus was poor.

But don't leave the Protestants out either. By far, I think one of the worst examples I've seen of an absolute scam is the preacher (who shall remain nameless) who is on television telling people to "Order your own personal prayer package today!" He also has the "red (colored) blood of

Jesus handkerchief... It is your point of contact with God", the red rag. "God has a special miracle for you, and all you need to do to receive it is to order your own personal prayer package! Watch God work supernatural miracles," he says. "But sometimes it *don't* work, because you didn't follow God's special financial instructions." (I didn't know God gave special financial instructions.) One older Southern woman called (I could tell by the sound of her voice), saying she had arthritis and a bad case of asthma. Screaming, and speaking in tongues, the preacher shouted a few words that sounded like gibberish, and told the woman she was healed. He asked his caller how she felt. Her answer, as expected, was "I can breathe! I can breathe! I been healed! It's a miracle!" (This all took place, including her healing, in less than forty-five seconds.) He goes on, "If you need a financial blessing you have to order your personal prayer package today. Somebody's at the phone lines right now just waiting for you to call for your financial miracle. But you got to move quickly! Move quickly! Move quickly! You got to be in a hurry!" And people actually called in a hurry, over and over. Another pastor sells "Blessed water."

As you recall, since I was a boy I have had a love affair with automobiles and been fascinated by them. As a young man in the '50s and later in the '60s, my friends and I would eagerly await New Year's Day and the annual family reunion at our house. My uncles and older cousins showed up in their flashy new cars, and my boys and I would go from car to car checking them out to see which one was "the baddest." An avid enthusiast, over the years I have owned exotic cars myself, including a 1935 Auburn Boattail Speedster, a baby Duesenberg (one of Liberace's cars in the movie, and the car featured in Madona's Argentina concert with Kanye West and Pharrell Williams.) The car preferred by rich playboys in the 1930s. Mine was a hand-built replica, because there are so few originals still in existence, and those remaining are quite valuable. My last exotic car was a red 2005 Ford Thunderbird, 50th Anniversary Edition, with both tops, convertible and porthole hardtop. Remember, I owned my first Corvette at twenty-three years old, almost fifty years ago. The point is that now anybody can own a Corvette. Today's hot cars are Bentleys and AMG Mercedes. "Rev" is a major player and that's one of the cars he drives.

Everybody knows about Creflo Dollar and the 60 million dollar jet he wanted. Bankrupt boxer Evander Holyfield claims to have paid him twenty million dollars in tithes, is broke, and reportedly still giving Dollar whatever he's got left. Dollar can even be seen in a video talking to his congregation, saying *"I'm not gonna be going to heaven and be broke when I get there."*

I believe when Coretta Scott King's body was flown back to Atlanta for her funeral, the jet we saw on television landing at the airport belonged to none other than disgraced Bishop Eddie Long, who likes being called "Daddy." I'm sorry. That's King Eddie Long. Or Bishop, King. Or maybe King, Bishop. (Eddie's congregation did actually make him a king.) One preacher even bragged about telling his congregation he needed a helicopter, but not just any ole' helicopter. He wanted a jet helicopter, so he could get where he wanted to go in a hurry.

Kenneth Copeland makes Eddie Long look like an amateur. Copeland has his own airport, the Kenneth Copeland Airport, situated right next to his 18,000 square foot, six million dollar mansion outside of Fort Worth. Inside the hangar he keeps a fleet of airplanes that are registered to the church. Including a twenty million dollar Cessna Citation, the fastest private jet money can buy. Copeland, an avid pilot who flies his own plane, said he needed the twenty million dollar jet "to better serve the Lord." When asked by Lisa Guerro, an investigative reporter for *Inside Edition*, how many jets do you have? Copeland answered "That's none of your business." Pointing his finger at her and walking away.

Several mega-church pastors have already been investigated by the United States Senate, including Bishop Eddie Long, Paula White, Kenneth Copeland and Creflo Dollar.

Before Hurricane Katrina, I understand that one bishop in New Orleans had a police motorcycle escort to accompany him from one church service to another. I suppose he didn't want to disappoint his faithful followers by being late.

But "Rev" works hard, we all know that. Part of his work today might be as a politician too, or no less than a quasi-politician. With tens of thousands of loyal followers eating out of his hand and very deep pockets, he can be counted on to deliver votes and cash at election time from the kind of members I talked about earlier, the ones who are too naïve or too lazy to think for themselves. In *Snakes in the Pulpit*, Reuben Armstrong's pastor misled him into believing he was called to preach the word of God. Armstrong says he was faith-filled and could not see the forest for the trees either, until the pastor started talking about getting the members to give more money. Why more money? The preacher nonchalantly told him he wanted to pay cash for a new BMW, and that it was the church's job to take care of him. He told Reuben, "*I will show and teach you how to manipulate these JACKASSES by using the word of God.*"

One preacher stood in front of his congregation and told them they owed him a new BMW for bringing the gospel to them, knowing Jesus said the gospel should be free. Matthew 10:8 says, "You received without payment; give without payment" (the 10 percent preachers are demanding, plus other collections and love offerings.) Now, at least once a year, some preachers want the congregation to give them ninety percent and keep ten percent for themselves.

Another preacher told his members he needed money for a new propeller for his helicopter. Who knows? Maybe "Rev" didn't hear Pope Francis say the gospel was free, or care that Jesus said it too. Being questioned by his own minister about why his tithes were coming up short, Adolph explained that he and his wife of nineteen years had finally separated, and he no longer had the same income. The minister's response, "have you considered a second job?" Not "how about some counseling for the two of you? Maybe I can help." *But get a second job because I need my money.* One member who had been missing from church was actually told "If you can't make it, just send the money."

Something you quickly learn in church today is "YOU GOT TO DANCE WITH THE ONE WHO BRUNG YOU." According to Reuben's explanation of what happened, this was a lesson that may have been learned by Prophetess Juanita Bynum after calling Bishop T. D. Jakes out and preaching against him a few years ago—then later seeking his forgiveness. Money, or the loss of it, is a powerful motivation that will help you keep it real. Quick, fast, and in a hurry. White prosperity minister Paula White really learned fast, buying Bishop Jakes, her spiritual father, a black Bentley convertible for his birthday in 2012. (Remember Psalm 22:6, call no man father.) Millions of children are living in poverty and going to bed hungry while preachers buy each other Bentleys. Money that was given by believers to do things like feed the poor and comfort the sick. (*If you're walking to church in your Sunday best and "Rev" drives past you with his head held high in his new Mercedes, what does that make you?... Probably a fool!*)

All too often we see that the minister, or rather the bishop—no, that's the apostle, I mean the prophet—is getting a kickback . . . I know, you don't have to say it. "IT'S PRETTY STUPID." The politician gets the kickback from the businessman. The minister gets his share from the politician and maybe the businessman. But then, preachers are politicians too, aren't they?

Some churches are so big that the minister doesn't know who you are, doesn't want to know you, and couldn't care less. Need to see him on a personal matter or for spiritual guidance, make an appointment. But even then he's probably busy so you'll have to see somebody else anyway, unless you're on his "A List".

Reverend, Doctor, Bishop, or King So-And-So. And he's already an apostle and a prophet. (Like doctors of God, how does one become a prophet or an apostle anyway?) Black churches have a history of pageants with kings and queens; you know, the person who raises the most money. But since the preacher is already the one who ultimately controls whatever comes into his little empire (the money), I guess he's already the real king, and not just king for a day. *Ministers are becoming millionaires while members of their congregations are left behind in ignorance and poverty. (Just like ancient times.)*

Then, there is the "first lady," the preacher's wife. I'm not sure, but if she is the "first lady" does that make him a "president" in the pulpit too? Maybe that explains his security team; the guys who look like secret service agents, complete with communication devices, Glocks and bad attitudes to boot. Those are the guys you've never seen in church before who surround him and keep you from getting too close. They never smile and look like assassins. *Why does a minister need bodyguards?* Even gangbangers don't waste bullets on preachers. Is Pope Francis right? Do protestant preachers think they're royalty too, like England's Prince William and Lady Catherine? Do preachers and first ladies really think they're that special?

Personally, if I were one of the other ladies in the church, I think I would be just a little bit perturbed. If simply by being married to the minister and giving him a little poonanny every now and then, or not giving him any, another woman becomes the first lady, then who are you? Nobody? *There's only one "true" first lady in America right now, and that's the president's wife.* Any other first lady is a joke, and I seriously doubt if you will ever hear of any preacher, no matter who he is, introducing his wife to the president as the first lady. Maybe *"his"* first lady, with a silly smirk on his face, but not *"the"* first lady. Even preachers are too slick to be that stupid. *But what "Rev's" first lady really is, is a spoiled, egotistical, opportunistic church diva.*

Let's not forget that as his co-pastor, you're buying those dresses, diamonds, and shoes she's wearing. Who knows, maybe some of the sisters have convinced themselves that by screwing around with him, they have somehow been anointed *"deputy first lady."* And maybe with all that extra cash just lying around, he's breaking her off a few thousand or buying her new cars too. At any rate, these "sickos" seem to love preacher man's two-day old dirty drawers, shamelessly waiting by the phone or dropping to their knees for his next command. *It's as if these Christian pretenders are racing to see who can get to hell first!*

Believe me, I only make these remarks because something as important in our lives as spirituality and perhaps religion are, is becoming a ludicrous abomination. Most of us who are decent human beings got our start at home during a time when we still had fathers and mothers, people around us who cared, and church. But again, today's church is primarily comprised of single women with children and men who are either less than a challenge or eager co-conspirators. Fran, another long-time friend of mine once told me, *"If I wanted to find a real man I definitely wouldn't be looking in church."*

The mayor or any other city official will receive Rev's calls without hesitation, as will many state officials, and in some cases even presidents, because of all the members of his church neatly tucked away in Rev's back pocket. Even the lazy media, when they have a question that is relevant to the black community, call Rev . . . Rev's on speed dial because he can always be counted on for a quick press interview. For some reason the media conveniently treats him as if he is moral and enlightened. *But we know better.*

As a reasonably intelligent, independent-thinking African American, I'm telling you, I'm thoroughly fed up with seeing black Baptist ministers presumably speaking for me. During staged televised press conferences, they (the ministers) gain both (free) mass exposure and perceptual legitimacy. They also make self-serving "media celebrities" of themselves. The ministers understand only too well that their black congregations love seeing them on television flexing their collective muscle under the tattered banner of enlightenment and righteousness. *Idiots becoming spokespersons.* Precisely one of the reasons I, and others like myself are estranged from the traditional black Baptist church is because it lacks progressive, intelligent, contemporary leadership. *It's a farce!*

Certainly the black church has done much for black Americans and for America as well, but perhaps like another once great church (you know which one I'm talking about), it too is no longer in touch with today's realities. Clearly, the Black church hasn't done anything notable in the last fifty years, surviving on its aging reputation.

As you recall, the black minister was the man of learning in the black community whose training and wisdom guided others. But today those others, including myself, know how to read too, and how to think and speak for ourselves. Many of us resent having individuals who frequently know less than we do standing in front of cameras voicing opposition or support for issues so complex that they have not yet begun to understand.

We live in a more sophisticated and specialized world. Black ministers, for the most part, specialize in religion. That should be their primary focus, because they often lack the vision and knowledge to appreciate and anticipate the long range consequences of possibly well-intentioned but ill-conceived pronouncements.

Surely spiritual development and human rights should be within their purview, but theologians are not authorities on every force that defines and shapes the human condition. And are we so naïve as to believe that ministers, or anyone else for that matter, know all there is to know about everything? (Some ministers may be learned men, but you wouldn't call one if you needed surgery, or if your plumbing malfunctioned.) Nobody knows it all. Most preachers should stay in the pulpit, and even there many of them are sorely lacking and have a long, long way to go. *Preachers should stick to preaching!*

A man of privilege, Rev also has his own table and his own waiter at all the best restaurants, never standing in any line. As Dr. Rosie always reminds me ... "That's why so many black men are becoming ministers ..." I believe she's right. Church can be a paradise for a man, especially when you're the boss. It's like having your very own island, an island where you can kick back, enjoy a warm tropical breeze and pick fresh fruit from lush trees while beautiful native girls wait on you hand and foot. (Well, maybe I'm exaggerating about the native girls.) I myself had once considered going to church to do a little one-stop shopping of my own. My buddy Noah and I had even considered opening our own church. We ran great nightclubs. What's the difference?

Unlike the sisters, however, I could not, not as a man, pay tribute to or worship another man (some fool) ... So, naturally we passed on the church thing ... And speaking of another man, exactly who is this other man, the Rev?

IF
An actor is one who performs
on the stage or in front of the camera ...
AND
A performer is one who gives a
performance before an audience ...
THEN
Is a television ministry complete
with makeup, lighting, cameras,

camera crews, and cues not a performance by an actor before an audience?

AND

Do actors not act? And do good actors not give powerful, emotionally charged performances?

IS

The minister wearing his diamond rings, and his elaborately striped robe giving a performance before the camera any different from Batman draped in his black cape, or SPIDERMAN?

IF

The peacock is a proud bird who struts and shows off its colorful feathers, is the minister dressed like a peacock not just one more proud, colorful strutting bird...? A dodo bird, perhaps. (The large, clumsy, flightless birds with small wings that lived on islands in the Indian Ocean that are now extinct.) Hey, maybe that's a cue for Rev to disappear too.

IS

Either the television minister with his co-minister wife by his side wearing her own expensive jewelry and dressed like Ivana Trump or Batman with his colorful sidekick

Robin any different from any
costumed World Wrestling Federation
television star and his ring girl?
IF
Batman is only an actor doing
a job (not a real superhero who
can leap from one building too another),
and if a wrestler is only a big
athlete performing stunts and doing a job
(not someone who can get slammed across
the face with a two by four
and continue wrestling fifteen seconds later),
then why do we not understand
that a television minister, dressed
in his costume, giving a performance
is also an actor doing a job?
A job that generally pays very well.

PROVERBS 14:7
(paraphrased)

If you are looking for advice, stay away from fools.

Luke 6:44, "each tree is known by its own fruit." If it walks like an actor, talks like an actor, and acts like an actor, it's an actor. *Rev's an actor y'all, and probably not a very good one at that.* In the past, ministers and pastors said that they were called by God. Today, I think visions of Jerry Maguire must be doing most of the calling, and you know what Jerry says, "SHOW ME THE MONEY!" The Bible says that THE LOVE OF MONEY IS THE ROOT OF ALL EVIL. If the person guiding your life loves money, material possessions, and himself just a little bit too much, and if you are no fool, maybe it's time you stopped acting like one. Move on.

PROVERBS 14:27
(paraphrased)

Stop listening to teachings that contradict
what you know is right.

Clifton, one of my business associates, once told me a funny little story about his childhood forty years ago out in the country. Clifton loves food, and at almost 300 pounds it shows. As was the custom back then, the preacher stopped by different members' homes after the service on Sunday to eat. The grown-ups were served first, while the children quietly stayed out of the way and ate later, after the adults had finished. Well, sometimes they might run out of something before the youngsters got a chance to eat.

On one occasion, the grown-ups had almost finished eating and Rev, with that big grin and chuckling with his deep baritone voice, was reaching for the very last biscuit. Clifton, who was only nine years old at the time, beat him to it. He popped up beside the table, snatched the warm biscuit, and ran out of the house as fast as he could. He ate every crumb, knowing full well that he was going to get the whipping of his life, insulting Rev and embarrassing his family like that. He was crying and trembling when his father found him, but instead of picking up a switch or pulling his belt off, his father hugged him tight and apologized. Until that day, he told Clifton, he had never really realized what he was doing. His son's actions reminded him that his family should come first. The minister was only a guest in their home, a frequent guest who was obviously eating well already.

The following is a passage referencing greed and power, and deals with what took place in Germany in the 1930s and 1940s. When Adolph

Hitler came to power in 1933 he met with his closest associates. They were worried about the impact the church was going to have, and Hitler indicated to them as he boasted of his prowess and his power, that the church was not something they had to be afraid of because of the pastors. These are the words Adolph Hitler spoke.

> I promise you that if I wished to I could destroy the church in a few years. It is hollow and rotten and false through and through. One push and the whole structure would collapse. WE SHOULD TRAP THE PREACHERS BY THEIR NOTORIOUS GREED AND SELF-INDULGENCE. We shall thus be able to settle everything with them in perfect peace and harmony. I'll give them a few years reprieve. Why should we quarrel? They'll swallow anything in order to keep their material advantages. The parsons will be made to dig their own graves. They will betray their God for us. *They will betray anything for the sake of their miserable jobs and incomes.*

A few years later the church in Germany experienced problems just as Hitler had predicted. According to Dr. Lawrence White, God's spokesmen must speak for God or the nation will be destroyed.

PROVERBS 28:12
(paraphrased)

A sensible man watches for problems ahead and prepares to meet them. The simpleton never looks and suffers the consequences.

There will be those who charge that I am unfairly picking on preachers and the church, which couldn't be further from the truth...I am only trying to help right a great wrong, and you know what they say...If you can't stand the heat, get the hell out of the kitchen. Shake things up a little and it's called persecution. Tell the Emperor he's naked and you're the bad guy. *Then they curse you out.*

Even Christians.

An excellent case in point, referencing corruption was the Rev. Henry Lyons, once leader of the multimillion-member National Baptist Convention U.S.A. Things were wonderful for the pastor and his cronies . . . until his wife Deborah Lyons lit a match, burning down a $700,000 waterfront home where she believed her husband was having an affair with Bernice Edwards, the convention's Public Relations Director for Corporate Affairs. Mrs. Lyons confessed, saying she became upset when she found her husband's clothing and other personal belongings inside.

The pastor's wife later said she dropped the match by accident, while her husband described Miss Edwards as a close friend of the family for several years.

It was discovered that Rev. Lyons co-owned both the house and a Rolls-Royce with Bernice Edwards, somehow overlooking a marriage document that failed to mention two previous wives, and a mortgage application listing him as single.

Bernice Edwards and another preacher shared commissions of over 75 percent on business deals cut in the name of the church. Lyons's response . . . "The commissions were a bit high. I made some mistakes."

I suppose he did make mistakes, like getting caught with his hand in the cookie jar, the candy jar and inside Bernice Edwards. He did not admit that it was immoral for a preacher to pursue money for the church, then pocket more than he was giving to the children's ministry, the building fund or the outreach ministry, and that it was wrong to funnel hundreds of thousands of unreported dollars into a discretionary fund. Instead, Henry Lyons played the race card, claiming that he was the victim. Reverend Lyons served a five-year prison term.

One of the top swindlers of all time is Rev. Gerald Payne, who headed Greater Ministries International, based in Tampa, Florida. Through a giant Ponzi scheme in the mid-1990s, Payne cheated nearly 18,000 unsuspecting believers "gifters," out of five hundred million dollars. Payne told them that God would make them rich. Saying God himself had anointed the plan he promised to double their investments in about seventeen months. The investors were told their money would be safe because the church owned gold mines, and was selling gold coins and gold rings. One woman gave her entire $20,000.00 life savings to the Paynes, not even keeping enough for food and rent.

The Rev and his wife were the ones who were getting rich, as he and Betty routinely cashed thousands of checks, just below the IRS's $10,000.00 required reporting limit. According to the Paynes the money was a gift. They also claimed that their First Amendment rights as a church were being violated. Betty Payne defiantly insisted that they had broken no laws, and that their actions were guided by the Holy Spirit.

Unfortunately for them the court didn't see it that way. The good Reverend got 27 years in prison, while his loving wife Betty was sentenced to 12 years. Three other church leaders also got time, about 20 years for conspiracy and money laundering. Church leaders, insiders, sometime received commissions of tens of thousands of dollars a month, which they referred to as "gas money". Reverend Payne was even selling "Greater Trust in God Bonds".

Payne and his cronies also sold a line of cancer treatments and herbal remedies, saying they pulled the cancer right out of your stomach. The supplements were called "Beta I" and "3rd Glucan", with promises that they would even help the buyer survive the "end times plague". Payne was also slick enough to try to establish his own independent country, free from laws like the Vatican, called "Greater Lands". (The Vatican's got it going on!)

In a world of seven billion people, do you really believe that God, who's probably busy in heaven solving real problems, takes the time to talk to the preacher living across the street from you, who pretends to be so holy? The same lazy man (or woman), who hasn't cut the grass in four weeks? Do you really think that the same individual who wouldn't take two minutes to help an old lady cross the street knows what God is thinking? That he can hit up God's digits and put in a good word for you? Most of today's preachers are little more than 21st Century witchdoctors. Like the Paynes, if Rev seems to be doing all right, the reason isn't that he's so smart or so spiritual. He's been picking pockets for years, including yours.

Three parables of the Black Christian Condition

I

"I love the Lord with all my heart" Linda beamed insistently, her tight black spandex dress cut 6 inches above the knee and at least two sizes too small for her forty-five year old body.
"God's been so good to me. I'm just so blessed. Praise the Lord". She said she was headed for a job interview and stopped by to see her minister for encouragement. The minister, a barber, was alone in his small shop when she arrived. The first thing he noticed was that she had recently had her hair and nails done. After counseling and a brief prayer the woman stood to leave, and as she turned, the minister noticed that there was a protruding bulge in back of the sister's dress. He diplomatically called it to her attention and suggested that she step into the back room to correct it.
"Oh, that's all right," she answered casually, catching the Reverend completely by surprise. She stood in the middle of the floor, lifted her dress, removed her underwear and laid back in one of the barber's chairs. Spreading her legs she offered herself to the minister saying, "I know you want some of this."

II

I had just walked into the lobby of the Sheraton Hotel in New Orleans when a man I had known during the days when I was involved in nightclubs excitedly approached me. His eyes flashed, darting back and forth as he spoke, searching, scanning the room as hundreds of women in town for the Essence Music Festival checked in.

"Don, man, it's been a long time. I haven't seen you since the club. I read your book. Man, it was deep, and I didn't even know you were a writer."

"So, what have you been up to?" I asked.

"Man, you got to come to church," he quipped. "I mean it's on, just like the old days when we was runnin' dem hoes. Fu*#in' women all over the place lookin' for a man. And check this out . . . You ready for this shit...I'm a deacon too. I'm tellin' you, you ain't gonna believe this shit!"

III

"Yeah, that mu-fuc#er' better take care of his mu-fuc#in' child, that's all the fuc# I know. I don't play that shit with him. He better stop playin' with me. I'm talkin' about my fuc#in' baby daddy.

"I bet I'll tell his fuc#in' wife that mu-fuc#er's still fuc#in' me too."

"But I thought you told me you weren't seeing anybody," I answered. "And why do you keep calling me?"

"Because you don't do right, that's why. I told you I wanted a pair of Tommy Hilfiger shoes. I still don't see 'em," she said, her neck snapping from side to side, with her hands on her extremely shapely hips.

"Unbelievable," I smiled to myself. And I still didn't buy the shoes.

"That's all right," she grinned. "I know how to get what I want, and believe me, I ain't nothin' nice. I got a new friend, anyway. He's married, but it's all good. I give him what the fu#k he wants, and he gives me what I want ... Yes, in mothafuc#in' deed."

She went on to graphically describe the nature of her illicit dalliances with each of the three men she boasted about being with. The first was a man of low character who only performed oral sex on her. She did not return the favor. The second was her "baby daddy," with whom she was having mutual oral, as well as anal and unprotected genital sex. The third individual was an older married man from her church, who was performing both oral and unprotected genital sex on her, unaware of her other sexual liaisons, both current and past. (Maybe he didn't care.) He did this in spite of the fact that he had an unsuspecting wife at home whose very life he was endangering by his reckless, irresponsible behavior.

These three parables are all true, but what amuses me most is that all three storytellers claimed to be good Christians. Like the minister, many in the congregation are acting, and if Jesus lives as they claim, he knows it and so does God.

PROVERBS 20:21
(paraphrased)

A fortune can be made from cheating, but there is a curse that goes with it.

Jesus referred to scribes and Pharisees as hypocrites. He was disgusted by them because of their fraud and deception. The term "hypocrite" is derived from the Greek word *hypokrites* which means actor under an assumed character; a stage player. At that time acting and lying were acceptable in storytelling, which was never assumed to be true in the first place. *They were stories!* During Jesus' day, right there in the Holy Land, many of the religious leaders and politicians were acting.

MATTHEW 23:13
But woe unto you scribes and Pharisees, hypocrites, for ye shut up the kingdom of heaven against men, for ye neither go in yourselves, neither suffer ye them that are gathering to go in.

If Jesus could see it and say it, why do educated and informed Christians today not see it or recognize it? Remember, a fool and his money are soon parted... THE TRUTH SHALL SET YOU FREE, BUT ONLY IF YOU HAVE THE DESIRE TO BE FREE.

All the world is a stage, and the men and the women in it only players.
—William Shakespeare

This includes bishops and preachers. Why do so many people who should know better find themselves in such precarious situations? That's an easy one. "IT'S STILL SHOWTIME BABY," and a lot of people are dying to get into the act, looking for their fifteen minutes of fame.

Everybody loves a winner, and secretly everybody wants to be a winner. In America, bigger is still supposedly better, so the biggest church may in essence appear to be the best church. As members, the congregation sees themselves as winners too.

In ancient times when pyramids were built the higher they were, like a stairway to heaven, meant the closer they were to God. Today's megachurches operate in a similar fashion by being bigger, with present day preachers seeing themselves as something akin to lesser gods. They are the ones holding power and human beings do identify with the strongest or the biggest.

Personally, I don't care to go to a church that feels like a motion picture studio or a football stadium. If I wanted to see a comedy, I would fly to New York to see *The Ellen DeGeneres Show* or to Chicago for *The Jerry Springer Show*. *The Real Housewives of Beverly Hills*, *Everybody Loves Raymond*, or *The Big Bang Theory* make more sense than some churches do. As Paul Harvey, the famous radio commentator might say, "What's the rest of the story?" Why do black people, as a race, continue to be so hyped up about religion, the slave master's religion, as that same steadfast beacon of hope in spite of its lunacy and abuses? For the slave master it was understandable. His beacon, the Bible, was written and interpreted from a similar dominant perspective. Its message gave both comfort and dignity to him! What did slaves get?

On his blog, Financial Juneteenth, Dr. Boyce Watkins talks about repetition in the church as a form of brainwashing. I made the same argument decades ago. Growing up in New Orleans, a very mystical city, I was casually familiar with Voodoo, which is somewhat trance-like and repetitive, a key element being spiritual possession. At Catholic and Protestant services I observed congregations mindlessly responding to cues like Zombies, especially Catholics, standing, kneeling, repeating, chanting and praying. Clutching prayer beads they echoed Latin words 99% of them didn't understand. Typically, white priests wearing ceremonial robes performed the mass as statues of white saints, and stained glass saints in windows overlooked pious believers. *I needed a smoke and a drink, or some of that ancient spiked communion wine!*

Dr. Watkins said that you can actually make a difference in your community by not giving all your money to the preacher, by not trying to buy your way into "Club Jesus". Watkins cautioned that some preachers are not spiritual leaders but entertainers. Creflo Dollar is reportedly worth 27 million dollars and T.D. Jakes 150 million dollars for being two of the best.

Is the purpose of today's church (especially the black church) to provide spiritual direction, or is it simply an opportunity to see and be seen? All dressed up in her Sunday best, once a week, could the sister who spends hundreds of dollars getting her hair and nails done and buying a new outfit for the Essence Music Festival, or for the church musical, have made a wiser choice had she used the money to prepare for a job interview instead, or perhaps double up on a mortgage payment? The same is, of course, true for the brothers who are busy getting their hair and nails done. Today Americans spend 70 billion dollars a year on lottery tickets. Their new God.

While they're busy getting all gussied up unforeseen forces are affecting their lives. One of those forces is the 15th Century "Doctrine of Discovery", justifying an oppressive decolonization policy of domination and dehumanization against indigenous people. *White colonization.* Not only had the Catholic Church labeled non-European, non-Christians beasts without souls, it sanctioned Christian enslavement. Pope Julius II, remember.

A series of papal decrees allowed Christian explorers to lay claim to property inhabited by indigenous people, saying their land *"nobody's land"* had finally been discovered. *Christopher Columbus.* With the Pope's blessings Christian explorers took property and possessions from poor natives. If the captives could be converted to Christianity they lived. If not they were disposed of, killed. Catholic Law!

In 2000 Pope John Paul II apologized for the church's mistreatment of groups like Native Americans, who were always depicted negatively as savages. But what about the suffering and generational wealth they were deprived of by Europeans and Americans for centuries, billions of dollars in land and minerals? Priceless resources stolen by the church and its friends who profit till this day. Why would anyone of non-European heritage ever become a Christian?

CHAPTER 22

Blind Obedience—A Slave to Religion

In previous chapters, I provided a glimpse into today's black church, with a brief look at the establishment of so-called organized religion during America's early settlement. I use the term "organized" loosely, because the Christians who landed in Plymouth found indigenous people already living there. Native Americans had a social order and homes for protection against the elements, as well as established spiritual belief systems of their own. They were neither primitives nor cavemen. *It was the ethnocentric, white, Christian, Anglo-Saxon who labeled the people they found "heathens," just as they later did with African slaves, calling them savages simply because they did not have the same social structure or believe in the same monotheistic God.* Color played its ugly role as well, because red men and black men were not made in God's *"white"* image. So called uncivilized savages were a gift blessed by God to be used.

It is still my aim to bring some reasonable degree of clarity and understanding into an appreciation of why black people and white people in this country think and do the things they do, after centuries of interacting with each other. Why do so many white people still maintain a feeling of privilege, entitlement, and superiority? Why do countless numbers of black people continue to feel either inferior, or that someday they will be vindicated as human beings when Jesus Christ returns? The authoritarian personality of many white people is real. The inferiority complex of many black people is also real. How do we all move forward together? If we can?

It is important to remember that the prevailing mentality which claimed that Columbus discovered America is the same one that said Native Americans and Africans were savages. Columbus supposedly discovered a place that was already inhabited, a place that had already been visited centuries earlier by Imhotep, the African navigator and genius, as well as others like Leif Ericson and the Vikings 500 years before Columbus' time. So Columbus didn't discover anything, at least not America.

The Native Americans the Europeans found were laid-back and living peacefully and in harmony with nature in an environment that provided abundantly for them. Europeans, on the other hand, were escaping from an environment that was anything but easy, an environment that was hostile, harsh, cold, and ripe with religious, social and political conflict. For the Pilgrims, fear and greed and not thanks became a motivating factor in what they believed. Fear, we know, does not make for wholesome, happy, healthy little campers. Fear often leads to paranoia and other mental disorders. Has that same paranoia become endemic in today's American psyche? Are we turning the world's populations against us, threatening preemptive military strikes against anyone who stands in our way? Have we become the world's policeman, deciding what is right or wrong for everybody else, based on an ethnocentric sense of entitlement and our own misguided pseudo-Christian values? As Americans, does life owe us painlessness, self-indulgence and happiness?

Has the fear of losing our lives and our land exhibited by our ancestors, both blacks and whites, seeped down (with some justification) through generations of Americans to the present? Are lessons (indoctrination and brainwashing) given to black slaves internalized in today's black child? Was there any intrinsic difference between a four-year-old black boy in 1715, 1815, 1915, or now? If he receives the same basic miseducation, and hears the same sunny Sunday school lessons in segregated churches and segregated schools four centuries later to guide his moral and spiritual character, with little emotional support, how can we possibly expect him be different, or new and improved? His neglect and miseducation began at birth with Christianity.

It has been said that insanity is doing the same thing over and over again and expecting different results. While "a rising tide raises all ships", keeping black people and brown people down doesn't actually lift anybody else up. Ignorance and crime affect all of us, ultimately bringing everybody down in one way or another, further exacerbating hostility and alienation. I guess that means we're all either insane or *"dumb as dirt."* It has also been said "if you want different results do things differently." I suppose we lose on that issue as well, because we never seem to recognize our mistakes or to make the necessary adjustments to correct them. "If I always do what I always did, I'll always get what I always got." *We unreasonably expect change without first changing and then doing things differently! You have to take that first step.*

It puzzles me when I see a preacher in a Baptist church or on television talking about Job, Jacob, Solomon, or somebody else, smiling the "smile", and speaking as though he really knows the person he is talking about. I mean *really* knows them, like his wife or his best friend. Who are they kidding? Are those holy men wolves in sheep's clothing, or simply egotistical, ignorant *brainwashed individuals* who are completely out of touch with reality? If you were to put this back in history, the black preacher would have been Pharaoh's black slave, shackled and working in the dirt and dust like an animal the same as everybody else, with no great friendship between himself and the king. How can any black preacher today profess to know what was in the mind of any Hebrew or Gentile twenty-one centuries ago, when the culture was entirely different? Again, how did people feel and what was important to them?

On plantations across America the same would have been true. How could any African, even if promoted by his master to the position of preacher, or overseer who sometimes killed his own people, have had any idea of what was going on in the mind of a man who viewed him like any other animal he owned? *How can you possibly understand the mentality of somebody who looks at you and sees a horse or a dog? What is truly in the mind of someone today who encounters somebody who is ethnically different and only feels hatred, loathing and contempt?*

During America's early days visionaries could see that slavery would someday produce serious consequences. While many saw slave labor as a necessity, others justified the policy by saying it was a way to introduce the African captives to God's grace. Disobedience carried consequences. Of the first 20 indentured Africans in the colonies, John Punch was declared a slave for life as punishment for running away. John Castor was made the permanent property of Anthony Johnson, a previously indentured free black tobacco farmer who owned 250 acres of land.

For over three and a half centuries black men and black women were brought to America, and over several generations they were exposed to Christian beliefs. As previously stated, *Christianity, in fact, became a fundamental tool used in perpetuating the institution of slavery.*

The Bible supports slavery. Exodus 21:2–4 "If thou buy an Hebrew servant, six years he shall serve; and in the seventh he shall go out free for nothing. If he came in [as a slave] by himself, he shall go out by himself; if he were married, then his wife shall go out with him. If his master have given him a wife, and she have born him sons or daughters; the wife and her children shall be her master's, and he shall go out by himself."

If it's true that the Bible was written by inspired men, did God actually inspire men to have slaves, the same way he supposedly inspired others to commit murder? Was slavery part of *"the good news"* they were writing about? And how could the Bible be God's perfect book when it supported and endorsed torture, slavery, murder, rape, the oppression of women and braking up families?

This particular chapter's purpose is to give you greater insight into why black people in America still continue to blindly follow the slave master's religion, a racist form of Christianity, no matter how much their lives are screwed up and their children's lives promise to be. In my opinion, the very best way to illustrate that is to provide excerpts from *Christianity, Islam and The Negro Race,* by Edward Wilmot Blyden, a negro educator, linguist, writer, and world traveler who lived from 1832 until 1912. *His book was first published in 1888.*

An eyewitness to those times, the following is taken from the chapter *"Christianity and The Negro Race,"* and deals with slavery's introduction to Christianity in America.

"The Christian Negro has, hitherto, as I have tried to show throughout this volume, rarely been trained to trust his own judgment, or to think that he can have anything to say which foreigners will care to hear. *His subordinate position everywhere in Christian countries has made him believe that what his foreign teachers think is the only proper thing to think and that what they say is the only right thing to say.* He is therefore, untrue to the natural direction of his powers, and attempts to soar into an atmosphere not native to his wing." [It was also impossible for the European to put himself in the place of the Christian Negro.] *"But it is evident that there can be hope for the future improvement of the African only as he finds out his work and destiny and as a consequence, learns to trust his own judgment.* Were it not for foreign interference, they would never, in any numbers, have left their ancestral homes for residences in other lands."

"Everybody knows how it happened that the Africans were carried in such large numbers from Africa to America; how one continent was made to furnish the labourers to build up another. Of course, the slaves who were introduced during the first hundred years, we may presume, died Heathens, or with only imperfect glimpses of Christian teaching. For the Christianization of their descendants, a system was invented which so shocked the feelings of John Wesley [founder of the Methodist Church] that, in view of its resulting enormities, he denounced American slavery as *"the sum of all villainies"*. [The most criminal act imaginable].

"*Generations descending from Huguenot and Puritan ancestry were trained to believe that God had endowed them with the right to enslave the African forever. And upon those Africans who became members of the Christian Church, the idea was impressed that it was their duty to submit, in everything, to their masters.* Christian divines of all shades of opinion, in the South, taught this doctrine and embodied it in books prepared especially for the instruction of the slaves, their "oral instruction," for they were not allowed to learn to read."

The Right Rev. William Meade, bishop of the diocese of Virginia, published a book of sermons, tracts, and dialogues for masters and slaves, and recommended them to all masters and mistresses to be used in their families. In the preface of his book the bishop remarks:

The editor of this column offers it to all masters and mistresses in our Southern States, with the anxious wish and devout prayer that it may prove a blessing to themselves and their households.

On page 93 he says:

Some He hath made masters and mistresses for taking care of their children and others that belong to them ... Some He hath made servants and slaves, to assists and work for their masters and mistresses, that provide for them; and others *He hath made ministers and teachers to instruct the rest, to show them what they ought to do, and to put them in mind of their several duties.* [The black preacher was to teach the others how to be good slaves as God commanded. Good niggers!]

On pages 94 and 95, he wrote, addressing the slaves:

Almighty God hath been pleased to make you slaves here, and to give you nothing but labour and poverty in this world, which you are obliged to submit to, as it is His will that it should be so. Your bodies, you know, are not your own; they are at the disposal of those you belong to.

On page 132:

When correction [punishment] is given you, you either deserve it or you do not deserve it. But whether you really deserve it or not, it is your duty, and Almighty God requires that you bear it patiently. [Surely the Jews were not told to be patient or to turn the other cheek as they were being sent to Hitler's ovens and gas chambers because they would be rewarded in heaven.] You may, perhaps, think that this is a hard doctrine [to be beaten and whipped], but if you consider right you must needs think otherwise of it. Suppose, then, that you deserve correction [to be whipped], you cannot but say that it is just and right you should meet with it [accept it]. Suppose you do not, or at least you do not deserve so much, or so severe a correction [beating] for the fault you have committed, you perhaps have escaped a great many more, and are at last paid for it all [being beating for the other things]. Or, suppose you are quite innocent of what is laid to your charge, and suffer wrongfully in that particular thing, is it not possible that you may have done some other bad thing which was never discovered, and that Almighty God, who saw you doing it, would not let you escape without punishment at one time or another? *[God saw what you did before, and that's why I'm beating the hell out of you now.]*

A clergyman of another denomination wrote a catechism for the use of slaves, in which we find the following:

Q. Is it right for the servant to run away, or is it right to harbour a runaway?

A. No.

Q. What did the Apostle Paul say to Onesimus, who was a runaway? Did he harbour him or send him back to his master?

A. He sent him back to his master with a letter.

(Brainwashing and fear were used to keep the slave in a constant state of submission.)

A right reverend prelate tells the slave, in another work written for his "oral instruction," that "*to disobey his master is to yield to the temptation of the devil.*"

Chancellor Harper, in his *Memoir on Slavery*, takes up the sentence of Thomas Jefferson, author of the Declaration of Independence, that "All men are born free and equal, and endowed with certain inalienable rights," and proceeds in a most elaborate, but false and sophisticated discussion, to demonstrate that Jefferson was wrong. But Thomas Jefferson actually argued that black people were inferior in both body and mind. He kept his slaves on his farm at Monticello until he died in 1826, guaranteeing his fine lifestyle even after his friends had freed their own slaves. Thomas Jefferson preached equality for land owning white males, but never freed anybody, including Sally Hemings his slave mistress and their six children. In *Notes on Virginia*, Jefferson stated that it was impossible to "encorporate the blacks into the state," because:

> deep-rooted prejudices entertained by the whites; ten thousand recollections by the blacks of the injuries they have sustained; the real distinctions nature has made; and many other circumstances, will divide us into parties, and produce convulsions, which will probably never end but in the extermination of one or the other race.

Thomas Jefferson firmly believed that eventually the black race and the white race would destroy each other.

One of Harper's references to slavery states that "the most audacious utterances we have read on this subject are those by General Hammond in his notorious *Letters to Clarkson*. That gallant and chivalrous gentleman says, on January 28, 1845, writing from Silver Bluff, South Carolina:"

"*I firmly believe that America slavery is not only not a sin, but especially commanded by God himself through Moses, and approved by Christ through His Apostles*. I endorse without reserve the sentiment of Governor McDuffie, that slavery is the corner-stone of our Republican edifice; while I repudiate as ridiculously absurd dogma of Mr. Jefferson, that all men are born equal. Slavery is truly the corner-stone and foundation of every well-designed Republican edifice" (Democracy, invented in Greece, and Capitalism).

"If the slave is not allowed to read the Bible, the sin rests upon the abolitionists; for they stand prepared to furnish him with a key to it, which would make it, not a book of hope, love, and peace, but of despair, hatred, and blood; converting the reader, not into a Christian, but a demon." [Truly learning about God would turn slaves into devils.]

"Such were the circumstances under which the Negro throughout the United States received Christianity. *The Gospel of Christ was travestied and diluted before it came to him to suit the "peculiar institution" by which millions of human beings were converted into chattels.* The highest men in the South, magistrates, legislators, professors of religion, preachers of the Gospel, governors of states, gentlemen of property and standing, all united in upholding a system which every Negro felt was wrong. *Yet these were the men from whom he got his religion,* and whom he was obliged to regard as guides. *Under such teaching and discipline, is it to be wondered at that his morality is awry, that his sense of the "dignity of human nature" is superficial, that his standard of family and social life is low and defective?"* [Black Americans are screwed up because their ancestors were lied to and bullshitted about God and their rightful place in the world.]

"Their emotions were their guides on Sunday and on Monday, in the conventicle and in the cornfield." Almost four centuries since the advent of slavery in America, many black people are still Christians driven by emotion rather than intellect. Others, who are not religious, but predatory, violently head in the opposite direction. What possible human dignity could there be in someone who kills without any regard whatsoever for human life? And what real moral standards exist within some blacks today because of incessant deprivation, created by systemic racism, which has become accepted as normal? A big part of the problem is that do-gooders waste too much time preaching to the choir. Evil-doers aren't listening and couldn't care less.

"Not so much by what Christianity said as by the way in which, through their teachers, it said it, were the Negroes influenced. *The teachings they received conveyed for them no clear idea or definite impression of the religion of Christ."* [Slaves never actually learned about the real Jesus or his teachings.] "As regards their religion, they were left less to their intellectual apprehension of the truth than to their emotional impulses." [Today's church is still guided by emotionalism (feeling good) rather than learning to use your mind to think and be analytical, which would ultimately inspire aspiration to a higher plane.]

"The influence of the Church was exerted continually to repress, to produce absolute outward submission. It produced an outward conformity to the

views and will of their masters, while it left the heart untouched. Or, perhaps, it might be more accurate to say that their whole nature was taken possession of, and all its capacities for thought and feeling, for love and hope, for joy and grief, were completely under the control of their taskmasters." *[Does this not also sound like today's church with the minister, as taskmaster, telling you what to think and how to act?]*

"As a rule, the Christianity of the Negroes is just such a grotesque and misshapen thing as the system under which they were trained is calculated to produce." *For slaves, there was a bizarre plan to abase and degrade them into submission. Through traditional Christianity blacks were being trained to be slaves to religion and their white masters. Forever!*

"Since the emancipation in the United States, the defective Christian character of the Negroes of the Southern states is constantly made the theme of essays, lectures, and newspaper articles. In the report of Dr. W. H. Ruffner, superintendent of the Public Schools of Virginia for 1874 we find the following:"

"Much of the glamour with which the Negro has been covered by philanthropic zeal, acting at a distance, has passed away as knowledge has increased; but the real character of this people can be learned only from those who have long lived among them. The Southern Negroes are polite, amiable, quiet, orderly, and religious; and hence it is hard to believe that as a class they are without moral character. And yet such is the unhappy fact ... occasionally a high type [Dr. Martin Luther King, Jr.—Barack Obama] is manifested by individuals; and while there is a great deal of religious sincerity and earnestness among them, and whilst the style of piety is modified by the character of the religious instruction they have received, and whilst families and congregations which have enjoyed special privileges exhibit better results [like today's black middle class], *yet with the masses of those who claim to be Christians, their piety is of an unintelligent, sometimes superstitious, and always spasmodic type, and it covers a multitude of sins.*" Is this not also true today? Are many black Christians not behaving unintelligently, superstitiously (shouting, fainting, dancing, and speaking in tongues), and committing a multitude of sins? This includes educated and so-called middle-class blacks.

The *America Missionary* newspaper published the following from a Northern teacher at work among the Negroes in Louisiana:

"Good teachers and preachers are very much needed in this State. I heard a preacher telling his hearers that they must go to *hell,* and leave their sins on the *mud-sills of hell* before they can say that they are born again. To prove this, he said that he would quote the fifty-third chapter of Isaiah. Now, what do you think he quoted? Why, Bunyan's *Pilgrim's Progress,* in relation to Christian's leaving the City of Destruction and the falling-off of his burden at the foot of the cross. *The mischief of the thing was that the people appeared to believe that what he was saying was really in the Bible.* What it is to be a pure Christian very few of these people understand. They profess to be religious, yet the Ten Commandments are a dead letter to them." [Preachers and teachers were lying, reading from other books and telling slaves they were Bibles containing God's word.]

"But even now, while white Christians in the North are shocked at the moral character of Southern Christian Negroes, they do not cease, by their practical teaching, to impress upon the minds of the blacks that *there is one standard of morality for white men and another for black men.* The shadow of the slave system still throws such a gloom over the land, that, where the Negro is concerned, right and wrong are only indistinctly seen."

"Many prominent Christians in the South still hold to the opinion that it is right to enslave the African, and these exert a degree of influence upon the North which, if it does not lead them to desire a renewal of the slave system, perpetuates among them the old feeling of contempt for the Negro." [So the poverty, ignorance, and degradation of blacks turned others against them, even people who weren't racist.]

"The advantages enjoyed by the Negro in the Western world, now that he is free, are hardly greater for the attainment of true manhood than when he was in bondage." [Being free didn't change anything]. "The Negro in Christian lands, however learned in books, cannot be said to have such a thing as self-education. And why? Because he is taught from the beginning to the end of his book-training, from the illustrated primer to the illustrated scientific treatise, not to be himself, but somebody else. *From the lessons he every day receives, the Negro unconsciously imbibes the conviction that to*

be a great man he must be like the white man. The Negro, under Protestant rule, is kept in a state of such tutelage and irresponsibility as can scarcely fail to make him constantly dependent and useless whenever, thrown upon himself, he has to meet an emergency." [The Catholic Church treated him no better than the Protestant church, also making blacks helpless and dependent.]

Slavery and the Jim Crow South were rooted in religion and white supremacy, which reserved the best for white people. What remains largely unknown today is that many Northerners also favored slavery. They didn't necessarily want to own slaves themselves but weren't opposed to others who did. Some Northerners, like Southerners, longed for bondsmen who could make their lives easier.

At one time slavery flourished north of the Mason-Dixon Line in cities like Boston, Philadelphia, and New York. Slavery was legal in all of the 13 Original Colonies. A Christian, Abraham Lincoln's great-uncle Isaac owned 43 slaves. His wife's family owned slaves.

One of the great ironies is how many free Negroes bought and sold slaves. Some bought family members to protect them because by law they were forbidden from remaining in the state after being set free. Others bought slaves purely for profit, often being just as cruel as white masters. Sometimes hiring themselves out and owning a business or land, even Christian slaves bought other slaves without hesitation.

In Cane River, Louisiana during the 1800s Nicolas Augustin Metoyer owned 12 or 13 slaves. Beginning with his mother Maria Theresa Coincoin, the slave concubine of Claude Metoyer, the family eventually owned 215 black bondsmen. Around the time of the Civil War Louisiana's free people of color, the Gens de Coleur Libres, in French, owned land, slaves and assets valued at $15,000,000. One in ten or ½ million black people were free.

The Gens de Couleur Libre were a class of people of mixed Spanish and French and African or West Indian blood whose families had been free for generations, whose language and culture were French. Many of them were wealthy fair skinned slave holders often indistinguishable from white settlers. By 1830 some 750 Creole (black families) owned among them almost 2,500 slaves.

Slavery in Louisiana was not as brutal as it was in the other American colonies. Many small farmers worked side by side with their slaves, the black code (code noir) requiring masters to feed, clothe, and house slaves adequately, even when sickness or old age prevented them from working, and they were not to be worked on Sundays and holy days. It was under the Spanish that free people of color began to be regarded as a separate class between whites and slaves and closer, in rights and status, to the whites. They did not associate with slaves or even newly freed blacks who had no education or manners. Many Gens de Couleur Libres were educated in France, or had French tutors.

White masters took slaves as their mistresses, choosing the best looking females, and over the years the whites preferred the lighter slave women. Many lived quietly as second wives to white men, keeping second homes for them, taking care of the children they had had together, registering them at The St. Louis Cathedral, using the father's name.

In the evenings, on different days, white citizens and free people of color went to the theatre d'Orleans. The silks, jewels and feathers on Creole women were as fine as those worn by white women. The most legendary aspects of this golden era for Creoles were quadroon balls, glamorous affairs held in the Orleans Ballroom, where beautiful young Creole girls, escorted by their mothers, attended hoping to meet a young Frenchman with whom they could form plaçage.

The most treasonous acts imaginable involved the Louisiana Native Guard, slave owning Free Men of Color (Creoles), who formed a militia to fight for the Confederacy, hoping to maintain their separate status. Like their own slaves they too were baptized and raised Catholic.

CHAPTER 23

American Negrophobia

Whatever the reason, whether it was his natural condition or environmental, a result of abuse and mistreatment, the black man's depravity became accepted as fact, especially Free Men of Color. Henry Clay, the American statesman once said, *"The free people of color are the most corrupt, depraved, and abandoned element in our population; but this is not so much their fault as a consequence of their anomalous condition"* [discrimination and being treated like garbage]. Considered a nuisance and a burden, most whites despised free Negroes. Many were living in poverty and couldn't find work. Free People of Color were accused of being a corrupting influence on society, with their begging, stealing, and smelling. Much like perceptions of black people who are denigrated today because of poverty. Remember, the prevailing sentiment among many whites was that slavery was the only way to get black people to do any work. Solomon Northup, an accomplished Free Man of Color who was kidnapped in Washington D.C., then sold into slavery for twelve years was visible proof that that wasn't true.

Sold for $650 after being drugged and beaten with a paddle until it broke, and then given 100 lashes with a cat-o-nine tails, he was told that he would be killed if he ever told anybody he was a free man. Northup, a violinist from New York, had been tricked into believing he would be performing at a circus and paid very well.

For twelve years his wife and two children, plus others who were close to him never knew what had happened or where he was, until someone working on the plantation got word to them. Northup was finally freed. But Washington law forbade black witnesses from testifying against white defendants and in Louisiana where he was held, nobody would ever be punished because of a two year term limitation for wrongfully selling somebody into slavery.

Because of such brutal acts, Henry Clay also predicted race wars, saying that "Negroes are rational beings like ourselves, capable of feeling and reflection and of judging what belongs to them as a portion of the human race. *By the very condition of the relation which exists between us, we are enemies of each other.*" [Eventually blacks would snap.] What would white people do if they were the ones who had been tortured and abused as slaves? Would black people have considered white people depraved savages? White people were never better, but always in a better place.

According to colonizationists like Calvin Colton, black degradation was a result of circumstance. Blacks were not automatically inferior to Europeans, some even arguing that blacks were actually superior. That white superiority was "accidentally derived" from an unequal historical relationship. *Blacks became criminals while whites became Negrophobes.*

Prejudice, which has never be eradicated, was the real problem as black people were disproportionately being thrown into jail and accused of causing an increase in crime rates (just like today). *There were also high rates of insanity among slaves and free blacks.* All the way back to the 1800s, it was proposed that educating black people would elevate them, but that never came to fruition, especially for slaves and former slaves. *The black man's color would always be a permanent sign of his heritage, and as a group, there would never be full acceptance in this country.* That is still true today, even for Barack and Michelle Obama, and Oprah Winfrey.

Democracy in America author Alexis de Tocqueville, while visiting the United States in 1831, wrote that the black and white populations were at war with each other and would never mingle because "American Negrophobia was widespread and deeply rooted, and racial prejudice actually increased with emancipation and was worse in the 'free' north than the slave South." (Just as animus and racism increased with Barack Obama's election to the office of President of the United States). *Skin color would always be an obstacle.* Today the Republican Solid South (Confederacy) is back, and meaner than ever. One of Tocqueville's observations was especially poignant, finding "*a problem of race more fundamental and difficult to solve than the problem of slavery.*" Slavery was structured while race was ambiguous.

Conservative "birthers" argued that Barack Obama was born in Kenya, Africa. Because he is not a natural born American citizen, he was never the legitimate president of the United States. Still, America suffers as legislators refuse to give even one inch, no matter what the consequences are or how catastrophic (possibly violent), they prove to be.

For abolitionist reformers like William Lloyd Garrison and Reverend Charles Grandison Finney slavery was a sin, and the only thing that might change things would be adherence to the gospels of Christ. *In contrast to Calvinism, through evangelical religion, anybody, including slaves, could be saved by becoming more like Christ.* For colonizationists slavery was a social and an economic evil, while abolitionist reformers saw it as a sin that should be repented of. Denying free blacks and slaves a chance to be saved was a sacrilege.

It was Reverend James Freeman Clarke who said in an 1842 sermon that

> "A worse evil to the slave than the cruelty he sometimes endures, is the moral degradation that results from his condition. Falsehood, theft, licentiousness, are the natural consequence of his situation ... *He goes to excess in eating and drinking and animal pleasure [sex]; for he has no access to any higher pleasures,* and a man cannot be an animal without sinking below an animal,—a brutal man *[murderers, rapists and muggers]* is worse than a brute. An animal cannot be more savage or more greedy than the law of his nature allows. But there seems to be no limit to the degradation of a man. Slavery is the parent of vices" [including today's elevated drug and murder rates].

So-called parental or guardian slave owners naturally had different sentiments about their domesticated blacks. Their slaves were more like children, part of the family circle and subjected to family government. And at least slaves who were being cared for, and who were no longer savages, were now happy and not eating anybody or in danger of being eaten. But men who were lovable as slaves would be monsters as freedmen. And not only were their slaves happy, (like Richard Pryor said), they were also grateful. Slavery was good for everybody, especially blacks, because it was the only thing that kept them from turning into heathens and savages again who were beastlike, immoral, ugly, and not fully human. As long as white people ruled them, using God's word.

The slave was still subhuman, a high type of domesticated animal to serve his master. Again, much the same as his horse or his hunting dog. Like other animals, they were also insensitive to pain. Negroes supposedly felt no family connections either, which justified breaking families up. But there was still a potentially serious problem. *Unlike his other property, slaves could rebel.*

According to Louisiana's Dr. Samuel Cartwright, physician to Confederate President Jefferson Davis, black people couldn't be overworked and didn't suffer compared to white people. One Southern writer went even further, writing that not only was it impossible to overwork a slave, because of their thick skulls, it was also impossible to knock one out. Cartwright believed that problems on the plantation with slaves resulted from either bad government or imperfect slavery. Similar to ancient Israelites, it was also Dr. Cartwright's pre-Adamite theory that the Negro was created before Adam and Eve and part of the dominion (beasts) over which white people were to rule. He hypothesized that Negroes were not descendants of Adam, but belonged to an inferior race that had already been created, as I previously explained. Cain's wife was one of them. Many Confederates believed those others were black savages who lived somewhere in Northern Africa, *East of Eden.*

In *The Wrong Of Slavery*, published in 1864, part of the Final Report of the American Freedmen's Inquiry Commission, authorized by President Abraham Lincoln, Robert Dale Owen compares white people and black people. Owen states that:

"The Anglo-Saxon race, with its great force of character, much mental activity, an unflagging spirit of enterprise, has a certain hardness, a stubborn will, only moderate geniality, a lack of habitual cheerfulness. Its intellectual powers are stronger than its social instincts. The head predominates over the heart. There is little that is emotional in its religion . . ."

And

"The African race is in many respects the reverse of this. Genial, lively, docile, emotional, the affections rule; the social instincts maintain the ascendant except under cruel repression, its cheerfulness and love of mirth overflow with the exuberance of childhood. It is devotional by feeling. It is a knowing rather than a thinking race. With time, if we but treat these people in a Christian fashion, we shall have our reward." [But, of course, they did not.]

It is interesting to note that in Germany, even today there is something called "softness training" to try to instill a greater sense of empathy, compassion, and sensitivity in the German people, who are typically cold and detached.

While there were many white people who did act in a Christian fashion to help abused and mistreated slaves, others remained pathologically true to their alleged character flaws, doing just the opposite. They continued to remain fixed on oppression and the exploitation of black people, both economically and socially. We know today that promises made to former black slaves were never kept. Remember, many Northerners opposed slavery but didn't like the idea of blacks running around freely any more than their ancestors had. They still wanted America to be all-white too, the debased, inferior black man gone and America purified. And if there were problems in the North, disorder and violence, it was only because the blacks had provoked the whites. In 1785 German philosopher Christopher Meiners coined the term "Caucasian", describing the white race.

As stated by Senator John C. Calhoun in 1848, "Ours is a Government of the white man." North America was to be a great Caucasian preserve, with John H. Van Evrie, writing, "The Negro is as much a product of the tropics as the orange or the banana." (In other words, as Anthony Browder said, they don't belong here.)

There was yet another problem created by Negroes, especially free people of color. Competition and antagonism. In an 1884 symposium on "The Future of the Negro," Senator John T. Morgan argued that:

> '. . . an increase in black wealth, intelligence, and capacity for industrial, commercial, and political activity was inevitable but potentially disastrous, because it could lead only to an increasingly bitter competition with whites. The greater their personal success may be, the more they will feel the pressure of caste, and their advancement in enterprises which may bring them personal honor and wealth will be checked by the jealousy of caste, so that race prejudice will forever remain as an incubus on all their individual or aggregate efforts." *Even today for successful black people.* [The only way Negroes could hope to advance would be to flee from white competition and antagonism by emigrating to Africa.]

To suppress competition between blacks and whites, fearing that black domination would replace white supremacy, a policy was spawned to deliberately hold black people back from the very beginning in America. Whites, afraid of successful blacks intermixing with their race, fought harder to restrict such liaisons. This, in turn, created greater black solidarity and forced violent collisions between the two groups.

Baltimore physician Edward W. Gilliam wrote:

"The advancement of the blacks becomes a menace to the whites. No two races, remaining distinctly apart, can advance side by side, without a struggle for supremacy."

As predicted, there was competition, but from a most unlikely source. Instead of dying out or disappearing because they were too lazy to work and could not sustain themselves, Negroes were producing children in record numbers. In the 1883 edition of *Popular Science* monthly, Dr. Gilliam wrote about the black population having grown by 30 percent in only ten years, addressing "the remarkable fecundity of the African." [Black people were baby-making machines, number one in the animal kingdom for determining who would survive and who wouldn't, suggesting that black people might overtake white people someday.]

Way back in the 1800s Dr. Gilliam predicted that when black numbers were large enough, black people would demand equality, but white people would continue to suppress them and that there would be "a point at which mere numbers must prevail over wealth, intelligence, and prestige, combined. This dark, swelling, muttering mass along the social horizon, gathering strength with education and ambitious to rise, will grow increasingly restless and sullen under repression, until at length, conscious through numbers of superior power, it will assert that power destructively, and bursting forth like an angry furious crowd, avenge in tumult and disorder, the social law broken against them." (Blacks who had been wronged would eventually awaken from their stupor and take over, demolishing whatever already existed and standing in their way.) Christianity could prevent that from happening.

Later, unfit populations had to be neutered, so organizations like Planned Parenthood came into being to "sterilize the unfit" and to purge America of "bad strains". *Eugenics!* Much of the above, relative to the state of Negroes and whites, was taken from *The Black Image In The White Mind: 1817 to 1914,* by George M. Frederickson.

As a follow-up, addressing the nature of white people versus black people, once again I reference Michael Bradley's *The Iceman Inheritance.*

Amusingly, Bradley asserts that in addition to laws, lies, and manipulation employed to dominate the world through racism, Europeans used religion to propagate the idea that God favored them over other people, turning God into a bigot, colonizing their image of being created in God's image, and colonizing the image of God and the Bible as well. (Bradley says that white Europeans hijacked Christianity too.)

As for the nature of the whites, while their primitive ancestors came from a cold, inhospitable environment where resources were scarce and survival difficult, developing one type of persona, blacks, who lived in an environment where resources were abundant and life somewhat easier, developed another. The white man needed fur for protection against the elements and a warm cave, hopefully one that wolves or bears hadn't already beaten him to.

In contrast, blacks wore very little and had only to reach up, stoop down, or climb a tree to retrieve a banana or some other delicious fruit or nut. A wide range of animals were another abundant food source. The white man evolved to be more materialistic and territorial, first needing the security of the cave, then the area surrounding the cave, and ultimately, the area around the area around the cave. (Some families today own hundreds of thousands of acres.)

There were physical alterations as well. Because of cold temperatures and thinner air at higher elevations where Caucasians lived, they developed more hair, thinner noses, and thicker legs and calves for climbing. Black people, living in more temperate regions like flat, grassy plains, had broader noses, less hair, and thinner legs and calves for walking and running. The most extreme areas produced light skin and blue eyes, or dark skin containing more melanin, and dark eyes. French physician Francis Bernier first divided races by skin color in 1684.

Settling down eventually led to rich and poor, the have's and the have-nots. The elites who had power controlled everything and thought they were invincible. (Like wealthy and powerful whites in America who are now in authority.) Staying put also meant more stress, plus diseases, and making sure nobody stole food or animals that had been acquired.

Divisions between the two classes became even greater. What the elites failed to understand, however, is that throughout history power structures always fail... Nobody stays on top forever.

Sigmund Freud even attributed Western man's psychosexual aggressions and ambivalences to glacial evolution and fighting harsh elements to survive and produce children. That, plus the challenges of sustaining and successfully rearing healthy offspring (today's issues of abortion, same-sex marriage, interracial relations, and possibly penis envy). Michael Bradley suggests that while 50% of white people claim superiority, they actually have an inferiority complex. If white people really felt superior, they wouldn't have to say it so much. Bradley tells how they had to make non-Europeans feel inferior to make themselves feel special. Europeans, who were naturally aggressive, reflecting their own nature, created gods and a God who was aggressive.

Hopefully, you now have a simple but clearer picture of the impact Christianity has played in the lives of black men and black women: how it was perverted to oppress and control them, and how it has been used to elevate white people. What's the rest of the story, the role of Christianity and domination versus subordination?

Religion and race have indeed shifted the more natural planes. *With a little help from God*, white people are typically viewed as leaders and rulers who dominate, while black people are seen as followers who must be controlled, subordinates. The challenge is to find out for yourself who and what you are, and then to decide which side of the bar is yours, the top or the bottom. Being on the bottom is easy enough, *except for survival*. For minorities being on top is another matter entirely, requiring courage and fortitude. If you think that's where you belong you'd better get busy, and stay busy! *Plan for the future now, so your precious life doesn't become one long, drawn out, never-ending emergency.*

Tragically, the lesson most young people receive is that when you mess up there is no second chance. Screw up, *just one time* and you're headed to tragedy. With an outlook for the future like that why even bother to try to do better? *They've already lost!*

While young white males who turn over cars, break windows and set fires are casually referred to as "college kids", economically deprived blacks who feel left behind and riot after reaching a boiling point, committing some of the same crimes as their white counterparts because there are no jobs (there will never be enough jobs), no educational opportunities, oppressive *"command presence"* policing, and crumbling neighborhoods are being branded, criminalized and labeled "thugs". The new "n-word." Without jobs black men are also unmarriageable, so 70% of black children are born to single mothers with little hope for the future.

Adding to their frustrations are the inequities used in prison sentencing schemes based on stereotypical perceptions of white victimization and black criminality. A lawful continuation of slavery. For example, unfair mandatory policies like "3-Strikes You're Out" for repeat offenders, implemented during the Clinton administration. Victims themselves of systemic racism that ignores their needs minorities are demanding that their voices be heard. It was Dr. Martin Luther King Jr. who also said "a riot is the language of the unheard."

Again, in the past guidance was provided by wise leaders like Dr. King and Malcolm X, but what most of today's leaders are passionate about is their own self interests. Some of today's preachers probably dream about topping the $9000.00 an hour (insane greed), McDonald's CEO makes.

Today's black youngsters are children of the oppressed and disenfranchised, young people who are often blamed for creating their own problems. They are living proof that praying and asking God for help, as their parents did, hasn't worked. *Maybe God's just not doing a very good job of doing his job anymore.* Was Dr. King's celebrated premonition, recounted by Mahalia Jackson during the March on Washington in 1963 just another cherished vision a tired Baptist preacher had one night, and not some divinely inspired supernatural message from God? Was Dr. King's dream simply subconscious brain activity that we all have, consolidating and processing information, hoping for a good outcome?

Christianity is supposed to be about hope, forgiveness and redemption. Black kids and other minorities who are waiting to get to heaven might as well give up now and they know it. Life means nothing because they have nothing. Not even hope. Everyday, because of generational poverty and racism, they experience the harsh realities of the unfair chaotic world they are living in. There's no time to wait for heaven! Not one day.

CHAPTER 24

Race, Sex and Homosexuality in History

Since I've already sparked your curiosity, at this point I would like to revisit the idea of homosexuality being involved when Lot wanted to surrender his two daughters to his neighbors instead of his three visitors, two angels and God at his front door. *There was a longstanding tradition in the ancient Mediterranean world that sexual acts were not to be performed between people who were of equal social status.* It was normal and expected for adult males to be attracted to both male and female teenagers of inferior status, but the dominant partner always had to be an adult male. A citizen could have sex with a slave or with a woman because both the slave and the woman already belonged to a lower station. Sex between men was not homosexuality as we know it today, but rather a matter of dominance or submission. *The penetrator or the penetratee.* Often during ancient times male-male sex meant "*I own you*". To them a man who was passive had become in essence a weak woman. Even today being sodomized and forced into the subordinate role of a female generally means you lose. Most men will do whatever it takes to avoid the perception of being effeminate, weak or not manly.

In the Assyrian dream omen series it states, "*If a man copulates with his equal from the rear, he becomes the leader among his peers and brothers.*" The Middle Assyrian law codes states that "If a man has sex with his comrade and they prove the charges against him and find him guilty, they shall have sex with him and they shall turn him into a eunuch." *If a man actually had sex with an equal, another man of equal status, and he was the penetrator he was to be raped and his penis cut off. The person he was sticking it to was already humiliated enough.* Those laws were written by men with money and power thousands of years ago who had secrets of their own.

What was important was domination and status. For Greeks it was totally different. The Greek Spartans saw things just the opposite. *The Spartans wanted men who were lovers fighting side by side, believing that would make them fight much harder.*

Centuries later sexual domination by warring factions has resurfaced. Attested to by United Nations officials, in the Congo rebels are now raping civilians using sexual violence against men to humiliate and demoralize them into submission, just as it was used during ancient times.

According to 2 Samuel 1:26, David, the young hero of David and Goliath, told Jonathan, the son of King Saul, how much he loved him. "I am distressed for thee, my brother *Jonathan: very pleasant hast thou been unto me: thy love to me was wonderful, passing the love of women.*" David told Jonathan that he loved him more than he ever loved any woman. They were only supposed to be best friends. Was it dominance or true love?

David also became Bathsheba's husband. While Uriah, one of his top commanders was off fighting the war, David, who had become king, saw Bathsheba taking a bath and said, "DAMN! I gotta' have that!" He found out she was married but sent for her anyway. That first night they knocked boots, and *wham*, a baby (Solomon) was on the way.

David sent for Uriah and told him to go to his wife (to cover up his pile-driving Bathsheba), but Uriah stayed with the other soldiers instead of going home and sleeping with Bathsheba. If they couldn't leave he wasn't leaving. David even got Uriah drunk, but he still didn't go home. Finally David couldn't take it anymore, so he arranged to have Uriah sent to the front of the battle knowing he would be killed. The husband's out of the way and he marries Bathsheba. David, the holy man, slept with another man's wife then had the man killed after knocking her up. He had somebody murdered so he could steal his wife, but he still had a boyfriend named Jonathan. It appears that King David, our Bible hero, was bisexual and murderous.

In Lot's case, however, his anxious neighbors in Sodom were simply not being very neighborly. The only way they could gain honor was for somebody else to lose theirs. Like today's drug dealers, they were protecting their turf. Being women, Lot's daughters were already expected to be used and dishonored. A man being attacked in his house, however, would have been unforgivable, an assault on male honor. The fact that the men wanted to rape and dominate God and a couple of angels was absolutely unthinkable, even if they didn't know who they were.

It is critical here that I add another historical piece to the Christian-black puzzle. During Shakespeare's time and the rule of famed King James, the curse of Ham was of particular interest to Englishmen in explaining the African's color, his genital size, and his beastly sexual appetite. Most Englishmen, including the king, were racists who hated blacks. *Englishmen who thought Africans were highly sexed brutes were the so-called inspired men who wrote the King James Version of the Bible.* Even if inspired, which they weren't, they were still nonetheless men first, with prejudices and insecurities the same as other men. It was a time when the English, the whitest men, were antagonistic toward Africans, the blackest men. Would you trust somebody who hated you to be a witness for you, or for somebody you care about? Or to tell you what's important in life and what's not, and how to live it? (Like asking David Duke to write a letter of recommendation for Rev. Al Sharpton or Rev. Jesse Jackson, or to tell them where to hide during an F-4 tornado or a Category-5 hurricane similar to Katrina as it approached the Gulf Coast.)

Color-conscious Englishmen were paranoid about black skin and black men being with white women. In William Shakespeare's *Othello*, one of the earliest literary works on race and racism, written around 1603, Iago, the play's main white antagonist said, "I hate the Moors and it is thought aboard twixt my sheets he has done my office." (I hate black people, *niggers*. Othello had sex in my bed with my wife.)

Othello is the enemy. Iago, a trusted soldier who fought by powerful General Othello's side, convinces Othello the black Moor that his hot young bride Desdemona (Dee) is cheating on him with Cassio, a handsome lieutenant. Iago's motive, he is vengeful and wants to destroy both Othello and Cassio. Iago feels that Othello unfairly passed over him for a promotion that was given to Cassio, who was coincidentally "Dee's" good friend. Cassio was the man who hooked her up with Othello. As far as Iago is concerned, that's how Cassio got the job that belonged to him. Besides that, Iago thinks that both men have been cheating with his wife, Emilia. Iago has already made up his mind that whether it's true or not, he's gonna do what he's gonna do. He intends to pay them back, no matter what. He wants to break up Othello's marriage and have Cassio demoted. Iago is jealous because Othello is more powerful and has a better marriage, even though he is a black outsider and is new in Venice. Cassio is young and has both looks and the new job.

To assist him in his scheme to make Othello jealous, Iago talks Emilia, the same wife he suspects of cheating, who happens to be "Dee's" handmaiden, into stealing her mistress's handkerchief, the first gift Othello had ever given "Dee," to use in his plot. He hides the handkerchief in Cassio's room. Bianca, Cassio's girlfriend finds it, and assumes that some other woman gave the handkerchief to him. Iago tricks Cassio into talking about his steamy hot relationship with Bianca, who is a prostitute, and Othello, overhearing them laughing and joking about the sex, including all the dirty little details, thinks they are talking about "Dee," his wife. Iago then convinces Othello that "Dee" gave Cassio (her boy-toy) the handkerchief. Iago mistreats his wife and has a low regard for women. He actually hates women and is possibly jealous of them.

Meanwhile, Roderigo, another soldier really is in love with "Dee," who is both rich and beautiful. A racist, he was already talking to her (hollerin' at her) before Othello, the big time black general came along. The only reason why Othello got Desdemona in the first place is because he was a famous military hero. (Like today's superstar black actors and black athletes. General Othello is also sophisticated and well-spoken like musician John Legend, a good catch for any woman.) Roderigo saw her first, but Othello had the advantage and quickly eloped with "Dee" behind his back. (That rotten sonofabitch Othello was sexing her while he wasn't looking.)

Othello is a proud black man who is overconfident, like many black men are today. He is especially proud of his fine, white prize (his trophy girl). "Dee's" powerful father, Brabanzio, a senator of Venice, doesn't like what's going on either, that his daughter has secretly run away with some black man and is married to him. While Iago and Roderigo say racist things behind Othello's back, Brabanzio, being Othello's superior, says whatever he wants to out in the open about good-for-nothing black people. Pops definitely doesn't believe that any nigger should be either a leader or a part of white society.

Talking to Brabanzio, an angry Roderigo says, "You'll have your daughter covered with a Barbary horse (because horses have gigantic penises), you'll have your nephew neigh to you" (a wild black animal will be on top of your daughter and everybody will make fun of you). Iago says that when Othello and "Dee" have sex, they will produce a "beast with two backs." (Your grandchildren will be disfigured half-human monsters, because blacks aren't really human.) Brabanzio is convinced that some worthless low-down black man is using magic to get to his daughter (with the magic snake). He wonders how she could fall in love with something so ugly if it wasn't for witchcraft. "Dee" knows that it's "against the laws of nature" for blacks and whites to be together, but does it anyway. (The snake, the snake!) Once Brabanzio finds out what the deal is, that the black man in question is Othello, he changes his mind. Everything's cool now, like the white father who finds out that his daughter has married Tiger Woods.

Iago convinces Roderigo that once they get rid of Othello and he's out of the way, he will help him, and "Dee" will come running back to him (if Othello hasn't already worn her out). Roderigo has his suspicions about Iago too, because he was already paying Iago to hook him up, knowing how much they both hated Othello. Roderigo felt double-crossed when Othello crept in, believing that if Iago had done his job the wedding might never have happened. Roderigo figured that Iago must have known about Othello and his girl, which he really didn't, because Othello and "Dee" had done a good job in keeping it on the "down low" about a black man screwing a white woman in the dark. What will they think of next? Oh no, I'm sorry. My bad. Not "next." That was centuries ago.

Some speculate that homosexuality is involved too, and that Iago is both jealous of Othello, and secretly in love with him. Maybe there's a little penis envy going on too. There are many twists and turns, especially since Iago is married but hates women.

As Othello's trusted adviser, Iago often counsels him and is known as "honest Iago," while he charms and tricks people (cons them) into believing him. Iago pretends to be a friend, but he is scheming to destroy them. That goes for anybody who gets in his way. A professional liar, he is always plotting and planning and enjoys ruining people's lives. For no reason in particular. As Richard Pryor might say, "cause they wuz there." Like Iago, Shakespeare, the author, understood people and knew how to manipulate them.

Iago claims to be loyal to Othello, but behind his back, shows that he is a racist when he says that Othello is "an old black ram tupping a white ewe", an old black male sheep-pile-driving a white female sheep. It is possible that Iago may not have been a racist against Othello, and is only saying such things below Brabanzio's window for Brabanzio's benefit, to piss him off, making him even angrier at "that black bastard," Othello. Roderigo calls Othello "thick lips," but like Iago, does it behind his back too. (He doesn't want to get an ass whipping either.) Shakespeare may not have been a racist, but is only writing about the brutal racist climate reflected at that time in England. England and Europe were even more racist before Othello's time. *The Bible was actually written by racists for racists!*

Falling for Iago's lie, Othello, now jealous and insanely insecure, is furious and orders Iago to kill Cassio. He promises him Cassio's position as lieutenant once Cassio is dead. Iago then tricks his friend Roderigo into a drunken fight with Cassio, but Iago double-crosses Roderigo and kills him before he can rat him out, while Cassio is only wounded. Even though he knew Iago was a liar, Roderigo still believed him to the end. (White men always make the mistake of trusting other white men, but Othello believed him too.) Iago had already double-crossed (ratted out) Roderigo by telling Othello that he was the one who had told Brabanzio about the marriage. Iago, the consummate schemer, even pretended to be so angry that he said he could have killed Roderigo for what he had done. Whoever wins or whoever loses Iago always plans to come out on top.

In a final fit of rage after beating her (being a black man), Othello smothers "Dee" to death as she continues to protest her innocence. ("I didn't do it! I didn't do anything! It's a lie. I love only you!") It's only a matter of time before Emilia tells Othello and the others about her role in Iago's plot. But she had already called Othello a "blacker devil" (black sonofabitch) for killing "Dee." Then Iago stabs her. Dejected and dishonored, Othello commits suicide, but only after stabbing Iago, not to kill him, but to make him suffer for the rest of his life. ("F" him up.) In the end, Iago is arrested, and when questioned, answers, "Demand me nothing. What you know, you know. From this time forth I never will speak a word." (Like the pope, I'm not sayin' nothin' about nothin'.) Shakespeare never reveals why Iago is such a treacherous bastard.

Earlier in the story, Iago said, "These fellows that flatter for their own purpose have some souls." (Even though somebody does a bad thing, that doesn't automatically make them bad.) Iago also says, "In following, I follow but myself." (I believe in me, and I always look out for number one.) When Iago says, "I am not what I am," it can clearly be taken to mean that things are not always what they seem (possibly a reference that includes the Bible and the characters in it, if you read between Shakespeare's lines).

A person need not feel bad or guilty about something he has done. That's especially true if it's beyond their control, like lying and deceit because you have been ordered by the king to do something. Just as Iago talks about the devil while he is the one who is evil, the Bible focuses on sin, while the corruption may be more a matter of distraction and misdirection by evil doers who orchestrated the whole thing. What about homosexuality, demonized in the Holy Bible that homosexuals were responsible for producing, and gays like David?

The word *honest* is used by Iago, and ironically means just the opposite. When it comes to the Authorized King James Version of the Holy Bible, what does the word *holy* actually mean? One source says *holy* means belonging to God, while another simply says dedicated or devoted to the service of God, the church, or religion. But *holy* is only a word, and people who are referred to as being holy can definitely have a few screws and scruples missing. It has been alleged, for example, that King James, who was a gay lover of Sir Francis Bacon, didn't even believe the Bible. *The utter hypocrisy and disingenuousness.* King James believed in witches and magic, but simply became the world's first great publisher. In addition to the Bible, King James published another book called *"Demonologia"*, telling how to identify and punish witches. Like Emperor Constantine, King James may not have been a real Christian at all.

Issues involving homosexuality are definitely problematic for conservative Christians, especially those living in the Bible Belt. Just how do they reconcile what they have been taught, with sexual acts they or a loved one may or may not practice? After all, the church, particularly the Catholic Church and the Protestant church, doesn't want Jesus to be either married or gay. All their lives Christians have been taught that there is only one way to get to heaven, and that's by following the straight and narrow. *Especially the straight part.* (Remember Briggs and the fact that times change.) So-called Christians passionately fight for family values, but Jesus can't have a wife and child. (That really is insane, since popes and disciples already had families living at home.)

We don't set people on fire or stone people to death for being gay anymore, or for being gay together (married). Same-sex relationships are said to offend God, but the Bible was written and compiled from a particular point of view by men centuries ago, some of whom were not straight themselves.

As Charles Briggs stated so eloquently in the 1800s, "all old dead dogmas must be cut away." Lesbians, gays, bisexuals and transsexuals are a reality, with the same rights everybody else has. *Remember, for Briggs God was alive, still at work, and flexible. According to Karen Armstrong, every generation has to create something that works for them, whether it's in the Holy Bible, written hundreds of years ago, or not.* Everything is open to interpretation, except for Fundamentalists. Fundamentalists see everything in the Bible as cold, hard teachings from God, even though the Bible supports slavery, rape, murder and genocide.

I purposely took time in telling Othello's story. I didn't just want to say the same thing others have already said, that William Shakespeare wrote parts of the Bible. I wanted to reiterate how smart he was and how detailed he was in developing plots. (A clay pipe containing marijuana and cocaine residue was dug up in Shakespeare's garden.) As you read your Bible, I want you to know how racist many of the people who wrote it were. *And even if not racists themselves, they were still surrounded by racists, racism and a culture of domination and subordination.* Men inspired by God may or may not have written the gospels. Men paid by King James did write "The Authorized King James Version of the Holy Bible." Could Shakespeare have written parts of it too? Shakespeare and King James were in the same place at the same time.

It is also believed that *Othello* may be an adaptation of *Un Capitano Moro* (*A Moorish Captain*) by the Italian writer Cinthio. Desdemona's name is used, as well as descriptions such as "the Moor" (Othello), "The squadron leader" (Cassio), "the ensign" (Iago), and "the ensign's wife" (Emilia). *Like Shakespeare, Cinthio's moral is that European women (white women) should stay away from wild niggers with huge penises.*

Othello's story is a lot like O. J. Simpson's. The famous ego-driven black superstar marries the white beauty, then has to pay for it after she's murdered. Is murder not also a true expression of hidden insecurity? It's like setting yourself up for your own lynching. You know what they say. If it looks too good to be true, it probably isn't true. Nobody gets it all, and most of us are reasonable enough to realize that up front. *Nobody is ever superior to anybody else, no matter what kind of evidence or rationale are provided to prove it, not even the Bible.*

There's an interesting little tidbit about Shakespeare's own sexuality. His *Sonnet 20* says, "But since she prick'd thee out for women's pleasure, Mine be thy love and thy love's use their treasure." Sam Greenspan says it basically means "You've got a nice penis that women really like, so go stick it to them but save the emotional love for me." His *Sonnet 126* begins with "O thou, my lovely boy". *Was Shakespeare gay too*? He often wrote about loving young men. He was married to Anne Hathaway and had children, but spent many, many years away from them going off to live by himself after the first three years they spent together. Some scholars believe he was bisexual. Things aren't always what they seem. Leonardo da Vinci, who was illegitimate, was flamboyant and paraded around Florence in rose-colored tights and a cape like a *drag queen*. One of the men who gave us pictures of the Bible's beautifully inspiring white characters loved painting naked men. Another was at least a bisexual. What about the other men who helped to create the Holy Bible? What kind of character flaws did they have?

A young man known as Andrea Salai moved into Leonardo's household at ten years old, becoming his student and his lifelong servant for more than twenty-five years. Salai was described as "a graceful and beautiful youth with curly hair, in which Leonardo greatly delighted." Others saw him as a liar, a thief, stubborn and a glutton. In stark irony, it is believed that Salai, Leonardo's "boy toy" was the model for Leonardo's painting of St. John the Baptist and possibly the Mona Lisa.

Salai himself painted a nude version of the Mona Lisa, the Monna Vanna. Leonardo's own painting "the Angel Incarnate" is of a nude young man with an erect penis. The model is believed to have been Salai. One of Leonardo's folios contains "Salai's bum," a hand drawing of an anus being chased by penises with legs. When Leonardo DaVinci died he willed his father's vineyard to Salai, who married at the age of forty-three and was killed in a dual by a crossbow a year later.

Women weren't allowed to be actors at that time, so Shakespeare's cast consisted entirely of men. It is said that one of the reasons why he and King James had problems with each other was because the king was constantly trying to get with Shakespeare's actors.

As for Leonardo's famous "Last Supper," there is no way he could have known what the apostles looked like. Leonardo probably used his favorite models (white lovers). It is believed that one of the disciples depicted may indeed be a self-portrait of Leonardo DaVinci. We know that Mark and Luke were not there, so two were missing, and there were no tables or chairs. People reclined on pillows to eat, or used a mat on the floor. The Last Supper is merely a symbolic painting. Not reality.

Because of Shakespeare we know about Othello, but who was King James, the man who would become king when he was only one year old. *Curiously, James IV of Scotland, who became James I of England, the man whose Bible most people read, commissioned 400 years ago in 1611 to be translated from Latin to English, was a homosexual or bisexual.* His father, Lord Darnley, was murdered and his mother, Mary Queen of Scots, married his daddy's murderer. Known to friends like Sir Walter Raleigh as "Queen James, while Elizabeth was jokingly called King." He had three male favorites (lovers), Esmé Stuart, Robert Carr, and George Villiers. Homosexuality at that time was strongly forbidden and being Scottish, the king wasn't liked by Englishmen very much. Lies definitely could have been made up to defame him by enemies like a man named Anthony Weldon. On the other hand, like so many others both then and now, King James certainly could have been married and on the "down low". In public he argued that sodomy was an unforgivable sin. We'll never know for sure, will we?

Esmé, who was 37, approached his younger cousin when he was 13. James gave Esmé all kinds of gifts and power, making him Duke of Lennox, in spite of the fact that they were both married, and Esme had five children. He even hugged and kissed Esme publicly. King James was once kidnapped returning from a hunting trip. His abductors blamed Esmé for all the bad things that had happened during James' rule, finally forcing the king to send his lover back to Scotland. When Esmé died, he left his embalmed heart to his lover, King James.

Robert Carr was a tall, athletic younger man the king actually hugged and kissed in public too, making him Groom of the Bedchamber. King James gave him gifts and political power the same as he had done with Esmé. He made him his private secretary in 1612 after commissioning the Bible, and eventually the Earl of Somerset. The king even paid for his wedding to Frances Howard, Countess of Essex. In addition to the king and his own wife, Carr was screwing around with a writer named Thomas Overly who knew way too much for his own good, and ended up in the Tower of London where he died of poisoning, murdered by Robert's wife Frances. Because of some old love letters between Robert and Overly, both Robert and Frances were sentenced to death. A couple of years later James pardoned both of them.

King James was seeing Carr and George Villiers at the same time. Before the king died, George seldom left his side. Three years later Villiers, the king's lover, was assassinated. George Villers is reportedly buried next to James and another of the king's lovers, Ludovic Stuart, Duke of Richmond and Lennox.

In 1617, the king addressed the Privy Council saying, "I, James, am neither God nor an angel, but a man, like any other. Therefore I act like a man and confess to loving those dear to me more than other men. *You may be sure that I love the Earl of Buckingham more than anyone else,* and more than you who are here assembled. I wish to speak in my own behalf and not to have it thought to be a defect, for Jesus Christ did the same, and therefore I cannot be blamed. CHRIST HAD JOHN, AND I HAVE GEORGE." *In other words, I'm gay like Jesus and I'm in love with George.* There was lying, deceit, cover-ups, and paranoia everywhere.

George was very handsome, and had risen from cupbearer to Gentleman of the Bedchamber like Robert Carr, before becoming Earl of Buckingham. James referred to him as his "sweet child and wife" and himself as "your dear dad and husband". I guess that's what he was being when he made George a Duke, giving him land and jewels too. He wrote to him saying "I naturally so love your person, and adore all your parts, which are more than ever one man had". Which parts was King James talking about?

King James also wrote to George saying "I desire only to live in the world for your sake, and I had rather live banished in any part of the world with you, than live a sorrowful widow-life without you. And so God bless you my sweet . . . wife, and grant that ye may ever be a comfort to (me) your dear . . . husband."

King James's friend, Sir Francis Bacon, the father of "the scientific method," was a bisexual who was married to Alice Barnham, fourteen, when he was forty-five. Bacon and the king were called pederasts (pedophiles), homosexuals who were interested in "buggery," or what was known as "masculine love," with boys who were twelve to seventeen years old, or until there was body hair. *King James and Sir Francis Bacon gave real meaning to the term "Sugar Daddy."* Remember, it was acceptable to exploit children if you were a type of benefactor. It is beyond fantastic that the world's top scientist and a king would be involved in manufacturing a homophobic book like the Holy Bible. Why? Was it obsession with power like Constantine? Was there another cover-up? The king (of the King James Bible) believed in witches, *and he was gay.*

Ham's curse, cited in the Bible, may indicate a gay factor. Some authorities now believe that it was not pronounced simply because Ham saw Noah naked, but because of some homosexual act that took place between the two of them. Others think that Ham may have had an improper incestuous relationship with Noah's wife because "seeing Noah's nakedness" could also have meant seeing his wife naked. And why were Ham's son and his descendants to be punished and not Ham? Were Ham's black children and descendants the result of scandal?

CHAPTER 25

Brainwashed?

If Englishmen were paranoid about black men and sex, and the King James Bible is an English creation, why do black people not believe that there is bias and prejudice in it? Prejudice against black people was as real as prejudice against gays. The King James Version of the Bible is a sexist, homophobic, xenophobic European creation. The following is testimony regarding English feelings about black skin during that time, taken from *The Black Image In The White Mind* by George M. Fredrickson.

From the first moment white Europeans came face-to-face with black Africans their differences were stark. Negroes were immediately viewed as "strangers" or as "the others." This perception of the Negro being different became one of the key arguments for maintaining slavery. The African's skin color and the way he lived automatically made him a savage heathen. Before the sixteenth century, the *Oxford English Dictionary* defined the word black as - a) "deeply stained with dirt, soiled, foul - b) having dark or deadly purposes, malignant, pertaining to or involving death, deadly; baneful, disastrous, sinister - c) foul, iniquitous, atrocious, horrible, wicked." Black was dangerous and disgusting while white was the opposite. White was directly related to innocence and God. Whiteness was desired while blackness was condemned. The black man's evil nature was undeniable and unmistakable because of his hideous color. On the English stage, as far back as the 1500s, the souls of those who were damned were represented by actors painted black or wearing black costumes. Christians were white, the heathens were nonwhites, Negroes. Blackness was a curse. In Africa the devil was white.

Many believed the Negro was a distinct order of being, the connecting link between men and monkeys. There was supposedly some logical relationship between the lowest man and the highest animal. The African was that missing link or connection; the only difference between him and the ape was that the African could speak. Ironically, both the black man and the anthropoid ape were discovered at the same time and in the same place. Men who resembled apes, and apes without tails who resembled men hinted that there may have been a sexual connection as well. Negroes were considered to be just as wild and equally as lustful as the African orangutan. What they were really comparing them to was the chimpanzee. Apes and men who had low, flat nostrils and comparably shaped skulls were too much alike for their similarities to be overlooked. Some even argued that the ape was the offspring of the Negro and some unknown African beast. Others believed the Negro and the ape were having intercourse; that the apes were having sex in the jungle with hot, passionate Negro women.

Because the ape was beastly and lustful, the Negro was also considered beastly and lustful. An early English writer, Samuel Purchas, in a segment of his writings wrote, "They are very greedie eaters and no less drinkers, and very lecherous, and theevish, and much addicted to uncleanness; one man hath as many wives as hee is able to keepe and maintaine." During the early 1500s, Leo Africanus, a Spanish Moor, wrote of Negroes that "there is no nation under heaven more prone to venery, principally addicted to Treason, Treacherie, Murther, Thaft and Robberie." Africanus further stated that "the Negroes likewise lead a beastly kind of life being utterly destitute of the arts. Yea, they so behave themselves as if they had continually lived in a forest among wild beasts. They have great swarms of harlots among them; whereupon a man may easily conjure their manner of living." One seventeenth-century traveler reported that the Negroes sported "large propagators" (penises), and another stated that Mandingo men were "furnished with such members as are after a sort Burdensome unto them." The implications were clear. The Negro was a well-endowed wild savage, an animal who had no control over his sexual appetite. If white people had such an extreme aversion to black people and black skin, what possible reason would black people have for believing anything they said, even if it was found in an ancient book called "The Holy Bible?"

Much of the Bible is written in allegorical form. These writings are stories in which people, places, and things symbolically represent higher moral truths which were known only to a select group of men.

I do not wish to argue the point that the Bible is the word of God or the word of God written by inspired men. When other faiths claim that their text is the "word of God," are they wrong? *Is God's word really only found in the Bible as many Christians firmly believe, or did God actually have important things to say to other people, too?* Is it really possible that in the entire universe there is only one God, and the only people He spoke to were the people in the Authorized King James Version of the Holy Bible? The one God made the entire universe, and then put white people who looked like him only on earth? What made earth so special? In the 21st Century do we still believe that?

Everyone is entitled to his or her own beliefs, and I certainly encourage everybody to believe in something, especially some higher power. We all need a moral compass, a spiritual reference point for contemplation, meditation and action. I personally think it would be too arrogant to think that everything just begins and ends with me, as mankind egotistically does, and that that's all there is. *That man alone is the most important creation in the cosmos, more special than any other living, breathing creature. Is it nature that is telling man he is so special, or is it religions such as Christianity, that were made up by egotistical man himself?*

Man is fallible; he makes mistakes. All men make mistakes. Men are also greedy. And about that word *inspired*, the word often used to describe the men credited with writing the Bible, men who they say were touched by God. What does *inspired* actually mean? The *Thorndike-Barnhart World Book Dictionary* provides several definitions: "to awaken or cause," "to influence with a thought or feeling," "to arouse or influence by a divine force," "to cause to be told or written." There is nothing mystical or magical about the word *inspired* in any of those definitions, relating to God himself. Watching Tiger Woods, I might be inspired to play golf, and with his genius, I'm sure there are those who probably think him divine, especially attractive, ambitious, entitlement driven young white women who play golf or admire rich athletes.

And what about that other word, *divine?* Well, it means "of God or a god." It also means "to find out or foretell by inspiration, by magic, or by guessing." *To find out by magic or by guessing!* Now, *that's* really deep. As a writer, I appreciate and understand the usefulness of buzzwords, just like politicians do, and as I'm sure the ancients did. It's obviously true by their choices to use such emotively powerful terms like holy, prophet, divine, scripture, angel, demon, devil, and so many others. Emotive words such as those are much more graphic and stirring than colorless words like cornflakes or typewriter. They get your attention. Two simple words, *holy* and *bible,* nine letters, together as *Holy Bible,* have even become sacred.

For the moment, let's accept that divinely inspired men wrote the Bible. It's still clear that others who were not divinely inspired, and possibly not even spiritual altered parts of it. In her book *Who Tampered with the Bible,* Pat Eddy says, "The ancients believed that the relative degree of the truth of a statement was a function of the prestige of the statement maker." In other words, to the ancients, an event such as the proverbial chicken crossing the road may or may not have been perceived as being true, depending upon who espoused it. Hence, as previously stated if an author really wanted something to be believed, it had to come from the lips of Christ, John the Baptist, Paul, Moses, etc. Thus, false attribution, pseudepigrapha, was extremely common and forms the basis for most of the tampering in the Bible."

To the ancient Semitic people the concept of time was just as fluid as the concept of truth. No clear-cut demarcation between past, present, and future existed in their mental processes. *This is seen by their proclivity to write history as though they were predicting the future.* The Old Testament book of Daniel is a clear demonstration of this. The sections of the book purported to be prophecy may actually have been written many years after most of the events took place. Future predictions were actually past events.

Many of today's Christians are indeed brainwashed, or victims of "Coercive Persuasion." Especially black people. They will believe anything when it comes to religion. Robert J. Lifton cites eight steps to what he calls "totalism," or complete involuntary conversion. They are:

- Milieu control: The purposeful limitation of all forms of communication with the outside world, sleep deprivation, a change in diet, control over who one can see and talk to. (Don't ask questions, especially about other faiths and stay away from non-believers.)

- Mystical manipulation: Teaching that the control group has a special *(divine)* purpose and that the subject has been chosen to play a special role in fulfilling this purpose. (Christians are God's children, and they must save sinners.)

- Need for purity: Convincing the subject of his former impurity *(before joining the church you were a sinner)* and the necessity of becoming pure or perfect as defined by the group. (Be godly and become more like Jesus.)

- Confession: Getting the subject to let down barriers and openly discuss innermost fears and anxieties. (Giving testimony.)

- Sacred science: Convincing the subject that the control group's beliefs are the only logical system of belief and therefore must be accepted and obeyed. (The Bible as fact, God's word.)

- Loading the language: Creating a new vocabulary by creating new words with special meanings understood only by members of the group, or by giving new and special meanings to familiar words and phrases. (Bishop, born-again, blessed and highly favored, etc.)

- Doctrine over persons: Convincing the subject that the group and its doctrine take precedence over any individual in the group or any other teaching from outside it. (God is the answer and believing in Him is the only way to receive his blessings.)

- Dispensing of existence: Teaching the subject that all those who disagree with the philosophy of the control group are doomed. (Only God guarantees salvation.)

Eric Merrill Budd, in *The Reality of Religious Abuse,* gives three examples of evangelical Christians who have suffered exploitation and emotional injury by abusive authoritarian churches and religious organizations:

- A young woman is too terrified to touch her electric toaster, convinced that she will be electrocuted because of her sins.

- A man is told to attend the same church as his wife, or he will never see his children again.

- When a couple tell their church leaders that they have placed a down payment on a new house, they are rebuked for not asking the leaders for advice and permission; later, the church leaders express even greater disapproval, because the location of the house doesn't fit in with the church's plans for evangelism.

It is tragic that our need to belong and our need to believe have led so many down destructive paths and away from the very thing they are seeking: *Truth.* It's even more dispiriting and disabling when we look at wars being fought against the Taliban, Al-Qaeda, and ISIS, all in the name of God, as well as those wars yet to be fought. It's insane to believe that there is a "winner" or a "victory" when so many are left crippled, countless lives are lost, and the ensuing economic burden is so apocalyptic. We have been intellectually desensitized and *dumbed-down* by profiteers using compact discs, as well as television, social media, and the media, a media which is increasingly being controlled by fewer and fewer oligopolistic companies with larger markets that are becoming more and more monopolistic. We watch the blood and gore of war or hate crimes from the comfort of our living rooms, nibbling on chips and sipping a Coke. Our reality is becoming artificial, a "virtual reality," and the church which controls so much of our lives is a major player, and complicit.

"Not Only Is Big Brother Watching You, You Are Watching Big Brother."

CHAPTER 26

What the Good Book Really Says

There are so many things in our lives that we take for granted. One is the Holy Bible. No matter who you are, if you live in America or anywhere in the world you are impacted by it. There is no "one" Bible. Because of politics there are at least 400 different Bibles. The texts of the Old Testament were written in Hebrew or Aramaic. *Jesus spoke Aramaic, not English*. Remember, the New Testament was originally written in Greek. Whether you are a Christian satisfied with listening to some preacher read from popular scriptures and verses, while he avoids the unsavory ones, or someone who couldn't care less, it may be in your best interest to at least try to understand something that daily affects your life.

Much of the Bible revolves around people like Moses, Abraham, Peter, and John, who are considered saints. One of the first things we need to establish is what a saint is, or is not. The *Thorndike Barnhart World Book Dictionary* defines a saint as a very holy person; one who is pure in heart and upright in life. I guess that settles it. There are no saints by that definition. Mother Theresa might genuinely have been a good person, but the Bible says "all have sinned" and are therefore not pure of heart. Rev, the priests and the bishops are some of those sinners too.

A second definition refers to a person thought of like a saint. Well, that's kind of weak too, isn't it? That definition could apply to almost anybody, including liars and con men wearing priestly robes.

Third, a person who has gone to heaven. And, of course, how would we know that?

Fourth, a person declared to be a saint by the Roman Catholic Church. The same guys who believed in slavery, who have abused tens, if not hundreds of thousands, or perhaps even millions of children and adults throughout the ages.

Lastly, a person belonging to any religious body whose members are called saints. Anybody can be called a saint as long as they belong to the right church, including me.

In *Let Us Prey* I am not trying to demonize or to put down any religion, and certainly not to denounce the importance of spirituality. I seek only to open your eyes, and my own.

One of the Bible's biggest shortcomings is that it distorts reality, in some instances lies, and sets forth an impossible reality, Santa Claus and the Easter Bunny for adults. *Storytime.* Standing in line to tell God how good you've been is a lot like children standing in line at Christmas to tell Santa how good they've been to get presents, for grown-ups going to heaven. The wise men didn't even bring gifts to Jesus on that first Christmas day. James, Peter, and Paul, three of the founders of the early Christian church may be called saints, but the word saint is after all, only one more label created by the Catholic Church to perpetuate an air of piety and legitimacy. *Many saints weren't innocent sheep or even decent human beings.*

It's curious too, that of all the religions in the world, only the Catholic Church and a couple of others have something called a saint. And like popes, saints are delegated by men. How can men make choices and decisions for God? Saints are one of those clever illusions that keep believers believing. A person's favorite saint is his personal contact with the Almighty. Their own angel perched atop their shoulder. Making Pope John Paul II and Pope John XXIII saints may even help to energize a declining Catholic population, while improving the church's bank balance. "Two for one" for the first time. Pierre Toussaint, a freed black slave who died in the 1850s will probably become the next American saint, or Louisiana's Creole Henriette Delille.

Another first is the Vatican displaying bone fragments, supposedly belonging to St. Peter, the first pope. (Another public relations move). For Pope John Paul II, it's really historic because sainthood usually takes centuries. Even Jesus wasn't a saint, and never knew any or spoke of any. Remember, sainthood means big business and even more people visiting the Vatican and buying souvenirs. Jesus was a Jew, and of course Jews didn't (and don't) believe in saints. *How could Jewish apostles become Catholic saints?*

The Roman Catholic Church maintains that it does not create saints, but recognizes them (finds them). All Catholics. Curiously, in the past 400 years it hasn't been lucky enough to recognize or find at least one African American. This, even though Pope John Paul II's sainthood happened so quickly. Followed by Mother Theresa.

According to one of the Church of England's Articles of Religion Of Purgatory, the Romanish Doctrine of Saints is "a fond thing vainly invented, and grounded upon no warranty of Scripture, but rather repugnant to the word of God." Anglicans generally believe that the only real Mediator between believers and God is his son Jesus. Jesus was a Jew who worshipped and believed in the God of the Hebrew Bible. Not saints or the Catholic Bible. He would have been dumbfounded by sainthood, especially kissing the pope's ring or his foot.

The Bible's scope is truly astounding, but what is really contained within its pages? Much of the following is also taken from *Scandalous Saints* by Frederick Heese Eaton. In Scandalous Saints he takes a look at homosexuality, incest, rape, and murder, all found in the Holy Book, and committed by so-called saints.

According to Eaton, "The fact of the matter is that many of the much revered Bible saints were less than saintly. Not only that, but many of the laws and teachings those saints promulgated were completely outrageous; certain laws that the clergy never discuss. But we will examine those unusual laws herein too, for your edification. And we will expose the wild and scandalous lives of these 'saintly' people, who are held up as examples to show us how to live uprightly, when they didn't live uprightly themselves." Again, the following is Eaton's account, and taken from *Scandalous Saints, published in 1994.*

Homosexuality and Incest

Getting back to the early church saint named Lot, who was the nephew of Saint Abraham. He is called "righteous Lot" in the Bible's New Testament, and those words were written by none other than the highly revered apostle Saint Peter, outstanding Judeo-Christian chosen by Jesus Christ himself. At 2 Peter 2:7 of the Bible, we read, "righteous Lot, greatly distressed by the licentiousness of the wicked." (With no morals, Lot was a freak.)

Perhaps you remember the Bible's story of the man called Lot; how he chose to live in a city called Sodom where homosexuality ran rampant. One day Saint Lot was visited by three men. Thereupon a gang of rapists assaulted Lot's house and attempted to drag out Saint Lot's male visitors to have homosexual intercourse with them. Usually we hear of rapists attacking women, but in this case the rapists wanted men.

Then the Bible tells us, "And Lot went out at the door unto them, and shut the door after him and said: 'I pray you, brethren, do not so wickedly. Behold now, I have two daughters which have not known a man [Some sources say Lot had four daughters]. Let me, I pray you, bring them out unto you, and do ye to them as is good in your eyes; only unto these men [my visitors] do nothing" (Genesis 19:6–8).

In other words, in Saint Lot's eyes, women and daughters were less valuable to him than men. Throw them to the rapist wolves. But leave his male visitors alone. Do you suppose Saint Lot was interested in these men for the same reason the mob was? [Even domination might be fun.] Either Saint Lot liked men more than he liked women, or he had something else working. Saint Lot may some day be known as the patron saint of homosexuals.

Also, Saint Lot invited the homosexual rapists to "Do to them [his daughters] as is good in your eyes." In other words, "If you're not satisfied with normal sex relations, then have anal sex with them, oral sex relations, or whatever. [Do your thing]. It's okay with me. But here they are. Rape them at your pleasure." This is a queer standard of morality that the Bible, and more particularly the Judeo-Christian New Testament holds up for people to follow, don't you think? With "Righteous Lot" as the saintly example.

Well, the homosexual rapist mob didn't want Saint Lot's daughters any more than Lot did. They wanted the visiting men. "And they [the mob] pressed sore upon the man, even Lot, and came near to break the door" (Genesis 19:9). According to the biblical account, Lot's visitors blinded the mob with tear gas or mace or pepper spray [the story doesn't say which], and this left them staggering about sightless and helpless outside.

Here the Bible story claims that Lot's visitors notified their host of the impending destruction of the city of Sodom and surrounding areas. They urged Lot to flee from there with his family. This Saint Lot did the next day, taking his wife and two grown daughters with him. It is doubtful that Lot fled Sodom because of any supernatural warning, however. He left town because he feared another attack by the mob, which might seek to take revenge on him.

Moses says in the Bible, "And he looked toward Sodom and Gomorrah and toward all the land of the plain, and beheld, and lo, the smoke of the country went up as the smoke of a furnace" (Genesis 19:28).

The Bible also tells us that Saint Lot's wife lagged behind him to watch the destruction of Sodom, and she was caught by the fringe of the blast, which fried her to a pillar of salt. So Lot was left without a wife. This is an important point to keep in mind as we consider the next sizzling episode of this story.

"And Lot went up out of Zoar and dwelt in the mountain, and his two daughters with him; for he feared to dwell in Zoar. And he dwelt in a cave, he and his two daughters Midrash and Aggadah.

"And the firstborn [daughter] said to the younger, 'Our father is old, and there is not a man in the earth to come into us after the manner of all earth [i.e., have sexual intercourse with us]. Come, let us make our father drink wine, and we will lie [sexually] with him, that we may preserve the seed of our father' [become pregnant] (Genesis 19:30. 32).

"And they made their father drink wine that night. And the firstborn went in, and lay [sexually] with her father. And he perceived not when she lay down nor when she arose" (Genesis 19:33).

Since he didn't know "when she lay down nor when she arose," the old man must have been lying there with all his clothes off, stark naked, because if she had to wrestle his clothes off him first, she might well have aroused him out of his drunken sleep.

There is still some question as to whether a woman can rape a man without his cooperation. [Especially an old man who needs extra help in getting it up.] But maybe old man Lot was not as drunk as his daughters thought he was. Maybe Lot was drunk with one eye open, and was just as anxious to have some fun as his daughters were." According to Eaton, Lot was obviously a bisexual and willing to take women when he couldn't get men.

The Bible tale continues: "And they made their father drink wine that night also. And the younger arose, and lay [sexually] with him [got some too], and he perceived not when she lay down, nor when she arose" (Genesis 19:35). Old man Lot was slick.

The Bible tells us: "Thus were both the daughters of Lot with child by their father. And the first born bare a son, and called him Moab; the same is the father of the Moabites unto this day. And the younger, she also bare a son, and called his name Ben-ammi. The same is the father of the children of Ammon unto this day" (Genesis 19:36–38). Here you have the account of a man having sexual intercourse with his own two daughters. (Daughters he may have been sexually abusing.)

"Drunkenness, incestuous pregnancy, and then deliberately lying about it are hardly righteous virtues, even though St. Peter says Lot was. And what do you think of a father who offered to turn his daughters over to a wild mob? Was Lot ever righteous? Did his daughters get him drunk, or was it the other way around? Did this dirty old man who was willing to see his daughters raped by a mob actually get them drunk instead? Lot was indeed scandalous but Christianity and the Bible consider him otherwise." There's definitely something wrong with this picture. (Even if one takes the domination-subordination argument into account, that doesn't mean that men in Sodom didn't enjoy sodomy when women were scarce. Domination could have been an excuse.)

Rape

Nowhere in the Bible is rape made a sin or a crime such as adultery or homosexuality. The only recourse in Bible law for rape was a civil suit for damages. A father whose unmarried daughter was raped could bring suit against the rapist, who was then required to pay the father fifty shekels of silver, but the raped woman got nothing. She didn't count.

The Bible says in Deuteronomy 22:28–29, "If a man find a damsel that is a virgin which is not betrothed and lay hold on her and lie with her [sexually] and they be found, then the man that lay with her shall give unto the damsel's father fifty shekels of silver, and she shall be his wife." This kind of law was worse than nothing. Can you imagine what kind of a marriage it would produce, with the poor girl married to her rapist for the rest of her life, or until he was tired of her, for only fifty shekels?

In Judges 19-21 a Levite has a big fight with his wife so she goes back to her father. The Levite talks her into coming back with him but they must spend the night away from home. Some men want to have sex with him but settle for his wife, viciously gang raping her all night. She dies the next day. The Levite cuts her up into 12 pieces which he sends to the twelve tribes of Israel. As punishment God slaughters 40,000 Benjaminites.

After the battle with the Midianites, Saint Moses wanted to reward his soldiers and himself, so he saved alive thousands of Midianite girls for himself and his soldiers to rape. The Bible again quotes Saint Moses' words, "But all the women and children that have not known a man by lying with him [have not previously had sexual intercourse] keep alive for yourselves" (Numbers 31:18). This was no small number of girls handed over to the soldiers for their sexual entertainment. The "Holy" Bible says there were 32,000 girls raped, a new beginning for Israel. "And thirty and two thousand persons in all, of women that had not known a man by lying with him" (Numbers 31:35).

Murder

Moses was up on top of the mountain desperately trying to engrave the Ten Commandments on small slabs of stone. Meanwhile, his long stay on the mountain stirred up rebellion among the Israelites. The Bible tells us, "And when the people saw that Moses delayed to come down out of the mount, they gathered themselves together under Aaron and said unto him, 'Up, make us gods which shall go before us. As for this Moses, the man that brought us up out of the land of Egypt, we wot not what has become of him." *We don't care what happened to Moses* (Exodus 32:1). After forty years who was left to remember some old man? The Hebrews definitely weren't thrilled about following Moses around the Sinai Desert all that time and nearly starving to death. But all their complaining about lousy food and no water was making God angry, so he sent poisonous snakes to kill a bunch of them. (God slaughtered his own people.) David said Nathan's God was a God without mercy.

Well, Aaron hesitated a bit, but he too was not sure about what had happened to Moses. Meanwhile, he didn't want to lose control of rulership over the Israelites, so he consented to their request. "And Aaron said unto them, 'Break off the golden earrings which are in the ears of your wives, your sons, and your daughters, and bring them unto me.'

"And he received them at their hand, and fashioned it with a graving tool, after he had made it a molten calf. And they said, 'These be thy gods, O Israel, which brought thee up out of the land of Egypt" (Exodus 32:2-4). Seventy Hebrews went to Egypt, 400 years later 3,000,000 returned.

In the midst of all the celebration, Saint Moses came down off the mountain, and when he saw what was going on he was enraged. They had returned to the pagan worship of El instead of Yahweh, worshiping the golden calf (Exodus 32:19–20).

The Bible related, "And he [Moses] said unto them, 'Thus saith the Lord Jehovah God of Israel, Put every man his sword by his side, and go in and out from gate to gate throughout the camp and slay every man his brother, and every man his companion, and every man his neighbor.' And the children of Levi [Moses' tribe] did according to the word of Moses. And there fell of the people that day about three thousand men" (Exodus 32:27–28). Genocidal terrorism.

Aaron made the golden calf for the Israelites, and caused them to be naked, but Moses did not order Aaron killed. He killed everybody who disagreed with him and taught his followers to do likewise, but not his own brother. Just as Abraham didn't kill Isaac. Angry, then breaking the stone tablets, Moses went back up Mt. Sinai to re-do The Ten Commandments. Like Babylonians, Jethro taught him about laws.

Also in Numbers 31:17, after the battle with the Midianites, Moses said, "Now kill all the boys. And kill every woman who has slept with a man . . ." (Moses was one of the greatest mass murderers ever.) When Joshua fought the battle of Jericho the Bible says (Joshua 6:20–21), "When the trumpets sounded, the people shouted, and at the sound of the trumpet, when the people gave a loud shout, the wall collapsed; so every man charged straight in, and they took the city. They devoted the city to the Lord and destroyed with the sword every living thing in it, men and women, young and old, cattle, sheep and donkeys."

There are several other things to remember about the King James and other versions of the Bible. Not one word was written by a black man or by a woman, as mentioned earlier. The Bible is deliberately biased against women and against people of color by omission. In the entire book it says nowhere that a father cannot have sex with his daughter, but a mother is forbidden to have sex with her son (Leviticus 20:11). Husbands were not prohibited from having more than one wife, but the wife was guilty of committing adultery if she had sex with any man other than her husband, and killed.

There are several questions you need to ask yourself again. Who was the Bible written by? Who was it written about? When the Bible was written, what was its purpose? Was it written for all men or was it written only for Hebrew genealogy and instruction? Is the Holy Bible by happenstance merely the first true product of globalization? Is it the world's first historical fiction "best seller"?

If you have not read the Bible, and if you are in any way interested in the underlying social factors that affect you it's time to read the Bible for yourself. Even if you're not interested read it anyway. There are people in the Bible (saints), who would absolutely be considered sociopaths and psychopaths today. *These sociopaths and psychopaths are being passed off as heroes and role models. The exact number of saints the Catholic Church recognizes is unknown, but one independent Catholic source puts it at approximately 921, while another estimate is over 2,500.* That's a lot of people, with sainthood costing up to one million dollars. Remember, there are no African American saints, and the only Native American was Kateritakewitha. Are white people the only miracle workers?

There are other characters who do not appear in the Bible, notable Christians who have been controversial and somewhat unorthodox, like Pope Joan, the Catholic Church's only female pope. Religious people have committed unimaginable deeds, all the while claiming to love God. In his illustrious book *Absolute Monarchs*, John Julius Norwich talks about the history of the Catholic Church and its extreme popes.

According to Norwich's sources, Joan was an Englishwoman referred to as John VII or John VIII, from 855 to 857. She became pregnant while pope and secretly had the baby during a procession. Some said she died after being attacked by an angry crowd. Others said Joan took her own life. The church of course denied that a female pope ever existed, but the rumor persisted for centuries.

Norwich says Pope John XII raped so many virgins and widows that women were afraid to visit the Shrine of St Peter for fear of becoming the next victim. The young pope, indifferent in his role, had turned the Palace of the Lateran into a harlot's brothel (whorehouse). Of his many mistresses, some were fat and some skinny, some rich and some poor, one he made governor of cities and gave the church's money to, another was Stephana, his father's concubine that he had gotten pregnant. Pope John XII was also using the city's money for gambling and even more screwing around.

Bishop Liudprand of Cremona called for a synod, or council, that the young pope didn't even see fit to show up for. There, testimony was given about John having ordained a deacon in a stable, being paid for ordaining bishops, blinding his spiritual father, castrating a cardinal subdeacon who subsequently died, burning houses down, drinking, and not celebrating canonical hours or making the sign of the cross.

When they threatened to get rid of him if he didn't come back to clear his name, the pope's reply was, "You can't do anything if I excommunicate you." They elected a new pope, Leo, but eventually John returned, cutting out tongues and cutting off hands, fingers, and the noses of anybody who had betrayed him.

Originally, his name was Octavian, before becoming pope and changing it to John XII. He was the bastard son of Alberic II, whose father Alberic I, an adventurer, had married his grandmother Marozia. Marozia, the young pope's grandmother, was a powerful aristocrat who had been labeled a shameless strumpet by Bishop Liudprand of Cremona. At 15 she became the mistress of Pope Sergius III, her father's cousin, having a son by him who became Pope John XI.

Marozia ruled Rome, and she hated Pope John X who was a former lover of both her and her mother Theodora. She and her second husband, Guy, Margrave of Tuscany, succeeded in having the pope's brother Peter killed in front of him, and Pope John X imprisoned, where he was found smothered to death.

Marozia got rid of Guy and married his half-brother Hugh of Provence, whose wife conveniently died just before the two of them were married by her son, Pope John XI, the only pope to ever officiate at his own mother's wedding. The pope's mom married half-brothers. But Marozia had underestimated Alberic II, the pope's half-brother who was successful in having Marozia and her pope son thrown into jail. Eventually Pope John XI was released, placed under house arrest, and treated like a personal slave by his half-brother Alberic II. Marozia was indeed scandalous. She was the mother of Pope John XI by Pope Sergius III, the lover of Pope John X, and the grandmother of Pope John XII, with a little incest and a few murders in between. If you watch the HBO series *Game of Thrones,* that is fiction, but this stuff is the real deal. These people and those in the Bible were ruthless, yet we think that they were pious and holy, and that we're so clever today. They were more cut-throat than we could ever be.

It was Giovanni de' Medici, Pope Leo X, who said "*God has given us the papacy, now let us enjoy it.*" Partying and having a good time were the Pope's religion. Making it easier, Leo X was a member of the powerful Medici banking family who controlled the city of Florence, Italy.

Another one of Norwich's outrageous popes was Cardinal Francesco della Rovere, who became Sixtus IV, and is said to have spent money like water. To raise money he sold unprecedented numbers of indulgences and high-sounding titles, even making an eleven-year-old boy Archbishop of Lisbon. One of the two nephews he bestowed red cardinal's hats on was even rumored to be his son by his own sister. The pope made his bastard son by his sister a cardinal. It is believed that Pope Sixtus IV fathered at least seven children, doing all he could to give them wealth and power. It was also believed that Sixtus IV was involved in the plot to overthrow the Medici family, ultimately excommunicating them after Giuliano Medici was stabbed at least a dozen times and dying. (Murder at the Vatican.)

Pope Julius II, who was said to be homosexual and widely accused of sodomy, actually fathered three daughters while he was a cardinal. Other popes like Eugenius IV liked to party, including horse racing, carnivals, and good-looking young men. Pope Alexander VI is also among those popes who fathered children. Before becoming head of the Church Pope Innocent VIII fathered at least sixteen illegitimate children, and possibly as many as one hundred by the time he was done. More bastard children than any other pope in history. (Was the name Innocent actually perverted sarcasm?) The Pope even cut deals to elevate two of his sons. His oldest, Franceschetto, married Lozenzo de' Medici's daughter Maddalena, so that Lorenzo's son Giovany could become a cardinal at 13, and then Pope Leo X. Three innocent boys were sacrificed, giving blood to try and save a gorged Innocent VIII's worthless life.

Pope Pius II had at least two children out of wedlock. Pope Clement VII, Giulio de' Medici, had one illegitimate son, Alessandro de Medici, while Pope Gregory XIII had one illegitimate son. It was alleged that Pope Paul III, who fathered four illegitimate offspring, three sons and a daughter, even delayed his ordination so he could keep screwing around. Although illegitimate, the children just mentioned were born prior to their fathers becoming popes.

Other popes however, have been denounced for being sexually active after they were ordained. Pope Sergius III was accused of being Pope John XI's father by Marozia and not her husband Alberic I. And of course Pope John X screwed around with Pope Paul XI's mother Marozia, and her mom Theodora. In addition to rape, Pope John XII was also accused of incest and adultery. Likewise, in addition to being accused of murder, Benedict IX held orgies that included rape, sodomy, and bestiality. Benedict V was eventually killed by a jealous husband after raping a young girl and escaping to Constantinople with the church's money.

Rodrigo Borgia, great-nephew of Pope Calixtus, became Pope Alexander VI, producing at least eight children by three different women, and according to Norwich, he made no secret of the fact that "he was in the church for what he could get out of it," including the orgies. Five of his children became cardinals.

Under Pope Alexander, who wasn't religious at all, nepotism ran wild and his oldest son, Giovanni, a twenty-year-old womanizer, was found murdered, his throat cut with at least nine stab wounds. By Norwich's account, the most likely suspect was his brother Cesare, who shared a crush on the same sister-in-law, Sancha, and Lucrezia, their own sister (murdering a brother or a brother-in-law to get to your sister-in-law or your own sister wasn't a problem). While some believed that Cesare killed Giovanni, others thought it was Gioffreo.

Wars and the church were costing a bundle, so Pope Alexander set out to shake things up. They were selling more indulgences than ever, as well as the sales of offices, but Alexander decided that enough was enough. No more transferring of church property to laypersons, only one bishopric (diocese) per cardinal, no more than eighty people and thirty horses per household, and no more hunting, theaters, carnivals, tournaments, and fancy funerals. And no more bribes or concubines. (They were spending a shitload of money.) The pope found a better way to make it all happen. It was an outspoken Dominican friar, Girolamo Savonarola, who hated what the church had come to represent, and so did Alexander's old enemies, the Medicis. Savonarola said that

> Popes and prelates speak against worldly pride and ambition and are plunged in it up to their seats (asses). They preach chastity and keep mistresses ... They think only of the world and worldly things; for souls they care nothing... they have made of the church a house of ill fame...A prostitute who sits upon the throne of Solomon and signals to the passers-by...O prostituted Church, you have unveiled your abuse before the eyes of the whole world, and your poisoned breath rises to the heavens. [They were sexual deviants. Perverts!]

After the Medicis were thrown out and Savonarola became the new leader of the city, he wanted mirrors, cosmetics, fine clothes, secular books, musical instruments, and gaming tables thrown out too. Pope Alexander excommunicated him and ordered him tortured, executed, stripped naked, hanged from the same cross with two other men, and cooked over a huge fire. The pope ordered the barbecue.

As Alexander aged, intent on building a Borgia family empire, the Borgias, under Cesare, the other woman-chasing son, took over the church, assassinating people and taking their property, and selling church offices to the highest bidder. Cesare Borgia was the first person to ever resign as cardinal. His father had made him Bishop of Pamplona at 15 years old and cardinal at 18. The Pope made his other son Giovanni captain general of the papacy military forces. And again, both brothers were guilty of screwing around with their 12 year old brother Gioffreo's 16 year old wife, Sancha of Aragon. Cesare died of syphilis at the age of thirty-one with eleven bastard children.

John Julius Norwich also quotes the diary of Johannes Burchard, the papal master of ceremonies during Alexander's reign:

> On Sunday evening, October 30th [1501], Don Cesare Borgia gave a supper in his apartments in the apostolic palace, with fifty decent prostitutes or courtesans in attendance, who, after the meal, danced with the servants and others there, first fully dressed and then naked. Following the supper, too, lampstands holding lighted candles were placed on the floor and chestnuts strewn about, which the prostitutes, naked and on their hands and knees, had to pick up as they crawled in and out among the lampstands. *The Pope, Don Cesare, and Donna Lucrezia were all present to watch.* Finally prizes were offered—silken doublets, pairs of shoes, hats, and other garments—for those men who could perform the act most frequently with the prostitutes. [The pope was in the middle of an orgy.]

Furthermore, there was a plot to murder the pope's son-in-law, Sforza, whom Lucrezia, his daughter, had married at thirteen. Her second husband, Alfonso of Aragon, actually was murdered by Cesare. To pay for Sforza's third marriage, this time to a second Alfonso, the Este duke of Ferrara, eighty new offices were sold and nine new cardinals appointed. At the same time, the pope appropriated the entire fortune of the Venetian Cardinal Giovanni Michiel, who had recently died, probably poisoned by Cesare.

It is important to also remember that the church was sometimes a family and even a state business, just like the shamans and the Hebrews. Pope Innocent VIII's half-brother was Pope Nicholas V, Pope Gregory VI was Benedict IX's grandfather and Pope Hormisdas was Pope Silverius father. The following is a short but incomplete example of family ties. There are many, many, more.

Papal name:	*Original name*
Benedict VIII:	Theophylact II of Tusculum
John XIX:	Romanus of Tusculum
Benedict IX:	Theophylact III of Tusculum
Calixtus III:	Alfonso de Borgia
Alexander VI:	Rodrigo Borgia
Sixtus IV:	Francesco della Rovere
Julius II:	Giuliano della Rovere
Leo X:	Giovanni de' Medici
Clement VII:	Giulio de' Medici
Pius IV:	Giovanni Angelo Medici
Leo XI:	Alessandro de' Medici

After all we have learned about church activities in the past, and what we know about cover-ups and pedophilia today, if the pope really does represent God there is something truly wrong with this picture. Again, there is much to be revealed, and for those who desire to learn more, there is no better reference than John Julius Norwich's *Absolute Monarchs*.

People are people, and while times and events may change, human nature overall remains consistent. Most of us want what we want, when we want it, and some of us are even willing to do almost anything to get it. People will also believe whatever they want to, no matter what the evidence is to the contrary. Once their minds are made up they look for anything that will support what they already believe, whether it makes sense or not. Confirmation bias, the tendency to interpret information in a way that confirms what someone already believes. That's the case with religion. People will continue to believe whatever they want to, no matter how ridiculous, far-fetched, or implausible. Many of Christianity's heroes were liars, scumbags, sociopaths, and even psychopaths, yet we are to revere them as icons. The only way to change implicit and explicit bias is by changing the culture, beginning with religion.

Speaking of iconic heroes, I want to give you a little something else to think about, or at least laugh about.

Jesus of Nazareth God-man	Clark Kent Super-man
Jesus worked supernatural miracles.	Superman had supernatural powers.
Jesus' father God lived in heaven.	Superman's parents Jor-El and Lara lived on Krypton.
Jesus promoted the Holy Scriptures.	Clark Kent worked for the Daily Planet.
Jesus' adversary is the devil.	Superman's adversary was Lex Luthor.
Jesus had Mary Magdalene.	Clark Kent had Lois Lane.

For Christians "God is a just God". Like being the lamb of God, is Jesus also an allegory or a metaphor for justice? Was Jesus (God), the original Superman for Hebrews? And let's not forget Superman's motto, "Truth, Justice, and The American way."

CHAPTER 27

Willie Lynch and Plato

⇥

As incredible as it might seem in the 21 Century, with the exception of a few scholars and people with an Afrocentric outlook, most people have probably never heard of either Willie Lynch or Plato. I'm sure more people at least know Plato's name, even though they may not know who he was or what he did. Very few, on the other hand, have ever heard of Willie Lynch, although both men, even deceased, have had a profound impact on our lives. While it was Willie Lynch who had a prescription for maintaining and keeping slaves, it was Plato whose philosophy and counsel could lead to real liberation. As Malcolm X suggested, we should be intelligent, or at least try. *If Abraham Lincoln's Emancipation Proclamation had not truly freed black people after the Civil War, why were they so quick to believe that another law, the Civil Rights Act of 1964 would have different results?*

We have seen the fortunes of people of color rise and fall and rise and fall time and again. We have watched as a few black people have done well, thinking that they have arrived or been delivered, only to realize that like everybody else, they still live on this planet and in racist America. Unfortunately, social change never actually changes very much. Is social change even real? Is it simply a superficial temporary form of pacification? An illusion?

Willie Lynch was the exception. He did indeed affect a kind of social permanence in America. In his words, his prescription would help to maintain a slave for 300 years or more. While there is often talk about what Mr. Lynch advocated, we seldom see the results he predicted from the inside out, looking in the rearview mirror from the perspective of the victim. How have we changed in nearly four centuries, 400 years, if

393

at all? Furthermore, how does Willie Lynch continue to affect me and you, blacks and whites alike? Naturally, there are also those who consider him a fabrication and modern-day myth. For anyone unfamiliar with Mr. Lynch, the following is from his letter distributed in 1712.

WILLIE LYNCH ADDRESS:

Gentlemen, I greet you here on the bank of the James River in the year of our Lord one thousand seven hundred and twelve. First, I shall thank you, the gentlemen of the Colony of Virginia, for bringing me here. I am here to help you solve some of your problems with slaves. Your invitation reached me on my modest plantation in the West Indies, where I have experimented with some of the newest, and still the oldest methods for control of slaves. Ancient Rome would envy us if my program is implemented. As our boat sailed south on the James River, named for our illustrious King, whose version of the Bible we cherish, I saw enough to know that your problem is not unique. While Rome used cords of wood as crosses for standing human bodies along its highways in great numbers *(crucifixion)*, you are here using the tree and the rope on occasions (lynching). I caught the whiff of a dead slave hanging from a tree a couple miles back. You are not only losing valuable stock by hangings, you are having uprisings, slaves are running away, your crops are sometimes left in the fields too long for maximum profit, you suffer occasional fires, your animals are killed. Gentlemen, you know what your problems are; I do not need to elaborate. I am not here to enumerate your problems, I am here to introduce you to a method of solving them. In my bag here, I HAVE A FOOL PROOF METHOD FOR CONTROLLING YOUR BLACK SLAVES. I guarantee every one of you that, if installed correctly, IT WILL CONTROL THE SLAVES FOR AT LEAST 300 HUNDRED YEARS. My method is simple. Any member of your family or your overseer can use it. I HAVE OUTLINED A NUMBER OF DIFFERENCES AMONG THE SLAVES; AND I TAKE THESE DIFFERENCES AND MAKE THEM BIGGER. I USE FEAR, DISTRUST AND ENVY FOR

CONTROL PURPOSES. These methods have worked on my modest plantation in the West Indies and it will work throughout the South. Take this simple little list of differences and think about them. On top of my list is "AGE," but it's there only because it starts with an "a." The second is "COLOR" or shade. There is INTELLIGENCE, SIZE, SEX, SIZES OF PLANTATIONS, STATUS on plantations, ATTITUDE of owners, whether the slaves live in the valley, on a hill, East, West, North, South, have fine hair, course hair, or is tall or short. Now that you have a list of differences, I shall give you an outline of action, but before that, I shall assure you that DISTRUST IS STRONGER THAN TRUST AND ENVY STRONGER THAN ADULATION, RESPECT, OR ADMIRATION. The Black slaves after receiving this indoctrination shall carry on and will become self-refueling and self-generating for HUNDREDS of years, maybe THOUSANDS. Don't forget, you must pitch the OLD black male vs. the YOUNG black male, and the YOUNG black male against the OLD black male. You must use the DARK skin slaves vs. the LIGHT skin slaves, and the LIGHT skin slaves vs. the DARK skin slaves. You must use the FEMALE vs. the MALE, and the MALE vs. the FEMALE. You must also have white servants and overseers [who] distrust all Blacks. BUT IT IS NECESSARY THAT YOUR SLAVES TRUST AND DEPEND ON US. THEY MUST LOVE, RESPECT AND TRUST ONLY US. Gentlemen, these kits are your keys to control. Use them. Have your wives and children use them, never miss an opportunity. IF USED INTENSELY FOR ONE YEAR, THE SLAVES THEMSELVES WILL REMAIN PERPETUALLY DISTRUSTFUL. Thank you gentlemen. [Some slaves would become hopeless degenerates while others would, in essence, become helpless fleas in a jar with no lid. Their descendants would follow the same model.]

LET'S MAKE A SLAVE
Frederick Douglass

"It was the interest and business of slave holders to study human nature, and the slave nature in particular, with a view to practical results. I, and many of them attained astonishing proficiency in this direction. They had to deal not with earth, wood and stone, but with men, and by every regard they had for their own safety and prosperity, they needed to know the material on which they were to work, conscious of the injustice and wrong they were every hour perpetuating, and knowing what they themselves would do, were they the victims of such wrongs. They were constantly looking for the first signs of the dreaded retribution. They watched therefore with skilled and practiced eyes, and learned to read with great accuracy, the state of mind and heart of the slave, through his sable face. Unusual sobriety, apparent abstractions, sullenness and indifference, indeed, any mood out of the common was afforded ground for suspicion and inquiry." Frederick Douglass' LET'S MAKE A SLAVE is a study of the scientific process of man-breaking and slave-making. It describes the rationale and results of the Anglo-Saxons' ideas and methods of ensuring the master/slave relationship.

LET'S MAKE A SLAVE "The Origin and Development of a Social Being Called 'The Negro.' Let us make a slave. What do we need? First of all, we need a black nigger man, a pregnant nigger woman and her baby nigger boy. Second, we will use the same basic principle that we use in breaking a horse, combined with some more sustaining factors. What we do with horses is that we break them from one form of life to another; that is, we reduce them from their natural state in nature. Whereas nature provides them with the natural capacity to take care of their offspring, we break that natural string of independence from them and thereby create a dependency status (today's illiteracy, broken families, welfare, food stamps, Section 8, incarceration and religion, etc.), so that we may be able to get from them useful production for our business and pleasure.

CARDINAL PRINCIPLES FOR MAKING A NEGRO

For fear that our future generations may not understand the principles of breaking both of the beast together, the nigger and the horse, we lay down the art. We understand that short range planning economics results in periodic economic chaos; so that to avoid turmoil in the economy, it requires us to have breadth and depth in long range comprehensive planning, articulating both skill and sharp perceptions. We lay down the following principles for long range comprehensive economic planning.

1. Both horse and niggers [are] no good to the economy in the wild or natural state.
2. Both must be BROKEN and TIED together for orderly production.
3. For orderly future, special and particular attention must be paid to the FEMALE and the YOUNGEST offspring.
4. Both must be CROSSBRED to produce a variety and division of labor.
5. Both must be taught to respond to a peculiar new LANGUAGE.
6. Psychological and physical instruction of CONTAINMENT must be created for both.

We hold the six cardinal principles as truth to be self-evident, based upon following the discourse concerning the economics of breaking and tying the horse and the nigger together, all inclusive of the six principles laid down above. NOTE: Neither principle alone will suffice for good economics. All principles must be employed for orderly good of the nation. Accordingly, both a wild horse and a wild or natur[al] nigger is dangerous even if captured, for they will have the tendency to seek their customary freedom and, in doing so, might kill you in your sleep. You cannot rest. They sleep while you are awake, and are awake while you are asleep. They are DANGEROUS near the family house and it requires too much labor to watch them away from the house. Above all, you cannot get them to work in this natural state. Hence, both the horse and the nigger must be broken; that is breaking them from one form of mental life to another. KEEP THE BODY, TAKE THE MIND! In other words, break the will to resist.

Now the breaking process is the same for both the horse and the nigger, only slightly varying in degrees. But, as we said before, there is an art in long range economic planning. YOU MUST KEEP YOUR EYE AND THOUGHTS ON THE FEMALE and the OFFSPRING of the horse and the nigger. A brief discourse in offspring development will shed light on the key to sound economic principles. Pay little attention to the generation of original breaking, but CONCENTRATE ON FUTURE GENERATIONS. Therefore, if you break the FEMALE mother, she will BREAK the offspring in its early years of development; and when the offspring is old enough to work, she will deliver it up to you, for her normal female protective tendencies will have been lost in the original breaking process. For example, take the case of the wild stud horse, a female horse and an already infant horse and compare the breaking process with two captured nigger males in their natural state, a pregnant nigger woman with her infant offspring. Take the stud horse, break him for limited containment. Completely break the female horse until she becomes very gentle, whereas you or anybody can ride her in her comfort. Breed the mare and the stud until you have the desired offspring. Then, you can turn the stud to freedom until you need him again. Train the female horse whereby she will eat out of your hand, and she will in turn train the infant horse to eat out of your hand, also.

When it comes to breaking the uncivilized nigger, use the same process, but vary the degree and step up the pressure, so as to do a complete reversal of the mind. Take the meanest and most restless nigger, strip him of his clothes in front of the remaining male niggers, the female, and the nigger infant, tar and feather him, tie each leg to a different horse faced in opposite directions, set him afire and beat both horses to pull him apart in front of the remaining niggers. The next step is to take a bullwhip and beat the remaining nigger males to the point of death, in front of the female and the infant. Don't kill him, but PUT THE FEAR OF GOD IN HIM, for he can be useful for future breeding.

THE BREAKING PROCESS OF THE AFRICAN WOMAN

Take the female and run a series of tests on her to see if she will submit to your desires willingly. Test her in every way, because she is the most important factor for good economics. If she shows any sign of resistance in submitting completely to your will, do not hesitate to use the bullwhip on her to extract that last bit of [b----] out of her. Take care not to kill her, for in doing so, you spoil good economics. When in complete submission, she will train her offsprings in the early years to submit to labor when they become of age. Understanding is the best thing.

Therefore, we shall go deeper into this area of the subject matter concerning what we have produced here in this breaking process of the female nigger. We have reversed the relationship; in her natural uncivilized state, she would have a strong dependency on the uncivilized nigger male, and she would have a limited protective tendency toward her independent male offspring and would raise male offsprings to be dependent like her. Nature had provided for this type of balance. We reversed nature by burning and pulling a civilized nigger apart and bullwhipping the other to the point of death, all in her presence. <u>By her being left alone, unprotected, with the MALE IMAGE DESTROYED</u>, the ordeal caused her to move from her psychologically dependent state to a frozen, independent state. In this frozen, psychological state of independence, she will raise her MALE and female offspring in reversed roles. For FEAR of the young male's life, she will psychologically train him to be MENTALLY WEAK and DEPENDENT, but PHYSICALLY STRONG. Because she has become psychologically independent, she will train her FEMALE offsprings to be psychologically independent. What have you got? <u>You've got the nigger WOMAN OUT FRONT AND THE nigger MAN BEHIND AND SCARED.</u> This is a perfect situation of sound sleep and economics. Before the breaking process, we had to be alertly on guard at all times. Now, we can sleep soundly, for out of frozen fear his woman stands guard for us. He cannot get past her early slave-molding process. He is a good tool, now ready to be tied to the horse at a tender age. By the time a nigger boy reaches the age of sixteen, he is soundly broken in and ready for a long life of sound and efficient work and the reproduction of a unit of good labor force. Continually through the breaking of uncivilized savage niggers, by throwing the nigger female savage into a frozen psychological state of independence, by <u>killing the protective male image</u>, and by creating a submissive dependent mind of the nigger male slave, we have created an orbiting cycle that turns on its own axis forever, *unless a phenomenon occurs and re-shifts the position of the male and female slaves. We show what we mean by example. Take the case of the two economic slave units and examine them close.*

THE NEGRO MARRIAGE

We breed two nigger males with two nigger females. Then, we take the nigger male away from them and keep them moving and working. Say one nigger female bears a nigger female and the other bears a nigger male; both nigger females—being without influence of the nigger male image, frozen with a independent psychology—will raise their offspring into reverse positions. The one with the female offspring will teach her to be like herself, independent and negotiable (we negotiate with her, through her, by her, negotiates her at will). The one with the nigger male offspring, she being frozen subconscious fear for his life, will raise him to be mentally dependent and weak, but physically strong; in other words, body over mind. Now, in a few years when these two offsprings become fertile for early reproduction, we will mate and breed them and continue the cycle. That is good, sound and long range comprehensive planning.

WARNING: POSSIBLE INTERLOPING NEGATIVES

Earlier, we talked about the non-economic good of the horse and the nigger in their wild or natural state; we talked out the principle of breaking and tying them together for orderly production. Furthermore, we talked about paying particular attention to the female savage and her offspring for orderly future planning, then more recently we stated that, by reversing the positions of the male and female savages, we created an orbiting cycle that turns on its own axis forever *unless a phenomenon occurred and reshifts positions of the male and female savages.* Our experts warned us about the possibility of this phenomenon occurring, for they say that the mind has a strong drive to correct and re-correct itself over a period of time if it can touch some substantial original historical base; and they advised us that the best way to deal with the phenomenon is to <u>shave off the brute's mental history</u> and create a multiplicity of phenomena of illusions (a black President, upper, middle and lower class blacks, Black on Black Crime, or getting rich through basketball, football, or rap), so that each illusion will twirl in its own orbit, something similar to floating balls in a vacuum. This creation of multiplicity of phenomena of illusions entails the principle of crossbreeding the nigger and the horse as we stated above, the purpose of which is to create a diversified division of labor; thereby creating different levels of labor and different values of illusion at each connecting level of labor. The results of which is the severance of the points of original beginnings for each spheres illusion (separation and isolation). Since we feel that the subject matter may get more complicated as we proceed in laying down our economic plan concerning the purpose, reason and effect of crossbreeding horses and niggers, we shall lay down the following definition terms for future generations. Orbiting cycle means a thing turning in a given path. Axis means upon which or around which a body turns. Phenomenon means something beyond ordinary conception and inspires awe and wonder. Multiplicity means a great number. Crossbreeding a horse means taking a horse and breeding it with an ass and you get a dumb, backward, ass long-headed mule that is not reproductive nor productive by itself. Crossbreeding niggers mean taking so many drops of good white blood and putting them into as many nigger women as possible, varying the drops by the various tone that you want, and then letting them breed with each other until another circle of color appears as you desire. What this means is this: Put the niggers and the horse in a breeding pot, mix some asses and some good white blood and what do you get? You got a multiplicity of colors of ass backward, unusual niggers, running, tied to backward ass long-headed mules, the one productive of itself, the other sterile. The one constant, the other dying, we keep the nigger constant for we may replace the mules for another tool, both mule and nigger tied to each other, neither knowing where the other came from and neither productive for itself, nor without each other. Today's powerless, helpless, egotistical upper and middle-class asses feel superior to lower class asses who are either passive or ambivalent, all going nowhere together.

CONTROLLED LANGUAGE

Crossbreeding completed, for further severance from their original beginning, WE MUST COMPLETELY ANNIHILATE THE MOTHER TONGUE of both the new nigger and the new mule, and institute a new language that involves the new life's work of both. <u>You know language is a peculiar institution. It leads to the heart of a people.</u> The more a foreigner knows about the language of another country the more he is able to move through all levels of that society. Therefore, if the foreigner is an enemy of the country, to the extent that he knows the body of the language, to that extent is the country vulnerable to attack or invasion of a foreign culture. For example, <u>if you take a slave, if you teach him all about your language, he will know all your secrets, and he is then no more a slave, for you can't fool him any longer,</u> and BEING A FOOL IS ONE OF THE BASIC INGREDIENTS OF ANY INCIDENTS TO THE MAINTENANCE OF THE SLAVERY SYSTEM.

For example, if you told a slave that he must perform in getting out "our crops" and he knows the language well, he would know that "our crops" didn't mean "our crops" and the slavery system would break down, for he would relate on the basis of what "our crops" really meant. So you have to be careful in setting up the new language; for the slaves would soon be in your house, talking to you as "man to man" and that is death to our economic system. In addition, the definitions of words or terms are only a minute part of the process. Values are created and transported by communication through the body of the language. A total society has many interconnected value systems. All the values in the society have bridges of language to connect them for orderly working in the society. But for these language bridges, these many value systems would sharply clash and cause internal strife or civil war, the degree of the conflict being determined by the magnitude of the issues or relative opposing strength in whatever form. For example, if you put a slave in a hog pen (raggedy shack), and train him to live there and incorporate in him to value it as a way of life completely, the biggest problem you would have out of him is that he would worry you about provisions to keep the hog pen clean (I need my voucher), or the same hog pen and make a slip and incorporate something in his language whereby he comes to value a house more than he does his hog pen, you got a problem. He will soon be in your house. (People who only know about the ghetto will always be happy there, like three generations living in the same housing project.)

"Henty Berry, speaking in the Virginia House of Delegates in 1832, described the situation as it existed in many parts of the South at this time: 'We have, as far as possible, closed every avenue by which light may enter their (the slaves) minds. If we could extinguish the capacity to see the light, our work would be complete; they would then be on a level with the beasts of the field and we should be safe. I am not certain that we would not do it, if we could find out the process and that on the plea of necessity." (*Brown America, The story of a New Race* by Edwin R. Embree. 1931 The Viking Press.)

I believe that I have been lynched. I think that every black man and every black woman in this country has been lynched. We were not physically beaten and dismembered or hung from a tree somewhere; we were psychologically, socially, politically, educationally, emotionally and economically mutilated. We had black parents and grandparents whose parents were black and lynched, as Willie Lynch prescribed. Even freed blacks or black people who were always free were still subjected to the harsh reality of racism. Black people who were fair enough to pass for white feared being discovered. They were lynched too.

In his book *"The Insane Nigger"* author Mack B. Morant quotes Bob Teague, who wrote *"Letters To A Black Boy"*. Teague explained that because of the inhumane way they have been treated *"all black men are insane"* and that *"there never has been a sane black man in this society."* Mack Morant says because of the way black people were forced to live they are socio-psychologically insane. Living the way they did on slave-ships, being sold on auction blocks as animals, naked, with people watching them, and then living in quarters similar to hog pens, muddy from the rain with hard dirt floors, being fed like animals, with rapes, beatings, castrations, eyes gouged out, burnings, lynchings, being fed alive to razor back hogs or being buried alive. Morant says that being black in a white America and being dominated by white people is no easy task as black people continue to try to prove to the world that they are intelligent. Trying to think white in an attempt to assimilate many are lost, confused, and plagued by feelings of helplessness (Du Bois' double consciousness). Morant called black men being denied good jobs, being fired from the best job they ever had and being denied loans "neo-lynchings".

Malcolm X went even further, saying the black man's color was like a prison, keeping him confined, not letting him go this way or that way, until he felt trapped in his own skin, ultimately leading to him hating himself. Remember, in *"In Search of Goodpussy"* I, too, talked about the fact that black people have learned to live successfully in an abnormal environment by pretending, concealing generations of abuse, frustration and anger.

I was unaware of my own scars and fears until Gerson, a Latino friend suggested that I was paranoid. Ordinarily I would have taken exception to any such suggestion, but for some reason, this time I decided to take a moment to think about it. Was I actually in denial? Because I was a so-called alpha male who always handled his business and had had his way, was it true that I might have been living in a state of fear without realizing it? *Brainwashed, and somewhat paranoid!*

I often thought about how easy it is for white people going about their affairs every day, not worrying about being stopped by the police for no good reason, or being mugged just walking to the corner grocery store for a coke. It's harder to get a job, so black men being in jail is a systemic problem. Inner-city schools are generally segregated and inferior, and the highest murder rate still exists among black people, exacerbated by unfathomable police brutality. Life for us has always been difficult in America, with the exception of people like President Obama, who was a political amateur, trusting Republicans too much, even after Bush Administration shenanigans. Was America truly ready for a black president?

In addition to everything else that may be unfair about today's criminal justice system, courts are now charging defendants "user fees". Joe Shapiro, NPR's investigation reporter says that "even getting a speeding ticket can land you in jail owing hundreds and even thousands of dollars." In Georgia a homeless man who had stolen a can of beer was charged $12 a day for a leg monitor. Some prisoners are even paying for room and board, while others are charged for juries.

Shapiro says most defendants are poor. In many instances they get put on payment plans that they can't possibly pay, and end up going deeper in debt. One man who was homeless and driving without a license ended up owing $10,000. People were going to jail because they couldn't pay their fines and fees, 21st Century debtors' prisons that were outlawed before the Civil War. A corrupt criminal justice system is quietly separating fathers and mothers from their families and leaving them unprotected, affecting seventy million Americans.

As a youngster, my mom ran the house while my dad worked. She and the other mothers all raised their sons to grow up to be good Christians.

The late Christopher Hitchens, author of *God Is Not Great* even posed the question "Is religion child abuse?" We had to go to Sunday School, 11 o'clock service, Bible School and Children's Choir rehearsals. As I stated earlier, we were obedient, well mannered, attentive, and good students. We didn't cause problems. Unknowingly, our mothers had learned Mr. Lynch's lessons, and they would make sure their sons were properly trained (emasculated), including me. To our detriment, we were all glued to our mothers at the hip, or the tit. *As an adult male, was my own self-confidence overrated?*

I was an excellent student, no fights, no smoking, no drinking, and no cursing, not until I started working at Delta Airlines with young white males who were my age. I had never even said the word *nigger* or gone into a bar before, not until I was in my 20s. During my youth, we had to be indoors by a certain time, and in bed by a certain time after doing homework or washing dinner dishes. If it was your turn and you forgot, my parents would wake you up, and see to it that you finished your chores or did your homework before you could go back to sleep. Mess up and a *whipping* was coming your way, administered by my mom. My father saved his energy for serious infractions.

Remember, my mother ran our home, my grandmother ran hers. The men were there, but the women did the rearing. I didn't realize it then but my mother was crippling me. We learned valuable lessons too, like respect, discipline, and work ethics. But she had no idea that she was training (conditioning) me and my siblings to be twentieth and twenty-first century pacifists, and it all started with church. Looking around, I see that most black men really are dependent on women in one way or another. And we know about black women and their so-called attitudes. She will kick your ass in a heartbeat, while the male lives in a perpetual state of fear where he is typically afraid to assert himself rationally or positively, which leaves basketball, football, rapping, criminal activity, and chasing women. Some Gen X males do appear to have found their voice and balls, even without strong men as models.

The average black male is in a state of confusion. Mother has taught him how to be a man, deciding what type of life he should live. Without knowing it, she has emotionally and psychologically castrated him. Even if mothers understood what they were doing, they would still choose emasculated sons instead of seeing them dead, victimized by psychotic "white animal cruelty." Mothers subconsciously teaching their sons to think like helpless, insecure women as Mr. Lynch prescribed.

I have, on far too many occasions, found myself relying on women. There were times in my life when I should have been more assertive, even aggressive, but chose instead to be cautious and to play it safe. And remember, I was one of those so-called non-conformist alpha males who wouldn't put up with too much. Including openly dating white women society told me to stay away from. I have been angry at times, often with myself, and not known why. I was literally and genuinely confused and didn't realize it. Why had I made some of the choices I made? Why didn't I ever put "me" first? Why didn't I ever look out for number one as so many others had? The answer is simple. *I was trained well by women, women who had learned Willie Lynch's lessons well.*

I was a true young gentleman, not realizing that being gentle and a man were not necessarily good things, not always compatible with the real world. Although it was generally a good thing in most women's eyes. I have learned the hard way that being tough really is a prerequisite for being a strong man who can protect himself and his home. After 400 years most Black Americans have truly lost both their way and their identity.

Being exposed and involved in the way white people live was truly beneficial. I honesty believe the most important thing I learned was how "not to only think and feel black." White people run the world. They have more money tucked away, power, information, connections and resources. Black people are limited, as their world was designed to be. We know they can compete with whites if the playing field is reasonably level, but it usually isn't. The first advantage is simply being born into a white family, presupposing superiority.

Because black people are generally on the outside looking in, they aren't even vaguely aware of what they don't know. *You've got to get inside!*

Former US Defense Secretary, Donald Rumsfeld calls them *"unknown unknowns"*. Things black people and white people don't know that they don't know. Especially all the *unknown unknowns* white people, who benefit without being racist themselves, don't know about black people.

If Willie Lynch was right, and he may well have been, how do we break the cycle? It has been said that to be a man you need to see a man. So, where are the men? I don't mean males who are severely damaged, but men who are independent, who act more or less on their own, and who are not afraid to break a few eggs if they must. I guess most of them are in a jail somewhere, the guys who bent or broke the rules, rules that were made up and then implemented by people with money and power to exploit and control everybody else. Higher-ups certainly had a reason for imposing them. Many of the men in jail don't know what some of those rules are anyway. Both rules and laws have something in common. Some are good while others are bad, making no sense at all, at least not to those who are intended to follow them.

Plato, in his *Republic*, relates an allegory in the voice of Socrates about a group of human beings, prisoners, who have lived in an underground cave with their necks and legs chained so they cannot move all their lives; in fact, since they were children. Beyond them is the mouth of the cave with a constantly blazing fire. Outside, as men walk past the opening of the cave carrying different things, their shadows are cast against the wall like a shadow cast against a plain white wall (or a movie screen), so those who are chained only see the shadows. They believe the shadows on the wall are actually reality. Whenever there is talking or conversation they think that is coming from the shadows on the wall too. After a while they take pride in the ability to recognize certain things, even establishing a type of hierarchy. Once, one of the cave people freed himself and got to the outside, where he still believed at first, that the shadows on the wall were the real people, and that what he faintly made out on the outside was not. Naturally, the daylight hurt his eyes and was confusing, just as experiencing this new reality or truth would leave him emotionally irritable and confused. In time, his eyes and understanding adjusted and he could appreciate the moon, the stars, the sun, the outside world, and even his own place in his new surroundings, this other world.

Homer once said, "Better to be the poor servant of a poor master, enduring anything, than think as they do and live after their manner." (It's better to know the truth, living with humility and dignity, whatever your cirumstance, than living the life of an ignorant tyrant or a racist.)

If the escaped prisoner goes back because he wants to rescue his friends, after being outside and going back into a dark cave, he's going to have trouble seeing and the others will think he has gone blind and believe that by going outside they will go blind too. The escaped prisoner, blind, has lost his mind, with outrageous tales about the moon, the sun, the trees, and the streams. They will kill him for trying to ruin anybody else. (To find truth, ancient Greeks drank kukeon, a psychoactive brew, eating and drinking god to become god). *Achieve Immortality!*

Most people choose to live in a world of fantasy or illusion where they are comfortable with partial truths and even outright lies. Such is the case with Christians, both blacks and racist whites, and their fantasies. They too will kill the messenger rather than see the light. Preferring a dark 2,000-year-old cave because they cannot free themselves from lifelong cultural, emotional and mental chains, choosing entertainment over critical information. For the prisoners the shadows are real. For Christians, the Bible, the priests, the bishops and the preachers are real, the people responsible for the lies, distortions and illusions. These days, if you believe in God in heaven, who 2,000 years ago had a son named Jesus, a son who is watching you at this very moment from up there in the clouds, who will sweep you up and take you with him one day, do you likewise believe in the Man in the Moon, a moon made of cheese?

Jesus said scribes and Pharisees sat in authority, calling them hypocrites seven times in Matthew. He cautioned everybody to listen to them but not to be like them. He said they'll see you working hard while they get rich and fat and not lift one finger to help you, sitting in the best seats in church and taking all your money. They look good on the outside but are rotten on the inside. Further quoting Jesus, "You serpents! You spawn of vipers! How can you escape the penalty to be suffered in hell?" If Jesus was right, there really are snakes, not just in the pulpit, but all around it. Are you seeing snakes too? In fact, are you actually surrounded by snakes and the only reason you're even sitting in somebody's church is you're afraid to admit that you might not want to believe or accept the fact that certain things are untrue? Are you afraid to leave the cave because you don't know what's on the outside?

Discipline, fortitude and direction, I believe, are essential in living your best life, the discipline that is necessary to learn life's valuable lessons and the fortitude to pursue a purposeful direction-driven life. *In today's world, even if you believe in God, can religion be trusted? Is Christianity actually little more than mythology esteemed as ancient history?*

Knowledge and truth are two of the first steps. We must first learn what is real and what is not, and then proceed earnestly toward realistic, meaningful goals. No fads, no hype, not because somebody else told us to do it, or because we're too afraid not to do it, but because we have taken the time to think for ourselves. Because we are willing and able to stand up for what is right, to face the truth. *There are no short cuts!*

Frederick Douglass and Marcus Garvey, two true American heroes basically espoused the same thing. Douglass said, *"A man without force is without the essential dignity of humanity.* Human nature is so constituted that it cannot honor a helpless man, it can only pity him. Even this, it cannot do long if the signs of power do not arrive. It was Marcus Garvey who said *"Power is the only argument that satisfies man. Man is not satisfied or moved by prayers or petitions,* but every man is moved by the power of authority which forces him to do, even against his will". Garvey also said "A race without authority and power is a race without respect", and "the only protection against injustice in man is power. Physical, financial, and scientific." *(Resist social, political and religious oppression.)*

Just as the Protestant Reformation took place during the 1500s throughout Europe and instituted separation from the Roman Catholic Church, there should likewise be a separation and reformation of many of today's churches, a separation from ignorance, stupidity, and superstition. In the 1500s the king and the people got tired of being controlled and pushed around. Inspired by men like Martin Luther, they decided to do something about it. Today, even an energized Pope Francis is calling for reformation in the Catholic Church. The time is long overdue for Americans to discover freedom, enlightenment, and their own spiritual and personal identities, escaping authoritarianism and out-dated dogma. Saving yourself is your responsibility alone, because your church and your government will not and cannot do it. Slavery and The Jim Crow system of racial separation and discrimination may be gone, but the Bible and traditional western Christianity live on, quietly reinforcing the same caustic, tribalistic agenda. Unconscious submission of the weak and defenseless to the strong and the powerful. Remember that power is never given, even when it comes to controlling your own life. It must be taken!

Ryan Bell, a life-long Christian and former Seventh-Day Adventist pastor really decided to test his faith. He is "trying on" atheism by living for one year without God. For 12 months he will live as if there is no God, doing things like not reading the Bible and not praying. And why? Because like so many others, including myself, he has questions and doubts. Bell believes that faith is one of those things people wrestle with.

Bell says "So I just decided not to fight it. I just decided to say, well, let me just give church a rest. And as I did that, I just began to wonder about the very existence of God". For most people faith (or superstition) is a hard thing to walk away from.

Dale McGowan, author of *"Parenting Beyond Belief"* and *Atheism for Dummies"* says* "Those whose will to know is stronger than the will to believe usually find their way out. And when they do, the most common emotion they describe isn't the anguish and despair they were told to expect—It's freedom and relief". That certainly describes how I feel.

Ryan Bell is not trying to get people to do what he's done. He simply wants them to find their own answers, just as I do. And it takes both strength and courage to do that. It is said that throughout human history progress was made, not so much because people have prayed and waited, but because they have taken action.

According to Howard Thurman, author of *Jesus and the Disinherited*, "Often there are things on the horizon that point logically to a transformation of society, especially for the underprivileged, but he cannot cooperate with them because he is spiritually and intellectually confused. He mistakes fear for caution and caution for fear. Now, if his mind is free and his spirit unchained, he can work intelligently and courageously for a new day." Quoting Alvin Toffler, futurist and author of *Future Shock*, "The illiterate of the 21st Century will not be those who cannot read and write, but those who cannot learn, unlearn, and relearn". It was Marcus Garvey who also said *"Liberate the minds of men and ultimately you will liberate the bodies of men."* Use your common sense and remember that patience and resilience are the keys to survival. Hopefully, *Let Us Prey* will help you with that.

Think, first! Just as I began with a series of quotes, I'd like to end with another of my own.

> Life is undeniably unforgiving.
> It will absolutely not hold your
> hand or do you any favors.
> Whatever happens is up to you.

—Don Spears

GET OFF YOUR KNEES!
IF YOU MUST PRAY,
PRAY STANDING UP!

WITH BOTH EYES WIDE OPEN

Food for Thought

America (the United States) is less than 300 years old. Except for Native Americans, who were curiously labeled Indians, the United States of America itself has no actual ancient history. America is, relatively speaking, still the New World.

Just as Europeans conquered inhabitants of other territories then claimed the land as their own, a similar format was used in taking possession of the ancient Israelite faith. Judaism was over-run by Europeans under the new heading of Christianity and expanded by The Catholic Church. *Jews had Moses, Christians had Jesus.* In America those expansionists were white Europeans. God loved white people so much he became one of them. Native Americans and blacks (heathens and devils) had no accepted, documented written histories, relying primarily on oral traditions. But actually white people in America didn't have an ancient history here either. Heroic fictional accounts (complimentary stories) were conveniently made up then recorded by them.

Again, was Man (the white man) really made in God's image, or is that genealogical legacy merely an ethnocentric delusion employed to justify unwarranted exploitation in the form of a kind of global manifest destiny, beginning with the Pilgrims. AMERICAN IMPERIALISM.

The belief that global expansion is only natural for whites who have been uniquely blessed by God with qualities of excellence, superiority and perfection. That it is their destiny and America's mission through Divine Providence to spread Christianity, democracy, and their culture across the globe, speaking one language and raising up the world's less endowed inferior peoples. That, of course was not the fate of Native Americans. The indigenous people were not raised up. Their land was *occupied and annexed*, while they at the same time were being reduced by *"ethnic cleansing"* (slaughtered), and *"Indian removal"* (shipped out).

"The Trail Of Tears." The excuse was to enjoin them to American society, the same rationale used at times with black people. We see how that's turning out too. Like Michael Brown's murder resulting in no indictment against Officer Wilson and no justice! No indictment against the officer who choked Eric Garner to death in New York. And 12-year-old Tamir Rice, murdered by Cleveland police while carrying a toy gun. Plus Freddie Gray's untimely death and so many others.

Christianity and the Holy Bible remain fundamental tools used in fostering such ridiculous notions of right and wrong, in spite of the fact that European roots and religion on the North American continent can be traced back no further than 1000 years ago. In the best seller *Our Country* written by Josiah Strong, a Protestant missionary in 1885, Mr. Strong says "My plea is not save America for America's sake, but save America for the world's sake". A white Christian America! (Like saving South Africa for whites only during Apartheid.)

In the year 3000 will that same sentiment prevail? Will America brashly continue to see itself as the world's policeman, still believing whatever it wants to? *A white Christian Robo-cop marching off to war to rescue humanity.* Or will man eventually awaken from his languid religious stupor and finally realize that it's only an illusion? That each individual's personal beliefs are actually his or hers alone to fathom.

Christianity and other religions often have little positive relevance when pressed against today's realities, mythologies that are the very quintessence of those subjugating religions (subliminal messages and images of white supremacy). For example Russell Crow starring in *Noah* and Christian Bale (*Batman*) playing Moses in *Exodus*. The simple truth is that as long as white people, especially believers singularly see themselves as God's special creation (based on lies and distortions), the world will remain rife with chaos and conflict. Is white supremacy the little engine that keeps Christianity, homophobia, sexism and racism chugging along and vice versa? Is America's white racist God real? Does the world's greatest conspiracy and hoax prevail, inspired by images of a white Jesus, bibles, crosses and Rebel flags?

"What is it men cannot be made to believe!"
Thomas Jefferson to Richard Henry Lee, April 22, 1786.

Quoting the Jamaican-American philosopher Charles Mills, "whites in general will be unable to understand the world they themselves have created," as consumers of racism with no self-awareness. It was Nietzsche who pronounced that "God is Dead," because "the belief in the Christian God has become unbelievable. Everything that was built upon this faith, propped up by it, grown into it is destined for collapse." America's Founding Fathers generally held three positions regarding religion. While Patrick Henry, John Jay and Samuel Adams were Christians, the others, Thomas Paine, Ethan Allen, John Adams, George Washington, Benjamin Franklin and James Monroe were either deist or Christian deist who didn't believe in miracles, but were disciples of Jesus' doctrine like Jefferson. Choosing to practice intelligent faith instead of blind faith.

In 1787 Thomas Jefferson famously advised his nephew Peter Carr to "Question with boldness even the existence of a god, because if there be one, he must more approve the homage of reason [deep respect for thinking and truth] than that of blindfolded fear." Of being manipulated and intimidated here on earth, then dying and expecting to spend eternity in heaven or hell. Jefferson believed that "your own reason [common sense] is the only oracle [wisdom] given you by heaven." He felt that religion was a matter between every man and his maker, and nobody else's business. Between a man and his God.

A deist, Thomas Jefferson could not accept orthodox Christianity because of what he referred to as its corruption. He was scientific, not superstitious. His God was not the personal God of Christianity. Jefferson believed in a Creator, "Nature's God", but not Jesus as the son of God. Nevertheless, Jesus' message inspired him. It was a simple, brilliant moral doctrine that he felt had been twisted by people claiming to be believers. By Christians and preachers who had at times accused him of being an infidel and an atheist. In writing to John Adams, he said "the greatest enemies of Jesus' teachings were some of those same people, and one day even the story of Jesus' miraculous birth by God in the womb of a virgin would be classified as a fable." As mythology. Thomas Jefferson felt that The Book of Revelations was merely the ravings of a maniac.

Jefferson said if Jesus, a Jew, ever came back even he wouldn't recognize what he supposedly preached and did. In writing to Timothy Pickering, he argued that "we have to unlearn everything which has been taught since his day to truly understand Jesus' mission." He called his approach Rational Christianity. It involved researching other sources outside of the Holy Bible and trying to put himself in the mind of a person who lived in another time to better understand things from their perspective and point of view, walking in their shoes. Not just believing what other people would later write. Jefferson said religion-builders had distorted and deformed Jesus' teachings with so many lies and fantasies that anybody with half-a-brain wouldn't believe them, or in Jesus either. He also understood full well that denying God's existence could undermine social order and lead to chaos.

John Adams declared that "the government of the United States is not, in any sense, founded on the Christian religion." This, as the United States continues to be lauded as the world's pre-eminent Christian nation. Most of American's Founding Fathers believed God and Christianity had no place in America's government. Nowhere in the Declaration of Independence is Christianity ever mentioned. The nation's motto "In God We Trust" wasn't adopted until 1956 when it was signed by President Eisenhower. "Under God" wasn't added to the United States Constitution until 1942.

Perhaps Jefferson and Adams were right. America was never intended to be a Christian nation because the consequences could permanently divide their country. As previously stated, Thomas Jefferson was an adherent of what he labeled Rational Christianity. Something I think of as Rational Literacy, more akin to the Golden Rule and critical thinking than Christianity's outdated mysticism and propaganda. Old-fashioned ideas maintained by today's Roman Catholic Church,

Evangelical Christians and others. Much of their exposition continues to be the deliberate exploitation of religion for personal, financial and/or political purposes. Americans, including black people, are Christians because they were born here, and of course slaves were forced to become Christians.

Remember that Jesus, "the prince of peace", who always spoke his mind, never said one word condemning slavery. As a staunch believer in the Old Testament, the Law and the prophets, he fiercely supported the concept of an eye for an eye, as well as the abuse, violence, and murder that was commanded. Revelations 19: 13-15 says that riding his white horse God's (Jesus') white robe is dripped in blood, and he has a sharp sword in his mouth. Matthew 18: 25-35 says you go to jail for being disobedient. Matthew 24: 45-51 tells that you will be beaten until you're cut and bleeding with the skin peeled off your back. Like Saul, Jesus obviously had no objection to cruelty or families being torn apart, having been considered violent and unstable himself. He believed that "anyone who practiced and taught the law would be great in heaven". That meant loving God more than your own mother or your own children. Paul said Jesus was adopted by God because he followed the Jews crazy laws so well, just as slaves and Gentiles who obeyed were adopted as children of God.

Keep in mind that there is no "thou shalt not have slaves" in the Bible. In Deuteronomy 20: 11-16 Israelites were actually commanded to invade and enslave distant cities. In places that surrendered peacefully kill all the men, but keep the women, children and animals as inheritance. If Jesus was truly divine he would certainly have known about the chattel slavery that was coming to America 2000 years later, and its dehumanizing consequences. Why didn't God inspire Jesus to speak out against slavery? If he had said something he could have saved millions of black lives. Is it possible that Jesus would have actually sided with slave-owning Andrew Jackson, Jefferson Davis and the Confederacy? If God is all powerful why didn't he end slavery? Couldn't God fix things?

Remember, tribalism in America (racism) actually began with two groups of religious zealots, Pilgrims and Puritans who believed in

Calvinism and Predestination. The beloved did not include heathens and savages who allegedly kidnapped and raped white women, like the Patuxet, the Pequot, or the Wampanoag who were wiped out by smallpox laced blankets, enslaved, shot, clubbed to death, burned alive and even beheaded. After every massacre days of thanksgiving were held to celebrate the victory and the acquisition of more land. In God's name. *(Not sitting around with Indians eating turkey dinners together and smoking peace-pipes.)* For Pilgrims and Puritans, God and Jesus were undoubtedly white, a belief based on "fake" Christianity and "fake" history. Fictitious depictions that most of America's Founding Fathers denounced.

Confederates, especially Christians, believed that by fighting to preserve slavery they were doing God's will. Opposing slavery was an attack against the word of God, a holy war against the Bible. It was a Christian's duty to defend and "perfect" slavery by obeying the Bible. Many whites saw themselves as prisoners in their own country, just as some white people today feel that they too are constantly being marginalized, disenfranchised and discriminated against. Is history repeating itself? Were Clay and Jefferson right? Will there be class or race wars? Of course Jefferson never expected white people to kill other white people because of slavery. Over 150 years after the Civil War it appears that we will always harbor ethnocentric delusions of white supremacy, nurtured by the media and subtly reinforced in separate, racially polarized schools and churches. American Christianity has never been, and never will be a black or non-white religion.

Were Jesus and his apostles real people, or perhaps an allegory, a story within a story? A surface story containing a symbolic hidden story, where an abstract idea may be described as a character, figure, or an event. Did the twelve apostles represent the twelve signs of the zodiac rather than twelve loyal followers? They could also have been metaphors; Jesus the Lamb of God, a perfect sacrifice. Not a real sheep. There is no evidence such as burial sites or family linages to prove that the Bible's heroes ever lived. Not Jesus, Abraham, Moses, or Paul. None of them. And everybody just disintegrated into thin air after they died, even Joseph.

In the context of a black man's perspective of American history, of slavery and Jim Crow, I see Christianity, especially the Christianity of the Puritans and the Calvinists as a mind-set imposed on captives by a foreign power, a white foreign power. Non-Christians, non-white outsiders were rarely afforded recognition as being human. Calvinists, formed under the notion of Predestination, even divided their membership into the Elect and the Damned, as manifested by their acquisitions, or lack of success in the material world. [True believers were blessed. Sound familiar?] Aside from the insult to Reason, try to imagine the sense of inferiority, the despair and hopelessness in the minds of those destined to Damnation. In the 1830s even Jim Crow was a minstrel characterized in the persona of a sketchy black slave who was lazy, dumb and untrustworthy, dressed in rags and wearing a battered hat and torn shoes, dancing a jig and destined to Damnation.

Try this little experiment. Every time you say the word "God" make it plural, "gods". For example: God loves me; the gods love me. Do the gods love you? Does God love you? Is removing one letter, an "s", really going to profoundly change your life? Will God make it better?

Dr. Ellen Langley, Professor of Psychology at Harvard University, has been studying mindfulness and mindlessness for decades. According to Dr. Langley, we usually pass on unquestioned what we all receive in our childhood classrooms. Like robots people mindlessly follow rules without ever thinking about what they actually mean, or what their implications truly are. Unconsciously and subconsciously accepting and learning what society teaches.

Dr. Langley explains that being mindful is constantly noticing new things and asking questions. Learning to make choices that are reasonable and empowering. One of the most important features of mindfulness is "being in the moment". This is especially true with Christianity, and the necessity of avoiding mindless outdated dogma and incongruent mythology. It's important to ask questions, like what makes one group or one individual claim to be superior to another group or another individual as religion does. Someday being mindful and self-aware could perhaps generate sentiments of cooperation and mutual respect.

Don't forget, for believers Christianity provides a calming false sense of security and closure. (But what will I do if there is no God who will keep me safe and take care of me?) Oftentimes it's easier to just remain mindless rather than ask questions and get answer you might not like. Suppose there is no heaven, at least not the one we've been told about. And were the Holy Scriptures inspired by psychoactive wine, hashish, and psychedelic mushrooms and used to contact God? Could answers to such questions change attitudes, affecting everything about life as we know it? John Adams felt that religion should be based on common sense and reasonableness, and should change and evolve. Suppose aliens are real, and something else besides God created the universe? What if angels actually referred to aliens, a word that did not exist 2000 years ago? Could aliens (angels), be human time travelers from the future?

As a mature adult I recall a time when black people said white people had a funny odor. White people claimed that black people had tails; they smelled bad too. Both groups, having very limited contact with each other, were equally guilty of being mindless, just as artificial intelligence is now making us less mindful, more out of touch with reality, and less human. Remember, most black people still have never been to a white person's house, and most white people have never been to a black person's house, even for a simple birthday celebration. Do we spend too much time occupied with the past (being tribal), instead of cooperating with each other and living in the present? Do pre-set biases determine what we accept and believe? Modern man survived because of cooperation, while Neanderthals who didn't work together became extinct.

Dr. Langley's observations about mindfulness and mindlessness are consistent with Thomas Jefferson's Rational Christianity and my own Rational Literacy, being aware and living in the moment. Americans, neither blacks, whites, Native Americans, Latinos, Middle Easterners nor Asians have ever been debriefed from this country's narcissistic, xenophobic legacy. Black people and other minorities in America, constrained by fear, have been bullied by white people everyday of their lives. Caucasians, for the most part, are unaware of the benefits they gained by simply being white, or the immeasurable damage they have inflicted on other people. Today, in the 21st century, 50% of white people who are comfortable with tribalism still feel superior and entitled, now embracing authority rule over majority rule, driven by a false sense of security. Remember, they will never move to the rear of the bus or back of the line, places where they've never been before. Laws will not eliminate racism, which is only the symptom of a much larger problem, not the cause! What would America be like today if black people had never become chattel slaves? Racism, self-centered entitlement and Double Consciousness will always be America's problem!

One of the first Enlightenment (conscious) thinkers was Baruch Spinoza, a Dutch philosopher born in 1632. He was a 17th century Jewish rationalist, a teacher of reality who questioned the authenticity of the Hebrew Bible and nature of the Divine. Vehemently attacking superstition and refusing to accept Jewish dogma, he was excommunicated and kicked out of Jewish society, but obviously never became a Christian. Spinoza said Catholicism and Islam were made *"to deceive the people and to constrain the minds of men"* as Robert Ingersol said. Naturally Spinoza's books were forbidden by the Catholic Church.

Like ancient Carpocratians and Sadducees, Spinoza denied the immortality of the soul. *No afterlife.* He also rejected the idea of the providential God of Abraham, Isaac and Jacob, or believe The Old Testament and The Ten Commandments were literally dictated to Moses by God. The same thing Aaron and Miriam doubted. Therefore Jews (and nobody else), had to follow laws God didn't give. Hoping that Judaism would prevail on earth, Jews were never to discuss religious matters with Christians, something that might create further doubts about Judaism. For Spinoza truth was <u>not</u> a property of Hebrew Scriptures. Always true because the Scriptures said so.

Spinoza argued that God exists but is abstract and impersonal. Remember Thomas Jefferson's Nature's God who was not personal and loving. For Spinoza God and Nature were two names for the same reality. That if mind and body were truly distinct (separate) how could they coordinate? God does not rule over the universe like something written in the stars, and nothing happens by chance or by accident. Everything that has happened or will happen is a long chain of cause-and-effect, happening because of necessity, which at a metaphysical level, human beings are unable to change, or is contingent on anything else. For instance whether believing in God, or being good or bad will or will not get you into heaven.

Everything is already connected to everything else. God, this abstract entity is everywhere and in everything, like atoms, molecules, and electrical charges. All things in nature proceed from a certain definite necessity with the utmost perfection. The world, which already functions perfectly looks imperfect to us because of our own limited perception of perfection. We are here, in this moment because everything is working the way it's supposed to, not by happenstance. Human beings think they have free will when they actually don't.

Spinoza also believed that reason (understanding), could not overrule emotion. *Intelligence is no match for stupidity.* Emotion can only be overcome by stronger emotion. Hate vs. love. Knowledge of true causes of passive emotion can transform it into active emotion. Sigmund Freud's psychoanalysis. Realizing that Christianity is a diabolical scheme orchestrated by church leaders for control can lead to liberating feelings of freedom and relief like those I experienced. The emotional wellbeing Spinoza focused on.

Even Albert Einstein admired Baruch Spinoza, the first secular Jew in modern times. Spinoza, a rationalist believed that reason, being rational, is the chief source and test of knowledge for everything, including God. Good and evil have no absolute meaning, and are only opinions and points of view. A lack of rationality however, can lead to dangerous reasoning. Tribalism, leading to hatred, leading to violence, even making religion dangerous. Spinoza believed the more we are conscious of ourselves, of nature and the universe, the more blessed we are in reality. Remember, heaven and hell are never mentioned in The Old Testament or Jesus' teachings. In Pelagianism the belief was that original sin did not taint human nature and that humans have free will to achieve human perfections without divine grace. (*Without God*). Get out of that "man-made-up" Christianity box. Don't waste your life away living a lie.

Baruch Spinoza was also admired by Rene Descartes, the French philosopher, mathematician, and scientist who famously said "I think, therefore I am." Descartes is also renown for his *"Dream Argument"*, suggesting that dreams can somehow help us see and understand things better than our senses, similar to Dr. King's and my own epiphanies. Does God reveal knowledge and truth, or is God the knowledge and truth revealed? Is God the conscious and subconscious energy that connects each of us with the unfathomable universe around us?

People always want quick simple answers. Are black churches failing African Americans? Is Christianity, especially Evangelical Christianity dividing America? Remember Abraham Lincoln's famous quote "A nation divided against itself cannot stand." And John Adams' "There never was a democracy that didn't commit suicide." Are Americans the damned, divided against themselves and doomed to destruction? Is the Holy Bible simply a historical fiction narrative where Jesus of Nazareth, the main character embodies white supremacy, with images showing white people what they want to see, attached to what they know. Like Evangelical Protestants who believe America should be white, even becoming violent. Adolph Hitler praised Jim Crow laws. Do wealthy privileged families like the Trumps and the Waltons (Walmart), somehow see themselves as supreme, as actual deities who are superior to everyone else? Like Henry Ford's Model T, has Christianity finally run its course? Is it time to move on? As Baruch Spinoza hypothesized centuries ago, are we exactly where we are supposed to be?

Waiting almost 2000 years, 20 centuries, was Jesus God's only begotten son? Is he ever coming back, riding a donkey, to be king of Israel? Are Paul, John the Baptist and James going to get their heads back when he returns? And what about Elvis? Will Jesus save us? *Stay woke!*

THE GREAT LIE

Bibliography/Recommended Readings

Armstrong, Karen, *A History of God*, Alfred A. Knopf, 1994.

Armstrong, Reuben, *Snakes in the Pulpit,* Reuben Armstrong Publishing, 2007.

Aslan, Reza, *Zealot,* Random House, 2013.

Atwill, Joseph, *Caesar's Messiah,* CreateSpace, 2011

Baigent Michael, Richard Leigh & Henry Lincoln, *The Holy Blood and the Holy Grail,* Jonathan Cape, 1982.

Barnstone, Willis, *The Other Bible,* Harper San Francisco, 1984.

Bolelli, Daniele, *50 Things You're Not Supposed to Know*, the Disinformation Company, 2011.

Barashango, Ishakamusa, *God, The Bible and the Black Man's Destiny.*

Baetzhold, Howard G. & Joseph B. McCullough (editors), *The Bible According to Mark Twain,* Touchstone 1996.

Battle, Michael and Tony Compolo, *The Church Enslaved*, Fortress Press, 2005.

Benedict XVI, *Jesus of Nazareth, The Infancy Narratives,* Doubleday, 2007.

Bennett, Lerone, *Before the Mayflower*, Penguin Books, 1982.

Berry, Mary Francis, *Long Memory*, Oxford University Press, 1982.

Blackmon, Douglass A., *Slavery by Another Name*, Doubleday, 2008.

Blassingame, John W., *Slave Testimony*, State University Press, 977.

Blyden, Edwin Wilmot, *Christianity, Islam and the Negro Race*, Black Classic Press, 1993

Bogle, Donald, *Toms, Coons, Mulattoes, Mammies and Bucks*, Viking Press, 1973.

Boteach, Stanley, *Kosher Sex*, Double Day, 1999.

Bradley, Michael, *The Iceman Inheritance*, 1978.

Browder, Anthony T., *Nile Valley Contributions to Civilization*, Institute of Karmic Guidance, 1992.

Browder, Anthony T., *From the Browder File*, Institute of Karmic Guidance, 1989.

Cleage, Albert B., *The Black Messiah*, World Press, 1995.

Cone, James H., *God of the Oppressed*, Orbis Books, 1997.

Cone, James H., *For My People*, Black Theology and the Black Church, Orbis Books, 1984.

Cone, James H., *Black Theology and Black Power*, Orbis Books, 1999.

Cone, James H., *The Cross and the Lynching Tree*, Orbis Books, 2011.

Cone James H., *Martin and Malcolm and America*, Orbis Books, 1991.

Cronon, David E., *The Story of Marcus Garvey*, University of Wisconsin Press, 1969.

Darkwah, Nanna Banchie, *The Africans Who Wrote the Bible*, Aduana Publishing, 2002.

Douglass, Frederick, *Life and Times of Frederick Douglass: Written by himself*, Collier Books, 1962.

Douglass, Kelly Brown, *The Black Christ*, Orbis Books, 1994.

DuBois, W.E.B., *The Souls of Black Folks*, A.C. McClury & Co., 1903

DeGruy, Dr. Joy, *Post Traumatic Slave Syndrome: America's Legacy of Enduring Injury and Healing*, Joy DeGruy Publications Inc, 2017

Durant, Will, *The Story of Civilization*, Simon and Schuster, 1993.

Eaton, Frederick H., *Scandalous Saint*.

Ehrman, Bart D., *Did Jesus Exist?* Harper Collins

Ehrman, Bart D., *Forged*, Harper Collins, 2012.

Ehrman, Bart D., *How Jesus Became God*, Harper One, 2014

Ehrman, Bart D., *Jesus, Interrupted*, Harper Collins, 2010.

Emmanuel, William Gilbert, *People of Color in the Bible*, Faith of Jesus Center, 1993.

Felder, Cain Hope (editor), *Stormy the Road We Trod*, Fortress Press, 1991.

Fox, Robin Lane, *Pagans and Christians*, 1986.

Frederickson, George M., *Black Images In The White Mind*, Wesleyan University Press, 1971.

Fox, John, *Fox's Book of Martyrs*, 1500s

Graham, Lloyd, *Deceptions and Myths of the Bible*, Citadel Press, 1975.

Greenberg, Gary, *101 Myths of the Bible*, Bristol Park Books, 2014.

Ginzburg, Ralph, *100 Years of Lynchings*, Black Classic Press, 1988

Harari, Yuval Noah, *Sapiens: A Brief History of Humankind*, Harpers Collins, 2015

Hare, Nathan, *Black Anglo-Saxons*, Third World Press, 1995.

Hare, Nathan & Julia, *The Endangered Black Family*, Black Think Tank, 1984.

Harik, Ramsay M., *Jesus of Nazareth*, Franklin Watts, 2001.

Harper, Chancellor, *Memoir on Slavery*, 1837.

Higginbotham, Evelyn Brooks, *Righteous Discontent*, Harvard University Press, 1994.

Hitchens, Christopher, *God is Not Great*, Warner Books, 2007.

Hollingdale, R. J., *A Nietzsche Reader*, Penguin Books, 1977.

Jocobovici, Simcha and Charles Pellegrino, *The Jesus Family Tomb*, 2007.

Jefferson, Thomas, *The Reverse Jefferson Bible*.

Jefferson, Thomas, *The Life and Morals of Jesus of Nazareth*.

Jordan, Winthrop D., *White Over Black*, University of North Carolina Press, 1968

Kreeft, Peter, *Heaven, the Heart's Deepest Longing*, Ignatius Press, 2013.

Kunjufu, Dr. Jawanza, *Countering the Conspiracy to Destroy Black Boys*, African American Images, 1985.

Kush, Indus, Khamit, *What They Never Told You in History Class*, Luxorr Publications, 1983.

Leary, Joy Degruy, *Post Traumatic Slave Syndrome*, Uptone Press, 2005.

Leedon, Tim and Albert Churchwood, *The Book Your Church Doesn't Want You to Read*, Truth Seeker, 1993

Lennox, J. Paul, *Fr. Marciel Maciel, Pedophile, Psychopath and Legion of Christ Founder*, Private Publication, 2012.

Lennox, J. Paul, *Our Father Who Art In Bed*, Private Publication, 2008.

Liebow, Elliot, *Tally's Corner*, Rowan & LIttlefield Publishers, INc., 1967

Lincoln, C. Eric and Lawrence H. Mamiya, *The Black Church in the African American Experience*, Duke University Press, 1990.

Lindenmeyer, Otto, *Black History: Lost, Stolen or Strayed*, Avon Books, 1970.
Lynch, William, *Willie Lynch Letter*.

Madhubuti, Haki R., *Black Men Obsolete, Single, Dangerous?* Third World Press, 1991.

Mannion, James, *Essentials of Philosophy*, Fall River Press, 2002.

McKenna, Terrence, *Food of the Gods: The Search for the Original Tree of Knowledge: A Radical History of Plants, Drugs, and Human Evolution*, Bantam, 1992

Meier, August & Rudwick Elliot, *From Platation to Ghetto*, Hill and Wang, 1966

Milligan, Rosie, *Nigger, Please*, Professional Business Consultants, 1996.

Milo, Gloria, *Secrets*, Professional Business Consultants, 2004.

Morant, Mack B., *The Insane Nigger*, R & M Publishing Company, 1982.

Muraresku, Brian C., *The Immortality Key*, St. Martin's Press 2020.

Norwich, John Julius, *Absolute Moncarchs*, Ramdom House, 2012.

O'Reilly, Bill and Martin Dugard, *Killing Jesus*, Henry Holt and Company, 2013.

O'Reilly, Bill, *The Last Days of Jesus*, Henry Holt and Company, 2014.

Pettiford, Hasani, *Pimpin' From the Pulpit to the Pews*, Blue Magic Publishing, 2003.

Quarles, Benjamin, *The Negro in the Making of America*, Collier Books, 1987.

Raboteau, Albert, *Slave Religion*, Oxford University Press, 2004.

Robinson, Eugene, *Disintergration: The Splintering of Black America*, Random House, 2010.

Rogers, J. A., *Nature Knows No Color Line*, Helga M. Rogers, 1980.

Spears, Don, *In Search of Goodpussy*, Don Spears, 1991.

Ruck, Carl A. P. and José Alfredo González Celdrán, *Mushrooms, Myth & Mithras: The Drug Cult that Civilized Europe*, City Lights Books, 2011

Smith, Delaney E., *Legacy of the Ancient Hebrews*, Truth in Publishing, 1994

Stowe, Harriet Beecher, *Uncle Tom's Cabin*, 1862.

Tabor, James, *The Jesus Dynasty*, Simon and Schuster, 2006.

Tate, Efelda, *Legacy of Tragedy*, Professional Business Consultants, 2001.

The Norton Anthology—American Literature

Thurman, Howard, *Jesus and the Disinherited*, Random House, 1996.

deTocqueville, Alexis, *Democracy in America*.

Watts, David Malik, *The Black Presence in the Lands of the Bible*.

West, Cornel, *Race Matters*, Vintage Books, 2001.

Wickham, Dewayne, *Thinking Black*, Crown Publishers, 1993.

Williams, Andrews L., *Six Women's Slave Narratives*, Oxford University Press, 1988.

Woodson, Carter G., *The Miseducation of the Negro*, African World Press, 1993.

Wright, N. T., *What Saint Paul Really Said*, William E. Eerdmans Publishing Co., 1997.

Wright, Robert, *The Evolution of God*, Little, Brown and Company, 2009.

*Recommended Viewing: Mia Maxima Culpa, *Silence in the House of God*, HBO 2012

INDEX

A

Aaron, 380
Abraham, 381
Adam, 12
Adams, John 13
Africanus, Leo, 367
Aitken, Jonathan, 285
American Exceptionalism, 194
Anastasius, Archbishop, 92
animism, 46, 150
Antipas, Herod, 38, 45, 61
Ark of the Covenant, 133
Armstrong, Karen, 289
Armstrong, Reuben, 301, 313, 417
Aslan, Reza, 47
Aurelius, Marcus, 96, 98, 118, 240

B

Baker, Henry, 175, 279
Baptist, John the, 38, 42, 62, 63, 110, 119, 140, 141, 157, 169, 183, 362, 369
Barashango, Rev. Ishakamusa, 224
Battle, Michael, 160
Batts, Valerie, 161
Benedict, Pope, 74, 79, 83
Berry, Mary Frances, 194
Bethlehem, 27, 30, 32, 260, 261
Bishop of Cyprus, 183
Blaine, David, 185
Blassingame, John W., 175, 194
Blease, Cole, 211
Bloomberg, Michael, 212, 214
Blyden, Edward Wilmot, 333
Boak, Josh, 191
Boehner, John, 190
Boteach, Shmuley, 285

Bradley, Michael, 207, 349
Briggs, Charles, 286
Browder, Anthony, 348
Brown, Michael, 217
Butler, Dr. Anthea, 223

C

Caiaphas, 61
Caiaphas, Joseph, 60
Calixtus II, 145
Calvin, John, 292, 297
Campbell, Joseph, 27
Campolo, Tony, 160
Celsus, 98, 99, 117
Charlie, 181
Chisholm, Shirley 11, 198
Christians, Pagans and, 95, 419
Churchwood, Albert, 421
Clay, Henry, 343, 344
Cleage, Reverend Albert, 237
Code of Hammurabi, 152
Colton, Calvin, 344
Commodus, 97, 98, 240
Condon, Bernard, 191
Cone, James H., 165, 168, 171, 181, 210, 285
Confucius, 182
Council of Cardinals, 207, 278
Cruz, Ted, 190
Curia, 66, 70, 91, 144, 278
Cyprian, 88
Cyprus, Bishop of, 183

D

Daniel, 56, 113, 261, 369
Davis, Jordan, 216
Derbyshire, John, 284
Dialogue of Pessimism, 152

431

Domitian, Emperor, 90, 94
Dorcas, 183
Douglass, Frederick, 172, 173, 175, 195, 393, 407, 419
Douglass, Kelly Brown, 181
DuBois, W.E.B., 197, 209, 210
Dunn, Michael, 216
Durkheim, Emile, 162

E

Eaton, Frederick Heese, 245, 246, 375, 378, 419
Eddy, Pat, 369
Ehrman, Dr. Bart D., 31
Elizabeth, 117
Emerentia, 34
emperor's new clothes, 264
Enuma Elish, 151
Essenes, 115
Eusebius, 33
Eve's Diary, 272

F

Father Marcial Maciel, 80
Finney, Charles Grandison, 345
Five Books of Moses, 186, 261
Flight Into Egypt, 30
Francis, Pope, 66, 67, 70, 73, 76, 79, 85, 87, 99, 109, 119, 256, 309, 310, 313, 408
Freeman, Morgan, 189
Freud, Sigmund, 27, 350

G

Gabriel, 24, 268
Garden of Eden, 141, 268, 269, 272, 282
Garrison, William Lloyd, 345
Garvey, Marcus, 209, 407, 419
Ginzburg, Ralph, 225
Glaude, Eddie, 306
Gnosticism, 118, 183
Gnostics, 42, 118, 119, 169, 183

Graham, Lloyd, 263
Great, Emperor Constantine the, 84, 88
Great, Emperor Theodosius the, 100
Great, Herod the, 29, 54, 56, 61, 63
Gregory, Pope, 91, 109, 117, 121, 385, 388

H

Hagar, 247
Hanina ben Dosa, 182
Hannibal, 206
Hannity, Sean, 172
Harrison, Joe, 184
Helena, Empress, 95
Herodias, 64
Herodotus, 206
Hillel Pharisees, 41
Hinkelammert, Dr. Franz, 167
Holt, Thomas, 209
Holy Grail, 117, 417
Homer, 265, 406
Honi the Rainmaker, 182
Houdini, 185
Hutchinson, Dr. Paul, 239

I

Ingersoll, Robert G., 224
Innocent, Pope, 146, 147, 384
In Search of Goodpussy, 9, 10, 422
Isaac, 110, 381
Ishmael, 247

J

James, King, 132
Jeantel, Rachel, 214
Jefferson, Thomas, 131, 136, 171, 299, 336
Jesus the Homeless, 99
Jones, Charles Colcock, 176
Joseph, 21, 23, 24, 27, 28, 30, 31, 34, 35, 38, 40, 56, 98, 106, 111, 113, 115, 122, 124, 157, 159, 247, 260, 261,

262
Jr., 163, 196, 209, 237, 306, 339
Jr., Thomas Holt, 209
Judas, 45, 49, 50, 53, 89
Julius, Pope, 21, 72, 84, 384

K

King Abimelech, 245
King, Dr. Martin Luther, 163, 196, 339
King Hammurabi, 152
King James, 57, 93, 94, 100, 101, 102, 265, 355, 362, 368
King Solomon, 24, 159
Kreeft, Peter, 284

L

Lane, Robin Fox, 95
Law, Cardinal John, 80
Leedon, Tim, 421
lestai, 49
letter of James, 136
Lillith, 266, 267, 277
Limbaugh, Rush, 172
Luke, 23, 49, 114, 157, 172, 175, 259, 260
Lynch, Willie, 390, 391, 405, 421

M

Magdalene, Mary, 28, 115, 117, 118, 121, 124, 125, 127, 132, 133, 145, 157, 169, 297
Magnus, Simon, 183
Mahoney, Cardinal Roger, 80
Malchus, 50, 53, 60
Marduk, 150, 151
Marozia, 383, 385
Marrocco, Brendan, 252
Martin, Trayvon, 214, 217
Mary, 21, 23, 24, 26, 28, 31, 32, 34, 47, 89, 98, 99, 100, 107, 113, 115, 124, 133, 134, 135, 141, 157, 169, 241, 247, 260, 261
McConnell, Mitch, 190

Mea Maxima Culpa, 83
Melchizedek, 150, 240, 242
Merlin, 185
messiah, 105, 111
Messiah, 25, 31, 40, 53, 64, 99, 108
Midrash, 262
Milligan, Dr. Rosie, 2, 193
Mithras, 240
money changers, 48
Moore, Garry, 238
Morant, Mack, 401
Moses, 17, 20, 22, 47, 61, 123, 133, 143, 148, 149, 150, 151, 154, 156, 159, 169, 183, 184, 185, 186
Murphy, ather Lawrence, 81

N

Nag Hammadi, 124
Nazarenes, 132, 138
Nazareth, 30, 31, 40, 106, 110, 113, 115, 131, 252, 260, 261, 281, 417, 420
Nietzsche, Friedrich, 20, 27
Noah, 122, 123, 159, 160, 269, 274, 276, 317

O

Obama, Barack, 344
Obama, Michelle, 315
Opus Dei, 73
Othello, 356, 357, 359, 361, 363

P

paganism, 38, 41, 43, 96
Paine, Thomas, 131
Pentateuch, 186
Perkins, Tom, 191
Pharisees, 36, 41, 61
Pharisee, Shammaite, 41, 44
Pilate, Pontius, 64
Plato, 390

Protoevangelium, 22, 23
Pryor, Richard, 202, 346, 358

R

Robinson, Eugene, 220
Roosevelt, Theodore, 182
Rugaber, Christopher S., 191
Rush, Benjamin, 181
Ryan, Paul, 190

S

Sadducees, 36, 61
Sarah, 245, 247
Scheindlin, Judge Shira, 214
sex on the shelf, 192
Shakespeare, William, 101, 327
shamans, 44, 45, 144, 254
Shamans, 39, 46
Shaw, George Bernard, 162
Sicarii, 41
Slaughter of Innocents, 29
Slave Testimony, 175, 279, 418
Socrates, 56
sons of God, 34
Sons of God, 149
sons of thunder, 60
Spears, Don, 6, 409, 422
Spyridon, 183
St. Francis, 88
St. Irenaeus, 265
St. Jerome, 33, 109
Stowe, Harriet Beecher, 297

T

Talpiot Tomb, 133
Tate, Efelda, 422
Tea Party, 223
Tertullian, 85, 109
Testament of Solomon, 24, 185
The Hindu Basket, 184
Torah, 41

Twain, Mark, 270, 272, 273, 274, 276, 417
Tyndale, William, 93

V

Vatican Bank, 69
Vatileaks, 71, 72
Vinci, Leonardo Da, 111
Voting Rights Act, 257

W

West, Cornel, 166
wise men, 31, 35
Wright, Robert, 45, 46
Wycliffe, John, 93

X

X, Malcolm, 11, 180, 390, 402

Z

zealot, 41, 47, 237
Zealot, 48, 417
Zechariah, 127
Zell, Sam, 191
Zoroaster, 240
Zoroastrianism, 240, 241

www.ingramcontent.com/pod-product-compliance
Lightning Source LLC
Chambersburg PA
CBHW071851290426
44110CB00013B/1104